Regimes of Description

In the Archive of the Eighteenth Century

Edited by John Bender

and Michael Marrinan

STANFORD UNIVERSITY PRESS

Stanford, California 2005

Stanford University Press
Stanford, California
© 2005 by the Board of Trustees of the
Leland Stanford Junior University

Library of Congress Cataloging-in-Publication Data

Regimes of description : in the archive of the eighteenth century /
edited by John Bender and Michael Marrinan.
    p. cm.
    Includes bibliographical references and index.
    ISBN 0-8047-4741-5 (hardcover : alk. paper) —
    ISBN 0-8047-4742-3 (pbk. : alk. paper)
        1. Description (Philosophy). 2. Aesthetics. I. Bender, John.
II. Marrinan, Michael.
B105.D4 R44   2005
121/.68 — dc22   2004008459

Printed in the United States of America
Original Printing 2005
Last figure below indicates year of this printing:
14   13   12   11   10   09   08   07   06   05

Typeset at Stanford University Press in 10/13 Galliard

Acknowledgments

This book first took shape among the organizing committee of a conference sponsored by the Stanford Seminar on Enlightenment and Revolution. We are indebted to Keith Michael Baker, Terry Castle, Eric Chandler, Hans Ulrich Gumbrecht, Timothy Lenoir, and J. B. Shank for their enthusiastic participation in the planning. We also thank members of the former Forschungsschwerpunkt Literaturwissenschaft, Berlin (today the Zentrum für Literaturforschung).

We are grateful for Helen Tartar's editorial advice early in this project. Peter de Bolla's sympathetic reading and critical comments helped us to shape and clarify the collection. A number of people have assisted in preparation of the manuscript. They include: Alexandra Arch, Lela Graybill, Annette Keogh, Joann Kleinneiur, John Perry, Kate Washington, and Molly Watson. Support for the Seminar on Enlightenment and Revolution, as well as for editorial expenses, came from the Peter and Helen Bing Trust for Teaching.

Versions of some essays in this book have been published elsewhere. By listing the sources, we gratefully acknowledge permission from the authors or their publishers for inclusion in this volume: Lorraine Daston, "The Cold Light of Facts and the Facts of Cold Light: Luminescence and the Transformation of the Scientific Fact, 1600–1750," *Signs of Early Modern France II: Seventeenth Century and Beyond*, ed. David Lee Rubin (Charlottesville: Rockwood Press, 1997), pp. 17–44; excerpts from Mary Poovey, *A History of the Modern Fact: Problems of Knowledge in the Sciences of Wealth and Society* (Chicago: University of Chicago, 1998), used by permission of the University of Chicago Press; Alex Potts, "'Sans tête, ni bras, ni jambes,' la description du Torse du Belvédère de Winckelmann," in *La Description*: *Actes du Colloque Archives de la Critique d'Art* (Chateaugiron: Printemps, 1997), pp. 19–33; "Imagining Flowers," from *Dreaming by the Book* by Elaine Scarry, ©1999 by Elaine Scarry, reprinted by permission of Farrar, Straus and Giroux, LLC; passages from the poetry of John Ashbery, cited in Elaine Scarry's "Imagining Flowers," used with kind permission of the author; Londa Schiebinger, various materials from *Nature's Body: Gender in the Making of Modern Science* (Boston: Beacon Press, 1993) and "Lost Knowledge, Bodies of Ignorance, and the Poverty of Taxonomy as Illustrated by the Curious Fate of *Flos Pavonis*, an Abortifacient," in *Picturing Science, Producing Art*, ed. Caroline Jones and Peter Galison (New York: Routledge, 1998), pp. 125–44.

Contents

Contributors   xi

Introduction   1
JOHN BENDER AND MICHAEL MARRINAN

Description: Fantasies of General Knowledge

Description by Omission: Nature Enlightened and Obscured   11
LORRAINE DASTON

Nature's Unruly Body: The Limits of Scientific Description   25
LONDA SCHIEBINGER

Mithridates in Paradise: Describing Languages in a
Universalistic World   44
JÜRGEN TRABANT

Between Political Arithmetic and Political Economy   61
MARY POOVEY

Describing: Imagination and Knowing

Problems of Description in Art: Realism   79
WOLFGANG KLEIN

Imagining Flowers: Perceptual Mimesis (Particularly Delphinium)   95
ELAINE SCARRY

Not Seeing the *Laocoön*: Lessing in the Archive of the
Eighteenth Century   118
WOLFGANG ERNST

Disparities between Part and Whole in the Description of
Works of Art   135
ALEX POTTS

The Undescribed: Horizons of the Known

Between Mechanism and Romantic *Naturphilosophie*:
Vitalizing Nature and Naturalizing Historical Discourse in the
Late Enlightenment   153
PETER HANNS REILL

Transparency and Utopia: Constructing the Void from Pascal
to Foucault   175
ANTHONY VIDLER

Aesthetic Media: The Structure of Aesthetic Theory before Kant   199
DAVID E. WELLBERY

Appendix   215
Notes   219
Works Cited   261
Index   285

Illustrations

1. *The Journeys of Linnaeus's Students between 1746 and 1796*, from
   Robert Elias Fries, *A Short History of Swedish Botany*   28
2. *Homo Sylvestris*, from Edward Tyson, *Orang-Outang, sive Homo
   Sylvestris: or the Anatomy of a Pygmie compared with that of a
   Monkey, an Ape, and a Man*   32
3. *Flos pavonis*, from Maria Sibylla Merian, *Metamorphosis
   Insectorum Surinamensium*   36
4. Lorenzo Hervás y Panduro, *Vocabolario poligloto con prolegomeni
   sopre più di cl. lingue*   52
5. Lorenzo Hervás y Panduro, *Saggio pratico delle lingue con
   prolegomeni, e una raccolta di orazioni dominical . . .*   54
6. *Laocoön*   120
7. Gotthold Ephraim Lessing, "Italian Notebook," entry for
   Rome, 26 September 1775   122
8. *Torso Belvedere* (front view)   140
9. *Torso Belvedere* (rear view)   141
10. Jeremy Bentham, Samuel Bentham, and Willey Reveley,
    Penitentiary Panopticon   177
11. Claude-Nicolas Ledoux, *Perspective View of the City of Chaux*   182
12. Claude-Nicolas Ledoux, *Cross Section and Plan of the Cemetery
    of the City of Chaux*   188
13. Claude-Nicolas Ledoux, *Elevation of the Cemetery of the City
    of Chaux*   190
14. Étienne-Louis Boullée, *Project for a Newton Cenotaph,
    Cross Section with Interior Effect of Day*   191
15. Étienne-Louis Boullée, *Project for a Funerary Monument*   194

Contributors

JOHN BENDER is Jean G. and Morris M. Doyle Professor in Interdisciplinary Studies at Stanford University in the Departments of English and Comparative Literature. He is Director of the Stanford Humanities Center and Anthony P. Meier Family Professor. His writings include *Spenser and Literary Pictorialism* (1972) and *Imagining the Penitentiary: Fiction and the Architecture of Mind in Eighteenth-Century England* (1987). He is editor, with Simon Stern, of *Tom Jones* (1996) and of two volumes with David Wellbery: *The Ends of Rhetoric: History, Theory, Practice* (1990) and *Chronotypes: The Construction of Time* (1991). He is currently working on *The Culture of Diagram*, a book co-authored with Michael Marrinan.

LORRAINE DASTON is Director at the Max Planck Institute for the History of Science and Honorary Professor at the Humboldt-Universität in Berlin. Her recent writings include *Wonders and the Order of Nature*, co-authored with Katherine Park (1998), and *Wunder, Beweise und Tatsachen: Zur Geschichte der Rationalität* (2001), as well as several edited volumes: *Biographies of Scientific Objects* (2000), *Things That Talk: Object Lessons in Art and Science* (2004), and, with Fernando Vidal, *The Moral Authority of Nature* (2003).

WOLFGANG ERNST is chaired Professor of Media Theories in the Seminar of Media Studies at the Humboldt-Universität in Berlin. His writings include *M.edium F.oucault* (2000), *Das Rumoren der Archive: Ordnung aus Unordnung* (2002) and *Im Namen von Geschichte: Sammeln—Speichern—Er/Zählen; infrastrukturelle Konfigurationen des deutschen Gedächtnisses*

(2003). He is also co-editor (with Georg Trogemann and Alexander Nitussov) of *Computing in Russia: The History of Computing Devices and Information Technology Revealed* (2001).

WOLFGANG KLEIN is Professor of Romanische Kulturwissenschaft at the University of Osnabrück in Germany. His books include *Schriftsteller in der französischen Volksfront* (1978, revised French edition as *Commune: Revue pour la défense de la culture*, 1988) and *Der nüchterne Blick: Programmatischer Realismus in Frankreich nach 1848* (1988). He is the editor of *Paris 1935: Erster Internationaler Schriftstellerkongreß zur Verteidigung der Kultur* (1988, enlarged French edition with Sandra Teroni as *Défense de la culture*, 2004) and *Heinrich Mann—Félix Bertaux: Briefwechsel 1922–1948* (2002). He co-edited *Nach der Aufklärung? Beiträge zur Kulturwissenschaft* with Waltraud Naumann-Beyer (1995), *Literaturforschung heute* with Eckart Goebel (1999), and, with Ernst Müller, *Genuß und Egoismus: Zur Kritik ihrer geschichtlichen Verknüpfung* (2002).

MICHAEL MARRINAN is Professor of Art History at Stanford University. His writings include *Painting Politics for Louis-Philippe: Art and Ideology in Orléanist France, 1830–1848* (1988) and *Romantic Paris: Histories of a Cultural Landscape, 1800–1850* (forthcoming). He is co-editor, with Hans Ulrich Gumbrecht, of *Mapping Benjamin: The Work of Art in the Digital Age* (2003). He is currently working on *The Culture of Diagram*, a book co-authored with John Bender.

MARY POOVEY is Samuel Rudin University Professor of the Humanities at New York University. Her books include *The Proper Lady and the Woman Writer: Ideology as Style in the Works of Mary Wollstonecraft, Mary Shelley, and Jane Austen* (1984), *Uneven Developments: The Ideological Work of Gender in Mid-Victorian England* (1988), *Making a Social Body: British Cultural Formation, 1830–1864* (1995), and *A History of the Modern Fact: Problems of Knowledge in the Sciences of Wealth and Society* (1998).

ALEX POTTS is Max Loehr Collegiate Professor and Chair of the History of Art Department at the University of Michigan, Ann Arbor. His writings include *Flesh and the Ideal: Winckelmann and the Origins of Art History* (1994) and *The Sculptural Imagination: Figurative, Modernist, Minimalist* (2000). He is currently working on a book about post-war European and American art.

PETER HANNS REILL is Professor of History at UCLA and Director of both the UCLA Center for Seventeenth and Eighteenth Century Studies and the William Andrews Clark Memorial Library. His books include *The German Enlightenment and the Rise of Historicism* (1975) and *Vitalizing Nature in the Enlightenment* (forthcoming). He is consulting editor for the *Encyclopedia of the Enlightenment* (1996) and co-editor of several volumes: *Aufklärung und Geschichte: Studien zur deutschen Geschichtswissenschaft im 18. Jahrhundert* with Georg Iggers et al. (1986), *Vision of Empire: Voyages, Botany, and Representations of Nature* with David Philip Miller (1996), *Wissenschaft als kulturell Praxis, 1750–1900* with Hans Eric Bödeker and Jürgen Schlumbohm (1999), *Republikanische Tugend: Ausbildung eines Schweizer Nationalbewusstseins und Erziehung eines neuen Bürgers* with Michael Böhler et al. (2000), and *What's Left of Enlightenment: A Postmodern Question* with Keith Michael Baker (2001).

ELAINE SCARRY is Walter M. Cabot Professor of Aesthetics and the General Theory of Value at Harvard University. Her books include *The Body in Pain* (1985), *Resisting Representation* (1994), *On Beauty and Being Just* (1999), and *Dreaming by the Book* (1999). *Who Defended the Country?*, edited by Joshua Cohen and Joel Rogers, collects her articles on the events of September 11. She has also edited *Literature and the Body: Essays on Populations and Persons* (1988), *Fins-de-Siècle: English Poetry in 1590, 1690, 1790, 1890, 1990* (1995), and, with Daniel L. Schacter, *Memory, Brain, and Belief* (2000).

LONDA SCHIEBINGER is Barbara D. Finberg Director of the Institute for Research on Women and Gender, and Professor of History of Science at Stanford University. She is author of *The Mind Has No Sex? Women in the Origins of Modern Science* (1989), *Nature's Body: Gender in the Making of Modern Science* (1993), *Has Feminism Changed Science?* (1999), and *Plants and Empire: Colonial Bioprospecting in the Atlantic World* (2004). She is the editor of *Feminism and the Body* (2000) and section editor of the *Oxford Companion to the Body* (2001). She has co-edited, with Angela Creager and Elizabeth Lunbeck, *Feminism in Twentieth-Century Science, Technology, and Medicine* (2001), and, with Claudia Swann, *Colonial Botany: Science, Commerce, and Politics* (2004).

JÜRGEN TRABANT is Professor of French and Italian Linguistics at the Freie Universität Berlin. His writings include *Elemente der Semiotik* (1976), *Apeliotes oder der Sinn der Sprache* (1986), *Traditionen Humboldts* (1990), *Neue Wissenschaft von alten Zeichen* (1994), and *Mithradates im Paradies* (2003). He is also the editor, with Sean Ward, of *New Essays on the Origin of Language* (2001).

ANTHONY VIDLER is Professor and Dean of the Irwin S. Chanin School of Architecture at the Cooper Union in New York. His books include *The Writing of the Walls: Theory and Design in the Late Enlightenment* (1987), *Claude-Nicolas Ledoux: Architecture and Society in the Ancien Régime* (1990), *The Architectural Uncanny: Essays in the Modern Unhomely* (1992), and *Warped Space: Art, Architecture, and Anxiety in Modern Culture* (2000).

DAVID E. WELLBERY is LeRoy T. and Margaret Deffenbaugh Carlson University Professor at the University of Chicago. His books include *Lessing's Laocoön: Semiotics and Aesthetics in the Age of Reason* (1984), *The Specular Moment: Goethe's Early Lyric and the Beginnings of Romanticism* (1996), and *Schopenhauer's Bedeutung für die moderne Literatur* (1998). He is the editor of *Positionen der Literaturwissenschaft: Acht Modellanalysen am Beispiel von Kleists "Das Erdbeben in Chili"* (1985) and the eleventh volume of Goethe's collected works (1988). His many co-editorial projects include two volumes with John Bender, *The Ends of Rhetoric: History, Theory, Practice* (1990) and *Chronotypes: The Construction of Time* (1991), as well as *Reconstructing Individualism: Autonomy, Individuality, and the Self in Western Thought*, with Thomas C. Heller and Morton Sosna (1986), *Traditions of Experiment from the Enlightenment to the Present*, with Nancy Kaiser (1992), and *Kunst—Zeugung—Geburt: Theorien und Metaphern ästhetischer Produktion in der Neuzeit* with Christian Begemann (2002). He is currently co-editor of the *Deutsche Vierteljahrsschrift für Literaturwissenschaft und Geistegeschichte*.

Regimes of Description

JOHN BENDER

MICHAEL MARRINAN

Introduction

> Today we are learning the language in which God created life. We are
> gaining ever more awe for the complexity, the beauty, the wonder of
> God's most divine and sacred gift. With this profound new knowledge,
> humankind is on the verge of gaining immense new power to heal.
>
> —President Bill Clinton[1]

Amidst the international excitement generated by the carefully staged joint
announcement of 26 June 2000 that two competing teams of researchers
had successfully completed a "working draft" of the human genome, both
the popular and specialist press claimed that a new era had opened in the
history and description of the human species.[2] Two years later, the Human
Genome Project drew to a close with delivery of "the instruction set that
carries each of us from the one-cell egg through adulthood to the grave."[3]
Yet even this final rendering of the human genome is far from complete
since sections of DNA near the center and at the ends of the chromosomes
contain so much repetitive data that they cannot be positioned with accuracy. The language of life championed by President Clinton still contains
many gaps: what kind of description of our human species has the genome
project made possible?

Ever since the discovery of DNA, and the double-helix model of the
chromosome, medical researchers have promised that mastering the genetic
code of life—whether human, animal, or plant—would offer the possibility
of a healthier, more productive world where one would be able to improve
species, eradicate disease, and clone favorite pets.[4] Genetics has seemed to
be on the verge of engineering the longevity that the Enlightenment
thinker Condorcet could only imagine in 1795 when musing on the future
of mankind: "will not the interval between the first breath that he draws
and the time when in the natural course of events, without disease or accident, he expires, increase indefinitely?"[5] Condorcet assumed that the
progress of knowledge would effect this benefit by gradually closing gaps in

our understanding of life. He probably never imagined that knowledge could be erected on gaps.

Condorcet dreamt a language of science that grew towards a perfection with no gaps or errors, "ever improving and broadening its scope" and "giving to every subject embraced by the human intelligence, a precision and a rigor that would make knowledge of the truth easy and error almost impossible."[6] By accepting a certain number of defined gaps, research on the human genome has undermined the persistent notion that the language of science is all-inclusive. It has also undermined the assumption that human beings are different in kind from animals. Researchers working with information from the genome project have arrived at some rather surprising estimates about the number of human genes. Backing away from original projections that the human genome might be comprised of more than 100,000 genes,[7] scientists began to extrapolate patterns from the genome project that predicted only about 30,000 human genes.[8] This number is uncomfortably close to the approximately 17,000 genes of *Drosophilia* fruit flies,[9] the completely tabulated 19,099 genes of the roundworm *Caenorhabditis elegans*,[10] or the estimated 15,000 genes of *Arabidopsis thaliana*, a plant related to mustard weed.[11] Current estimates are even lower—perhaps 24,500 or 23,299.[12]

Even such revised numbers assume that a mass of chromosome material in the human genome is "junk," the origin and purpose of which remains a mystery. Sydney Brenner, who coined the phrase, was quick to say "junk, and not garbage, because there is a difference that everybody knows: junk is kept, while garbage is thrown away."[13] Research on the Y chromosome has demonstrated Brenner's point.[14] The Y chromosome is unusual because it does not have a twin against which to check genetic integrity. Rather, it exchanges genes with two adjacent sequences—mirror images of one another—that otherwise carry no genetic information. In this way, seemingly useless material performs an essential backup function, allowing the Y chromosome to replicate with a minimum of error. One day, other seemingly useless material may figure in our accounts of the complexity of human life relative to that of flies and roundworms. It might turn out that proteins and enzymes peculiar to the junk material in the human genome determine much of who we are.

Many of the issues fueling publicity around the genome project strike us as germane to the problem of describing. The popular notion, echoed by President Clinton, is that sequencing the human genome brings us closer to understanding the essence of humanity. This might be true, although recent studies have revealed that the chimpanzee's genome is 98.8% identical with that of humans, a startling discovery seeming to imply that variables like diet might, for instance, have affected the relatively recent genetic adaptation of humans to speech.[15]

The genome project has produced an extremely useful research tool, but it seems unreasonable to think that the essence of humanity has been captured in its strings of code. Its techniques were too limited to yield a definition of the human, whether physical or metaphysical. The project's computerized technology and algorithms of probability assume gaps in the sequence that do not threaten the usefulness of the resulting tool. High-speed sampling machines, designed to read "snippets" of stained chromosome material five-hundred thousand positions at a time (known as an "expressed sequence tag" or EST), converted the visual spectrum of each snippet into a sequence of four letters that became the "code" of each position. A somewhat controversial method to interpret this cornucopia of data, developed by J. Craig Venter's team at Celera Corporation, used a powerful computer algorithm to "splice" the snippets into a continuous thread: rather than working steadily from one end to the other, they scanned strips in a kind of "shotgun" approach and relied upon a battery of computers to produce the billions of comparisons and cross-checks to assemble the parts—very similar to how compact audio disks over sample the music to produce relatively error-free reproduction of complex sound waves.[16] The sequence of the genome was produced by a sorting operation guided by probabilities made possible by reducing the genetic material to a code of very few elements, and by accepting the inevitability of extensive gaps. Those gaps raise some general questions about our contemporary fascination with, and belief in, the power of digital bits to encode fully the material world.

What strikes us as worthy of comment in all of this is the unflagging belief that this sequencing technology has fully "mapped" the genome, even though an inordinate and surprising surplus of "junk" material remains. Some researchers believe this material might be chromosomes damaged by disease or altered by evolution throughout the long history of humankind, forming in a peculiar way a living archive of our species.[17] If this is so, our current understanding of the human genome relegates much of our genetic history to the scrap heap. But our point is slightly different. An explanatory shortfall is a problem only for those who fantasize the utopia of a completely defined code.[18] By contrast, if we define "description" rigorously— meaning to represent rather than to replicate an object materially—it becomes clear that digital technology of the sort used to sequence the human genome is also a form of representation and does not free us from the hermeneutic constraints of describing. What are some of those constraints?

The topic demands more than a cursory treatment, and the long meditation on description produced by the authors of the *Encyclopédie* (see Appendix) testifies to the historical and disciplinary complexity of the question. At least three conditions seem to govern descriptions. First, and perhaps foremost, is the simple fact that things do not describe themselves, meaning that descriptions are produced from particular perspectives or situations, and are based upon a finite and selective body of features— whether perceived by humans, measured by machines, or produced in the imagination. Leaving aside questions of use-value, we see no differences between descriptions of "real" things and those of imagined things. The corollary is that technical descriptions based on perceptions have no greater intrinsic claim to objectivity than the descriptions of a novelist or a painter. The second condition is that descriptions do not replicate objects, but rather employ different media to transmit the salient characteristics of those objects across time and space. To send a poem or a drawing of roses to one's lover will always be a different kind of present than an actual bouquet. The third condition is historical variability produced when the technology used to register descriptive features changes so dramatically that things previously invisible become newly visible. An uncanny example of this would be the earliest daguerreotype views of Paris that are mysteriously devoid of people—not because the streets had been cleared for the photographer, but because the medium was simply unable to register the presence of anything or anyone that moved.[19] Within a few years, thanks to the huge improvements in light sensitivity produced by exposing daguerreotype plates to bromide vapors, people began to repopulate those strangely empty streets.

The essays in the present volume sketch some of the historical circumstances tied to these three qualities as they were articulated in the late eighteenth century. Michel Foucault's groundbreaking work on this period, which clearly affects our own thinking, emphasized the rupture between disciplines of synthesis and analysis—a separation of deductive and formal sciences from empirical sciences that "detached the possibility of synthesis from the space of representation."[20] But the surprising aspect that emerges from these essays is the degree to which their archaeology of the "regime" of description does not reveal a rupture so much as three interlocking arenas, which we have used to divide and organize the volume. First, and probably closest to Foucault's line of thought, is the section we have called "Description: Fantasies of General Knowledge." The recurring issue in this first group of essays concerns the utopian idea that knowledge is stable and generally impervious to the vicissitudes of time. Taken together, the essays counter this idea by demonstrating the historical nature of fact (Daston), the cultural, geographical, and gendered specificity of descriptions (Schiebinger), the emergence of a relational theory of language (Trabant), and the mutability of the border between quantitative and rhetorical disciplines that Foucault thought unbreachable (Poovey).

The essays gathered in "Describing: Imagination and Knowing" explore questions related to our assertion that descriptions of imagined things are technically indistinguishable from those of objects in the world. On one hand, realism in art—notably as a form of literature—is not isolated from the practices of science, but emerges historically where empirical modes of analysis are deployed in the construction of an imagined world (Klein). On the other hand, under highly specialized conditions in which the perceptual apparatus and imagination fall into perfect congruence, realism is forestalled by the emergence of an absolute mental reproduction (Scarry). Between these two extremes lie the physical encounters, recorded in various archives, which engender descriptions that might be both empirical and shaped by discursive constraints (Ernst), or sensual and driven by desire (Potts).

Attention to gaps and voids in the archive lead to our final section, "The Undescribed: Horizons of the Known." The three authors included under this rubric reconnoiter the historical breadth and reach of *Aufklärung* by drawing attention to the edges of our understanding. This includes revealing the emergence of a vitalist, organicist science that parallels both the mechanist, rationalist practices of empiricism, and the affective domain of *sentiment*, without intersecting either of them (Reill). In a like manner, the lucidly massed, geometric volumes of the architecture of Boullée and Ledoux, or the pervasive transparency of Foucault's Panopticon model, cannot be described without recourse to the voids that throw solids into relief, or the opacity that gives transparency its brilliance (Vidler). Finally, for those who believe that modernist immanence extends in an unbroken line from the Enlightenment, an archaeology of aesthetic description reveals a complex, unstable attention to both medium and message that Kant and Hegel cut short, but which has reemerged as the central concern of postmodernist theory (Wellbery).

Today, scientists regularly refer to the sequence of the human genome as a "map" of the human chromosome, and we believe that word is appropriate, though "description" would be more precise. Maps remain within the realm of classical description, which we have defined as intrinsically different from its object. Maps are representations that include many gaps and ellipses, yet one is still able to sail from Southampton to Rio using a map as an instruction set. This is how geneticists and drug companies are using the human genome—as a map to locate a relatively small number of genes amidst a vast sea of material where one hopes to find remedies for the diverse maladies that plague humankind. The promise of great commercial profit incites researchers to patent their genetic findings on speculation, even before knowing the eventual import. Nonetheless, sequencing of the entire human genome, including its lengthy runs of "junk" material, remains a long-term goal of some researchers, even though the genome project has been officially ended. The idea of an eventual success raises another kind of question: will the entirely sequenced human genome retain the approximation of a map, or will it actually approach the truth about life? Will it, in other words, remain within the realm of description? Recalling our three governing conditions, our answer would be yes. If a complete genome sequence is eventually achieved, it will be the product of a particular perspective determined by a given array of equipment and analytic procedures, it will employ a different medium than that of human cellular tissue, and—ultimately—it will be the result of a different technology of measurement and analysis than used at present. If today's incompleteness follows from limitations intrinsic to current technology, then closing those gaps will involve more than spending a lot of time on the problem: the technology itself will be forced to evolve. Finally, any added value derived from a fully sequenced human genome will emerge from its use as a tool in research or treatment, not from the mere fact of its completion.

Much has been made of the "digital revolution" and its potential to blur and to mix media, or to fabricate new realities—a nightmare envisioned in popular culture by the *Matrix* films. Yet we continue to believe that classical descriptive modes will not disappear, although they might very well be *absorbed*.[21] In saying this, we recall the troublesome "junk" material that eludes explanation and fills the gaps between genes along the extraordinary length of human chromosomes. One day those gaps will probably be filled with meaning—the way the streets of Paris eventually recovered their life and animation from those early daguerreotypes. Conceptual distinctions between representation and replication will surely remain viable in that brave new world, but functional differences may collapse. In our most pessimistic moments, we can imagine that a cloned and re-engineered human species will find untidy analog descriptions to be merely pleasant diversions. But we also believe that the power to describe is one of the great achievements of human thought, and that an archaeology of description is order: the essays of this book are a beginning.

Description

Fantasies of General Knowledge

Description by Omission

Nature Enlightened and Obscured

In its very first volume of proceedings, the botanists of the Paris Académie Royale des Sciences (est. 1666) announced that their mission consisted in the description of particulars about plants, and that these descriptions would be prolix: "Among plants, there are some which encompass such a large number of circumstances, that it is not possible to describe them in a few words. We have therefore decided that, after we have given an idea of the whole plant, it will be good to describe exactly each of the parts that merit treatment in more detail." The French language was not always adequate to the exacting descriptions the botanists desired. Somewhat apologetically, perhaps mindful of the vigilance of their colleagues at the Académie Française with regard to neologisms, the botanists took "the liberty of introducing several new ways of speaking when we lack appropriate words in usage," even at the expense of "a little less civility [un peu moins de politesse]." For the description of colors in particular, the botanists turned from the polite society of books to the shop talk of artisans: "we have in French many quite suitable words [mots significatifs] in this matter [of color], but which are not in any books, and which only painters, dyers and weavers appear to have introduced into their common usage." Such linguistic slumming was essential to botanical description, for colors were key to the identification of plants, and "could not be replaced in any manner" by figures alone.[1]

Some seventy years later, the Swedish botanist Carl von Linnaeus railed against the verbosity and excessive prolixity of botanical descriptions: "[The French botanist Joseph Pitton de] Tournefort enumerates 93 Tulips (where there is only one) and 63 Hyacinths (where there are but two), and others have often been no less extravagant." He reproached his fellow botanists in scathing terms for their preoccupation, verbal and visual, with the details of color: "How many volumes have you written of specific names taken from colour? What tons of copper have you destroyed in making unnecessary plates? What vast sums of money have you enticed fraudulently, as it appears, from other men's pockets, the purchasers to wit, on the strength of colour alone?" Only "Number, Shape, Position, and Proportion" counted in the identification of plants, and each species could be described with an economical label of two words. Linnaeus went so far as to elevate verbal parsimony to a principle of ontological perfection: "The All-Wise Author of Nature shared such conciseness making all things. . . . The fewer elements are used in making anything, the more perfect it is." A quadruped was superior to a six-legged insect, a two-legged man to a quadruped, and Linnaeus boasted that he could "distinguish these 100 [plant] species by no more than six adjectives each."[2]

The shift from the prolixity of the Parisian botanists to the parsimony of Linnaeus is emblematic of a far broader transformation in the ideals and practices of scientific description that occurred between circa 1660 and 1730. Whereas naturalists in the late seventeenth century had chosen "to make our descriptions very particular," in the belief that "nature is variable and inconstant,"[3] the *Encyclopédie* article on "Description" in natural history warned that "[a] book which contained so many and such long descriptions, far from giving us clear and distinct ideas of the bodies which cover the earth and which compose it, present to the mind only indeterminate and colossal figures scattered without order and traced without proportion." In this paper I will argue that this shift in the ideals and practices of the description of nature was symptomatic of a more fundamental shift in the category of the scientific fact in the early decades of the eighteenth century.

That the factual should have a history is an uncomfortable notion. Facts are the alpha and omega of modern scientific experience, the beginning and the end of all of its most exacting experiments and its most elaborate theories. Since we equate "the facts" with the totality of all that exists and happens, the claim that facts per se come into being and pass away seems outrageous, akin to that of the wild-eyed skeptic who denies the existence of the external world. What I mean is, however, nothing so metaphysical. It is facts as a way of sieving and parsing experience rather than experience per se (or whatever external reality may give rise to human experience) that is my quarry here. Although historians and philosophers of science have worried that facts may be "contaminated" by theory or "constructed" by society, and although they have charted the changing content and credibility of particular facts, the *category* of the factual has remained curiously unanalyzed. This or that fact may have a biography; facts in general may not be as neutral and detached as they seem; but the concept of what kind of thing or event qualifies as a scientific fact, and when and why it does, has escaped investigation. I would like to suggest that the *category* of the factual, as well as the particular facts that instantiate it, has a *history*, and that this history is rich in implications for how description creates a texture of experience—granular with particulars and riotous with colors, or smooth with generalizations and as angular as a woodcut (to return briefly to the botanists).

More specifically, I shall argue that the prototypical scientific fact mutated between circa 1660 and 1730, from a singular and striking event that could be replicated only with great difficulty, if at all, to a large and uniform class of events that could be produced at will. The texture of description of nature changed accordingly, from long accounts bristling with particulars to concise reports made deliberately bland by summary, repetition, and omission of details. Nature was not yet universal and eternal at the turn of the eighteenth century; my story of the transformation of the scientific fact is part of how it came to be so by mid-century. Examples might be taken from any number of scientific disciplines, from botany to meteorology to optics. For reasons of space, I have chosen to concentrate on a single case, symbolically resonant of the Enlightenment: the late seventeenth- and early eighteenth-century investigations of luminescence, or "cold light." Within the history of luminescence during this period, I shall focus on the writings of the English chemist Robert Boyle and the French physicist Charles Dufay, both because their work set contemporary standards of experimentation, and because their similar scientific temperaments, both wary of hypothesis, permit a more closely controlled comparison of how each drew the contours of the scientific fact.

I. *"Shining Instances"*

When Robert Boyle published his observations on his "aerial noctiluca" or on "a diamond that shines in the dark" or on "shining Flesh, both of veal and pullet," he was contributing to a collection of singular phenomena that he and his contemporaries hoped would eventually unlock the best-guarded "secrets of nature." The annals of the earliest scientific societies founded in the seventeenth century abound with such oddities: the *Saggi* of the Accademia del Cimento in Florence, the *Philosophical Transactions of the Royal Society of London*, the *Mémoires de l'Académie des Sciences* in Paris, and the *Miscellanea Curiosa* (later *Ephémérides*) of the Collegium Naturae Curiosum in Germany all routinely carried news not only of things that glowed in the dark, but also of anatomical anomalies such as monstrous births, unusual weather such as cyclones or "rains of blood," heavenly rarities such as the aurora borealis or a new star, and a great deal that defied ready classification—a man who slept for three weeks at a stretch, a well that emitted a searing heat, ants from Surinam that "marched in formation."[4]

It was just this miscellaneous quality that seventeenth-century natural philosophers valued in these strange phenomena, which were meant to serve two principal purposes in what they called the "new experimental philosophy." First, they would help destroy the old, Scholastic natural philosophy by confronting its sweeping generalizations and neatly parsed species with a crowd of exceptions. Second, they would help to build a new natural philosophy by laying bare the otherwise inaccessible deep structure of nature, and by furthering the labor of induction.

Strange facts would not only defy Aristotelian explanations, straddle boundaries between Aristotelian natural kinds, and contradict Aristotelian axioms; they would also lead the new natural philosophy to the hidden causes of all we observe in nature. Why should the phenomena that Aristotelians thought *least* suited to serve as the raw material of science—odd, variable, rare phenomena—have struck their seventeenth-century critics as the phenomena *best* suited to the purpose? In part, because they thought the fundamental causes in nature were likely to be beyond the grasp of human senses; Aristotle's forms can be discerned by perception, but not Francis Bacon's "latent configurations" of René Descartes' microscopic mechanisms or Isaac Newton's "active principles." Nature had "secrets," in the parlance of the day, and was thought most likely to divulge these when caught by surprise, or when deviating from her wonted paths. As in medicine, seventeeth-century natural philosophers (many of whom had medical training) expected to understand the normal by careful study of the pathological.

For a natural philosophy that above all was wary of facile generalizations and conventional wisdom and that sought the "secrets" of nature, the facts of strange phenomena were peculiarly enlightening. Even the wonder they evoked made a minor contribution to spreading the new science, for wonder, as Descartes observed, stimulates us to probe the causes of all that appears to us "rare and extraordinary."[5] Both the typical characteristics of these atypical phenomena—rarity, singularity, variability—and the emotional responses they evoked—wonder, surprise, and occasionally fear—would, it was hoped, work to estrange the observer from the habitual, the familiar, and the conventional, and to open the mind to an empiricism without preconceptions.[6] These were the alleged scientific advantages of wondrous facts, and in the context of seventeenth-century natural philosophy they were estimable.

We are now in a better position to understand how and why Boyle and his contemporaries studied luminescence. Like the study of monstrous births in anatomy or double refraction in optics, luminescent substances were the anomalies that would reveal true natures—in this case, the nature of light. Luminescent substances like Boyle's noctiluca or the celebrated Bologna stone were examples of Bacon's prerogative instances, "shining instances" in every respect. In contrast to the familiar light of flame or of the sun, these glowing objects were cold to the touch, decoupling the customary association of light and heat. Moreover, each instance of luminescence was a singularity in its class. The "carbuncle" (from the Latin "little coal") that Benvenuto Cellini claimed to have seen glow at night on the finger of one Biagio de Bono was a singularity among gemstones; the radiant mutton that the Danish physician Thomas Bartholin saw at the Montpellier market was a singularity among meats; the shining fungus described by the Swiss naturalist Conrad Gesner a singularity among plants.[7] However much these individual singularities strained the boundaries of received categories, they could nonetheless be gathered together into a single class of "substances of whatever kind, that generate light," as Bacon headed his *Topica inquisitionis de luce et lumine* (1612). The facts of strange phenomena simultaneously dissolved homogeneities and united heterogeneities—separating heat and light, but bringing together the stars, rotten wood, and "some stockings [that] shine while you are pulling them off."[8] I shall call this outlook "militant empiricism."

Although there were several comprehensive seventeenth-century treatises devoted to luminescence, the bulk of the literature of this period dwells on a single type of luminescence, or even a single instance. Typical of these narrow-gauge publications was Boyle's "A Short Account of some Observations . . . about a Diamond, that shines in the Dark" (1663), which describes the properties of a single gem when rubbed, warmed, plunged into oil, gouged with a steel bodkin, and spat upon. Throughout these observations, Boyle never lost sight of his broader goal, namely explaining the nature of light. But, in keeping with the metaphysics and methods characteristic of the facts of strange phenomena, he approached this unifying goal by carefully marking the differences—rather than the similarities— among luminescent substances. This preference for differences over similarities among luminescent phenomena runs through almost all of the seventeenth-century literature on the subject, even those more compendious treatises meant to encompass the whole range of known phosphors. It worked to undermine the integrity of the class of luminescent phosphors, despite their common property of being cold light-bearers. This splintering tendency was strengthened by the fine-grained descriptive detail also typical of seventeenth-century observation reports. Boyle for example records which side of the diamond he rubbed, and with what color cloth.[9] He admitted his narratives were prolix and "particular," but refused to sacrifice even the most minute detail to the reader's impatience.[10]

This strenuous heed to particulars stemmed from both the demands of militant empiricism and the sensibility it fostered. Determined to begin natural philosophy afresh, without preconceived notions, Boyle and his contemporaries could not afford to neglect the slightest detail, for who could tell a priori whether or not a red or white rubbing cloth, or the direction the wind was blowing that day, might make a difference? (In the case of capricious phenomena such as luminescence and electricity, such minutiae sometimes *did* make a difference.)[11] For fear of missing a tiny but crucial detail, the natural philosopher cultivated a state of exaggerated attention that attempted to focus simultaneously and with equal sharpness on every aspect of the sensory field. When reading the observational reports of Boyle and his colleagues, one is irresistibly reminded of the impossible accuracy of some of Dürer's animal paintings, in which every tuft of fur of the rabbit or squirrel is as crisply outlined as every other: there is no background in these pictures, only foreground. In natural philosophy, this heroic effort of observation was fueled by curiosity, which in the seventeenth century connoted not only an omnivorous and impatient appetite for knowledge, but also painstaking, even excessive care (recall the Latin root *curare*) lavished on each and every particular.[12]

The open-mindedness required by militant empiricism, sustained by the typically seventeenth-century sensibility of curiosity, also predisposed natural philosophers to lend a sympathetic ear to marvelous tales ridiculed by their more skeptical contemporaries. In reviewing the many ancient and modern accounts of carbuncles and other wondrous gems, Boyle trod a fine line between credulity and skepticism: "though I be very backward to admit strange things for truths, yet I am not very forward to reject them as impossibilities."[13] After all, both the voyages of exploration and recent scientific research on phenomena like luminescence and electricity had vindicated or even surpassed many a traveler's tale with new wonders. As Pierre Potier wrote in his 1622 account of the Bologna stone: "Daily there emerge new things in nature, in which its great miracles are appearing."[14] The worst fear of empiricists—denying a real fact to save a false hypothesis—was not without grounds. For example, the French Cartesian Jacques Rohault doubted the carbuncle stories in his *Traité de physique* (1671) because "if it were true, what they say of a *Carbuncle* and a *Diamond*, viz. that they shine in the Dark; I should freely own, that I am mistaken in all that I have said about Light. . . . But it is certain, that these are only idle Stories, told without any Proof, and received by credulous Persons, for I have often times experienced the contrary myself."[15]

In Rohault's "contrary" experience lay the greatest disadvantage of the facts of strange phenomena. Successful as they were at debunking old theories and blocking a too ready acceptance of new ones, they were also devilishly difficult to produce and reproduce. The very singularity that the militant empiricists valued and emphasized in their treatment of these facts wreaked havoc with attempts to replicate them. They frustrated the most careful controls, and their idiosyncrasies baffled explanation. The seventeenth-century literature on luminescence abounds with examples of capricious phenomena: Gottfried Wilhelm Leibniz related how the Wittenberg chemist Johann Kunkel could only sometimes synthesize phosphorus;[16] even in Bologna there was almost no one who could calcinate the stone so that it would reliably glow;[17] Boyle puzzled over why some rotten fish shined and others did not, even though "they were brought by the same person I was wont to employ, and hung up in the same place where I used to have them put";[18] Boyle's correspondent John Clayton wondered why the petticoat of one Mrs. Susanna Sewall sparkled when she wore it, but not when her sister did.[19]

Because the facts of strange phenomena were capricious, chance played a large role in their replication and a fortiori in their discovery. All three of the artificial phosphors discovered in the seventeenth century were lucky byproducts of alchemical puttering: Vincenzo Cascariolo was trying to extract silver from Monte Paterno ore when he calcinated the Bologna stone; the Saxon magistrate Baldewein was trying to collect the *Weltgeist* when he instead made "phosphorus hermeticus"; the Hamburg alchemist Hennig Brand was looking for gold when he distilled phosphorus from human urine. Natural phosphors like the Montpellier mutton or Boyle's diamond depended at least as much as these artificial ones on a mysterious conjunction of circumstances which researchers could not manipulate. The discoverers of phosphors often had difficulty reproducing their own results, and their would-be imitators were in even worse straits. Only with numerous hints and after a long string of failures was Boyle able to reproduce Brand's phosphorus, or something like it. Although Boyle published his method to spare others the same pains, he warned that even with the recipe "he, that shall, at the first attempt, succeed in preparing this liquor, shall be thought by me, either a very skilful, or a lucky operator."[20]

These formidable difficulties of variability and dexterity were compounded by the secrecy that surrounded the preparation of phosphors. The ethos of openly communicating results had only an unsteady foothold in seventeenth-century science. This was in part because secrets could be sold for a tidy sum: for example, Herzog Johann Friedrich bought the secret of Brand's phosphorus by successfully outbidding the Duke of Mecklenburg with the help of Leibniz's shrewd negotiating.[21] In part, secrecy bred secrecy: Boyle was glad he had withheld his "uncommon mercuries" from publication so that he could trade that information for a hint as to how to prepare the German phosphorus.[22] But secrecy could also be defended on scientific grounds. Boyle long hesitated to publish his recipe for phosphorus not because he wanted to sell or trade it, but because he believed that if other experimenters were "obliged to employ their own industry, their trials may, as mine have done, produce an instructive diversification of effects . . . and thereby both inrich the yet wanted and designed history of light, and assist the speculative, to accommodate a good hypothesis to them."[23] From a twentieth- (or even an eighteenth-) century viewpoint, nothing could have seemed less desirable than to diversify further the already wildly diverse phenomena of luminescence. But for the militant empiricists of the seventeenth century, the best prospect for solving the riddle of light lay in collecting as many facts as possible, even if each was in itself singular and capricious—or rather, especially if they were—for these seemed to be the most revealing of the nature of things.

Natural variability aided and abetted by human secrecy made for rarity, and rarity made for wonder. The facts of strange phenomena were wonders and evoked wonder from those who studied them, wonder that was often admixed with delight at nature's variety and with admiration for its beauty.[24] The aesthetic as well as the aristocratic associations of light intensified the aura of wonder surrounding luminescent phenomena. Boyle could hardly restrain his pleasure at his first viewing of phosphorus, "which shone so briskly, and looked so oddly, that the sight was extremely pleasing, having in it a mixture of strangeness, beauty, and frightfulness, wherein yet the last of those qualities was far from being predominant."[25] The writings of Boyle and other seventeenth-century natural philosophers abound with such reactions, as if the testimony not only of the outer but also of the inner senses were part and parcel of a full description.

It should be noted that the sensibility, which delighted in the facts of strange phenomena, was a cultivated one, not shared by most people. Boyle observed with "wonder and delight" that the veal shank intended for Sunday dinner was glowing in several places, but the servant who brought him the news was terrified.[26] It was a sensibility that set the natural philosopher apart from the crowd and also set the phenomena most cherished by that sensibility apart from the rest of nature. Circa 1700, the facts of luminescence were in all senses Baconian "shining instances" of the facts of strange phenomena. But by 1723, when Dufay published his first paper on luminescence, the prototypical scientific fact was no longer an anomaly. Between 1723 and 1735 Dufay presented four papers on luminescent substances to the Paris Académie des Sciences. Taken together, they transformed the field of investigation, not by proposing a new theory, or by discovering a brilliant new phosphor, but rather by vastly expanding the list of substances that could be made to glow in a modest way, by expanding the range of methods that could accomplish this and, finally, by making these methods so simple, cheap, and reliable that almost anyone could succeed with them.[27]

The new factuality of uniformity stamps these memoirs, each of which is characterized by: first, the aim of replacing chance discoveries with surefire replications; second, a determination to render facts cumulative, both by means of retelling history and by means of replication; and third, the will to generalize over large classes of instances, even in the face of manifest exceptions. A few passages from Dufay's memoirs will make vivid the contrast between the factualities of singularity and of uniformity on each of these counts.

Dufay opened his memoir on new phosphors with the by-then standard observation that heretofore most discoveries in the field had been made by chance. But he drew the quite non-standard conclusion that this accounted for the neglect of such phenomena by chemists.[28] The seventeenth-century history of new phosphors such as the Bologna stone, Brand's phosphor, and the hermetic phosphor of Baldewein—chance discoveries all—would in fact suggest just the opposite: these were objects of intense interest to chemists. This discrepancy measures the distance between seventeenth- and eighteenth-century styles of investigation. The perpetual secretary of the Académie des Sciences, Bernard de Fontenelle, agreed wholeheartedly with Dufay that rare phenomena in general, and chance discoveries in particular, were of meager interest: "one hardly deigns to observe them, because they lead to nothing."[29] This claim would have astonished Boyle and his contemporaries, who had lavished considerable attention on such rarities in the belief that they were the royal road to a reformed natural philosophy. But for Dufay and his contemporaries, rarity made impossible the systematic investigation that they had come to believe was the only kind worth pursuing.

Dufay's lifelong concern with making reliable replications of hitherto singular or isolated instances went hand-in-hand with his campaign to save the phenomena, albeit in a more literal sense than was originally meant by the Greek phrase. Phenomena were first to be saved in scientific memory, and only eventually in hypothetical explanations. In order to make science truly cooperative and cumulative, it must be possible to transcend local conditions. Otherwise, the journals of learned societies could hope at best to entertain their readers with a stream of novelties (and their resemblance to and simultaneous emergence with the first newspapers and novels was no accident), but not to unite them in a common scientific undertaking.[30] Dufay's scientific career illustrates how varied were the requirements for cumulative science, extending beyond the laboratory to the literary genre of the scientific article and the social organization of the scientific community.

First and foremost, facts had to be replicable by everyone, not just the lucky or the supremely skillful. Dufay not only eschewed all forms of secrecy and obscurity in publishing his techniques, he also strove to make them as simple and as insensitive to local variations as possible. Where Boyle fretted endlessly about the proper degree of fire required to extract phosphorus from urine, Dufay blithely reassures his reader not to bother with such details, "for it is nearly impossible not to succeed in all these operations."[31] This nonchalance was made possible by severely editing out phenomena that failed to meet Dufay's exacting standards for regularity, and his manuscript notes are peppered with results he refused to publish—results which "philosophical sincerity" would surely have compelled Boyle to divulge in their entirety.[32]

Almost overnight, Dufay's memoirs had multiplied by a factor of a hundred or more the handful of phosphors known to Boyle. Indeed, Dufay went so far as to claim that where it used to be that luminescent substances like the Bologna stone were singularities, it would now be "a very singular phenomenon" to find a substance that *could not* be made luminous.[33] Wonder itself had been displaced, as Fontenelle remarked apropos of Dufay's discoveries: "Almost everything has become a phosphor, and if everything doesn't become so right away, we will be in a state of surprise opposite to that induced at first by the Bologna stone."[34] The facts of singular phenomena had emphatically become the facts of regular phenomena.

Why did Dufay succeed in generalizing luminescence where Boyle had failed? The difference between the two did not lie in scientific goals. Both hoped to use luminescence to explain the nature of light. Nor did their use of mathematics differ: both were innocent of quantitative measures, much less mathematical models. Both were meticulous observers who could afford assistants and equipment. Their theoretical allegiances were similar, for both subscribed to a Cartesian explanation couched in terms of escaping particles of the "first element." Rather, the distinction lay in the brand of empiricism each embraced, and the factuality dictated by each empiricism. Boyle's militant empiricism fixed upon singularities as the phenomena most revealing of the nature of things; Dufay's inductive empiricism systematically tamed singularities into regularities that he, in turn, believed to be the phenomena most revealing of the nature of things. Dufay's a priori conviction that such regularities not only existed but were also the premier object of scientific study allowed him to take liberties with the description of luminescence that Boyle could not have countenanced.

This contrast emerges most clearly in their respective treatment of exceptions and variability. Dufay's sweeping claim, cited above, that all substances would turn out to be luminous, considerably overstated his actual findings. He candidly admitted that agates, jaspers, rock crystal, talc, and a fair number of other substances had resisted his best efforts to make them glow in the dark.[35] His results with electrophosphorescent gems were equally mixed.[36] But where Boyle had gone on to catalogue these exceptions in exquisite detail and to forswear generalization on their account, Dufay waved them aside and confidently generalized to all phenomena anyway. Both men were consummate observers. Dufay was just as sensitive as Boyle to the nuances and variability of the phenomena, duly noting that yellow diamonds are very luminous but only weakly electric when rubbed, and that green diamonds were just the opposite.[37] For Boyle, such detailed descriptions had been an indispensable part of observational reporting, full of potential revelations, while for Dufay they hardly merited mention in a scientific article. Although Dufay privately exclaimed over "How different bodies behave which seemed so similar, and how many varieties there are in effects which seemed identical,"[38] his *published* memoirs repeatedly summarized results, in order "to avoid boring detail."[39] By deleting this swarm of detail, Dufay was able to create the impression of a uniformity in nature that Boyle's scruples precluded.

II. Nature Universalized

Dufay enlightened the study of cold light by systematically obscuring the details of the phenomena. Although Dufay's brand of inquiry was arguably more public than Boyle's had been, it would be wrong to describe Boyle's science as private. Boyle may have withheld some things from publication, but those he did publish were recounted in exquisite, indeed excruciating detail. He would have been heartily shocked at Dufay's routine editing of his laboratory notes to delete individuating particulars and variability: according to Boyle's code this was nearly tantamount to scientific dishonesty. Our received distinction between public and private knowledge hardly does justice to the moral differences between Boyle and Dufay. Each professed an openness of a different sort: Boyle was open about the slightest variation of circumstance in the phenomena; Dufay was open about the means to reproduce and multiply the phenomena. This meant that the facts they presented had to be accordingly culled and trimmed from nature.

It was this culling and trimming, this stuffing and evacuating of details that wove such different descriptive textures into their accounts of nature. Late seventeenth-century scientific experience had been bumpy with singular phenomena described in rich detail, and as dizzyingly various as the contents of the cabinets of curiosities. By contrast, mid-eighteenth-century scientific experience was smooth, blended of regular phenomena that resembled each other everywhere and always. Note that the uniformity of nature in time and space does not follow necessarily from a metaphysics of nature governed by natural laws. Boyle was as firm a believer in such laws as Dufay, depending on their initial conditions and interaction, but he recognized that they could produce considerable variability with no violation of mechanical determinism.[40] By the 1740s, a belief in inviolable natural law had come to be conflated systematically with a belief in the uniformity of nature. Neither singularities nor variability disappeared from nature—two-headed cats were still born on occasion and certain diamonds only sometimes glowed in the dark—but they were no longer the stuff of which facts were made. A raft of scientific practices, literary and material, created and sustained the smooth texture of nature: descriptions that summarized rather than particularized events; cabinets and vitrines in which objects of the most disparate provenances—plants from Brittany, plants from Brazil—were arranged to maximize resemblance rather than diversity (as in the cabinets of curiosity); illustrations of type specimens in natural history rather than of individuals; systems of classification and later museum displays arranged to show the plenitude of nature as a continuous series rather than as an astonishing miscellany. There was a close harmony between Linnaeus's miserly way with adjectives in botanical descriptions and his project to transplant exotic plants, including tea, to Sweden for domestic cultivation.[41] Local specificity had officially disappeared from nature along with all other forms of diversity and variability.

What was at stake in the laborious project of universalizing nature over space and time? To answer this question we must go beyond the sciences of nature to the symbolism of nature in the early eighteenth century. In his critical commentary on Montesquieu's *L'Esprit des lois* (1748), Marie Jean Antoine Nicolas Caritat Condorcet countered Montesquieu's emphasis upon local customs and national characters with projects for the universal reform of weights and measures, and of civil and criminal legal codes, that are gathered under the heading "Ideas of Uniformity." Such ideas, contended Condorcet, "please all minds, especially precise minds."[42] In a still more pointed passage in his biography-cum-eulogy of Anne Robert Jacques Turgot, Condorcet insisted that since property rights are natural, they are therefore universal, and the laws derived from them "may not be arbitrary, may not depend on the constitution, the climate, the customs, or the opinions of the people."[43] In this effortless slide from nature through universality to inalienable and immutable property rights, Condorcet appealed to a new kind of political and moral authority. The wars of religion waged in Italy, France, England, and Germany during the sixteenth and seventeenth centuries had destroyed the claims of any church to universal authority; universal nature rushed in to fill the void in the arguments of Enlightenment social theorists. First reform, then revolution, and finally conquest were all justified by recourse to *universal* nature, which superseded all local tradition and authority. The metric system (allegedly nature's own measure), the "Droits de l'Homme" (proclaimed as "natural, imprescriptible, and inalienable rights"), and the Napoleonic wars that attempted to export both of them from Milan to Moscow were ultimately all anchored in the universality of nature. A slender but strong chain connects the smooth-textured descriptions of Dufay and his fellow savants to the voyages of exploration that imposed a grid of uniformly executed measurements over the entire globe, the division of revolutionary time and space into units of ten, and what the Assemblée Nationale was pleased to call the "inviolable and sacred" rights of property.

To explain how nature was universalized does not explain how nature became sacralized: why should nature, whether local or universal, exercise an authority over the human polity? Fontenelle, Dufay's colleague and admiring chronicler at the Académie Royale des Sciences, dimly understood that the authority of universal nature required an ersatz religious faith. In his posthumously published account of utopia, *La République des philosophes, ou Histoire des Ajaoiens* (1768), Fontenelle described the fortunate island of the Ajaoiens. Here the countryside is beautiful because of its "order and symmetry"; the women are industrious and content because they are taught to read but not write, thus not mixing "in any manner in [matters of] government, nor justice"; and the men are pampered and content because each takes two wives who compete with one another to make his life more pleasant. The Ajaoiens worship nature, but are not burdened with any religious observances: "these peoples have neither temples, nor altars, nor priests. . . . Nature is not capricious, they say, to change her order for [the sacrifice of] a few quarters of beef or roast mutton, or for the smoke of a few grains of gum [i.e. incense], or a prayer from the mouth of a hypocrite. Her laws are immutable, her revolutions are always made in the same order, and nothing can in the least divert her from her ordinary course." Fontenelle, long-time Perpetual Secretary of the Académie Royale des Sciences, had read his share of marvelous reports: perhaps this is why he allowed marvels if not miracles in the Ajaoien religion, albeit marvels extraordinary for their very ordinariness. The children of Ajaoia chant an "Ode to the Marvels of Nature" with a refrain that might serve as epigram for the universal nature built up of smooth-textured facts: "The same Nature, always similar to herself, demonstrates to us her eternity. Let us give her all our admiration."[44]

Nature's Unruly Body

The Limits of Scientific Description

In a moving passage in her magnificent 1705 *Metamorphosis insectorum Suri-namensium*, the German-born naturalist Maria Sibylla Merian records how the African slave and Indian populations in Surinam, then a Dutch colony, used the seeds of a plant she identified as the *flos pavonis*, literally "peacock flower," as an abortifacient:

> The Indians, who are not treated well by their Dutch masters, use the seeds [of this plant] to abort their children, so that their children will not become slaves like they are. The black slaves from Guinea and Angola have demanded to be well treated, threatening to refuse to have children. In fact, they sometimes take their own lives because they are treated so badly, and because they believe they will be born again, free and living in their own land. They told me this themselves.[1]

Merian's passage is remarkable for what it reveals about the global politics of plants in the early modern period, specifically the culturally induced loss of certain craft-botanic knowledge traditions. In the explosion of knowledge generally associated with the scientific revolution and global expansion, European awareness of herbal anti-fertility agents, such as Merian's *flos pavonis*, declined dramatically. Contrary to other trends, where naturalists assiduously collected local knowledges of plants for medicines and potential profit, there were few attempts to introduce into Europe new and exotic contraceptives and abortifacients gathered from cultures around the globe. European mores and mercantilist policies guiding global expansion did little to define trade in such plants as a lucrative or desirable business, nor did the policies of the great East and West trading companies often place women in the field.

Merian's work offers but one example of how Enlightenment naturalists came to value certain types of knowledge over others. This essay explores some of the limits on scientific description—both recognized by and unknown to naturalists at the time—by looking at what Europeans collected in their forays into other cultures, what they left behind, who did the collecting and for what reasons, whose observations were validated, and whose not. We turn first to natural history traditions within Europe—the engines that sent explorers into the field.

I. Mediations: Natural History in Metropolitan Europe

As strange as it may seem in our high-tech big science world, natural history was one of the premier sciences of the eighteenth century. Denis Diderot, in his *Encyclopédie* article on natural history, reported that the popularity of natural history replaced a taste for abstract sciences and experimental physics.[2] Indeed, members of the cultivated leisured classes considered a cabinet of natural history an essential part of their households (there were over 230 such cabinets in Paris at mid-century).[3] These cabinets contained, among other things, pickled specimens of brains, embryos at different stages of development, monstrous fetuses, skulls, skeletons, and one legendary whale penis measuring "a Yard and a Quarter" in length.[4] Wealthy patrons established botanical gardens, menageries, and museums. The English Duchess of Queensberry was so taken with nature's riches that she commissioned a dress designed to make her appear a walking botanic garden.[5] Natural history books were popular and widely read: the initial printing of Buffon's voluminous *Histoire naturelle* sold out in six weeks. Naturalists also came to reap new rewards: the renowned Swedish naturalist Carl Linnaeus, a parson's son, was the first man of letters awarded the title "Knight of the Order of the Polar Star," an honor usually reserved for military men.[6]

Eighteenth-century natural history is often portrayed in this innocent light, but it was also big business, an essential component of Europe's commercial and colonial expansion. Natural history cabinets groaned with scientific spoils collected from around the globe: Egyptian mummies extracted from their tombs or exotic animals and peoples brought to fill European menageries. Large private collections symbolized the huge fortunes amassed during this period in European capitals.[7] Naturalists collected nature's bounty with self-professed disinterest but also with an eye to profit. Voyages, financed by trading companies like the Parisian *Compagnie des Indes* (whose headquarters long housed the Bibliothèque Nationale), had to be profitable to be feasible. As described by a naturalist of the day, men of science competed with one another to discover some previously unknown island that might contain new and exotic spices to add to the riches returned by Indian cargoes.[8]

Europeans approached nature in the eighteenth century with confidence and relish. Diderot, in his article on natural history, reveled in the vastness and richness of the great kingdoms of nature—animal, plant, and mineral—and exuded confidence that nature could be known and understood. He praised natural history cabinets for allowing the curious to "approach the most savage animals without fear or harm, to study birds without their taking flight, to peruse the innermost parts of flowers, the minutest insects," and so forth. At the same time Diderot admonished students of nature to leave their chambers and see nature for themselves. One must experience nature as it lives and breathes.

All of this was good advice. Naturalists, however, rarely had the immediate access to nature that Diderot took for granted. Knowledge, as we shall see, was mediated in a variety of ways that answered and informed many spheres: national and global priorities; opportunities for funding and patterns of patronage; the structure of academic institutions, markets, and information networks; personal and professional experiences; technologies for collecting and preserving specimens; and relations with foreign culture.

Personal enthusiasm for particular hypotheses often funneled funds into peculiar projects. It is difficult for us today to recapture the excitement and confusion of naturalists as they sought to understand the natural world. Carl Linnaeus, for example, shook the learned world when he declared to have found a second species of man—*Homo troglodytes*—the golden-eyed nocturnal cave dwellers described by Pliny the Elder. He was heartened by the news of a possible specimen, a female, being exhibited in London in 1758, and he dispatched a student with a list of investigations to be performed: did she have a clitoris and well developed "nymphae" (labia)? Did she have the *membrana nictitans*, that characteristic feature of the troglodyte eyelid? And so forth. The investigation was thwarted when the "troglodyte's" keeper refused to allow her garments to be removed for a perusal of her private parts (the specimen was an adolescent girl from Jamaica). Linnaeus was personally so convinced of the reality of his hypothetical *Homo troglodyte* that he persuaded Swedish Queen Louisa Ulrika to invest considerable resources in a three-year expedition to search for one in the wild.[9]

One powerful mediator of knowledge in the early modern period was

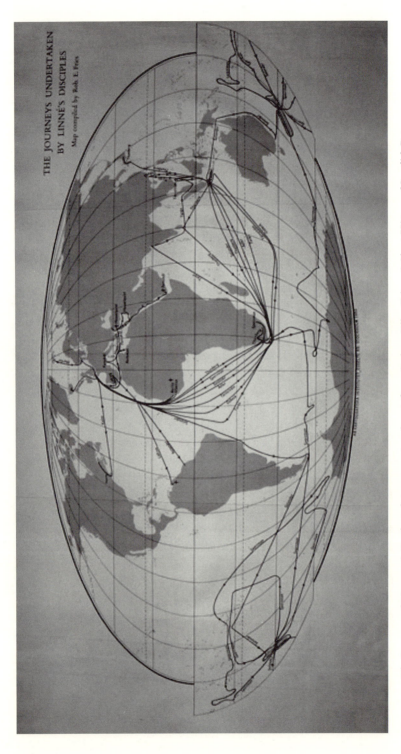

THE JOURNEYS UNDERTAKEN
BY LINNÉ'S DISCIPLES

Map compiled by Rob. E. Fries

FIG. 1. *The Journeys of Linnaeus's Students between 1746 and 1796*, from Robert Elias Fries, *A Short History of Swedish Botany* (Uppsala: Almqvist & Wiksells boktr, 1950). Photo: author, used with kind permission of the publisher.

the availability of specimens. Few specimens from far-off places survived transport: glass vessels containing pickled specimens broke easily; dried plants often spoiled aboard ship; living specimens—plants and animals and even humans—frequently succumbed to disease. Dutch colonial botanists in Ceylon (Sri Lanka), who sent regular shipments of seeds, cuttings, and seedlings to Leiden and Amsterdam throughout the eighteenth century commonly expedited identical consignments by different ships to ensure safe delivery.[10] Europeans' preference for the study of skulls and skeletons that emerged in the late eighteenth century may have had to do at least in part with the durability of those specimens during transport.

When specimens did arrive safely, they often required close scrutiny. When the first platypus arrived in Europe (from Australia) in 1799, George Shaw of the British Museum suspected that the odd creature had been fabricated by foreign taxidermists, already notorious for their willingness to feed European curiosity by producing "mermaids" from the heads of monkeys sewn to the tails of fish. Shaw satisfied himself that the creature was authentic on the evidence of a stuffed skin. Three years later he received another platypus—this time an entire animal pickled in spirits—but deterioration of the animal made analysis difficult. Crucial structures of the platypus, such as the mammary glands, were not identified for another twenty years.[11]

The organizational structures of botany also set limits on scientific description. Despite Diderot's admonitions to experience nature first hand, some naturalists never actually saw many of the plants and animals they so diligently classified. The great eighteenth-century naturalists—Carl Linnaeus, his contemporary and rival Georges-Louis Leclerc, comte de Buffon, and the great German Johann Blumenbach—worked at centers of scientific empires ordering nature but rarely traveled into it. Linnaeus, it is true, traveled throughout Lapland in his youth, but in his later years he declined passage to Surinam, the Cape of Good Hope, and Canada, preferring instead to gather materials through his network of students. It is interesting to see how this worked. In 1745, nineteen of Linnaeus's students—his traveling "apostles" as he called them—left on voyages of discovery to all possible parts of the globe: Japan, Java, Sri Lanka, the African Cape, South America, the Caucasus, Western Siberia, and China (fig. 1). Linnaeus helped fund the voyages and armed his students with lists of plants and animals to be collected and specific details to be gathered about them.[12] Johann Blumenbach, who may never have left his native Germany, followed suit. In 1797, when Friedrich Konrad Hornemann was sent into Africa by the Association for Promoting the Discovery of the Interior Parts of Africa, Blumenbach gave him a list of forty-five questions, including a request for first-hand observations about whether Africans flatten their children's noses or whether they were born with wide noses (Blumenbach was an environmentalist who held that climatic conditions and life experiences shaped racial characteristics) and a query about whether African women give birth more easily than European women (Europeans tended to consider Africans closer to nature, that is more primitive, and so it was assumed that African women experienced little pain in childbearing).[13] Had Linnaeus and Blumenbach traveled themselves, they might have encountered new conceptual systems rather than merely receiving answers to questions that responded to European intellectual frameworks and political debates.

Others naturalists did travel in pursuit of nature's bounty. Many of these self-fashioned botanists and zoologists were not academics, keepers of major gardens or menageries, or members of fashionable elites, but missionaries, employees of the great trading companies, and traders in spices or slaves. In Surinam or Indonesia, as they came into direct contact with other peoples and their ways of life, they often came to cultivate and to depend upon local knowledges for the success of their colonial enterprises and their own well-being.

II. Colonial Connections

It is rarely possible to discern what Europeans left behind when collecting specimens and knowledge from abroad; naturalists tended not to reflect on the knowledges they discarded or devalued. I want to develop in the next two sections examples of how conflicting traditions—inside and outside Europe—structured knowledge.

My first example comes from studies of the great apes. Europeans were often aware of the difficulties awaiting them upon entering foreign cultures. Language presented obvious problems; differences in values and conceptual frameworks made communication, even when using similar words, difficult. The French naturalist Foucher d'Obsonville remarked on how his attempts to secure reliable information were often disappointed: "because of our European air of eager admiration, they [the Asians] make serious and important objects which otherwise would have drawn no particular attention, and demand an exorbitant price."[14] Native guides were essential, however, for tracking down, capturing, or killing the desired animal for exhibit or study in Europe, and Europeans sometimes took at face value the information provided by their guides. Foucher d'Obsonville believed his

Malaysian guide, for instance, when he was told that the orangutan is "a wild man of the same genus as humans, though constituting a very distinct species" (he obviously imputed to his guide the classificatory apparatus of European taxonomy).[15]

What transpired between European naturalists and their local informants went for the most part unrecorded. One incident, however, provides rare insight into negotiations between differing traditions of knowledge in this period. In 1739 the Englishman Thomas Boreman recorded a dispute over the average height of an adult chimpanzee. The dispute arose in 1738 following the arrival in London of the celebrated "Madame Chimpanzee" from Angola. Thomas Boreman related that the Angolan who procured "Madame Chimpanzee" did so by shooting her mother—an animal he claimed to be five feet tall. Boreman contrasted the report of the Angolan with that of the English anatomist Edward Tyson, who declared these animals to measure a little over two feet, literally "pygmies" as described by the ancients.

The dispute—whether the average height of the animal in question was five feet or two feet at maturity—was already influenced by the European convention of thinking of these animals as standing erect. The overwhelming majority of illustrations of anthropoid apes in the seventeenth and eighteenth centuries show them either standing erect or seated in a human manner. Tyson apparently believed that his "pygmie" (actually a chimp) walked on its knuckles only because it was sick; in good health, he believed, it would have walked erect, and that is how he had it drawn (fig. 2).[16] While it is true that apes can walk on two legs for short periods of time, naturalists in the eighteenth century tended to exaggerate this capacity. Jean Audebert criticized the overly erect posture of the male chimpanzee shown in Buffon's *Histoire naturelle*, saying that the engraver "tried very hard to make him a man."[17]

It is important to put this dispute into perspective. European knowledge of great apes was extremely limited in the early modern period. Tyson, according to his text, had studied two apes—a male and a female (he chose the male as the subject for his pioneering 1699 *Orang-Outang, sive Homo Sylvestris: or the Anatomy of a Pygmie Compared with that of a Monkey, an Ape, and a Man*). He had never seen these animals in the wild and, as was common in this period, mistook his chimpanzee for an orangutan. Knowledge of the great apes commonly depended on second-hand information. Jacob Bontius's fanciful description of a female ape in his 1658 *Historiae Naturalis* records characteristics reported to him. All in all, perhaps ten illustrations

FIG. 2. *Homo Sylvestris*, from Edward Tyson, *Orang-Outang, sive Homo Sylvestris: or the Anatomy of a Pygmie compared with that of a Monkey, an Ape, and a Man* (London, Printed for T. Bennet and D. Brown, 1699), fig. 1. Photo: The Wellcome Library, London.

of the great apes circulated in Europe in the seventeenth and eighteenth centuries. Few Europeans had seen these animals in the wild.

Despite a lack of information, Thomas Boreman went on to resolve the clash between the reports of the eyewitness and the learned European. He remarked: "If what the Negro related, who shot the Mother of this Chimp ['Madame Chimpanzee'] be true, viz. that she was upward of five Foot high, it will quite overthrow the Ingenious conjecture of Dr. Tyson." Boreman boldly announced that "for my own part I am inclined to believe Tyson . . . who has with much labor, learning, and good reasoning upon the subject made it so evident that I think everyone who reads him impartially, will acquiesce with him in that opinion." Boreman, unsure how to judge the misinformation provided by the African, wondered "Whether the Negro-man, who reports this, understood our measure, or was faithful in his account? Or whether to get a better price for the young, he did not paint the old one to be such a huge fierce beast? Or to imagine his own courage and skill in killing the one and taking the other?"[18] Even in an age of empiricism, Boreman accepted Tyson's estimate based on the writings of the ancients over reports by native peoples who had actually seen these animals alive.

It was Tyson who was misinformed. When standing erect, an adult chimpanzee typically measures around five feet in height. Tyson's error was based partly on the fact that he falsely regarded the immature chimp he dissected in his London home in 1699 to be nearly full-grown.[19] It is striking that many of the apes brought to Europe in this period were very young, usually only a few months old. Travelogues recount how difficult it was to take adult animals alive. Consequently, most of the apes transported to Europe were captured only after their mothers had been shot. Stephen Jay Gould (as did James Prichard before him) has pointed out that the fact that so many of the apes studied by Europeans were immature served to heighten their human appearance. Young apes have many humanlike characters that adults eventually lose.[20]

We have almost no knowledge of the "Negro man" to whom Boreman refers. We do not know if he was learned in the ways of chimpanzees, or if he was merely a hired tracker. This example illustrates how Europeans privileged certain types of learning—the exactitude of dissection—over others. In the eighteenth century, the body, stripped as clean of history and culture as it was of clothes and often skin, became a privileged object in natural history, politics, and the European mind more generally.

III. Women's Traditions

A second example of how conflicting traditions formed knowledge concerns the practices of women. As naturalists fanned out across the globe, only a few exceptional women undertook voyages in pursuit of nature's bounty. Jeanne Baret sailed with Louis-Antoine de Bougainville around the world disguised as the male valet of Philibert Commerson, the ship's botanist and her fiancé.[21] "A little virgin" saved the English slave-trader Richard Ligon's ship and crew by spinning thread from a cargo of cotton to mend the sail.[22] Other women, like Lady Charlotte Canning, collected as an adjunct to their main occupations as colonial wives, traveling where their husbands happened to take them.[23] Maria Merian was one of these rare women travelers, and perhaps the only European woman to travel on her own as a naturalist in the eighteenth century.

Maria Merian was indeed bold in traveling to Surinam in search of exotic flora and fauna. Moral and bodily imperatives kept the vast majority of Europe's women close to home; the German anthropologist Johann Blumenbach was typical in warning that white women taken to very warm climates succumbed to "copious menstruation, which almost always ends, in a short space of time, in fatal hemorrhages of the uterus."[24] There was also the often-expressed fear that women giving birth in the tropics would deliver children resembling the native peoples of those areas. The intense African sun, it was thought, produced black babies regardless of the mother's complexion.

Despite warnings from the mayor of Amsterdam, who had lost four daughters in Surinam, Maria Merian deposited her will and set sail in 1699 at the age of 52, only a decade after political upheavals in that colony had left the governor dead, shot by his own soldiers. Maria was accompanied by her daughter, Dorothea, trained from an early age to work as her mother's assistant. Maria Merian was not schooled, as many of Linnaeus's students would be, to be sent into the field, nor had she been commissioned to make the journey by a trading company or scientific society, as were many of the botanists in this period. Her interest was self-generated and largely self-supported, part of her life-long quest to find another variety of caterpillar as economically significant as the silkworm. During her sojourn in Surinam, she drew and catalogued plants and insects. As was common at the time, she was aided by "her slaves," who, with great machetes, hacked paths for her through the thick tangle of the jungle and who supplied her with rare and unusual plants and insects. For two years, Maria gathered specimens in the cool of the early day and studied, prepared, and drew them in the evening.[25]

Naturalists in the field were often more sympathetic to native knowledges than systematizers in Europe. Merian followed the common practice of field naturalists by cultivating a keen interest in what her local informants had to tell her. Like the Englishman Hans Sloane, who worked in the Caribbean around the time of Merian's voyage to Surinam, she collected "the best information" concerning the exotic plants and insects from "books and the local inhabitants, either European, Indian or Black."[26] Like the astronomer Peter Kolb, who wrote an early ethnology of the Africans at the Cape of Good Hope, Merian developed warm friendships with several Amerindians and displaced Africans in Dutch Guiana who provided her with desirable specimens.[27] She tended to record, often verbatim, what these people told her, and provided, among other things, tasty recipes for preparing wine and brandy from pineapple or bread from the cassava root.

Many of Merian's practices were similar to those of her male colleagues. One area of divergence, however, was her sympathetic interest in and access to information about contraceptives and abortifacients. In the moving passage quoted at the beginning of this essay, she recorded the use of a plant she called *flos pavonis* as an abortifacient (fig. 3). She tells us that she learned about the abortive virtues of the peacock flower directly from the enslaved females of Surinam. Did male naturalists have the same access to and interest in this type of information?

Interestingly, Hans Sloane, working as physician to the governor in Jamaica, also reported the abortive qualities of a (different) plant he called the "flour fence of Barbados, wild sena, or Spanish carnations." He mistakenly took this plant to be the same as Merian had described, and he cited her work in an appendix to his book (the flat, broad seed pods of the two plants are, however, quite distinct). Sloane compared his "flour fence" to savin (*Juniperus sabina*), a shrub widely regarded at that time as the most powerful herbal abortifacient in Europe.[28]

How did Sloane procure information about the uses of the plant he took to be the peacock flower? Certainly not from the many European texts he studied about West Indian flora before sailing to the Caribbean: although the flower was known to Europeans (mostly in an East Indian context) from about 1660, none of these printed sources reported its abortifacient qualities.[29] Sloane may well have encountered slave women who had

F I G . 3 . *Flos pavonis*, from Maria Sibylla Merian, *Metamorphosis Insectorum Suri-namensium* (Amsterdam, 1705), pl. 45. The Wellcome Library, London. Photo: The Wellcome Library, London.

aborted their embryos, a practice common enough in the Caribbean to alarm plantation owners. Unlike Merian, however, he did not record the source of his information.

While both Merian and Sloane mentioned abortifacients, only Merian emphasized the importance of these types of plants for the physical and spiritual survival of the slave women of Surinam. Slaves in Surinam endured extreme brutality: John Stedman, the inveterate observer of colonial Surinam, reported in the 1770s a "revolted negroe" hung alive upon a gibbet with an iron hook stuck through his ribs, two others chained to stakes and burned to death by slow fire, six women broken alive upon the rack, and two slave girls decapitated.[30] While Sloane was well aware that slaves "cut their own throats" to escape such treatment, he did not see his "flour fence" in this context. The future president of the Royal Society of London wrote rather drily, "it provokes the Menstrua extremely, causes Abortion, etc. and does whatever Savin and powerful Emmenagogues will do."[31]

Sloane's discussion of abortion does not reveal his interest in collecting these types of herbs for introduction into English *materia medica*, but rather the growing conflict between doctors and women seeking assistance in this matter. In his text he discussed how, as a physician in Jamaica, he refused treatment to women seeking abortions:

> In case women, whom I suspected to be with Child, presented themselves ill, coming in the name of others, sometimes bringing their own water, dissembling pains in their heads, sides, obstructions, etc. thereby cunningly, as they think, designing to make the physician cause abortion by the medicines he may order for their cure. In such a case I used either to put them off with no medicines at all, or tell them Nature in time might relieve them without remedies, or I put them off with medicines that will signifie nothing either one way or other, till I be further satisfied about their malady.[32]

He finished with a strict warning: "if women know how dangerous a thing it is to cause abortion, they would never attempt it. . . . One may as easily expect to shake off unripe Fruit from a tree, without injury or violence to the Tree, as endeavor to procure Abortion without injury or violence to the Mother." The few learned men who did discuss anti-fertility herbs in the seventeenth and eighteenth centuries tended to do so in order to warn about their dangerous consequences.[33] Sloane himself noted that when an abortion was absolutely necessary to save the life of the mother, "the hand" was preferable to herbal preparations.

It is unclear who might have sought out Sloane's services in this regard. Caribbean plantations generally had a hospital for slaves run by a female of this class (who often employed medical traditions carried with her from Africa), several younger aides (mostly female), and a midwife (either slave or free). These hospitals were most often supervised by a local white surgeon who visited but twice a week.[34] It was commonly known that the "herbs and powders" slave women used for abortion were obtained from healers known in Jamaica as "obeah men and women." Reverend Henry Beame wrote concerning slave abortions in Jamaica in 1826, "white medical men know little, except from surmise."[35]

I do not want to make too much of the contrast between Sloane and Merian. Merian, to my knowledge, discussed only one abortifacient. Her chief interest was insects, and she described plants primarily in their relationships to them (in the passage cited at the beginning of this paper, she devoted an entire paragraph to the caterpillars living off the plant's leaves). Whether women "do science differently" is currently a topic of heated debate; distinctions, however, should not be drawn too sharply between individual men and women in this regard. Many European women—plantation owners or governors' wives, for example—had little interest in their newly adopted countries, and most came and went without collecting any information from the indigenous populations or cultivating any special sympathies toward the women of the region.

Larger historical forces, however, can make gender an important factor. Although Merian and Sloane differed in their attitudes toward abortion, they were unusual in providing knowledge about abortifacients from abroad.[36] Colonial administrators were often interested in medicines to protect traders, planters, and trading company soldiers, among whom few women were found. In the colonies, abortion among slave populations was seen by plantation owners as nothing less than a threat to their property. Within Europe itself, mercantilist expansion mandated pro-natalist policies celebrating children as "the wealth of nations, the glory of kingdoms, and the nerve and good fortune of empires."[37] In such climates, agents of botanical exploration—trading companies, governments, scientific academies, or directors of university botanical gardens—had little interest in expanding Europe's store of anti-fertility pharmacopoeia. Collecting and cultivating new and exotic abortifacients and contraceptives would not be of interest to either academic botanists or medical doctors. In this instance, gender served as a potent mediator of knowledge.

Customary divisions in physical and intellectual labor within Europe had long left fertility control in women's hands.[38] Though physicians like Sloane occasionally reported on abortifacients, few had an intimate knowledge of their use. Effective employment of the plants required knowledge of the parts appropriate for use (root, sap, bark, flowers, seeds, or fruits), the proper time for harvesting, when to administer the drug within the menstrual cycle and in relation to coitus, in what amounts, with what frequency, and so forth.[39] As medical men gradually displaced midwives across Europe, the use of herbal abortives and contraceptives declined among the general population.[40] As states began to overturn the traditional Aristotelian notion that early abortion was acceptable when a mother's life was in danger, pregnant women lost the prerogative to judge for themselves when "ensoulment" took place—that is, when they truly were with child.[41]

Though threatened, the use of herbal anti-fertility agents did not disappear entirely. Despite priestly admonitions and legal warnings, these practices continued, though more and more hidden from public view. Court records in early-modern Italy speak of aborted embryos pushed into cracks in church walls or thrown into cemeteries.[42] An unusual set of records gathered in seventeenth-century Lancashire, England, reveals an abortion rate varying between 10 and 30 per 1,000 live births; the rate of unrecorded abortions would most certainly be higher.[43] Common abortifacients (rue, savin, squirting cucumber, and pennyroyal) were increasingly discussed in code as "menstrual regulators," as herbs to "promote the menses," "bring down the flowers," "purge the courses," or "restore menses obstructed."[44] Knowledge of anti-fertility agents, while still available to women, was destined to remain "folk" knowledge, tried and tested by long use and experience, but not something that was to be valued and cultivated by the new sciences.

IV. Epilogue: Taxonomic Mediations

The history of Maria Merian's *flos pavonis* is also interesting for what it reveals about emerging European systematics, in particular botanical nomenclature. Although Merian was very much aware of the social conflict involved in the use of this plant as an abortifacient, she was largely oblivious to the complex politics involved in the naming and renaming of this plant as it was assimilated into European conceptual frameworks.

A long-standing narrative in the history of botany has emphasized a kind of liberation from the practical, usually medical focus of pre-modern botany.[45] Several botanical traditions coexisted in the eighteenth century, which later became more sharply distinguished: applied botany, which consisted of economic and medicinal botany along with horticulture and agriculture, and what is today called theoretical botany, especially nomenclature and classification.[46] In the seventeenth and eighteenth centuries, economic and medical botanists tended to value and collect vast stores of local knowledges along with specimens from diverse cultures around the globe. System builders, by contrast, tended to discard the local names of plants and preferred to devise European names or conceptual schema to encompass even exotic plants. This development is epitomized in the linguistic history of *flos pavonis*.

As mentioned above, it was not uncommon for naturalists in the field to collect native names for plants and animals. Maria Merian emphasized more than once that she retained the native names for the plants and insects she studied while in Surinam. In the introduction to her *Metamorphosis*, which she advertised as the "first and strangest work done in America," Merian wrote: "the names of the plants I have kept as they were given by the natives and Indians in America."[47] It is curious, then, that Merian chose to continue to use the Latin name, *flos pavonis*, for the abortifacient she described.[48] Given that she recorded the personal experience of her informants in vivid detail, why did she not report a local Arawak or transplanted Angolan or Guinean name for the plant?

Merian may have chosen the name *flos pavonis* because she had seen this tropical tree in the Hortus Medicus, Amsterdam's ostentatious (by standards of the time) botanical garden. The plant was cultivated there beginning in 1684. Most of the names known to Europeans for this brilliantly flowering plant associated it with the peacock. Jakob Breyne, a Danzig merchant and sometime botanist, reported that in Ambon, an island of Indonesia, the luxuriant tree was called *crista pavonis*, "crest of the peacock," for its "distinguished stamen . . . that bursts forth to form the proud crest of the peacock."[49] Paul Hermann, a German medical officer who served in Ceylon for the Dutch East India Company and later taught botany at Leiden, called the flaming red, yellow, and orange flower the *flore pavonino* (peacock flower) and *flos Indicus pavoninus*.[50] The Dutch living in the East Indies called the plant "peacock tails" (*paauwen staarten*); the Portuguese labeled it the *foula de pavan*. Less poetically, the plant was sometimes also known by the Latin *frutex pavoninus*, or "peacock bush."[51]

The peacock flower enjoyed other, even more exotic, names. Merian, whose knowledge of Latin was weak, employed Casper Commelin, a friend and director of the botanical garden in Amsterdam, to add bibliographical references to the text of her *Metamorphosis* to place the Surinamese plants and insects she so elaborately recorded and illustrated into the world of European classical learning. What Commelin added to her paragraphs discussing the *flos pavonis* was the term *tsjétti-mandáru*, a Latinization of the Malayalam name for the flower that also associated it with the peacock.[52] In addition, the plant was also known by names in "Brahmanese" or Konkani (transcribed as *tsiettia*), Arabic, Portuguese, and Dutch. This flower was also occasionally called in Europe by its colorful "Zeylonese" (Sinhalese) name: *monarakudimbiia*.[53]

These exotic names and the cultural traditions they embodied were to be discarded, however, when the plant was placed within Europe's emerging systems of taxonomy. In 1694, Merian's *flos pavonis* was included within Joseph Pitton de Tournefort's abstract typology, the classification widely regarded today as one of the forerunners of modern systematics. Tournefort, director of Jardin du Roi in Paris, included the plant in his Class 21, Section 5, encompassing "trees and shrubs with red flowers and seed pods." As was typical of the new schema, Tournefort's classification focused on the physical characteristics of the plant: namely, the corolla and the fruit. The plant's Asian connections and its medical uses—both of which had played a significant role in earlier European accounts—were not discussed.

In the process of anchoring Merian's *flos pavonis* in the European world, Tournefort devised for it a wholly new name, *Poinciana pulcherrima*, a scientific name still in use today.[54] This term celebrated his countryman, Louis de Louvilliers Poinci, governor of the French Antilles, rather than the plant's own virtues, its East Indian heritage, the peoples who used it, or those who "discovered" it and supplied Europeans with information about it—all features of the other names given at one time or another to the plant.

Carl Linnaeus, whose system is considered the beginning point of modern botany, followed Tournefort's lead, mentioning only that *Poinciana pulcherrima* grows in the Indies, apparently both East and West, and under the sign of Saturn (!), for its woody character.[55] In his effort to stabilize botanical nomenclature, Linnaeus drew up a series of rules for acceptable names and designators. Expressly targeting earlier collectors who had relished local names, Linnaeus declared all foreign names and terms "barbarous" and ruled that "generic names not derived from Greek or Latin roots are to be rejected."[56] Linnaeus's extensive rules for botanical nomenclature banished many things: European languages except for Greek or Latin; religious names (he did allow names derived from European mythology); foreign names; names invoking the uses of plants; names ending in *-oides*; names compounded of two entire Latin words; and so forth.[57] To fill the void, Linnaeus promoted generic names designed to preserve the memory of botanists who have served well the cause of science. Men immortalized in the Linnaean system included Tournefort (*Tournefortia*), Hendrik Van Reede (*Rheedia*), the Commelins (*Commelina*), and his own modest self (the *Linnaea* is a small flowering plant indigenous to Lapland). Discussing this practice, Linnaeus asserted that such men were martyrs to science, having suffered wearisome and painful hardships in the service of botany.[58] Linnaeus also promoted generic names celebrating European kings and patrons who had contributed to the cost of oceanic voyages, botanical gardens, and textual illustrations.

In their reform of botanical nomenclature, European systematizers broke the ties with other cultures that naturalists like Maria Merian had begun to establish. Rather, European nomenclature highlighted the deeds of the great men of European botany. The French botanist Michel Adanson, working some years after Linnaeus, pointed to the absurdity of Linnaeus's naming a colonial plant *Dillenia* after Oxford's Johann Dillenius rather than retaining one of its traditional names.[59]

↬

In the course of the seventeenth and eighteenth centuries, European natural history took on a distinctive physiognomy. Academic realignments within Europe placed medical botany (still vigorously collected, but now more often disparaged as applied science) on a lower rung of the disciplinary ladder. Gender politics created conditions that discouraged knowledge of abortifacients from becoming a part of mainstream academic botany or medicine. Women, both inside and outside Europe, continued to regulate their fertility but did not benefit from the resources that Western science might have offered research in this area. In the nineteenth century, hardening colonial relations brought local knowledges into greater disrepute among European elites. Naming practices developed in the consolidation of European taxonomic systems tended to discourage conceptualizing the world fauna and flora in other than European terms. European systems of classification were ratified in the early twentieth century when international congresses established Linnaean nomenclature as the starting point for both botany and zoology.[60] In failing to become international coinage, other systems of conceptualizing and naming nature were submerged. They reemerge from time to time as poorly understood alternatives.

The limits to description—the limits to what was chosen to be described, the limits to who did the describing, and how that information was received—lent recognizable contours not only to distinctive bodies of knowledge but also to distinctive bodies of ignorance.[61] Ignorance is often not merely the absence of knowledge, as Robert Proctor has suggested, but the project of protracted cultural struggles.[62] Bodies of ignorance, in turn, can mold the very flesh and blood of real bodies.[63] European women's loss of easy access to contraceptives and abortifacients curbed their reproductive and often professional freedoms; Europe's devaluing of local knowledges made easier the destruction of colonial peoples and their ways of life. Limits to knowledge can also define limits to ways of living.

Mithridates in Paradise

Describing Languages in a Universalistic World

Mithridates, 1555 and 1809

In 1555, in his book *Mithridates. De differentiis linguarum,* the Swiss erudite Conrad Gesner starts writing about the English language by quoting the Lord's Prayer:

> De anglica lingua
> Oratio dominica Anglice conscripta
>
> Our father whiche arte in heaven, halowed be thy name. Thy kyngdome come. Thy wyll be done in earthe, as it is in heaven. Geve us thys day our dagly bread. And forgeve us our trespasses, as we forgeve our trespassers. And leade us not in temptacion. But delyver us from evyll. Amen.[1]

He remarks that all the words of the prayer are Germanic [sunt autem vocabula Germanica vel Saxonica omnia], either somehow distorted or unaltered [sed aliquo modo detorta, vel immutata]. As distorted Saxon names he quotes the words *arte* and *be,* the conjunction *but,* and the noun *heaven.* He notices French words [Gallica vocabula], *trespasses* and *delyver.* And he states that in former times French and Latin words had been less common in the English language, but that they are now—due to snobbism that kept the *vulgus* from understanding—mixed into conversation. Two hundred or three hundred years before, the books were written completely in Saxon. Gesner seems to ignore totally the Norman conquest of the island. He adds a quotation about the origin of the *anglica lingua*: "Anglica lingua (inquit Seb. Munsterus) mixta est ex multis linguis praesertim Germanica & Gallica. Olim vero mere fuit Germanica" [The English language (according to Sebastian Munster) is a mixture of many languages, primarily German and

French. Earlier it was actually entirely Germanic].[2] And to prove the Germanic past of the *anglica lingua*, he quotes a passage from the Venerable Bede.

Gesner's book, called *Mithridates* after the famous king of Pontus who, according to a venerable historiographic tradition, spoke twenty-two languages, is the starting point of the modern enterprise of the description of the world's languages in the sixteenth century.[3] Conrad Gesner knows from Saint Augustine and tradition that after Babel there were seventy-two different languages in the world, and he writes down what he knows about them.[4] It is rather little. Sometimes this eminent European intellectual has a text, a paternoster or another prayer, sometimes he has a short word list, sometimes he has just the name of the language and a geographical indication. Old and modern languages are mixed in his alphabetical list. Only the European, Asian, and African languages of the Old World are mentioned. A short mention is made of the New World, the *orbis novus*, which was really quite new in 1555.

The information Gesner gives about those languages he knows well is rather restricted. If he has a text, he sometimes makes lexical remarks, or more exactly remarks about the origin of the words. The viewpoint of his presentation is clearly that of a German-speaking person, as one can see, for instance, because he does not bother to explain which words in the "oratio dominica anglica" are Germanic. There are no remarks on grammar. Even for languages on which one might expect grammatical explanations, there is nothing. Gesner reproduces for instance the Ave Maria as well as the paternoster in Hungarian, which is grammatically quite different from Latin or German. But there is not a single word about the grammatical structure of that language. Instead, there are remarks about the history of the Hungarian migration. The origin of the people who speak a language rather than the language itself seems to be the real scope of interest. Languages are considered as vocabularies, and the "differentiae linguarum" are lexical differences or, better, differences of signifiers.

What Gesner writes about English or Hungarian might be termed a "description" of those languages if we take the term "description" in a very weak sense of the already weak "belles lettres" meaning of "description" in the *Encyclopédie*:

DESCRIPTION, (*Belles-Lettres*) Imperfect and not very precise definition, in which one tries to make a thing known by means of enough specific properties and conditions to give an idea of it, and to distinguish it from other things, but without explaining its nature and essence. Grammarians are satisfied with *descriptions*; philosophers want definitions.[5]

Gesner enumerates some "specific properties and conditions" of a language. But one wonders whether those properties are sufficient to give an idea of that language and to distinguish them from others. If Gesner's unsystematic remarks constitute a description, it surely is a very poor one. The poverty of that description is first of all due to the poverty of the linguistic archive. In the sixteenth century, practically only the European and the Mediterranean languages were known and documented. And the archive is rather messy. The alphabet is introduced to give a certain order to the chaos. The presentation of knowledge, made possible by the printing press and by erudites like Gesner, favored the alphabetical order. If we apply a geographical order to the material assembled by Gesner, we see that whole shelves are empty: Europe still does not know very much about the globe. This is still very much the same world as that known to Greek and Roman antiquity. The New World is mentioned, but is still completely unknown. Gesner writes that Columbus has brought some men from Hispaniola and some of their words have been written down. Africa is present only through the Ethiopian, Egyptian, and Arabic languages. Asia does not stretch very far: a *lingua indica* is mentioned.

In a book with the same title, *Mithridates,* published 254 years later by Johan Christoph Adelung and Johann Severin Vater, we have in the second volume not only one English paternoster but sixteen versions of the Lord's Prayer in English, from 875 to modern times, and in different dialects.[6] The information about the English language has increased considerably. More diachronical and more diatopical information is available. Adelung and Vater have an exact knowledge of the history of the English language from the Anglo-Saxons, via the Danes, the Normans, and the melding of French and Germanic. They know of the dialects of English. And there are some very pertinent remarks about the grammatical structure of English. The bibliography has visibly increased: Gesner quotes only one book, Adelung and Vater have 50 books on English in their bibliography. The number of "specific properties and conditions" of the object described has been enormously enhanced.[7]

As far as the whole of the archive is concerned, Gesner's *Mithridates* is a booklet of 150 pages; Adelung and Vater have five volumes of 500 to 800 pages each, more than 3,000 pages altogether. The order is geographical. The Adelung and Vater *Mithridates* starts with a part on the Asian languages; part two is on the European languages; part three (in two volumes) has three sections: III,1 (Africa); III,2 (South America); III,3 (Middle and North America). Part IV contains addenda and corrections.

But, even if the linguistic archive is incomparably better furnished at the end of the eighteenth century, it is far from complete. And even if the descriptions of the individual languages in the Adelung and Vater *Mithridates* are much more detailed, even if they now certainly satisfy the *belles-lettres* concept of descriptions, they will be considered unsatisfactory. They will be criticized as being biased portraits, caricatures more than true images of the individuality of the described object. The whole *Mithridates* will still be regarded more as a cabinet of curiosities than a scientific collection. What will be stipulated are descriptions in the stronger and more systematic sense of natural history:

> DESCRIPTION, (*Hist. nat.*) To describe the different products of nature is to draw their portrait, to make a picture that represents them, as much the inside as the outside, from all sides and in different states.[8]

Since there is the danger of not coming to an end with the description and creating monstrous descriptive figures instead of clear and distinct ideas of the object under scrutiny, descriptions have to be limited and they have to be made systematically: "Descriptions can be useful only to the extent that they are confined to proper boundaries and subject to fixed laws." The indispensable prerequisite for this systematicity—delimitations and laws—seems to be comparison:

> When one describes a creature, one must pay attention to its affinities with other natural beings; it is only by comparing them in this way that one is able to discover the resemblances and differences that exist among them, and to establish a set of facts that yield general knowledge.[9]

Systematicity based on comparison will be the basic postulate of Wilhelm von Humboldt's project of comparative linguistics [vergleichendes Sprachstudium].

I. From Linguistic Catholicism to Protestantism

In order to understand the shortcomings of linguistic description around 1800, but also the enormous increase of linguistic knowledge, we have to have a look at the rather dramatic developments between 1550 and 1800.

It is an amazing fact that Europe, before the sixteenth century, knows so little about languages, her own languages (with the exception of Latin) as well as the languages of the rest of the world. It is amazing because linguistic diversity was a daily experience and because one does not need any sophisticated technical device like microscopes, stethoscopes, or telescopes for linguistic research. But the Greeks had no curiosity about the languages of their neighbors, the *bárbaroi* (those who produce animal-like sounds: "brrbrr"); the Romans (who did not even think a great deal about their own language) were not interested in the languages of the peoples of their huge empire; and the middle ages were deaf to the different voices of Europe and were therefore somehow monolingual in Latin. So, generally speaking, besides Latin grammars, there were no descriptions of languages until the Renaissance.[10] The reasons for this state of affairs seem to be the following.

In spite of the tower of Babel and in spite of the daily experience that languages are different and that these differences are serious obstacles to communication—certainly also in order to forget Babel—Europe was deeply convinced, for thousands of years, that languages are profoundly identical and that language differences are only superficial ones, differences in *sound*—and that therefore, they do not matter. This belief is still today the naïve conviction of people with little experience of linguistic alterity. But also in linguistics today, after a short period of stressing, and perhaps exaggerating, the differences of languages, the belief in the identity of languages has become a common and even aggressively promoted modern conviction.[11] This belief has deep historical roots in our tradition.

Aristotle, the *Philosophus Maximus*, has taught the West that thought is identical for all humans and that languages are only different sounds with which humans communicate their thought. The famous passage in *De interpretatione* reads as follows:

> And as not all men have the same letters, they do not have the same sounds [phonai]. But the affections of the soul [pathemata tes psyches] of which these sounds are signs [semeia] in the first place, are the same for all, as the objects [pragmata] are the same, of which those are images [homoiomata].[12]

Cognition is extra- or pre-linguistic and the same for everybody. Language, on the other side, is only a phonetic device for the purpose of communication. And this phonetic device comes in different forms. The different sounds are linked arbitrarily with the universal content: the Aristotelian term is *kata synthéken*, which means "according to tradition" and which has been translated into Latin as *secundum placitum*, or *secundum arbitrium*, hence "arbitrary."

This is the European standard model of the relationship between language and thought. And it is a serious obstacle to think about human languages, to grasp the differences of languages: Why bother with languages if they are only a secondary medium for the real thing behind it—for (universal) thought?[13] Why bother with languages if they are only arbitrary signs of what really matters? Why bother with languages if they are only materially different signs for the same? Why this completely superfluous tinkling of sounds? Would it not be much better to do away with it, since it only hides the universality of thought and since it is only an obstacle to the universal communication of the same?

This Greek conception of a universal unity of thought is confirmed by the other tradition of the West, by the Biblical story: before Babel, there was one language, and, hence, behind all existing languages there is one language, the *lingua adamica*. Even if, contrary to the Greek linguistic conception, the Babel myth tries at least to reflect about linguistic diversity and to take linguistic differences seriously, diversity of languages is considered as a punishment. As a nostalgic story about the loss of the original unity, it establishes the necessity of redemption, of a return to the *lingua adamica*. Pentecost shows one way: the diversity of languages is unimportant and can be overcome, because the speakers are inspired by the same (holy) spirit. But, deep down, Europe does not believe in Pentecost; it remains profoundly nostalgic for the universal language of paradise.

Antiquity and the middle ages are clearly universalistic, catholic in every respect. Differences of languages are not perceived, there is a blindness—or, better, deafness—for languages. And—what we should not forget—there is a deep contempt for all those who do not speak the language of the dominant culture, for the *bárbaroi*.

The general renewal of science in the sixteenth century, the media revolution that goes with it, the invention of the printing press and the diffusion of knowledge, and the Copernican revolution are certainly the bases of the constitution of a linguistic archive. But within this complex of changes, two reasons seem to be decisive for the rise of an interest in the differences of languages. The first one is Europe's encounter with real alterity—that is, the first encounter with America. Europe has to deal with the experience that there is an *orbis novus* and that there are human beings who are really different from Europeans. And a noticeable difference is the difference of language which turns out to be a profound difference, namely one of thinking. The second reason for the rise of an interest in languages is the loss of that language of paradise that practically prevailed during the middle ages: the loss of Latin. In the sixteenth century, Europeans started to write more and more in their national languages, leaving behind Latin as the language of the old church and the old culture.

This is the moment when Francis Bacon discovers the "idols of the forum." He realizes that there are "prejudices" sedimented in everyday words of the vulgar languages, and that those prejudices are a source of misunderstanding and a cognitive obstacle to true knowledge. This insight is nothing other than the recognition that something in the natural languages has to do with thinking, even if this thinking is not welcome to the new scientist. For Bacon (and the whole analytical tradition after him) the philosopher has to get rid of those linguistic prejudices through science and enlightenment—that is, he has to get rid of the semantics of natural languages. Paradoxically, this fight against linguistic prejudices is the beginning of linguistic research: the new scientist has to study the languages in order to know the enemy and to build a new scientific language without those prejudices.[14]

John Locke, who discovers profound semantic differences between languages (and who in this context was perhaps the first philosopher to allude to American languages), was only deepening the Baconian language criticism when he claimed that a language reform based on scientific insight and cooperation should overcome the "mist" that the natural languages spread "before our eyes." And also Étienne Bonnot de Condillac—even if he has more sympathy for the "genius of languages"—ends his *Essai* with propositions on "how to make our ideas clear," ideas obfuscated by the semantics of individual languages. He ends with proposals for how to overcome the semantic particularity of natural languages.

The growing sensibility for linguistic particularities first strengthened universalistic tendencies in linguistic reflection. It seems as if the differences between languages had become so dangerous that it was time to stress their uniformity: as Wolf Peter Klein has shown, the concept of the *harmonia linguarum* in the sixteenth century—a study of the one original word behind the many words of the different languages—was such a universalistic project in the field of the vocabulary.[15] Later, in the seventeenth and eighteenth centuries, when the *harmonia linguarum* turned out to be of little plausibility, universal or philosophical grammar represented the universal nucleus of all languages, from the Port-Royal Grammar to Destutt de Tracy's *Élémens d'idéologie* (1803). Thus, the experience of a cognitive impact of language differences creates first a negative reaction. Bacon wants a new *lingua philosophica*, and the Port-Royal intellectuals look for the common core beyond the differences: "Grammaire générale et raisonnée . . . qui contient tout ce qui est commun aux langues."[16] The *grammaire philosophique* is a reaction against the catastrophe of the loss of the unity of the Human Mind, and an attempt to save its catholicity.

But philosophical grammar (and *harmonia linguarum*) is only one reaction—the catastrophic reaction—to the ever-growing insight into semantic differences among languages. The other possible reaction is the celebration of those differences which—*cum grano salis*—might be called the German (or Protestant) way of dealing with the discovery of the *idola fori*. I am alluding to the fact that Gottfried Wilhelm Leibniz reacted differently to the discovery of prejudices sedimented in natural languages and to semantic differences among languages. Against the Baconian or Lockean lament over the different languages as obstacles to the truth, as "mist before our eyes," Leibniz, in the *New Essays*, considers linguistic differences a cognitive wealth. Languages are documents for the knowledge of the human mind. Leibniz therefore advocates a study of all the languages of the world, not in order to fight the enemy but in order to discover ourselves. We have to store and to describe all the languages of the world: "to put all of the world's languages into grammars and dictionaries" because the *idola fori* are nothing to be lamented about, but documents of the wealth of the human spirit.

> In due course, all the languages of the universe will be recorded and put into dictionaries and grammars, and they will be compared to one another; this will be used in many ways, as much for understanding things . . . as for understanding our intellect and the marvelous variety of its operations.[17]

To enhance "understanding our intellect and the marvelous variety of its operations" is the explicit—and in my opinion still the only valuable—reason for the study of the languages of the world. This is the birth certificate of linguistics as an autonomous *descriptive* science.

But Leibniz adds a second reason for linguistic study: "to say nothing of the origins of people, which will be understood by means of reliable etymologies that the comparison of languages will best provide."[18] The knowledge of languages yields insights into the history of peoples. Languages are also documents for history. Linguistics can be an auxiliary science for history. This was the chief reason Leibniz put forward in his 1710 article on considerations about the origins of nations deduced from the evidence of languages, *ex indicio linguarum*.

II. Toward the Marvelous Variety

The Leibnizian enthusiasm for language studies—"to put all of the world's languages into grammars and dictionaries"—was rather successful: it was taken up by French erudites like de Brosses and Court de Gébelin

Lingue.	Acqua.	Anima.	Animale.
Persiàna.	ab.	revvan.	davvar.
Curdistàna.	ave.	ghiàne. ruhh.	ahhivàn.
Turca.	su.	gian.	hajvan.gianvver.
Greca letteraria.	ydor.	psychi.	zóon.
Dialetti della Greca volgare.	nero. sferò.	anèmos. psychi.	zò. zòon. empsychon.
Epirotica.	vie.	spijpti.	eresüe.
Albanese.	ui.	spirt.	staas.
Greca Siciliana.	újë.	scpirte.	animáal.
Ungherese.	viz'.	lèlek.	èlo.állat.
Russiana.	voda:	ducha. spijpti.	givotnoye.
Moscovita.	voda.		
Polacca.	vvoda.	dusza.	zvvierze.
Boema.	vvoda.	dusse.	zvvirzata.
Dalmata.	voda.	dusa.	zvir.
Gotica.	vvate.	saivvala.eaiyala.	
Islandese.	versla. krap.	saal. ande.	dir.
Svedese.	vatn.	skiel.	diur.
Danese.	vand.	siel.	
Inglese.	vvater.	soul.	animal.
Fiamminga.	vvatter.	siele.	dier.
Olandese.	vvate.	ziel.	beest.
Tedesca,	vvasser.	seel.	thier.
Svizzera.	vvasser.	seel.	thier.
Val-Cimbria, o de' sette Comuni.	bazzar.	seel.	animaal.
Cèltica.	avved. aa. au. dour. dur.	ane. ene.	aneval.
Bretòna.	douv.	ene.	pen-moh.
Wallèse, o Gallèse.	dvvr.	enaid.	anifail.
Irlandese.	isee. ishe.	anm.	ainbhigh.
Erse.	visge.	anam.	beoch. bruide.
Guipuzcoana, o Bascuenze.	ur.	arimì.	animalí.
Biscaglìna.	ur.	animí.	animalí.
Latina.	aqua.	anima.	animal.
Portoghese.	agoa.	alma.	animàl.
Gallèga.	agüa.	alma.	anemale.
Spagnuola.	agua.	alma.	animàl.

Valenà

F I G . 4 . Lorenzo Hervás y Panduro, *Vocabolario poligloto con prolegomeni sopre più di cl. lingue* (Cesena: Gregorio Biasini, 1787), p. 165. Photo: author.

and, more important, by the Russian empress Catherine II, who was a German princess. She fostered the recording [enregistrement] and the description of the languages of her vast empire. The most famous result of those linguistic activities is Peter Simon Pallas' *Vocabularia comparativa*. And Adelung also depends upon the Russian enterprise—which he considers as completely insufficient and therefore wants to complete and to improve.

Adelung—and Vater, who continued his work later—makes great use of that marvelous other archive that had been collected in Rome by Lorenzo Hervás. I do not know whether Hervás had any knowledge of Leibniz, but it seems that, by the end of the century, the Leibnizian project to make records of all languages of the world was in the air. Hervás had the richest archive of the languages of the New World. He had collected information about the languages of the Americas from his fellow Jesuits who had been chased from the Spanish part of the continent. This missionary linguistics is one of the richest stocks of linguistic material. It is still available, by the way, at the Vatican. Furthermore, Adelung's archive was completed by the collection of linguistic materials brought over from America by Alexander von Humboldt and completed by Wilhelm von Humboldt.[19] Here we see again the impact of the American experience for the description of languages.

It is important to remark that the main motive of the Russo-German enterprise to collect languages was, however, not so much the first Leibnizian motive, that of documenting and describing the marvelous variety of the human mind; but rather the second one, the historical one, to show the genealogical parental connections between the nations—the origins of nations *ex indicio linguarum*. Therefore, Pallas's work is a comparative vocabulary, the idea being that by comparing the most important words of languages— God, man, woman, water, and so forth—one can see which words they have in common, which languages belong together and, hence, which nations have common roots. The historical aim does not favor linguistic description. In Pallas there is definitely no description of individual languages. The research for origins automatically reduces variety to unity,[20] a fact immediately visible in a schema from the *Vocabolario poligloto* of Lorenzo Hervás y Panduro (fig. 4).[21]

Adelung is also explicit about his historical aim. In his introduction to the *Mithridates*, he states that it is certainly interesting to have knowledge about many languages, but that the higher aim of all this is to know their parental relationships. Nevertheless, the structure of the *Mithridates* rather favors the other Leibnizean aim, the demonstration of the "marvelous variety" of the operations of the human mind. Adelung's *Mithridates* is not any

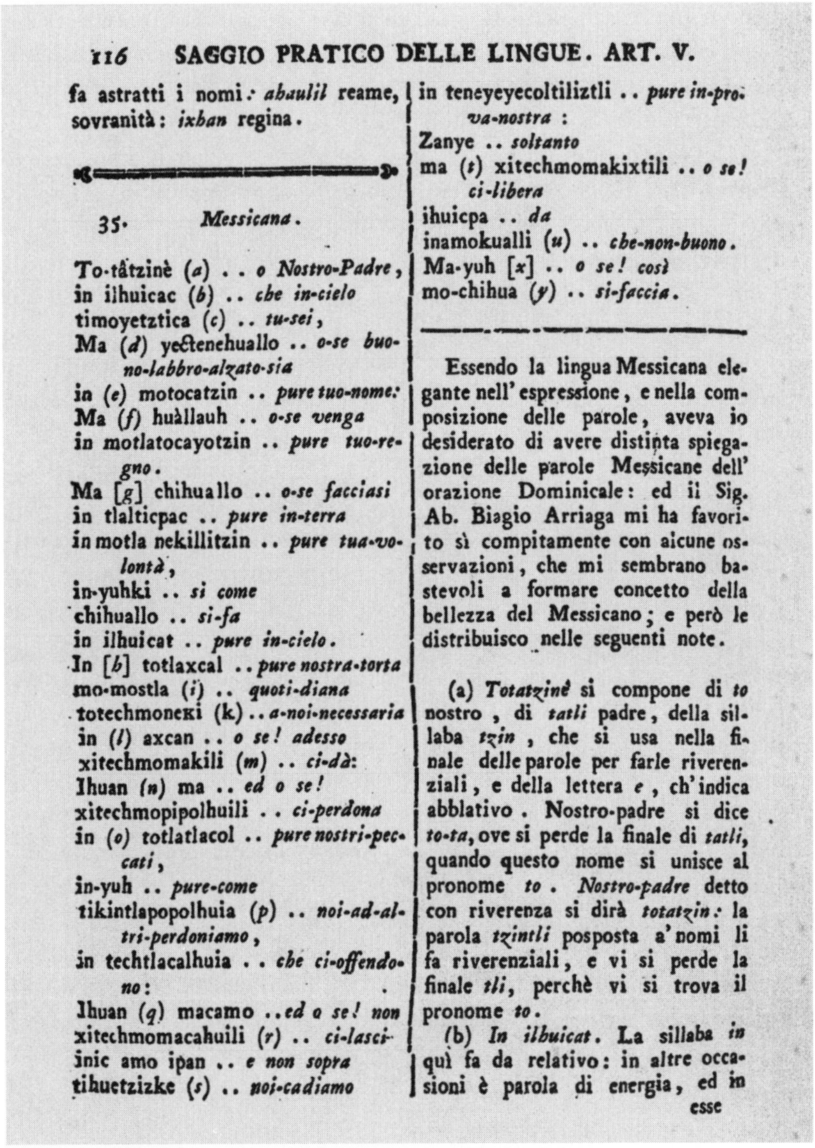

fa astratti i nomi: *abaulil* reame,
sovranità: *ixban* regina.

35.   Messicana.

To-tâtzinè (*a*) .. *o Nostro-Padre*,
in ilhuicac (*b*) .. *che in-cielo*
timoyetztica (*c*) .. *tu-sei*,
Ma (*d*) yeêtenehuallo .. *o-se buo-*
   no-labbro-alzato-sia
in (*e*) motocatzin .. *pure tuo-nome:*
Ma (*f*) huàllauh .. *o-se venga*
in motlatocayotzin .. *pure tuo-re-*
   gno.
Ma [*g*] chihuallo .. *o-se facciasi*
in tlalticpac .. *pure in-terra*
in motla nekillitzin .. *pure tua-vo-*
   lontà,
in-yuhki .. *si come*
chihuallo .. *si-fa*
in ilhuicat .. *pure in-cielo*.
In [*h*] totlaxcal .. *pure nostra-torta*
mo-mostla (*i*) .. *quoti-diana*
totechmoneKi (*k*) .. *a-noi-necessaria*
in (*l*) axcan .. *o se! adesso*
xitechmomakili (*m*) .. *ci-dà*:
Ihuan (*n*) ma .. *ed o se!*
xitechmopipolhuili .. *ci-perdona*
in (*o*) totlatlacol .. *pure nostri-pec-*
   cati,
in-yuh .. *pure-come*
tikintlapopolhuia (*p*) .. *noi-ad-al-*
   tri-perdoniamo,
in techtlacalhuia .. *che ci-offendo-*
   no:
Ihuan (*q*) macamo ..*ed o se! non*
xitechmomacahuili (*r*) .. *ci-lasci-*
inic amo ipan .. *e non sopra*
tihuetzizke (*s*) .. *noi-cadiamo*

in teneyeyecoltiliztli .. *pure in-pro-*
   va-nostra :
Zanye .. *soltanto*
ma (*t*) xitechmomakixtili .. *o se!*
   ci-libera
ihuicpa .. *da*
inamokualli (*u*) .. *che-non-buono*.
Ma-yuh [*x*] .. *o se! così*
mo-chihua (*y*) .. *si-faccia*.

Essendo la lingua Messicana ele-
gante nell'espressione, e nella com-
posizione delle parole, aveva io
desiderato di avere distinta spiega-
zione delle parole Messicane dell'
orazione Dominicale: ed il Sig.
Ab. Biagio Arriaga mi ha favori-
to sì compitamente con alcune os-
servazioni, che mi sembrano ba-
stevoli a formare concetto della
bellezza del Messicano; e però le
distribuisco nelle seguenti note.

(a) *Totatzinè* si compone di *to*
nostro, di *tatli* padre, della sillaba *tzin*, che si usa nella finale delle parole per farle riverenziali, e della lettera *e*, ch'indica
abblativo. Nostro-padre si dice
to-ta, ove si perde la finale di *tatli*,
quando questo nome si unisce al
pronome *to*. *Nostro-padre* detto
con riverenza si dirà *totatzin:* la
parola *tzintli* posposta a'nomi li
fa riverenziali, e vi si perde la
finale *tli*, perchè vi si trova il
pronome *to*.
(b) *In ilhuicat*. La sillaba *in*
quì fa da relativo: in altre occa-
sioni è parola di energia, ed in
   esse

FIG. 5. Lorenzo Hervás y Panduro, *Saggio pratico delle lingue con prolegomeni, e una raccolta di orazioni dominical* ... (Cesena: Gregorio Biasini, 1787), p. 116. Photo: author.

more a series of comparative word lists for the same concept, but a series of portraits of languages in a geographical order. And the main reason for the improvement of the descriptive art is certainly the shift of the focus of attention from the lexicon to grammar. This barely responds to Friedrich Schlegel's insight of 1808 that grammar has to be the core of comparative language study, but it is certainly indebted to Lorenzo Hervás's *Saggio pratico*. Hervás has no theory of linguistic description but a revolutionary descriptive intuition which seems to be a result of handling not only word lists but texts in an impressive series of languages. He discovers specific grammatical traits of languages by a kind of dissection of the syntactic sequences, which had not been done before. Taking into account that modern descriptive linguistics considers grammar as the structural core of language, this is a decisive step towards descriptive adequacy in a modern sense.

In Hervás we also have both Leibnizian motivations. His relevant linguistic work comprises three books, the *Catalogo delle lingue*, the *Vocabolario poligloto*, and the *Saggio pratico*, which represent three different kinds of approach to the languages of the world. The *Catalogo delle lingue*, his most famous work, is what the title says: a catalogue of the names and the geographical situation of the languages of the world. The second book, the *Vocabolario poligloto*, consists like Pallas's comparative vocabularies, of lists of important words in different languages—in order to highlight their kinship. And the third book, the *Saggio pratico*, which presents the Lord's Prayer in 326 languages, is a new *Mithridates*, but differs from Gesner's in that it adds grammatical remarks to the text. And here, Hervás uses a very ingenious and powerful, even if not completely new, analytical instrument: the interlinear version.[22] This tool analyzes the sequences, segments the string, and thereby detects structural qualities that are meant to be specific properties of that language with the intention of drawing a portrait—even if somewhat sketchy—of the language. Nahuatl will be our example for the demonstration of this new element of description (see fig. 5). In the Mexican paternoster, the line meaning "hallowed be thy name" is *ma yectene-huallo inmotocatzin*. The first part is literally translated by Hervás in the following way:

> Ma yec ten ehual lo
>
> o-se buono-labbro-alzato-sia[23]

The Italian interlinear version would be in English: o-if good-lip-elevate-be. This morphemic segmentation and syntactic imitation gives a first impression of the structural proceeding of the foreign language. The European reader who certainly knows the underlying synthetic Latin form, namely *sanctificetur* (third person singular subjunctive passive), immediately grasps the fact that the grammatical content of the subjunctive passive is rendered by two morphemes: *ma* (modal) and *lo* (passive), or a discontinuous morpheme *ma . . . lo?*, and that the semantic content of *sancti-ficare* [make holy] is composed by the agglutination of lexemes meaning "good," "lip," and "heighten." This immediate insight into the structural traits of the sequence given by the interlinear translation is then confirmed by further notes that explain the structural analyses.[24]

Adelung and Vater now combine the information Hervás gives in three different parts of his work in order to draw more complete pictures of individual languages. In the case of Nahuatl, they first have a rather long paragraph on the history of Mexico and its language. Second, they give information about linguistic affinities. Third, they make considerations about the grammatical character of the language by proceeding in the following way: they check the linguistic categories which are known to them—that is, the categories of the Indo-European languages—and they note what is different in the language under description. It is, hence, clear that those remarks are made from the standpoint of their normal grammar—that is, Latin- and Greek-based grammar—or even more specifically from the viewpoint of Spanish which is the background language of their sources. The latter can be clearly seen from what they say, for instance, about the phonemes of Nahuatl: they remark that there is no /ñ/ and no /l/ in Nahuatl. They do this because the background is Spanish—that is, because the Spaniards who wrote the Nahuatl grammars—of course for practical reasons—noted that there is no /ñ/ and no /l/ as in Spanish. The same is true in the paragraph on the tenses of the verb: Adelung and Vater say that there is no difference between imperfect and preterite. From the standpoint of their native German such a remark makes no sense. Here too, the background is Spanish, because there is the opposition of *imperfecto* and *pretérito perfecto* in the Spanish grammar: Spanish Nahuatl grammars note this as a deviation from the Spanish norm. After this grammatical characterization, Adelung and Vater add bibliographical indications of the grammars and dictionaries used, which stem mainly from the seventeenth century. And finally, they present the Lord's Prayer with grammatical explanations that are practically copied from Hervás.

III. Representing Organic Beings

Even if this kind of description of a language is incomparably more complete than Gesner's sketchy remarks of 1555, it still presents some methodological problems to which I have already alluded. It certainly presents "specific properties and conditions," but it lacks the systematicity, "confined to proper boundaries and subject to fixed laws," required by the other concept of description in the *Encyclopédie*. This is what Humboldt will postulate for his project of a new descriptive linguistics or, better, of a "comparative language study."

> What the general linguistic study is still lacking, is that one has not yet sufficiently penetrated into the knowledge of individual languages, without which the comparison of many languages is not very useful. It was believed that it was enough to remark single deviant particularities of the grammar and to compare more or less numerous series of words with each other. But the dialect of the rudest nation is a work of nature too noble to be broken into accidental pieces and presented fragmentarily to the contemplation. It is an organic being and has to be treated as such.[25]

The term organic being [organisches Wesen] shows that we are already deep in the new century: in 1820, Humboldt is presenting a new and huge program for future linguistic research, for a new *Mithridates*. What he had in mind, already in 1811, was "a complete encyclopedia of every language." For this project new standards were being developed.

According to Humboldt, what Adelung and the others did was premature. They did not have sufficient knowledge about the structures of individual languages to do what they did. On a shaky basis, they made remarks about "deviant particularities" of the languages, thereby destroying and fragmenting a living object. Those particularities deviate from a norm which is not even consciously reflected as such: the grammar of the describer or—most of the time—the generalized Latin and Greek grammar is considered as a general grammar and taken as the measure for the descriptions of languages of a completely different kind. As a collection of deviant linguistic traits, these descriptions are caricatures rather than portraits. The *Mithridates* thus is more a teratology, a collection of monstrosities, than a beautiful art gallery.

How can this be changed? The remedy is, as Humboldt says, to treat a language as an organic being. This means nothing else than to treat it as a whole or—as Humboldt puts it—in its "inner coherence" [in ihrem inneren Zusammenhang]:

It is an organic Being, and one must treat it as such. Thus, the first rule above all is to study each known language in its inner coherence, so as to pursue and to order systematically every detectable analogy.[26]

"To study inner coherence . . . to order systematically" clearly refers to a complete, holistic, systematic, structural presentation of a language. The first step towards that study of the inner coherences and analogies has to be to get rid of that presupposed general norm from which languages seem to deviate. Two years later, in another academic discourse, Humboldt is explicit about the distortion of the "inner coherence" through the unreflected standpoint of another language, mostly that of the traditional Latin grammar or the grammar of a mother tongue (for instance, Spanish in the case of the Amerindian languages):

> Since one normally approaches the study of an unknown language from the perspective of a known language, one's own language or Latin, one sees how the grammatical relationships of these languages are designated in the foreign language and one names the flexions and positions used for those relations exactly with the terms of the grammatical forms which serve in our language or according to general linguistic laws. Very often, however, these forms do not exist in that language but are substituted or circumscribed by other forms. In order to avoid this error, one therefore has to study every language in its particularity in such a way that one recognizes, through an exact segmentation, by which definite form it designates grammatical relations according to its own structure.[27]

In this passage, Humboldt demands an exact segmentation in order to find out the forms that belong to its proper structure. Now, interestingly enough, the most important tool for getting to the "inner coherence" is Hervás's interlinear version. The interlinear version helps to find the grammatical units of a language since it is the tool for the precise segmentation through which one avoids the error of projecting a foreign structure on a language. Humboldt's most famous example is the following form of the Caribbean language: *aveiridaco* is said to be "2. pers. sing. imperf. conjunct." of *to be*: "you were," lat. *esses*.[28] But there is no such form in that language. The form means "on the day of your being" or:

a	veiri	daco
you	be	that day

After a proper segmentation of its own categories and lexical units, a systematic description of the whole would depict the individual language according to its proper laws. And this is what Humboldt tries to do in his *Mexican Grammar*, the only grammar Humboldt really completed (all the other grammars of mainly Amerindian languages are not finished, but very interesting sketches) and which was published in 1994 as the first volume of the new edition of Humboldt's linguistic work.

But with this new and complete structural description the task of the linguist is not completed. We have two new problems: first, the holistic description is too detailed to grasp the whole as a whole, a danger already hinted at in the *Encyclopédie*.[29] And second, also this "exact segmentation" [genauere Zergliederung] which generates the structural grammar and the scientific lexicon of that language cannot help destroying or killing the language, that living being. Humboldt is explicit about it: grammars and lexicons are only *skeletons* of languages [todte Gerippe]. Therefore, a further step has to be taken which again seems to draw Humboldt toward the *Mithridates*: Humboldt strongly recommends to take into consideration texts [Sprachproben], because only texts—discourse [verbundene Rede]—contain the living spirit of the language and are able to give life back to the skeleton. Only on the basis of texts can one attain the ultimate aim of the study of languages, can one grasp the character of a language. But this characterization, which is clearly considered an artistic activity—a painting [Charaktergemälde, Charakterschilderung]—must be made on the basis of a thorough knowledge of the single language, i.e. on the basis of the structural description of the structure or the organism. The *Charaktergemälde* explicitly transcends any scientific discourse. Humboldt asks himself whether this kind of "investigation of the individuality" of languages "should not be excluded from the sphere of scientific linguistic study," because the contours of that individuality can only be "felt and intuited." But he answers that—whatever the epistemological status of such an enterprise—the linguist has at least to venture this attempt because only this audacious intuitive grasping of individuality gives sense to the tiresome descriptive work.[30]

Humboldt does not fulfill this request in his own presentation of the Mexican language. It is true, he writes a Mexican grammar, a complete description of that language. And at the end of that grammar he has a chapter, "Character der mexicanischen Sprache," which is a well-founded alternative to Vater's chapter on the "grammatical character" of Mexican. But Humboldt does not really reach his ultimate aim: the characterization of Nahuatl on the basis of texts. He has no texts. The Lord's Prayer is not an acceptable Nahuatl text since it is only a translation of a European text. Humboldt looks for the real thing, for true Mexican texts. The portrait of the character is possible only on the basis of the living object, the "organic Being," and this means on the basis of autochthonous texts. This is, by the way, very probably the reason why he abandons the project of writing his book on the American languages, a project pursued for more than twenty years, and dedicates the last years of his life to the study of Malayo-Polynesian languages, where texts were available.[31]

IV. Mithridates Lost, Paradise Regained

Looking back on nearly 200 years of descriptive linguistic work after the second *Mithridates*, one might say that Humboldtian—structural—principles have been largely adopted in the descriptive work of modern linguistics. Descriptive linguistics—which by the way was the historical mission of American linguistics (America had to describe the native languages of the continent)—has fulfilled the task of describing the languages of the world.[32] The *Mithridates* of our times is not one little book of 150 pages, nor a five-volume digest of 3,000 pages, but the ensemble of the "monographs of languages," as Humboldt calls them, thousands of books describing thousands of human tongues. But most of the time, linguistics has not gone beyond the skeletons of grammar and lexicon. Therefore, portraying living languages—or let us say languages in action, because life metaphors are not fashionable any more—on the basis of structural descriptions *and* on the basis of texts [Sprachproben], might still be a valuable task for linguists. But this dangerous hermeneutical and poetical approach to languages is not considered as a worthy task for linguists anymore.

Therefore, since everything seems to be done—that is, since the *Mithridates* seems to be accomplished—linguistics has chosen to disappear, to dissolve itself in the philosophical or rather psychological universality of the cognitive sciences. Faced with the dramatic diversity of languages, linguistics, as in the sixteenth and seventeenth centuries, has become extremely critical of the *Mithridates* and the *differentiae linguarum* and is going back to the old Catholic universalistic mainstream of Western thought, to researching the Language of Paradise lying underneath all those different languages. Linguistics is back to the *harmonia linguarum*, to a universal vocabulary called "mentalese," and it is back to the *grammaire générale*, radicalized as an innate Universal Grammar. The theological dream of the *lingua adamica*, of the primitive and final universal linguistic unity, has largely triumphed over the joys of diversity.

Between Political Arithmetic and Political Economy

In the second half of the seventeenth century, William Petty, member of the Royal Society and aspirant to royal patronage, advocated redefining value, streamlining government, and institutionalizing something like an economic index to determine national well-being. The key to all these reforms, according to Petty, was the collection and presentation of reliable information about rates of mortality, the size and wealth of the population, the numbers of people killed in the Irish uprising, the numbers of "teeming"— that is, reproductive—women, and so on. The form in which this information was presented was also important to Petty. Figures of arithmetic, Petty declared, which displayed only "number, weight, and measure," were more trustworthy than figures of speech, because language, which depended on imprecise metaphors, was inherently susceptible to manipulation. According to Petty, the "science" founded upon the collection and presentation of numerical information, which he christened political arithmetic, would enable legislators to determine the regularities of the population they governed, and this determination would facilitate efficient, and therefore (cost-) effective government.[1]

In 1825, J. R. McCulloch, who aspired to public, not royal, approval, confidently asserted that many of the goals Petty had identified had been realized: value had been defined as the amount of labor necessary to transform a natural article; government had been disciplined to intervene in economic matters only when non-interference would be more deleterious; and, although an exact standard for quantifying national well-being had yet to be determined, the science capable of providing that standard had been perfected. Indeed, in McCulloch's account, political economy, as "the *sci-*

ence of values," had become the most useful, as well as the most modern, of all sciences.[2]

I want to make two points about the relationship between Petty's political arithmetic and McCulloch's political economy. The first is that the latter was not, in any direct sense at least, the disciplinary descendant of the former. Despite the fact that practitioners of both political arithmetic and political economy claimed to draw upon the methods of natural philosophy, political arithmetic belonged to an Enlightenment discourse known as the science of *police*, whereas political economy derived from eighteenth-century moral philosophy. The science of police was essentially a science of government; it focused on such subjects as health, highways, public order, and trade.[3] Moral philosophy, by contrast, contained elements of what we would call psychology, logic, ethics, jurisprudence, history, and rhetoric.[4] Practitioners of police, whose foremost concern was efficient rule, were interested in collecting numerical information to facilitate centralized administration, while moral philosophers deployed a combination of historical analysis and introspection to determine the nature of man, for whom government was a necessary, but secondary concern.

My first point about the relationship between political arithmetic and political economy is that, in Britain—as opposed to much of Europe—the kind of government-sponsored data collection associated with political arithmetic was cordoned off from the predominant form of philosophizing about society that Hume called the "science of man." Indeed, in 1825, McCulloch specifically distinguished between statistics, which was the obvious disciplinary descendant of political arithmetic, and political economy, which was, in his eyes, self-evidently superior to the mere collection of particular facts. "The object of the statistician," McCulloch explained, "is to describe the condition of a particular country at a particular period; while the object of the political economist is to discover the causes which have brought it to that condition, and the means by which its wealth and riches may be indefinitely increased. He is to the statistician what the physical astronomer is to the mere observer. He takes the facts furnished by the researches of the statistician, and after comparing them with those furnished by historians and travelers, he applies himself to discover their relation."[5]

My second point about the relationship between these two disciplines is suggested by McCulloch's account of their difference. Despite the marginalization of the kind of data collection germane to political arithmetic and police in eighteenth-century England,[6] the nineteenth-century science of wealth resembled political arithmetic in some striking ways. In addition to sharing methodological claims, political arithmetic and political economy were both concerned with the aims and limits of legislation, both sought to understand and maximize the conditions that generated human happiness, and both focused on society. Indeed, one could say that, taken together, these two disciplines constituted society as an object of knowledge. Practitioners of both political arithmetic and political economy, moreover, played similar cultural roles: they made policy recommendations and they sought to describe the regularities of aggregates like the population. More to the point, perhaps, the two disciplines shared not only a claim about method but the problematic associated with that method. Examining this problematic will enable us to understand the implications of the fact that political economy performed the social function Petty outlined for political arithmetic but performed that function differently—as an extension of the philosophy of mind, not a practice derived from counting.

The problematic central to both political arithmetic and political economy concerned the relationship between particulars or "facts" and generalizations or theory.[7] The heart of the problematic can be captured by two questions, the first of which has two parts: (1) were theories derived from particulars, which were observed, or were (what counted as) particular "facts" determined by the theoretical position of the observer? And (2) if theories were not simply constructed from particulars, which, in turn, were not the products of simple observation, then what did theories reflect—something inherent, but not quite observable, in nature, or something originating in the mind of the theorist? I suggest that even though McCulloch depicted political economists as beginning with the "facts" straightforwardly furnished by the latter-day political arithmetician, practitioners of both political economy and political arithmetic were entangled in this problematic. I also suggest that these questions *became* problematic because, by the beginning of the nineteenth century, apologists for political economy had severed the connection between particulars and theory, demoted the former on the grounds that particulars were irrelevant to theory, but then recast theoretical statements as descriptive of particular "facts."[8] What simultaneously underwrote the claims of apologists like McCulloch and rendered those claims a problem for nineteenth-century critics of the "dismal science" was the detour that questions about society took through Scotland. This "detour" culminated in the revision of moral philosophy initiated by its most famous late eighteenth-century professor, Dugald Stewart.[9]

To begin this chapter in the genealogy of modern knowledges, I need to take up the methodological claims central to the work of the Scottish moral philosophers whom Stewart called "conjectural historians," because these writers specifically adapted the "experimental method" also used by Petty to the study of society. According to Stewart's *Account of the Life and Writings of Adam Smith* (1793), the dilemma that would-be historians of society faced was that "many of the most important steps" in the "transition" from "rude" to polished societies were made "long before that stage of society when men began to think of recording their transactions." Writers like Adam Smith, David Hume, Dennis H. Robertson, and Adam Ferguson solved this evidentiary problem, Stewart continued, by combining empirical observations of children and contemporary "savage" societies with conclusions deduced from assumptions about the principles of human nature. These assumptions, in turn, were derived from observations about the human being most immediate to the observer—himself.[10]

Before I take up Stewart's interpretation of the conjectural historians, let me briefly consider one of the clearest statements of the conjectural method, John Millar's introductory remarks to his *Observations Concerning the Distinction of Ranks in Society* (1771). Millar's first assertion is that the historians' only reliable evidence consists of particular observations provided by travelers who have "no speculative systems to warp their opinions."[11] From such accounts, he continues, the moral philosopher will be able to abstract "those rules of conduct, which, independent of all positive institutions, are consistent with propriety, and agreeable to the sense of justice." Implicit in this leap are several assumptions: that human nature is universal, that what he calls propriety and justice are immediately recognizable by the universal light of reason, and that individuals reproduce in small the universal characteristics of the species. If we have what he considers reliable reports about *any* societies, especially "rude" societies like those in America, we can conduct what Millar calls "real experiments." By real experiments, Millar explains, "not by abstracted metaphysical theories, human nature is unfolded; the general laws of our constitution are laid open; and history is rendered subservient to moral philosophy and jurisprudence."[12]

For the contemporary reader, the challenge is to understand how Millar could have understood the opposition he sets up here—between "real experiments" and "abstracted metaphysical theories"—in such a way as to place his assumptions about human nature—which *we* might well call "abstracted metaphysical theories"—in the category of "real experiments." The kind of experiment that Robert Boyle performed with his air pump, after all, could not be conducted with vanished—or even existing—societies. In order to appreciate Millar's distinction between experiments and theories, it is necessary to pose two questions: (1) from what epistemological assumptions did Millar derive what he thought of as an experimental method? And (2) in opposition to what philosophical positions did he formulate his claims?

The answer to the first question takes us back to what P. B. Wood has called the "scientistic belief" that the experimental method developed in relation to the seventeenth-century natural sciences could be applied to morals, and to moral philosophy more generally.[13] This belief, in turn, points to two features that distinguish the eighteenth-century concept of science: (1) despite Boyle's efforts, and partly because of the mathematical contributions of Isaac Newton, what counted as a legitimate experiment considerably exceeded the laboratory trials we associate with that term; and (2) even the most rigorously experimental philosophical method drew upon Aristotle's association of structure with function and his insistence that an organism's purpose follows from, because it originates in, an essential nature.

For the Scottish historians, the laboratory capable of providing evidence about the structure and therefore the function of human nature was history. By looking at past societies, they argued, the philosopher could identify the aspects of human behavior that remained constant and from these he could deduce the universal principles of "man." Looking into the laboratory of history, however, was not a simple task—both because evidence was lacking and because particular details could not easily be assigned to final causes. Largely to guide their observations about past societies and by analogy to observations made about the natural world, most conjectural historians supplemented their descriptions of particular details with the assertion that these details could be referred to an ultimate final cause—the providential design written into human nature by God. For Lord Kames, for example, belief in a providential design was sufficient to set aside not only doubt but also all problems relating to evidence. According to this reasoning, if one lacked evidence to support a theory, this might signify the current limits of human knowledge rather than the error of the theory. "As men ripen in the knowledge of causes and effects," Kames confidently declared, "the benevolence as well as wisdom of a superintending Being become more and more apparent. . . . Beautiful final causes without number have been discovered in the material as well as the moral world, with respect to particulars that once seemed dark and gloomy. . . . Is it too bold to maintain, that an argument from ignorance . . . is altogether insufficient in judging of divine government? How salutary is it for man, and how comfortable, to rest on the faith, that whatever is, is the best!"[14]

Eighteenth-century conjectural historians actually derived their "experimental" method not from Boyle but from Newton, especially as his work had been popularized through public lectures in the early eighteenth century. This method was "scientistic" rather than (what we would think of as) "scientific," because it was as prescriptive as it was descriptive.[15] Indeed, prescription—the inculcation of moral values—was considered one of the principle duties of moral philosophers, especially those who taught in universities, where boys between the ages of twelve and seventeen were being trained to be good citizens and churchmen.[16] The prescriptive element in both conjectural history and moral philosophy more generally was intended in part to counter philosophical positions considered dangerous to young souls. Among these were Cartesian rationalism and Hobbesian nominalism. This is the answer to my second question: in opposition to what philosophical positions was experimental philosophy formulated? Conjectural historians claimed that their method was "experimental" partly to avoid the charge that their theories were affiliated with Descartes and Hobbes. This claim was plausible, in turn, for two reasons: first, because one of the legacies of seventeenth-century English natural philosophy was the assertion that English science was unlike continental science in being experimental, that is, non-hypothetical;[17] and second, because, despite the resemblance between these writers' "conjectures" and the explicitly hypothetical method of Hobbes, the eighteenth-century writers could refer their descriptions of the state of nature to existing "rude" societies, which they claimed were like the societies whose records did not exist.[18]

For the majority of the Scottish historians, the assertion that their method was empirical, or founded on "experiment" and the observation of particular facts, did not conflict with their theories, which were typically derived from a variant of providential design. This was true because what we might see as an unstable compound rested on the double authority of Aristotle and Newton and derived additional strength from its repudiation of Descartes and Hobbes. Before turning to one of the two eighteenth-century historians for whom this conjuncture was more worrisome, let me note that the conviction that God had designed the world to manifest His purpose did not entail any assumptions about the tendency of society to "progress," much less commitment to the idea that commerce inevitably tended to improve human nature. The eighteenth-century conjectural historians were interested in the relationship between virtue and commerce, and especially in the ethical role of private property, but the majority of these writers thought that commerce had as great a tendency to corrupt as to improve, and most, following Hume, identified in human history not a straightforward progression from "rude" to "civilized" societies, but cycles of improvement and decay.[19]

For two of the writers whom Stewart identified as conjectural historians, the conjuncture between an empiricism based on particulars and the kind of a posteriori reasoning epitomized in the argument from design did not seem quite so stable as it did to Millar, Ferguson, and Kames. Even though the most notorious eighteenth-century skeptic was surely David Hume, for brevity's sake, I will discuss only Adam Smith, whose "History of Astronomy" Dugald Stewart nominated as one of the best examples of conjectural history.[20] In the opening pages of this history, Smith addresses the question of why human beings are drawn to philosophy, which he defines as "the science of the connecting principles of nature." We take up this discipline, Smith explains, because only seeing the bewildering array of particular natural phenomena as parts of a coherent whole can counter the debilitating effects of the "wonder" that variety provokes. "Philosophy, by representing the invisible chains which bind together all the . . . disjointed objects [in nature], endeavours to introduce order into this chaos of jarring and discordant appearances, to allay this tumult of the imagination, and to restore it [the imagination], when it surveys the great revolutions of the universe, to that tone of tranquillity and composure, which is both most agreeable in itself, and most suitable to its nature."[21] In passages like this, Smith seems to be saying that orderly philosophy *reflects* the order of nature; by the end of the essay, however, Smith has introduced a note of doubt. In concluding his history, Smith admits that in describing the Newtonian system, whose simplicity satisfies the human need for order, he has "insensibly been drawn in, to make use of language expressing the connecting principle . . . *as if* they were the real chains which nature makes use of."[22] In making this admission, Smith allows for the possibility that the order that philosophy introduces may not actually reside in the natural world but simply project the imagination's ideal coherence onto the world whose proliferating particulars are so troubling.

That unsettling "as if," at the very least, brackets the question of the accuracy or adequacy of any theories. Like other conjectural historians, of course, Smith lacked sufficient evidence to check the adequacy of past astronomers' theories or even, in some cases, to reconstruct these theories.

Unlike most of the other conjectural historians, however, Smith was not consistently committed to the argument from design, which his peers typically relied on to offset the insufficiency of data. Despite his famous references to an "invisible hand" and "the natural course" of society, Smith was as evasive about whether design is providential as he was about whether the design we imagine exists in nature.[23] Smith elevated theory over the observation of particulars not by reference to providential design and not because particular observations are sometimes impossible, but because theory can soothe the psychological distress generated by too many particulars. This offers a psychological account of the priority of theory—the need for coherence is part of human nature—that renders the work of the conjectural historians normative, not a response to a regrettable, and exceptional, historical dilemma.

When Dugald Stewart began to revise moral philosophy in the early 1790s, he introduced two significant alterations. First, he retained—indeed, elaborated—Smith's commitment to theory over facts *by restoring* the providentialism that Smith had bracketed; and second, he shifted the emphasis away from history and toward a kind of visionary politics.[24] Both of these revisions articulated Stewart's conviction that God's plan was not only pervasive but benevolent; this optimism, in turn, constituted a significant revision of the eighteenth-century historians' stoical providentialism. To understand these revisions, we need to remember that Stewart developed his interpretation of moral philosophy in the very early years of the great political experiment in France.[25] Some of his optimism and much of his disdain for particulars came from Stewart's enthusiasm for the theoretical writing of Condorcet and from his desire to answer the kind of conservative objections to such theory that were formulated by Edmund Burke. Stewart's answers to such conservatism were to caution that dwelling too long on past failures would only discourage the political theorist and to claim that the philosopher's *duty* was to "forward . . . the gracious purposes of [God's] government" by offering optimistic projections about the future.

By way of demonstrating Stewart's characteristic moves, let me cite two passages from his work. The first comes from his *Dissertation: Exhibiting the Progress of . . . Philosophy*, which was published in 1820 in the *Encyclopedia Britannica*. In it, Stewart explains that the conviction that the providential order must, by design, be benevolent requires the philosopher to devote his efforts to realizing this benevolent design in the political world. By such efforts, Stewart insisted, the philosopher could actively contribute to the progress he also described.

A firm conviction . . . that the general laws of the moral, as well as of the material world, are wisely and beneficently ordered for the welfare of our species, inspires the pleasing and animating persuasion, that by studying these laws, and accommodating to them our political institutions, we may not only be led to conclusions which no reach of human sagacity could have attained, unassisted by the steady guidance of this polar light, but may reasonably enjoy the satisfaction of considering ourselves, (according to the sublime expression of the philosophical emperor) as *fellow-workers with God* in forwarding the gracious purposes of his government.[26]

My second passage comes from Stewart's *Elements of the Philosophy of the Human Mind*, which was published in 1792. After paying obligatory homage to "the examination of particular objects and particular facts," Stewart cautions that too much attention to particular details can actually be deleterious to judicious conclusions: "It is by no means necessary to pay the same scrupulous attention to minute circumstances, which is essential in the mechanical arts, or in the management of private business. There is even a danger of dwelling too much on details, and of rendering the mind incapable of those abstract and comprehensive views of human affairs, which can alone furnish the statesman with fixed and certain maxims for the regulation of his conduct."[27]

These two statements, published almost three decades apart, express the same epistemological, ethical, and methodological commitments: Stewart maintained throughout his life that the only form of experimentalism relevant to moral philosophy was introspection, because when combined with belief in providential design, it alone could reveal the universal principles of human nature;[28] that "particular accidents" were inessential, in an Aristotelian sense; and that the moral philosopher was a kind of statesman whose duty was to advance "improvement." From these commitments came a theory of legislation that would have freed "society" from all unnatural restraints. Because "the social order is . . . the result of the wisdom of nature, not of human contrivance," Stewart insisted, "the proper business of the politician, is . . . to remove every obstacle which the prejudices and vices of men have opposed to the establishment of that order which society has a tendency to assume."[29] These commitments—especially Stewart's providentialism—also underwrote his repudiation of history. "In the course of these latter ages," he explained, "a variety of events have happened in the history of the world, which render the condition of the human race essentially different from what it ever was among the nations of antiquity; and which, of consequence, render all our reasonings concerning their future fortunes, in so far as they are founded merely on their past experience, unphilosophical and inconclusive." In 1792, when he wrote this statement, Stewart had in mind only one "event," the invention of printing. Printing, he maintained, was the "single event, independently of every other," that has been "sufficient to change the whole course of human affairs."[30] By 1820, Stewart had added to printing a second agent of progress: commerce. Taken together, he proclaimed in his *Dissertation*, printing and commerce combine "all the varieties of intellect, natural and acquired . . . into one vast engine, operating with a force daily accumulating, on the moral and political destiny of mankind."[31] Whereas for Adam Smith, the psychological need for coherence was the machine or engine whose workings were visible in human speculation, for Stewart, the engine has become society; with this shift of emphasis, agency has passed from the language and mind of the theorist to the object whose operations he describes.[32]

Although it was to have profound consequences for nineteenth-century developments in political economy, Stewart's elevation of commerce to the status of divine agent was an incidental outcome of his debt to the French *economistes*. For Stewart, political economy was a capacious science, which encompassed jurisprudence, excluded politics per se, and included—but was by no means limited to—the study of wealth.[33] In 1792, in fact, Stewart's comments about commerce were cast as a kind of thought experiment, not as a policy recommendation. That Stewart's speculations were neither policy recommendations nor whole-hearted endorsements of the details of the French economic program is clear in his depiction of the *economistes'* plan as an ideal, not a realizable goal. "To delineate that state of political society to which governments may be expected to approach nearer and nearer as the triumphs of philosophy['s] extend[t?], was, I apprehend, the leading object of the earliest and most enlightened patrons of the economic system," Stewart declared. "It is a state of society, which they by no means intended to recommend to particular communities, as the most eligible they could adopt at present; but as an ideal order of things, to which they have a tendency of themselves to approach, and to which it ought to be the aim of the legislator to facilitate their progress."[34]

If Dugald Stewart took over the *economistes'* emphasis on commerce in order to enlarge the domain of political economy, then in 1825, J. R. McCulloch constructed a taxonomy of disciplines having to do with government and wealth that completely transformed the definition and role of political economy. McCulloch's taxonomy, which assigned the lowly task of data collection to statisticians and the higher office of theorizing to politicians and political economists, constituted one solution to the problematic conjuncture of observed particulars and theory that characterized the moral philosophical project.

Paradoxically, however, and in a move that will require close attention, McCulloch also enhanced the claims of political economy by demoting the kind of political theory essential to the French writers. In his discussion of the new taxonomy of disciplines, McCulloch simultaneously paid lip service to the superiority of political theorists and assigned political economists a more important intellectual role. "The sciences of Politics and of Political Economy are, therefore, sufficiently distinct," McCulloch explained.

> The politician examines the principles on which government is founded; he endeavours to determine in whose hands the supreme authority may be most advantageously placed; and unfolds the reciprocal duties and obligations of the governing and governed portions of society. The political economist does not take so high a flight. It is not of the constitution of the government, but of its ACTS only, that he is called upon to judge. Whatever measures affect the production or distribution of wealth, necessarily come within the scope of his observation, and are freely canvassed by him. He examines whether they are in union with the just principles of economical science. If they *are*, he pronounces them to be advantageous, and shows the nature and extent of the benefits of which they will be productive; if they *are not*, he shows in what respect they are defective, and to what extent their operation will be injurious. But he does this without inquiring into the constitution of the government by which these measures have been adopted.[35]

By repudiating inquiries "into the constitution of the government," McCulloch decisively severed whatever link remained between political theory and political economy. In separating those "measures that affect the production or distribution of wealth" from "the constitution of the government by which these measures have been adopted," McCulloch simultaneously reinforced the semi-autonomous domain that would eventually be called "the economy" and transformed Stewart's didactic providentialism back into what the conjectural historians had claimed to provide: a scientific "experimental" approach that could generate a reliable account of events that had actually occurred.

In McCulloch's various descriptions of political economy, the law-abiding domain of "commerce" was depicted not only as ideally immune from government interference; it was also depicted as real—neither a projection of the theorist's desire for order nor simply an expression of optimistic providentialism. Although McCulloch voiced the optimism intrinsic to Stewart's didacticism, he did so in such a way as to negate the conjectural historians' anxieties about the effects of commerce on the virtue of modern society. The result, which *was* political economy for most readers in the early nineteenth century, was a science that claimed to arrive at principles from experience while actually reaching them through deduction—that is, by reasoning from an a priori confidence in commercial freedom that derived from what had once been a posteriori providential assumptions about the tendency of human nature to improve.

I can only point here to three of the salient features of McCulloch's revision of Stewart and the conjectural historians: his elevation of commerce to a position of unrivalled importance, the effects of his secularization of the argument from design, and his complex reconsideration of the relationship between particulars and theory. The first two of these revisionary moves appear in McCulloch's brief survey of Torrens's idea that there is a "territorial division of labor" in the world.

> Providence, by giving different soils, climates, and natural productions, to different countries, has evidently provided for their mutual intercourse and civilization. If all restrictions on commerce were abolished, each people would naturally devote themselves to such employments as are most beneficial to each: And this pursuit of individual advantage is admirably connected to the whole. By exciting industry, by rewarding ingenuity, and by using most efficaciously the peculiar powers bestowed by nature on different countries, commerce distributes labour as best suits the genius and capacities of each. It gives us new tastes and new appetites, and it also gives us the means and the desire of gratifying them.[36]

In this passage, agency originally resides, as it did in Stewart's work, with "Providence" ("Providence . . . has evidently provided"). Almost immediately, however, and by means of a shift from a geographical description to a prescription for policy ("if all restrictions . . . were abolished"), McCulloch shifts the agency to "commerce" ("commerce distributes labour"). With this shift, "commerce" becomes not only an agent that distributes the bounty of Providence but also an independent creative force, which "gives us new tastes" and thus directs humans to carry out what now seems only distantly a providential plan ("by using most efficaciously the peculiar powers bestowed by nature on different countries, commerce distributes labour"). By the end of this passage, commerce has become the moral agent—indeed, the "engine"—that the social system as a whole was to Stewart (and that the possibly fictitious "invisible hand" was to Adam Smith); and what would have been conjecture for the eighteenth-century historians, projection for Stewart, and psychological necessity for Smith has become what looks very much like a straightforward description of historical particulars.

One effect of secularizing—or rather de-Christianizing—Stewart's political economy and of turning it into a science of wealth was to reinforce the tendency, *which we also see in early nineteenth-century advocates of police*, to look at aggregates rather than individuals or classes.[37] Unlike Stewart, who was interested in tracing the effects of providential design on both collective *and* individual prosperity (which could be calculated) *and* morals (which could not), McCulloch judged "progress" as primarily commercial and therefore as always amenable to calculation—but only in the aggregate. Thus, according to McCulloch, the political economist's role was "not to frame systems, and devise schemes, for increasing the wealth and enjoyments of *particular classes*; but to apply himself to discover the sources of *national wealth*, and *universal prosperity*, and the means by which they may be rendered most productive."[38] Emphasizing calculations about "the public" rather than moral assessments of individuals demoted ethical issues and carried over the universalism that Stewart and the eighteenth-century historians had associated primarily with human nature to an abstraction called "society" or the "nation." The quantifiable prosperity of the latter, according to this logic, was "universal" not because it could be calculated through addition or ratios (like the "greatest happiness of the greatest number"), but because the prosperity of the nation realized for the aggregate the desire universal to human nature *but not simultaneously realizable for every individual*: the "wish to augment our fortunes and to rise in the world."[39]

McCulloch's relative indifference to individual happiness was also expressed in his tendency to conceptualize individuals as interchangeable parts of the great machine of commerce. According to McCulloch, these parts could be interchanged both because they were simply repositories of abstract labor and because, as an abstraction, labor (like "prosperity") could be quantified. "Every individual who has arrived at maturity," McCulloch declared, ". . . may, with perfect propriety, be viewed as a machine which it has cost twenty years of assiduous attention, and the expenditure of a considerable capital to construct."[40] This tendency to reduce human beings to embodiments of abstract labor, then parts of a commercial machine, which could be subdivided *and quantified*, made McCulloch's science of wealth seem to hostile readers like an adjunct of or supplement to statistics, instead of being a different, albeit compatible science. When critics like Charles Dickens and Robert Southey conflated political economy with statistics, they could criticize what Carlyle called "the dismal science" *either* for reducing knowledge to quantification *or* for encompassing all of the ills associated with the "manufacturing system."[41] Indeed, one reason that McCulloch's version of political economy was so vulnerable to so many kinds of criticism was that he was carried, by a combination of his desire to present the "science of values" *as* a science of wealth and his desire to negotiate his culture's pervasive ambivalence toward theory, to an undecidable position on the very issue that his epistemological taxonomy had been devised to address: the relationship between observed particulars and general theories. This is true *even though* McCulloch presented his theoretical positions as descriptions of actual—that is, particular—historical "facts."[42]

McCulloch's claim that observed particulars were necessary *but not sufficient* for adequate theory is clearest in his *Principles of Political Economy*, which was published in 1825. Immediately after he declares that the focus of the political economist should be "the public," not "particular classes" or individuals, McCulloch denounces another form of particularism—the marshalling of particular observations against the judgments of the political economist. In defense of his position—that no concatenation of particular facts can afford an adequate "means of judging of the truth or falsehood of a general principle"—McCulloch summons an authority from the world of the medical sciences, the renowned Dr. William Cullen:

> "There is," to use the words of the celebrated Dr. Cullen, "a variety of circumstances tending to vitiate the statements dignified with the name of experience. The simplest narrative of a case almost always involves some theories. It has been supposed that a statement is more likely to consist of unsophisticated facts, when reported by a person of no education; but it will be found an invariable rule, that the lower you descend in the medical profession, the more hypothetical are the prevailing notions. Again, how seldom is it possible for any case, however minutely related, to include all the circumstances with which the event was connected. Hence, in what is commonly called experience, we have only a rule transferred from a case imperfectly known, to one of which we are equally ignorant. Hence, that most fertile source of error, the applying of deductions drawn from the result of one case to another case, the circumstances of which are not precisely similar. *Without principles deduced from analytical reasoning, experience is an useless and a blind guide.*"[43]

This suggestion that the relationship between particularized experience and theory *constitutes a problem* suggests why what McCulloch presented as the self-evident truths of political economy did not seem self-evident to all of his contemporaries. The context for understanding McCulloch's formulation is simultaneously historical and epistemological. Indeed, historical developments early in the century reinforced an epistemological bias already evident in many British writers of the mid- to late-eighteenth century. In the first two decades of the nineteenth century, British revulsion from the revolutionary events in France seriously compromised the kind of optimistic providentialism voiced by Stewart in 1792 *by interrogating the theoretical method* from which it derived.[44] The political danger with which theory became associated in the wake of the Revolution dovetailed with the "common prejudice" against conjecture, hypothesis, and theory more generally that British proponents of experimental moral philosophy claimed to have learned from Newton.[45] The hostility toward theory, which had become widespread by the first decades of the nineteenth century, meant that political economy might seem suspect precisely because it was theoretical. By the same token, opponents of political economy could derive considerable cultural clout from appeals to experience and the observation of particulars, whether those observations were made by the kind of first-hand experience preferred by Dickens or second-hand, from the evidence published in government-sponsored Blue Books.[46]

Despite this general cultural suspicion of theoretical speculation, however, appeals to theory could still be powerful rhetorical weapons for champions of new sciences, especially when the science in the making had less than a self-evident relationship to the kind of experimentalism that had become been conventionalized in the natural sciences. Even though a variant of the debate about "induction" also occupied natural scientists, appeals to the importance of theory functioned to legitimate scientific expertise by distinguishing between mere observation, which anyone could provide, and explanation, which required a form of theoretical knowledge irreducible to the observation of particulars.[47] McCulloch sought to negotiate these complex cultural currents—to make his way between the suspicion cast on theory and the imperative to delineate professional expertise—when he constructed his taxonomy of knowledge in 1825. By distinguishing between statistics, which consisted of data collection, and political economy, which epitomized theory, McCulloch proposed a way to retain both methodological imperatives *and*, by subordinating the former to the latter, he argued forcefully for the professional superiority of the political economist.

Because McCulloch simply asserted that the relationship between the particular facts that the statistician "furnished" and the theories the political economist produced was self-evident, and because he did not yoke the two together with the kind of providentialism that underwrote the methods of Stewart and the eighteenth-century historians, the teleological nature of his argument did nothing but enrage contemporaries who did not share his a priori faith in the beneficial tendencies of commerce. In presenting his argument as if it were a description, while denigrating whatever particular observations contradicted his foundational assumptions, he antagonized his contemporaries by impugning both their method and their loyalty to a nation whose virtue he equated with its prosperity. McCulloch presented his secular and theoretical position as if it were simultaneously a theological argument from design and an unbiased description of past and distant events. By the 1820s, this compound, which had seemed unproblematic to the eighteenth-century Scots, could no longer be defended. At least partly, this was because the combination of a more secular interpretation of society, the example of a national survey actually based on first-hand observations, and a larger, and more diverse, reading public made claims about knowledge as controversial as claims about politics had always been.[48]

McCulloch's description of the relationship between observed particulars and theory as problematic more nearly accords with the late twentieth-century view of these things than does the complacency of eighteenth-century experimental philosophy, which now seems, at best, curious and, at worst, hopelessly politically incorrect. My account of these historical and epistemological developments is not intended to contribute to a Whiggish narrative of progressive enlightenment, but rather to interrogate the conditions in which modern disciplines have emerged *alongside* the problematics that distinguish them. Recognizing that a forerunner of one of the most influential modern social sciences descended from a version of the philosophy of mind *that was conceptualized in theological terms* should, at the very least, alert us to the historical roots of the grandiosity that modern critics of economics so thoroughly resent.

Describing

Imagination and Knowing

Problems of Description in Art

Realism

The conference statement, "Regimes of Description," raised the following question: "What might we learn from those eighteenth-century thinkers and researchers, who forged . . . the principles of description upon which most—if not all—of the specialized disciplines of modern inquiry were erected?" (See Appendix.) If we turn to the history of realism with this question in mind, we discover first that artists, too, are among the intellectuals referred to as thinkers and researchers. Artistic modes of perception and knowledge did not evolve independently of the general context of realism; in fact, they took an active part in shaping this period and its forms of knowledge. Second, we can ask if Jean-François Lyotard's assertion that the logic of the bit—with its privileging of the fragment and its tendency to dispense with reasoning, argument, and mediation—really marks the inauguration of a new age of knowledge. The history of realism suggests that the logic of the bit is the radical expansion of a viewpoint that the Enlightenment (i.e., the modern) paradigm already contained, but one situated in a conceptual network different from ours. If this conjecture is correct, one could learn from eighteenth-century thinkers and researchers not to sever the relationship between fragment and argument, fact and generalization, observation and relation, description and knowledge, but to treat these relationships as governed by what Lyotard termed the *différend*. Should mankind attempt to extend the age of description while, as Lyotard suggests, no longer knowing "what it is" we are describing? Or can we deal with it in another way? The following comments assume that so long as description remains fundamental to knowledge, it is premature to declare an end to modernity.

I.

"The best and most reliable way of philosophizing," wrote the young Isaac Newton to an acquaintance in 1672, "seems to be that we first carefully investigate the characteristics of things, confirm through experiments and then gradually advance toward hypotheses in order to explain them."[1] To the present-day reader, Newton's reflection is not particularly remarkable, although it was almost unheard of at the time and aroused vehement protest. Newton's pronouncement reversed the deductive foundation of knowledge that had seemed assured in human efforts to understand nature and society. The results were remarkable. Sixty years later, Voltaire wrote that before Sir Francis Bacon man was capable of much, but knew nothing of the circulation of the blood, the weight of air, or the number of planets, and that "any man who defended a thesis based on the categories of Aristotle, on the universal (*a parte rei*) or other such foolishness was considered a prodigy." For Voltaire, such "astonishing contrivances" were not the greatest achievements of the human mind. Rather, he appreciated the person who examines gradually what we would like to know instead of defining all at once what we do not know.[2] The modern concept of description came into being amidst these debates. Increasingly, it seemed that general knowledge could be gained only from exactly described detail rather than from general intuitions about the qualities of God and his presence in every aspect of nature. Description became the first step toward knowledge.

Significant variations eventually emerged as later generations tested empiricism's newly determined distinctions between particular and general, fact and concept, phenomenon perceptible to the senses and essence, or detail and whole. G. W. F. Hegel believed that "totality" could only be gained if "the external material for itself, in its particularity and external appearance" was pervaded by the "significations of the intellect."[3] Auguste Comte, on the other hand, sought to establish "the preponderance of observation over imagination" and to derive comparative generalizations from observation and experiment.[4] In empiricist circles, inductively processed descriptions protected one from excessive speculation. In German Idealist circles, the accent lay on a transcendence that exceeds facticity. A general respect for phenomenality attended both approaches, despite the different valuations ascribed to it. Whether treated nominalistically or essentially, exactitude of observation and description were mandatory. Description was indispensable and yet did not get at the essence of reality. In short, descriptions required supplement.

In practice, the ideal of object-related exactitude in description has been reshaped by the anthropological, historical, or socially determined forms of subjectivity. Some lament this as an unavoidable loss of truth, while others welcome it as a gain in human sovereignty. An awareness of reduction, fuzziness, and breaks in the transitions from particulars to generals defined the epistemological problems inherited by the modern age. Recently, however, a new dimension has emerged: the subject-determined a priori seems to have been pushed into the background by a new technological, media-related a priori. If so, descriptions of objects no longer depend on man, but are produced and encoded by a second-order objectivity: only machinery can produce digitally encoded knowledge. The perception "that forms of knowledge in every sector of contemporary culture are being fundamentally reshaped by the digital revolution" is irrefutable (see Appendix).

How these new forms will affect traditional notions of description that link truth and subjectivity in the pursuit of general knowledge is open to question.[5] What are the implications for description if language is not a neutral medium? What will remain of Newtonian experimental philosophy if exact analyses of scientific procedures lead to the conclusion that all experiments "begin and end in a matrix of beliefs"?[6] To what extent can we retain the Enlightenment's positive view of general knowledge in light of the scientific and social totalitarianism that some find lurking in its depths?[7] Such questions make it clear that description, as a basic concept of knowledge, is in crisis.[8]

"Realism" became the term for applying the Newtonian mode of cognition to the sphere of art.[9] Parallel to the development of an empiricist concept of description, the concept of realism was given its modern form. In scholastic disputes about *universalia*, representatives of the general (*realistae*) provided a link to universals. The term disappeared completely when the concept of reality was secularized. It re-emerged, wholly inverted, at the end of the eighteenth century as the opposite pole of Idealism, now linked to the particular and to phenomena. Empiricism's new concept of reality enabled this wondrous peregrination. The core of the concept of realism centers on the modern (Enlightenment) conception of the relation between empirical facts and general knowledge in the work of art.

Later definitions of artistic "realism," very much more circumscribed, have occluded its early use in the works of Immanuel Kant, Friedrich Schiller, and Johann Wolfgang von Goethe, where the term designated those aspects of authors, representation, and functions of the arts referring to phenomenality. The different accents that Hegel and Comte placed on the definition of "description" also led to further variants in the concept of realism: in the French-English sphere of positivism, "realism" was considered from the 1850s to be the reductive attempt, unworthy of art, "to represent nature as it is, without seeking to idealize it."[10] In Germany and Russia, on the other hand, the synthesizing efforts of Hegel to bring empirical reality into the realm of art continued to exercise influence—Karl Marx, Vladimir Ilyich Lenin, and Georg Lukács are examples.

I will pursue my discussion of the concept of "realism" with an historical example from its heyday. Then I shall return to the eighteenth century and its aftermath, before concluding with the question of whether the bell has tolled for realism in a "digital age" where "description" has become problematic. Does the current crisis in description require the radical solution of dissolving the relation between the general and the particular, or might this relation simply be redefined?

II.

"Descriptions. There are always too many of them in novels."[11] Gustave Flaubert's remark, uttered late in life, appears to disparage description and to confirm anti-realist sentiments he expressed previously. Flaubert's statement appears to support Eugene Donato's claim about the place in literary history of Flaubert's last novel, *Bouvard et Pécuchet*: "the emblematic literary landmark of fiction's necessary incapacity to raise the description of reality to intelligibility."[12] Because of his obsessive work with detail in language, Flaubert was long a favored example of the claim that description and realism were on the wane because writers wanted to concentrate on "the infinite auto-referentiality of language" instead of describing the world out there.[13] More than thirty years ago, Michel Foucault had gone beyond questions of style to justify a similar claim on the basis of the structure of Flaubert's novels. Above all in *La Tentation de Saint-Antoine* and *Bouvard et Pécuchet*, Foucault perceived "a literature that exists only in the web of the already written and as a result of this web."[14] Donato did not entirely ascribe to Foucault's position, for he argued that not all the insurmountable obstacles the two anti-heroes encountered can be explained by "the incapacity of linguistic and symbolic representation to account for reality."[15] Yet Donato did not reconnect language to reality—on the contrary, he justified an ever more assiduous concealment of the external world. Donato based his assertion principally on the development taking place in thermodynamics at the time that *Bouvard et Pécuchet* was written. He argued that an epistemological break had occurred, and went on to say that ever since, nature and history have been "given to us only in the form of senseless fragments without a memory, and any attempt of ours to reconstruct a history is nothing but vain fabulation . . . . In this sense, beyond language, Flaubert is an epistemological nihilist."[16] It is, therefore, only logical that Donato finds the idea that Flaubert was a realist to be a "naturalist myth."[17] Clearly, Flaubert did not engage in descriptions for their own sake. This, however, is not enough to count him as believing that constructions of sense and the objectivity of history were obsolete. Rather, it seems to me that a particular relation of construction to description—problematic to be sure, but nevertheless there—constitutes realism.

To elaborate this relation, I take Flaubert's words quite seriously: "Descriptions. There are always too many of them in novels." This is to be found in the *Dictionnaire des idées reçues*. We know that Flaubert did not record there what he himself thought, but rather opinions of the time that appeared to him to be particularly obtuse. He must have thought it idiotic to claim that novels always contained too many descriptions. Was Flaubert therefore a fan of description? Yes, but in a specific sense.

Letters written when Flaubert was working on *Bouvard et Pécuchet* elucidate his views. "I need a cliff," he wrote in October 1877 to his young protégé Guy de Maupassant, who had grown up in Etretat. "Give me a description of the whole coast from Barneval to Etretat."[18] This must have been done very thoroughly and by return post, for only six days later, Flaubert thanked him: "Your information is perfect. I comprehend the whole coast as if I could see it." But—and now for the words of real interest—"it is too complicated. I need something simpler." He had allotted three pages for the corresponding passages, two of which were to be devoted to dialogue and the psychology of the characters. Having explained this to his budding colleague, Flaubert continued: "This is my plan, and I cannot change it. It is necessary that Nature lend herself (the difficulty lies in not going against her, in not arousing sentiments of revolt in those who will have seen the place). . . . More details would get in the way. . . . I need to keep as much as possible to a Normandy cliff in general."[19] The next letter reinforces this idea: "The coast at Etretat is too specific."[20] Of the three other place names mentioned, only one appeared in the text of the novel, and the concluding sentence of the scene explicitly excludes the particularity Flaubert temporarily sought in his original request to Maupaussant: "They forgot Etretat."[21]

Description was important for Flaubert when he was involved in the writing process. Even in old age, he did not intend to carry out the project formulated in his much-quoted 1852 play on words: to write "a book on nothing, a book entirely unconnected with anything outside itself." He always remained the "old fellow . . . who likes to bring out the small fact as strongly as the larger one, who would like to make you feel almost materially the things he is reproducing."[22] Flaubert declares that "it is necessary to keep the horizon in view and at the same time, to look at what is at one's feet. Detail is atrocious, especially when one likes detail as much as I do."[23]

Detail was dear to Flaubert, yet his reference to the horizon is important. Flaubert assigned mainly functional value to description. Nature was not simply to be reproduced; it had to submit to a plan—his plan. Flaubert visited an agricultural show before he described it in *Madame Bovary* but when he arrived home, he was not delighted to have filled a notebook as one imagines Émile Zola would be later on. Instead, he was disgusted by the characters he had seen, even made "physically ill."[24] Flaubert's will to construct personae and worlds determined what he brought to the fore. But personae and worlds were already given, independent of the author. The general idea was to be culled from details lying within a specified horizon, not randomly selected. Here was a will to "intelligibility" and in this regard, Flaubert was a realist.[25] His struggle with an excess of information before the digital age returns us to the Age of Reason.

III.

Flaubert's positions assume qualities of Enlightenment in the historical sense, if viewed in conjunction with the article on "Description" in the *Encyclopédie*. This article covers several kinds of knowledge and disciplinary practice. It begins by elaborating on "Histoire naturelle" and, after a paragraph on geometry not here discussed, explains problems of descriptions in "Belles-Lettres." The views in these two sections are not identical. The *Encyclopédie*'s editors were less interested in differences of form and structure among kinds of knowledge than in a universalistic approach. From beginning to end, the article concerns a single question: how can a large "sequence of facts" yield "general knowledge"?[26] This is the question Flaubert posed when he was faced with the cliffs of Etretat.

The article on description says that unlimited description testifies only to "frivolous curiosity" and demands "the greatest efforts of imagination." Something different was needed to comprehend the "arrangement," the "laws," the "mechanics," the "relations" of what was being described. A call for constructive efforts in the face of an incoherent reality is unmistakable. The reverse is also true: without some empirical data, the "more real object" necessary to the "advancement of true knowledge in Natural History" would come to a standstill. Detail, as point of departure, is relativized by reference to the efforts of reason, but it is not obliterated by reason.

Questions about the relation of facts to general knowledge were among the most important of the time. For example, John Bender has pointed out that around the year 1750, the English novel abandoned its claim to be the embodiment of literal historical truth in favor of rendering higher truths perceptible through the transparent fictional construction of particular versions of the "real" world. Likewise, in the natural sciences of the time, fictionality played a role in the legitimization of reality.[27] Such problems had long vexed those who claimed that the acting, knowing modern subject could appropriate the world, whether in productions that surpassed "the direct relation to nature," or in thought that abandoned the certainties of divine revelation.[28] As early as the Renaissance, Leonardo da Vinci had taught his students that "there are innumerable real things, and our memories have not sufficient capacity for them."[29] General knowledge no longer could tame the facts. Attempts to master the resulting chaos included: theories of art, from Leon Battista Alberti to Abbé Charles Batteaux, about the choice among beauties; seventeenth-century regulations specifying the terms for verisimilitude; and René Descartes's insistence on the "logical capacity of the subject."[30] Increasingly, however, industrial capitalism, the natural sciences, and the exploration of the earth opened different ways of defining facts: "curiosity, laden with desire, about the infinite world of empirical objects," became the basic attitude.[31] "We are still only on the shores of an immense ocean: there are so many things yet to be discovered!" concluded Voltaire in his 1738 work on Newton's philosophy; his serenity was undisturbed by the knowledge that many "things will always be outside the sphere of our knowledge!"[32]

Voltaire was commenting on Newton's famous remark, "hypotheses non fingo." Voltaire's enthusiasm and self-confidence no more can be overlooked than his distance from naive universalism. Newton's thought cannot be summed up as a mere belief in facts, for the novelty of his conception was to emphasize how general knowledge emerged from observations through induction. Newton forced speculation in the natural sciences into the background. Likewise, the new empiricist epistemology of John Locke and David Hume gave priority to the inductive process.[33] As Ernst Cassirer observes, a "new methodic ordering" of thinking was introduced, no longer leading "from concepts and principles to phenomena, but rather from the latter to the former. Observation is the 'Datum,' the principle and the law, the 'Quaesitum.'"[34] In this new order, it became possible to link the human action of material production to inductive processes.

These changes were momentous for the history of realism at its inception. Soon facts were assigned new dignity in the novel, the least regimented genre and, for that reason, also the one with the lowest standing. Daniel Defoe recommended *Robinson Crusoe* (1719) to the hearts of his readers as "a just History of Fact" without "any Appearance of Fiction."[35] Alain-René Lesage's *Gil Blas* (1715/35) tried to "represent life as it is."[36] Johann Heinrich Merck gave dignity to the gift of "really sensual people" to see and to tell: "he does not rush quickly to the end . . . he embroiders."[37] And finally, Nicolas-Edme Restif de la Bretonne endeavored to depict the lives of the lower classes. It is not surprising, then, that realism emerged in tandem with the new epistemology. Seventeenth-century Dutch painting also attempted to describe the world in an unhierarchic manner and was not afraid of unresolved complexity. Svetlana Alpers has demonstrated the connection between the Keplerian belief that the retina of the eye reproduces true-to-life pictures of the world and the inclusive realism of Dutch painting.[38]

The seventeenth-century enthusiasm for facts runs through the eighteenth and nineteenth centuries, right up to the narrower concept of realism prevalent in our own time. Witness Wilhelm von Humboldt's illuminating report of his attempt to explain Kant's philosophy to the *idéologues* in Paris in 1798: "it is impossible really to understand each other, and there is a very simple reason for this. Not only have they no idea, but they do not have the least notion of anything beyond appearances."[39] "Unquestionably, they are better realists than idealists," was Schiller's comment to Goethe on this report.[40] The French penchant for realism continued throughout the nineteenth century. Positivism, underwritten by the natural sciences, was at work. The step from facts to general knowledge was thought to be relatively simple. Underlying Zola's zeal for description, for example, was a universalist worldview, according to which descriptive detail could symbolize larger unities. Champfleury's descriptive asceticism was actually the result of a considerable naiveté: he no longer described because the whole could be deduced from any detail.[41] Such views inform the polemic of Roland Barthes and many others against the referential nature of realism. This polemic would have driven Flaubert mad. For the "poor devil" Flaubert, the "sensuous content," the "outer *Dasein*," the "externality distinct from the mind" seemed highly significant.[42]

In emphasizing the strong epistemological influence of Positivism in nineteenth-century France and Positivism's origin in Enlightenment empiricism, I counter Foucault's influential thesis that the paradigm of representation shifted around 1800 in the wake of the Kantian critique of man's cognitive faculty.[43] For France and England, such an absolute paradigm shift cannot be claimed. My objection is not based on the simple truth that representation did not end with the epistemological rupture identified by Foucault in *The Order of Things*.[44] Rather, my point is that representation and reasoning were conceived as neither identical nor separate since Newton and others established the modern notion of reality. The two categories form a problematic yet indivisible matrix, a fact equally reflected in the efforts of the *Encyclopédie* to connect facts with general knowledge and Flaubert's interest in the cliff of Etretat.

The emerging "realistic" literature of the eighteenth century, especially its masterpieces, is characterized by an intuition or understanding of the problematic interdependence of representation and reasoning. This literature tried in various ways to come to terms with what Jakob Michael Reinhold Lenz called "paralyzing fear": on one hand, "the shaky craving to circumscribe the whole with your reason," and, on the other, "the incessant striving to unroll and separate out all our collected concepts again . . . to make them vivid and present."[45] This line of realism, which took the connection between facts and general knowledge to be a complex problem, proceeded from this fear and, at the same time, attempted to overcome the paralysis.

For Henry Fielding it was crucially important to keep "within the rules of probability" in his "search" through the "holes and corners of the world." His turning away from old romances led him to the view that anything "supernatural" was only to be used "with the utmost caution"—like "arsenic." Yet Fielding took a free hand with the Aristotelian distinction between poetry and history. Is poetry a self-evident truth because "the thing related is really matter of fact?" Fielding's answer was that the author should only represent what could credibly lie "within the compass of human agency."[46] Fielding transposes the Enlightenment quest for general knowledge into a quest for generally used knowledge.

Laurence Sterne took a less stringent view. He took great enjoyment in exact observations of daily life. In *Tristram Shandy*, he describes with delight someone's removing a wig with his right hand while taking a striped Indian handkerchief out of his right jacket pocket with his left. Sterne personified the poles of the *Encyclopédie*'s approach to knowledge in his novel. Tristram's uncle "took everything as it happened," while his father busied himself with "reasoning upon everything which happened, and accounting to it too."[47] Sterne did not seek to connect the poles, and his characters operated on a different principle. Sterne's novel is written as a train of association in Tristram's thought, and so chance sweeps general knowledge aside again and again, making it ridiculous. As David Wellbery writes, Sterne's novel achieves "a valid principle of narrative form from the domain of the contingent."[48]

In turning now to France, and passing over the English gothic novel, which gave facts a new place by substituting the old "miraculous" for general knowledge, we do not find a new perspective on our problem. Denis Diderot referred to the opposition between general knowledge and facts when he praised Samuel Richardson for showing "both the general course of things" and "all the variety of circumstances of life." But in defending Richardson's longueurs, he merely turned the Aristotelian classifications around and, in this manner, proclaimed an easy solution to the problem without explicitly having thought it through.[49] It was remarkable to assert that, in contrast to the "abstract and general rule" of French literary maxims, "the details of Richardson" were characterized as "the art of the great poet."[50] Diderot seems not to have considered the implications of his own "Éloge de Richardson," for characteristics of the French novel such as "order and wisdom," though highly esteemed at the time, escaped his notice.[51] The *Petit Larousse*'s simple concept of realism mentioned earlier was in this way predetermined.

In one extreme case, the paralyzing fear of which Jakob Lenz had spoken led, in France at least, to individual failure and to the social interdiction of speech. The Marquis de Sade, who "felt that strong urge to paint everything," and yet censured Rétif for "a long-windedness . . . for which only the pepper-merchants would thank him," himself wrote manically.[52] In *Les 120 journées de Sodome* (1785), for example, Sade's ambition was to write a comprehensive fictional description of his object; in the end, though of great length, the novel was able barely to register all the facts in brief. Formulating general knowledge as the sum of detail turned out to be both impracticable and rejected by a society that sought to condemn Sade's texts to non-existence. Imprisoned in the Bastille, he could not know that while he failed in his universal claim, hundreds of kilometers eastward, the work of thinking about the relation between facts and general knowledge had reached a new stage. This new thinking would become so influential—first in Germany and subsequently in Russia—that Foucault's thesis of a rupture with the age of representation works much better for these two nations than for France and England.

In Königsberg, as Kant reflected on Hume's empiricism, it appeared to him crude and even restrictive to liberty to accept all phenomena "as things in themselves."[53] Kant elaborated the notion of "transcendental idealism,"[54] which meant—in practical endeavors—deriving the "legitimacy of rule" from the "achievements of the subject itself,"[55] and in theoretical considerations of knowledge based on the rational processing of experience—thinking by pure reason about objects "not given in experience at all."[56] Rather than following Hume and outlawing the question about relations of cause and effect, Kant asserted that it can

> be thought very well . . . that I do not prove the concept of cause alone in accordance with its objective reality in consideration of the objects of experience, but rather could also deduct it as an a priori concept because of the necessity of the synthesis that it brings with it, i.e. demonstrate its possibility through pure reason, without empirical sources.[57]

Kant also acknowledged the significance of "exterior objects of the senses" as the basis of knowledge, including the formulation that one could well be an "empirical realist."[58] His new use of the term "realism" to designate the empirical bases of knowledge reworked and updated the Enlightenment's bipolar schema: he restored the transcendental as "idealism," but insisted on the a prioris of reason, which divorced the transcendental from direct knowledge of the divine. Kant's structure of the particular and general was synthetic: neither side obliterated the other, for they were mutually interdependent. "Thought without content is empty, perceptions without concepts are blind."[59] This dialectical thought enabled realism to detach itself from facts and could be said to have spared Flaubert from a journey to gather material for his description of the French coast at Etretat.

Kant's ideas were first applied to art by those already cited here, as critics of French dependency upon facts. In 1794, Schiller, still entirely in the grip of a first personal encounter with Goethe, offered a Kantian solution to the *Encyclopédie*'s problem. "At first glance, it is true that it appears as if there could be no greater opposition than the speculative spirit which takes unity as its starting point, and the intuitive, which starts with diversity. If, however, the former seeks experience with chaste and faithful sense, and the latter seeks the law with the autonomously acting power of free thinking, then the two cannot fail to meet each other halfway."[60] This thought is found again and again in Schiller's correspondence, just as in his published work. It is important for this essay that a possibility existed for overcoming the horror "of the sheer size of the empirical world," of "the million-headed hydra of empiricism."[61] The artist could pass "from intuition to abstraction" and then, "in reverse, change concepts into intuitions and thoughts into feelings."[62] Ernst Cassirer described this sequence of steps as characteristic of enlightened thinking. Such thinking, for Schiller, required "genius"—"the highest that man can make of himself"—and consisted in "generalizing his intuition and making his sensibility the rule."[63] Hegel later formulated this as an aesthetic principle, and set the stage for those authors of the nineteenth and twentieth century whose realism could later be called "critical."

Schiller also emphasized that his great friend—surrounded from his youth by "figures lacking in substance"—had undertaken to correct "vile nature according to the better model that your formative spirit created for itself."[64] Those who believed this corrective was too important to be delimited by nature had no time for realism, regardless of its critical powers. They turned instead to the autonomy of art.[65] The opposition between realistic and romantic (Baudelaire called it modern) literature began around 1800. In a world becoming newly problematic, the realist concept of art as a complete representation of the world became problematic too.

The fresh ennobling of general knowledge intimated by Schiller had significant support from the past. Following the tradition of French classicism, the account of "Belles-Lettres" in the *Encyclopédie*'s article on description did not take the empirical line but an older one. Detail was relatively unimportant, and sensuous perception counted merely as the point of departure for the ideal in art with genius at its center.[66] Following upon the new-fashioned section on "Histoire naturelle," description in the arts was turned over to grammarians and orators, while definitions were entrusted to philosophers. By contrast, a writer "who describes from imagination, has all the economy of nature to hand, and can give it the charms that he wants," although he must not "reform it too much." Nonetheless, detail is still clearly subordinated to the subject.

As a creator of worlds, the author was elevated above reality. This was consonant with Enlightenment discourse. Lessing, writing shortly later, pleads for an art world "whose coincidences are linked together in a different order . . . to the world of a genius which . . . shifts, changes, reduces, increases the parts of the present-day world in order to make for itself its own whole, with which it connects its own intentions."[67] As Wolfgang Heise remarks: "The genius . . . creates a 'world,' forms a 'whole,' which has in common with the real world general laws which, however, reshape the real as material for his intentions."[68] Description here is entirely subordinated to the intention of the author.

The idea of the autonomy of art became increasingly important. Schiller argued in one of his last texts, "that art is only true through departing from the real entirely and becoming purely ideal."[69] Aesthetic criticism of reality from a practical perspective gradually lost its significance. Friedrich Schelling claimed that Romanticism was interested in the generation of worlds: "in regard to that which is absolute, the question of reality as it is constituted in the common consciousness is meaningless."[70] Baudelaire praised the imagination as opposed to the real: "Nature is ugly, and I prefer the monsters of my fantasy to the triviality of the real."[71] Realism may be linked to the "Histoire naturelle" section of the article on description, whereas the close of the part on "Belles-Lettres" invokes genius and consequences that go beyond the scope of realism.

It remains to be said that Flaubert, with his critical, even dogged reference to the triviality of the real, cannot be subsumed under the category of the autonomy of art. Yet it is also important to recognize at least two threads in the history of realism: first and foremost, those who took the outer world so seriously that they erected their constructions using its details; second, those who sometimes oriented their constructions to produce a general knowledge of the outer world. This knowledge, which could be as naive as Champfleury's, as universalistic as Zola's, or as astute as Flaubert's, is determined by a movement from the particular to the general, not the other way around.

The later unfolding of concepts of realism cannot be traced here, but at least one great moment requires mention. Georg Lukács's theory appeared to many readers to contain prescriptions for art that were for the most part rather narrow and that ignored the aesthetic of the avant-garde—propagating instead novels with a conventional world-view. Upon closer examination, however, Lukács as philosopher of society focused on the concerns we have observed in the *Encyclopédie*: how can a sequence of facts yield general knowledge? Against the "conception of the world as a chaos, a meaningless confusion of irrational and hostile powers," it was the task of art, according to Lukács, "to portray the inherently rational essence of the world" and to liberate it "from the confusing ornament of the merely empirical."[72] Thus for Lukács, realism was "not one special style among many others . . . but the artistic basis of every valid creation."[73] He faithfully followed Schiller in noting that such creation consists of two steps: "first, the laying bare in thought and the showing in an artistic design of this connection [to social reality]; second, though, and inseparable from it, the artistic covering of the connections gained through the effort of abstraction—the cancellation of the abstraction" in such a way that a "new immediacy conveyed by form" comes into being.[74] The "type" thus became the center and "criterion of the realistic conception of literature." "Particularity" formed the epistemological focus of great art's endeavor toward "a unique in-between region that organically unites the immediate appearance of life with the world of appearances becoming transparent, with the radiance of the essence."[75] Nineteenth-century critical realism was for Lukács the peak of such an art.

While it is true that Lukács's conception of realism was used for ideological education in *Realsozialismus*, such an assessment is unduly reductive. Lukács's enlightened insistence on the interconnected structure of social reality through art remains at odds with the resignation that Karl Jaspers felt before the growing fragmentation of reality: "if there is a question of the whole, we are powerless, Monsieur Lukács as much as all of us."[76] Even admitting that Lukács's claims to truth were ideologically tainted, that they were fettered by unabashed absolutism, and that certain adepts tried to use them to legitimate their own pretensions, his statements remain valid. "Petrified, fetishized things," is how Lukács formulated his humane intentions, "wreathed about by an essenceless atmosphere," until the "real knowledge of the driving forces" is won from them through "composition."[77] His texts were an attempt and a call to overcome a dread of the empirical (which had its nadir in German Fascism) by constructing it anew: practically, through the workers' movement; later, by an art called realistic. For Lukács, realism was defined in the broad sense of a relationship between general knowledge and facts.

Right up to the present day—at least where I come from—forms of art have existed that tried to do just this: to construct reality on the basis of descriptions in order to grasp it critically and to advance public discussion. A few years ago, Wolfgang Mattheuer, a Leipzig painter, formulated the hopes attached to this project: "A politician who wants to turn the realists into his helpers' helpers [is] soon revealed, and he will be surprised how much difficulty he is in for."[78] Those who occupy such positions often regard themselves as continuing the Age of Reason, and one might say they really are.

IV.

Is this Enlightenment tradition a thing of the past in a digital age characterized by questions about subjectivity, the linguistic turn, and the critique of representation? The digitalized media, in which thoughts increasingly are produced today, claim the power to make an unreasoning "freely and evenly floating procedure of attention" into a new age of thought that links fragments freely instead of according to their logical, ethical, or aesthetic value. As Lyotard said, "One describes it. One does not know what it is. One is sure only that it refers to some past."[79]

Such changes must have an effect on realism. Where the unconscious is determinative, the goal-oriented author has a hard time. If language is always constituted from previous speech, a view that bases art on a natural or social reality becomes untenable. If the production of meaning is the production of power, the construction of general knowledge can no longer claim to be liberating. If thought today is itself necessarily fragmented and interconnections disintegrate, realism then becomes old-fashioned.

The question that I want to pose with regard to these changes, but that I shall not answer, is about their degree of importance. Some see the changes as having ushered in a new age. Absolute sentences have been composed, heavy with pathos, severing the relations between reality and fictionality established after the Renaissance: "The time has now come for the due insight that the dematerialization of the world, its transformation in images, in conceptions, in signs has turned into an imaginary obsession without equal, which tendentiously annuls all differences between reality and fiction."[80] This annulment would lead to something very different from those interactive relations between the domains of the natural sciences and fiction described by John Bender for the time of the Enlightenment. With this annulment, the domains would flow into one another and it would make no sense to distinguish between facts and general knowledge. An order of simulation would then prevail, in which "signs, arbitrary and unlinked to anything, circulate in the world of artificial reality."[81] Jean Baudrillard wrote of the hyperreal, i.e. the "generation of a real without origin or reality."[82] Should we remember Schelling? Norbert Bolz has asserted that "sexual relations are today no more intimate than switching between the gadgets of the electronic world, and the word 'personal' does not mean any more than the personal computer."[83]

One is tempted to say, "Poor Bolz." I shall make only two remarks, in order to question whether a bit more intimacy could be accorded him. First, if we think of "the virtualization of space and time," we are not obliged to imagine the sheer dissolution of every space-time reality.[84] In the automobile industry, techniques of virtual reality have been developed to test future products, including all relevant information, before their actual manufacture.[85] This is the Age of Reason with new methods, not the Digital Age. And second, in Lyotard's *L'Inhumain*, we do not find just reflections on "immediately linked" scraps or units of information. Lyotard mentions elsewhere that Hubert L. Dreyfus has concluded that "human thought does not think in binary oppositions. It does not work with units of information ('bits'), but with intuitive and hypothetic constructs . . . . It can distinguish the important from the unimportant without going through all the data."[86] Perhaps one cannot speak of the beginning of a Digital Age after all, as long as such reflective forms of thought for dealing with vast bodies of information remain important. Perhaps humankind is giving up too much—namely itself—when it proclaims a Digital Age that makes it impossible for humanity to describe and understand the interactions among nature's different productions. As Baudrillard exclaimed after describing "the disintegration of the real world": "Of course I hope that it will not come to this."[87]

Imagining Flowers

Perceptual Mimesis (Particularly Delphinium)

I wrote in an earlier essay about the problem of vivacity—about the ghostly enfeeblement of images under the ordinary exercise of daydreaming and, in contrast, the mysterious (or difficult to account for) vividness of mental images when we are under the instruction of the verbal arts—and I ended with lines by John Ashbery:

> Something
> Ought to be written about how this affects
> You when you write poetry:
> The extreme austerity of an almost empty mind
> Colliding with the lush, Rousseau-like foliage of its desire to
> communicate

Ashbery returns often to this subject and when he does, the image that he again and again uses to express the image-making power of the mind under poetry's sway is—as in the lush foliage of the lines above—that of the flower: "Now, / About what to put in your poem-painting," he writes, "Flowers are always nice, particularly delphinium."[1]

In his prose poem "Whatever It Is, Wherever You Are," Ashbery speaks about the invention of writing, "the cross-hatching technique which allowed our ancestors to exchange certain genetic traits for others," and he continues:

> Probably they meant for us to enjoy the things they enjoyed, like late summer evenings, and hoped that we'd find others and thank them for providing us with the wherewithal to find and enjoy them. Singing the way they did, in the old time, we can sometimes see through the tissues and tracings the genetic process has laid down between us and them. The tendrils can suggest a hand, or a specific color—the yellow of the tulip, for instance—will flash for a moment in such

a way that after it has been withdrawn we can be sure that there was no imagining, no auto-suggestion here, but at the same time it becomes as useless as all subtracted memories. It has brought certainty without heat or light. Yet still in the old time, in the faraway summer evenings, they must have had a word for this, or known that we would someday need one, and wished to help.[2]

In its very vivacity, in the conviction it at once compels, the sudden yellow flash of the tulip seems to have come neither by "imagining" nor by "auto-suggestion" but by perception. Ashbery's turn to its yellow, or to the particularity of the delphinium blossom, or to the lush, leafy foliage of the mind's desire to communicate is striking, yet also widely shared. Both José Ortega y Gasset and Walter Benjamin have called attention to "the vegetative life" of Marcel Proust. And Seamus Heaney repeatedly pictures poetic consciousness entangled with sweet pea, cow parsley, and meadow grass. Verbal creation, he writes, is an archaeological dig, "a dig for finds that end up being plants."[3]

I have elsewhere argued that the imagination consists exclusively of its objects, that it is only knowable through its object, that it is remarkable among intentional states for not being easily separable into the double structure of state and object. Fear, for example, though certainly describable in terms of such objects as earthquakes and examinations, is also recognizable in terms of the intentional state, the felt experience, with its familiar bodily and psychological attributes. The same is true of other states such as joy and surprise, which are recognizable in terms of both their objects and the felt experience. In contrast, imagining is only its objects.[4] There exists almost no account of the felt experience of image-making. This does not mean that we lack accounts of the action of imagining; we have a number. But in almost every case, the action is wholly derived from whatever object happens to be put forth as its representative. If Pegasus is the example, then the discussion will be centrally about the capacity of the imagination to take what is given in the natural world—such as horses and wings—and rearrange them into a new combination. If the representative object is the face of an absent friend—like Jean-Paul Sartre's Annie and Pierre—then the discussion will be centrally about the presence of imagining in everyday acts of perception (as it is for someone like Mary Warnock). If the representative object is Yahweh—an object that explicitly prohibits any specification of attributes—then the discussion will be about the near impossibility of imagining without imagining something, a project made barely possible by the ability of "objectlessness" to itself be taken as an object. I want in this essay to contemplate the implicit account of the action of imagining that comes before us when the representative object is a flower; or perhaps more accurately I should say, I want to contemplate the implicit account of the action of imagining that comes before us in the yellow flash of the tulip or the particularity of the delphinium. For, unlike the images of Pegasus and Yahweh, the flower has the feature of forever shattering into scores of specified surfaces.

It is not irrelevant to this enterprise to notice that a blossom lends itself to being imagined, to being mentally captured in nearly the same degree of extraordinary vivacity it has in the perceptual world. If one takes the four representative objects a moment ago introduced—Pegasus, Yahweh, the faces of Annie and Pierre, and the flower—it is clear that the first two illustrate the counterfactual sweep of the imagination and the second two, what can usefully be called its counterfictional impulse.[5] Pegasus and Yahweh express the imagination's originary power, the power to bring new things into the world, though they do so to varying degrees: Pegasus conforms to Samuel Taylor Coleridge's fancy or secondary imagination, its capacity to reassemble in an unprecedented form elements that in isolation are part of the natural given; Yahweh conforms to Coleridge's primary imagination, expressing the capacity to create that which is in its entirety without precedent. The second two objects in contrast—the faces of absent friends, on the one hand, and the yellow tulip and blue delphinium on the other—both express the counterfictional, the aspiration of imagining to bring about a mimesis of perceiving. Rather than wishing to turn away from the world and create a new one, or to supplement the existing world with features it does not yet have, all the imagination's longing is instead directed toward being able to bring about things (or a certain set of things such as vivacity and givenness) sensorily present in perception. But the daydreamed face expresses the lapse of the imagination from the perceptual ideal it has taken as its standard, whereas the daydreamed blossom, as I will try to suggest, expresses the capacity of the imagination to perform its mimesis so successfully that one cannot be sure an act of perception has not actually taken place: "The yellow of the tulip . . . will flash for a moment in such a way that after it has been withdrawn we can be sure that there was no imagining, no auto-suggestion here."

Two questions are central. Why do flowers so often come to be taken as the representative object of imagining? It may be because, of all objects in the world, they are most beautiful.[6] Should anyone wish to press this explanation, I will be eager to assent and happy to forgo the speculative descriptions that follow. But it has been noticed—Immanuel Kant, for example, noticed it—that the world is covered with beauty. So the question is, why, among all these beautiful things, do flowers so often push themselves forward as our primary candidates.

The second question looks at the specific revelations about the counterfactual and counterfictional that the particular image might expose. The content of a given image calls attention to the structural attributes of the imagination. We might notice, for instance, that Pegasus expresses not only the mind's ability to reassemble already existing parts into new wholes but also its action of producing weightless images. One is tempted to say that due to the thinness or weightlessness of mental images, Pegasus could lift off the ground even if he did not have wings. (But perhaps he needs them to move forward: without wings, he could float; only with wings can he fly.) Visible also in Pegasus, therefore, is the imagination's aspiration to lift us above the material world, to disencumber us of given restraints. The flower, no doubt, makes visible the opposite movement of the imagination, its willful re-encumbering of itself, its anchoring of itself in the ground—its aspiration, in other words, to rival material reality in its vivacity. What else is at stake, or what is more literally at stake, is the second question to be addressed.

Presumably flowers come forward because they are imaginable: faces express the labor of perceptual mimesis; flowers seem to express its ease. Probably everyone has, at least once in this lifetime, heard someone echoing Marcel's lament in *Remembrance of Things Past* of not being able to picture a certain face with a vivacity commensurate with one's affection for the person. But has anyone ever encountered someone complaining that though she loves columbine above all other flowers, or meadow rue best in the world, she just cannot get an image of it clearly in mind? In fact, people seem to spend long languorous conversations describing to others the flower they that morning most love, as well as the precise shades of pinks among the astilbes, which among the many-flowers-promised-to-be-blue are actually blue or instead purple or lavender, which shape of the columbine they like best, all this on the telephone, or by letter, that is, all occurring without the actual material objects in view. (Jean-Jacques Rousseau, in his botanical letters, sometimes refused to give the name of the flower he was that day describing, insisting that he could plant so precise a picture in his correspondent's mind that she would at once recognize it when she later came upon it in the meadow or garden.)[7] Flowers lend themselves to long, highly charged, and highly judgmental aesthetic conversations. But why is this? What accounts for the picturability of columbine or for the ease of imagining meadow rue?

I. The Space of Imagined Blossoms

Flowers, unlike the faces of human beings, appear to be the perfect size for imagining. An imaginary object does occupy an identifiable location, and that location is in part determined by the size of its perceptual counterpart in the material world. For example, if the picture is occurring outside the boundary of the body, it is usually somewhere in the field that is encompassed by vision. If the object is the size of the flower it will probably appear immediately in the small bowl of space in front of one's eyes: this may be in part because in the perceptual world flowers are continually being lifted up off the ground into the space before our faces by vases, window boxes, and the paintings of vases and window boxes by Matisse, Manet, Renoir, van Gogh. But this phenomenon also occurs because flowers fit into that space in the way that a horse, with or without wings, clearly does not. If the horse were placed there, one would only see a small patch of him. In order to see a great deal of him, he would have to be placed, let's say, at least ten feet away. The only way he could be placed immediately in front of our eyes would be through radical miniaturization. The same is true if the picture has been placed inside the boundary of the body. When we think of images somewhere on the inside of the body, we habitually think of them as residing inside the head. In fact, however, it turns out to be remarkably easy to carry out one's imagining in other parts of the body: while, for example, one may picture Pegasus in one's forehead, one can imagine him instead in one's forearm, or instead in one's forefinger.[8] This is of course true even if one is picturing a changing image such as a man sitting by a window with apple-tree shadows playing across his face as he performs weight experiments with a leaf and books: all this can take place with almost equal ease in the interiors of forehead, forearm, forefinger. But as can be quickly apprehended, both Pegasus and the man in the chair change their size depending on the physical location in which one's imagining of them takes place. In the forefinger, for example, they become exceedingly small: Pegasus can barely fly, and the leaf in the man's experiments, and the shadows across his face are almost too small to see. In fact the whole point of that experiment with apple-tree shadows is lost since its purpose was to watch the gradual materialization of his face (its mobility and solidity) and, here in the forefinger, once can barely make out even the outline of his head. An image almost always contracts or expands to fill the physical space specified. It is useful to acknowledge this, because if we now leave aside forefinger and forearm and return exclusively to the habitual space of interior imagining—the forehead—it inescapably appears that, unlike men sitting in chairs or Pegasus or most other things (all of which suffer the radical miniaturization they underwent when placed in the exterior space close to the face), unlike all these other things, the yellow tulip of John Ashbery or Geoffrey Chaucer's daisy or William Wordsworth's celandine or William Blake's lily or Rainer Maria Rilke's opium poppy or most other blossoms fit precisely into this interior space without any alteration in the size they have in the external world.

When a poet describes a flower, even (I think) when a poet merely names a flower, it is always being offered up as something that after a brief stop in front of the face can immediately pass through the resisting bone and lodge itself and light up the inside of the brain. In Rilke's "The Bowl of Roses," a poem that will be returned to several times, he places the roses directly in front of us:

> before you stands the full bowl of roses,
> which is unforgettable and filled
> with that utmost of being and bending

As he continues to describe the intricacies of the blossoms themselves, they seem to have already passed into the interior of our imagining, that at once accommodates their size and contours:

> Soundless living, endless opening out,
> space being used without space being taken
> from that space adjacent things diminish,
> existence almost uncontoured, like ground left blank
> and pure within-ness, much so strangely soft
> and self-illuminating—out to the edge:
> is there anything we know like this?[9]

The most unexpected thing about the flower as the representative object of perceptual mimesis is that—as I will try to show at a much later point—it is precisely here that one begins to get the very thing I started this essay by saying we never get in accounts of the imagination, namely the felt experience of image-making. "Is there anything we know like this?" Surely Rilke means us to be able to say "yes" at this moment, to undergo an act of recognition—to understand where we have seen this before and where we are seeing it now, to understand what it is we see in "the ground left blank," "the pure within-ness," the "much so strangely soft and self-illuminating." It is as though the soft, self-illuminating petals are the tissue of the mental images themselves—not the thing pictured, but the surfaces on which the images will get made. The poet gives us the easily imaginable flower (the object that we can fairly successfully imagine even in daydreaming) and does so in order to carry onto that surface other, much less easily imaginable images. In the poem "When Lilacs Last in the Dooryard Bloom'd," Walt Whitman for fifteen stanzas moves us hypnotically back and forth from the night-lit lilacs (every heart-shaped leaf "a miracle") to the dropping star in the night sky (lilac, leaf, and star) and only in the sixteenth stanza does there suddenly appear the face of the person mourned, "O comrade lustrous with silver face in the night."[10] The night-lit blossom has acted as the template on which the image of the face gets made. It is the work table on which the less easily imagined becomes imaginable. The petal is, in effect, the substance, the "mental retina" on which the others are formed.[11] The same is true of the lines from Ashbery. The yellow flash of the tulip makes not only itself visible; it is the surface on which that entire summer evening passage is carried into the mind, for when we look again we see that it comes to us as though written on a flower or a leaf: "singing the way they did, in the old time, we can sometimes see through the tissues and tracing. . . . The tendrils can suggest a hand." Here, as everywhere in Blake, it is as though the vegetative tissues, tracings, and tendrils are the illuminated manuscript on which the picture of the writing gets carried.[12]

II. Sympathetic Shape, Faultless Curvature

The kind of claim I am making about a literal match between the size of the physical body and the size of its favored object may seem overly literalized. (In fact, I can already hear the wry formulations of this that will return to me.) But the claim is borne out by experiments in cognitive psychology that show that in image-making "people spontaneously tend to image smaller objects as if they were closer."[13] When people in one experiment were asked to imagine animals of ten different sizes, the larger ones were consistently placed farther away than the smaller ones, though it turned out that small animals could not be seen in detail by the experimental imaginers because small animals (unlike flowers) do not often come close enough that we can really learn their features. An imagined elephant is placed farther away from the imaginer's face than an imagined rabbit, just as in visual perception an actual elephant must be placed father away from us so that we can see its entire surface.[14]

In the realm of perception—as opposed to that of daydreaming and imagining-under-authorial-instruction—it would be unthinkable *not* to take centrally into account the fit between perceiver and perceived. For ex-

ample, most objects are too small or too large to be seen, and there is nothing surprising about the requirement that something be within the perceiv-
able scale in order to be apprehended, just as there is nothing surprising
about the very precise match between the size of certain sounds we hear
with great acuity, such as a baby's cry, and the size of the mechanisms of the
inner ear. In fact, in the realm of perception, claims about a match between
the physical contours of the body and of favored objects even extend to the
felt pleasures of perceiving. Joseph Addison, for example, speaks in his *Spectator* papers of the special love we have for "the concave and the convex" because those shapes are sympathetic with the shape of the eye itself: "Look
upon the outside of a dome, your eye half surrounds it; look up into the inside, and, at one glance, you have all the prospepect of it; the entire concavity falls into your eye at once." Addison elaborates this: "There are, indeed,
figures of bodies, where the eye may take in two-thirds of the surface; but,
as in such bodies, the sight must split upon several angles, it does not take
in one uniform idea, but several ideas of the same kind." He concludes:
"For this reason, the fancy is infinitely more struck with the view of the
open air and skies, that passes through an arch, than what comes through a
square, or any other figure."[15]

Addison's account of the sympathy between the physical curve of our
eyes and the "entire concavity [that therefore] falls into your eyes at once"
has not been chosen at random, since many blossoms have this very shape,
and, like size, shape surely contributes to the special imaginability of flowers, the phenomenon I am trying to understand at this moment. In one of
Virginia Woolf's short stories, the narrator cries out in exasperation over
"the rapidity of life, the perceptual waste and repair; all so casual, all so hap-
hazard" but then suddenly moves to a paradisal image: "But after life. The
slow pulling down of the thick green stalks so that the cup of the flower, as
it turns over, deluges one with purple and red light."[16] The shape pours in
on one's imagining mind as in one's perceiving, and the imagination, as
though absorbing the curvature of the eye into its own recesses, seems to
yearn for it and find it nowhere so often as in flowers. John Ruskin's small
book *Queen of the Air* (the work that ignited Marcel Proust's intense infat-
uation with Ruskin)[17] devotes one-third of its pages to the description of
individual blossoms, blossom by blossom, noting the concave shapes (the
"cups" and "vases," the "tubes" and "phials") of campanula, foxglove, the
asphodels and Draconidae; and writing of the great group of Drosidae:
"The delicacy of the substance of their petals" enables "them to take forms
of faultless elastic curvature, either in cups, as the crocus or expanding bells,
as the true lily, or heath-like bells, as the hyacinth."[18] Rousseau continually

describes the "vases," "parasols," "pavilions" of individual blossoms, as in his three-page inquiry into the five petals of the sweet pea blossom.[19] The concave blossom also reappears in D. H. Lawrence's account of the rape of Persephone, pursued by the underworld in the flowers that suddenly emerge on the surface of the ground and seize our attention as they seize Persephone herself: "purple anemones / Caverns / Little hells of color, / caves of darkness."[20] The ungraspable expanse of the underworld can suddenly (as Addison promised) be taken-in in a single glance in the shape of the anemone. So too, and more happily, the shape reappears in Rilke's poem "Opium Poppy," whose blossom is "willing, open, and concave." The shape of self-delight is audible in the last hyphenated word of the poem, "poppy-cup."[21]

In "On Vivacity" I wrote about how the attributes of the imagined object in daydreaming are discontinuous with the imagined object elicited by the verbal arts. The daydreamed object has the Sartrean features of two-dimensionality, inertia, and thinness. The image elicited by the verbal arts, in contrast, has some of the vivacity, solidity, persistence, and givenness of the perceptual world, attributes that can in part be accounted for by the instructional quality of writings, the explicit directions for how to construct the image that replace our own sense of volition with the sense of something there for the taking. The vivacity of objects imagined under authorial direction can also be attributed to a set of such specific phenomena as the mimesis of the material antecedents of images, the enlisting of the imagination's own expertise in generating certain odd attributes (such as gauziness), the sensory experiments carried out by fictional persons within the text, and the uneven distribution of these techniques (their capacious presence for persons the author directs us to imagine, their absence from the persons or places longed for by fictional persons within the text). To this list we can add the fact that in rare cases where an image, for whatever peculiar reasons, can in fact be vividly apprehended by the daydreaming mind, the verbal arts will of course enlist that image into a major part of their strategies; my work at the particular moment is simply to identify one such peculiar image, the easily daydreamed flower, and to specify what makes it exceptional, what makes it easy.

III. Locality Rule: Color and Compositional Surface

The imaginability of the flower can in part be attributed to its *size*, which lets it sit in the realm in front of our faces and migrate into the interior of what Aristotle called "our large moist brains." It can in part be attributed to the flower's cuplike *shape* breaking over the curve of our eyes, whether in actual acts of seeing or in mimetic seeing. A third feature is its intense *localization*. The experimental literature in cognitive psychology suggests that "there is only a limited amount of energy or 'processing capacity' with which to construct images," with the result that a smaller image will also be a more "filled-in image."[22] We can ourselves test the accuracy of this insight. If one closes one's eyes and pictures, for example, a landscape that encompasses the imaginative equivalent of our visual field, it is very hard to fill in its entirety with concentrated colors and surfaces. If, in contrast, one images the face of a flower—a much smaller portion of the visual field with its sudden dropping off at the edge of the petals where no image production is required—the concentration of color and surface comes within reach.

We might call this the ratio of extension to intensity. The flower brings the work of imagining into the compass of our compositional powers. If this observation seems odd or unfamiliar, it is certainly familiar in the analogous work of painters. During the last months of his life in 1883, as well as in periods of illness and weakness during the two years before that, Manet painted a series of oils, mostly of sprigs of lilac in a water glass or vase, sometimes of roses and other flowers. If Manet was weak (and it is said that he was very weak) his weakness shows itself not in any diminution of the intensity of the paintings but only in their scale. The paintings are extremely small. The canvas of *Lilacs in a Water Glass*, for example, is approximately 10 inches by 8 inches; *Roses in a Champagne Glass* is approximately 12 inches by 9 inches; *Lilacs and Roses* is 12 inches by 9 inches. Further, the actual area of imagistic localization is much smaller than the canvas, for the lilacs (in some pictures, lavender; in others, white with light green; in one, deep navy blue) are the size of actual lilac sprigs (four- or five-inch ellipses), and at their edges the backgrounds fall away into uniform lavender-gray or black. Their small size may be compared to the scale of paintings such as Manet's *Luncheon on the Grass* (83 inches by 106 inches), to *Olympia* (51 inches by 74 inches), to *The Execution of Emperor Maximilian* (99 inches by 120 inches), as well as to the painting considered his "final great achievement" and completed a year before his death during a brief period of strength, *Bar at the Folies-Bergère* (38 inches by 51 inches). In all of these, in contrast to the small pictures of lilacs and roses, it is not some localized object, but the entire surface that is filled in.[23] The last day of Pierre-Auguste Renoir's life, when he was very fatigued with pneumonia, he painted a small "study" of anemones that a maid in the household had brought in to him from the garden. Renoir's final words—"I think I'm beginning to understand something about it"—refer to those flowers.[24] (Some popular accounts incorrectly, but comprehensibly, claim that "flower" was the last sentence he spoke.) These examples underscore the obvious point that the labor of construction has a certain radius: in imagining, as in painting, the localization of intensely filled-in surfaces becomes possible with a smaller surface.

We can also find equivalents for what can be called the "locality rule" in the verbal arts. There is a moment in *Far from the Madding Crowd*, for example, when Thomas Hardy is instructing us in the construction of a certain scene where he notes that the temperature behind every piece of furniture in the room is slightly different. Local for Hardy means not neighborhood, not house, not even room, but each pocket of air hovering around each chair or table. Nothing about the work of this detail is accounted for by explanations that say vivid writing piles on more and more details: on the contrary, the accumulation of detail leads only to what Edward Tufte, in his analysis of visual information in maps, timetables, and architectural drawings, calls "visual noise" or "color junk." Further, what Hardy does at that moment is subtractive rather than additive. He takes the overall visual field, then gathers all the diffuse compositional labor we are at that moment engaged in distributing over its entire surface, and now folds it into one exquisitely narrow ribbon of specification that runs across the circumference of the room designating the variation of the single sensory dimension, temperature. If one were to take that narrow strip and calculate its total surface area, it would probably be about as big as a flower.

Here is another instance. It begins with a sentence Addison would appreciate: "[Norcombe Hill] was a featureless convexity of chalk and soil— an ordinary specimen of those smoothly-outlined protuberances of the globe which may remain undisturbed on some great day of confusion." The picture we are instructed to make is diffuse and, save for the dome outline, it has none of its surface filled in. But now again Hardy begins to harvest all the ambient pastel light and concentrates it on one small patch whose composition is within the magnitude of our power:

> The hill was covered on its northern side by an ancient and decaying plantation of beeches, whose upper verge formed a line over the crest, fringing its arched curve against the sky, like a mane. To-night these trees sheltered the southern slope from the keenest blasts, which smote the wood and floundered through it with a sound as of . . . .[25]

And here begins an extended description of the spinning of leaves and stormy wind, all of which has been explicitly marked off from the largest surface of the composition (the entire southern slope has been excised) and which therefore has a radius that permits the intensity of disturbance Hardy now assigns to it. The overactivity of description occurs in a space that then has a rapid falloff to zero; all the compositional energy we might devote to the full picture is instead drafted into the storm on the northern slope. In the same way, when one pictures (or even looks at) a flower, there is an intense localization of color with a sudden dropping off at the edges.

The high ratio of intensity to extension—what I'm calling the locality rule when it occurs as a feature of Hardy's prose—is already at work in the flower, even when it is only daydreamed and certainly when it is composed under authorial instruction. The concentration of a small patch of high coloration explains why variations in the surface of the flower are always attended to. Aristotle, for example, who sometimes seems to have written his essays in a garden, says in his treatise on color that "the petals of the poppy are crimson at their ends, because the process of maturation takes place quickly there, but at their base they are black, because this color is already predominant at the end." He attributes the color shifts to varying ripening speeds within the flower, to the uneven rapidity of maturation; but what is crucial at the moment is not the accuracy or inaccuracy of his explanation but his ease in specifying the surface he wishes us to picture. While the variable color of the fruit can also be explained this way, "[It] is still more evident in the actual blossoms . . . . The best example of all is the iris; for its blossom shows a great variety of hues according to the different states of maturation in its different parts . . . . Therefore the extremities of blossoms always ripen most completely, whilst the parts near the base have much less colour."[26]

The specificity of the poppy and iris petals can be contrasted with various accounts of the nonspecificity of the daydreamed face. Sartre opens his description of Pierre's face by noticing that it presents itself without any specificity of angle "like the silhouettes drawn by children; the face is seen in profile, but both eyes are nevertheless drawn in . . . . They are 'presentable' under an all-inclusive aspect." When we imagine a face, we "obtain these objects in their entirety."[27] If Sartre's observation is accurate, what makes it especially startling is that the face is the part of the human being where the greatest concentration of features occurs, since all the perceptual systems except touch are located here. Henri Bergson states this observation in a more expansive form, talking about objects in general as well as faces in particular. He criticizes "cerebral explanations" of memory that speak as though our "visual recollection of an object" entailed a physical impression or trace that "subsist[s] in the brain as it were on a sensitive plate or a phonographic disk." This could not be the case because then there "would be thousands or even millions" of traces for each stable object and even more for a continually mobile human face. What we "unquestionably" have instead is a "unique image, or . . . a practically invariable recollection of the object or person."[28] Whether or not we imagine a face as such a unitary and generalized object is debatable, but the description seems generally true of faces as well as of many objects of imagining: Pegasus and Yahweh, for example, both seem to present themselves as unitary rather than from a hundred points of view. But the flower, in contrast, immediately breaks into the specificity of lilacs, roses, and delphiniums, and each of these in turn, into a specification of a precise disposition of color at a certain moment in its maturation, its variations from center to edge. And this is true not only in the images we produce under authorial instruction (some of which I will turn to before long) but even in everyday daydreaming and conversation, hence under the verbal instruction of friends or the cheerful recommendations of gardening books.

The reliance on language, rather than photographs, in flower catalogs such as *Gilbert Wild's Daylilies* displays the same confidence in the flower's describability—that is, in the reader's ability to construct from a set of phrases a clear mental image.[29] The entry for daylily "Satinique" begins, as do all entries in this catalog, with a coded specification of the month of the bloom, the size of the blossom, the length of a single petal, the length of the stamen, followed by several lines of description. The specification of the size of the blossom (in the case of Satinique, 5-inch bloom, 2 3/8 petal, 1 5/8 stamen) is important because it designates the compositional surface on which the description that follows takes place. Here is that description:

> Ruffled, slightly creped deep burgundy with slightly raised rib of same color, blue violet veining and shading, slight magenta eye, gold throat and slightly green heart. Beautiful satin finish. Sepals recurve giving blooms flat triangular look. Opens well after cold night.

The slender catalog gives approximately twenty such verbal descriptions per page for ninety pages, presenting sixteen hundred daylilies with a precision that makes it possible to distinguish any two, such as Oriental Garden, which is "soft yellow dusted with rose," and Oriental Influence, which is "buff yellow with lavender overlay on heavily diamond dusted segments." The way colors shift with the sky light—both because of changing weather and the changing hours of the day—is specified, as in the case of Iffy, whose "smooth melon" becomes under the sun "a snow pink," and again of Oakleigh, which "under completely cloudy skies" becomes a "rolled back pale peach with orchid overlay," or Copper Canyon, which looks most lovely after "hot, windy days." Sometimes the gradations in color under a given sky light are even specified by mysterious color charts: the daylily Real Wind (as perhaps you already know) has "vivid colors under clouds (6/28/77) Light orange 2,5 YR 8/6, Munsell Hue, with rose halo which is split by orchid rib going deep into gold green heart";[30] whereas, "under sun, Munsell Hue: moderate yellowish (10 R 8/6) to strong yellowish pink (10 R 7/9). Cupped bloom." The passages just cited are misleading because they are fragments, so let me give the full account of one daylily, say, American Revolution:

> Midseason, Repeat bloomer, 5 1/2-inch bloom, 1 7/8 petal; 1 3/8 sepal. Very velvety black wine red, tiny green heart blends into a bit of yellow before meeting the black red segments which gently fold back: they seem to have a fine line on edges. Velvety finish . . . remains good at night. Buds are black red on outside . . . top multiple branches which is good with so many rebloom scapes coming.

I will stop here, though I would very much like to recite Raspberry Dream, Raspberry Wine, Raindrop, Raining Violets, and Random Wit, as well as School Girl, See Here, and Someday Maybe. (I sense that there is one person in the country who names all the daylilies, the racehorses, and the lipsticks.)[31]

IV. Thinness of Petals

In addition to size, shape, and localization, there is a fourth feature that contributes to the flower's imaginability. As I said in "On Vivacity," the imagination has a special expertise in producing two-dimensional gauzy images. Phenomena in the actual physical world that have those same attributes of transparency or filminess (such as thin curtains, fog, and mist) can be more easily imitated in the mind than can thick or substantive phenomena. The gossamer quality of many flowers (columbine, companula, foxglove, sweet pea, rose of Sharon), the thinness and transparency of the petals (that lets one see the sunlight though them or see the shape of another overlapping petal coming from behind), gives them a kinship with the filmy substance, the substancelessness, of mental images. In this respect Gilbert Wild's daylilies are not the perfect instance of the ease of imagining flowers; for, although in the realm of fabrics satin and velvet are judged delicate, in the realm of flowers the satin of Satinique and the velvet of the American Revolution seem too substantial. Many of the catalog entries for daylilies in fact directly specify that a particular flower has "good substance," a term not used for other species. Daylilies do not have the thinness of ordinary flowers, the airiness of Cobweb and Peaseblossom.

Aristotle called this thinness of plants their "rarity." It is, he argued, their rarity, their lack of material density, that lets them suddenly grow to maturity in a single day: "The material of which the plant is formed is near at hand, and therefore its generation is quick, and it grows and increases, because it is rare, more quickly than if it were dense."[32] Aristotle conceives of rarity not as an absence of something, but as a positive possession; the plant "has rarity." Thus he writes, "Any body which *has* considerable *rarity* tends to rise upwards, for the air supports it. This we often see when we throw a gold coin or some other heavy substance into the water and it immediately sinks; whereas if we throw in a piece of wood, which *has rarity* in it, it does not sink . . . . That which has rarity can never altogether sink."[33]

But the rarity of petals is more often conceived of as a subtractive process, and I want to quickly sketch out three forms of the subtractive. The first is a straightforward verbal instruction to erase what is there; the second is the lifting of the color off the face of the flower; the third is the placing of the flower in an arc between the material and the immaterial, so that its passage back and forth is implied. To be fair to Gilbert Wild's beautiful daylilies, they are not so substantive, so thick or so coarse, as I a moment ago implied. Even here the subtractive quality is key, as is audible in the catalog's constant recourse to the word "slightly." Satinique, one may recall, is a "slightly creped deep burgundy with slightly raised rib" and has a "slight magenta eye" and "slightly green heart." Oriental Garden does not have rose but merely a dust of rose, as Oriental Influence has not quite lavender but merely its overlay. And Oakleigh, "under completely cloudy skies," is not pale peach but "a *rolled back* pale peach." Its pale peach must once have been there but has apparently been taken away. The four- or five-inch blossoms become small pools of color that appear and disappear in front of our eyes.

What I was earlier calling the flower's localization and what I now want to call its rarity may seem to urge us in two different directions, since I was then attending to the saturated quality of its surface, its being filled in, and I now appear to stress its quality of subtraction. But the two are compatible, for it is the vivacity (or filled-in) quality of color that remains and the substance that falls away. In Ashbery's yellow flash of the tulip, the color lifts off the already delicate surface and passes, still more rarefied but completely filled in, into the mind, retaining its petal shape. The breaking away

of color from substance also recurs in many of Rilke's poems. Rilke says of
the umbelled blossoms of the blue hydrangea that they

> are a blue
> they do not bear, only mirror from far away.[34]

Detached and dematerialized, the shapes of color pass into our mental
space. At the end of the poem, a detached color-patch of blue touches a detached color-patch of green and is suddenly vivified, an event that can be
felt palpably in the mind as the caress of one color glances over, touches
down on, the surface of the other. Rilke describes the revivification of the
blue as the "delight" it feels in touching the green, and this same account of
self-experiencing pleasure as colors lift away or touch one another occurs in
"The Bowl of Roses." Here Rilke combines the Aristotelian account of
color (changing as the flower matures) with an account that emphasizes the
arc from material location to dematerialized image:

> And was opening-out too much for this one,
> since in the air its indescribable pink
> took on the bitter aftertaste of violet?
> And that cambric one, is it not a dress
> in which, still soft and breath-warm, the chemise
> clings, both of them cast off at once
> in the morning shadows of the old forest pool?[35]

The second form of subtraction, then, the lifting of the color off the face
of the flower, sometimes comes to be inseparable from the third form of
subtraction, the placing of the flower in the arc between material and immaterial. Rousseau's many-pages-long dictionary entry for *flower* opens
with a statement about the irresistible ease of imagining a flower ("If I
should let my imagination surrender to the sweet sensations which this
word seems to evoke . . .") and then proceeds to the way the flower eludes
formal botanical definition because it remains even after each seemingly essential part has been subtracted: "The essence of the flower lies not in the
corolla," since the corolla is either missing or almost invisible in wheat,
mosses, beech, oak, alder, hazel, and pine, which are nonetheless flowers;
nor can the flower lie in the calyx, which is missing in the tulip and lily
("and one will not say that a Tulip or a Lily is not a flower"); nor can it lie
in the pistils and stamens ("Now in the whole of the Melon family . . . half
the flowers are without a pistil, the other half without stamens; yet this deprivation does not prevent them from being called and from being, each
and every one of them, flowers").[36] Friedrich Schiller, too, in one of the rare
invocations of a concrete object in *Aesthetic Education of Man*, places the

flower in the space of passage between material and immaterial: "In saying that the flower blooms and fades, we make the flower the thing that persists through the transformation and lend it, so to say, a personality [eine Person] in which both those conditions are manifested."[37]

This explanation of the easily imagined as something that can enter the mind precisely because it is always already in a state of passage from the material to the dematerialized was present, but hidden, in the account of solidity I gave in "On Vivacity." I cited there a sequence of passages in which the passing of a film over an object asserted to be solid worked through the processes of complete and incomplete kinetic occlusion to produce the mimesis of solidity. A filmy object conferred solidity on the surface beneath. I did not have occasion to mention how frequently the filmy object associated with this process is a flower. The "palpable iridescence," for example, that Des Esseintes intends to have permanently moving back across his floor in Joris-Karl Huysmans's *Against Nature* emanates from the jewels implanted in the shell of a tortoise. Des Esseintes's choice of jewels is determined by the quality of light they throw outward: the purplish reds and "sharp bursts of fire" from uvarovite and translucent minerals; the icy blues and deep sea greens flashing deceptively from sapphirines, cymophanes, and Ceylon cat's-eyes; and finally the "feeble luster" emanating from the stones selected for the "edging of the shell" so as not to compete with the brilliance of the arrangement of the interior.[38] That arrangement at the interior, the arrangement that orchestrates the hurling of the jeweled light, is in its specified design a bouquet of flowers.

In Virginia Woolf's short story "The Mark on the Wall" a woman watches an unidentifiable shadow on the wall progress through successive materializations: first a mark, then a small residue from a rose leaf, then a "gigantic old nail driven in two hundred years ago," then a rent in the wood itself, then a garden snail. During this progressive solidification, the woman herself metamorphoses into a tree. Film, flower, and wall are brought into rapid companionship even in the story's opening sentences: "Perhaps it was the middle of January in the present year that I first looked up and saw the mark on the wall . . . . So now I think of the fire; the steady film of yellow light upon the page of my book; the three chrysanthemums in the round glass bowl on the mantelpiece."[39] In William Wordsworth, too, the solidity of earth is established by the small galaxies of floral starlight continually hovering several inches above its surface. Stars of the day is how he imagines the field flowers in "Evening Voluntaries," with their "dazzling sheen" until twilight restores the green. Another poem addresses the daisy, "Yet like a star, with glittering crest / Self-poised in air thou seem'st to rest." The "glittering multitudes" reappear wherever the daisies grow.[40] There are many other instances: Rilke's filmy piece of lace whose interior pattern is a flower; Kant's tiny inventory of the instances of pure beauty—flowers, birds, crustaceans, music, geometric form—that expands to include the tonally anomalous "foliage . . . on wallpaper"; the red-gold river of light in Dante's *Paradiso* that when it runs between flower-covered banks, "issue[s] living sparks, which settled on the flowers on all sides . . . and then, as if intoxicated with the odors, they again plunged [back] into the amazing flood."[41]

Flowers can be taken as the representative of the imagination because of the ease of imagining them. That ease is in turn attributable to *their* size and the size of our heads, *their* shape and the shape of our eyes, *their* intense localization and the radius of our compositional powers, *their* rarity that lets them rise and enter our brains and our willingness to receive them as the template for the production of other, more resistant compositions. It is clear: we were made for one another. No wonder the kind of cross-species desire that Ovid recommends turns out to be key to imaginative life, to the bringing forth of what is fresh. (Homer shows us "what is great," said Addison; Virgil, "what is beautiful"; and Ovid, "what is new.")[42]

When a long period elapses between *reading* Ovid and *thinking* about Ovid, one can make the mistake of believing that humans turn into trees and plants simply to resist pursuit, to bring to a decisive end the troublesome lovemaking. But even after the transformation into bark-covered, branching laurel, or into reedy grasses, the lovemaking goes on in graphically vegetable detail; the rumor that these trees and flowers used to be humans seems merely an excuse to let them love each other now. Though we are now, by comparison, more prudential and constrained in our sexual preferences, cross-species desire has not wholly disappeared: Diane Ackerman points out the odd fact that when human beings want to attract other human beings, they usually wear not their own scent but the scent of flowers.[43]

I want to turn, very briefly, to a final question: What is it about imaginative cognition that the image of the flower displays?[44] I have suggested that in some very serious way the tissue of the flower is the work table on which imaginative life gets processed; and this point needs to be unfolded in more detail.

V. Perceptual Mimesis

Aristotle said that what distinguishes human beings from other creatures is our capacity to love something without wanting to ingest it. All animals, including human beings, he writes in *Sense and Sensibilia*, have the power to smell in order to eat; humans alone have a second reason to smell, namely to smell flowers, with no interest at all in eating them. Our smelling of food, says Aristotle, is discontinuous and contingent—whether something smells good depends on whether we are hungry—whereas our smelling of flowers is noncontingent and ongoing.[45] (The citizenry of California and several other regions have somewhat confounded these categories by their habit of eating flowers, but in many places in the world the Aristotelian distinction still holds true.) Of course smelling the flowers, seeing the flowers, touching the flowers, imagining the flowers is also a way of ingesting or at least interiorizing them, since we carry them in as objects of perception and imagining. Ludwig Wittgenstein said that when one sees something beautiful—an eyelid, a cathedral—the hand wants to draw it.[46] Like smelling, like imagining, this too is an act of interiorization, the yearning to incorporate, to make a residual image.

What I want to argue is that we interiorize the flower—we seize upon the flower as the proper object of the imagination—because it expresses the distinct quality of cognition at work in imagining. The formal properties of the act are displayed in the content of its object. It is important to stress that I am not here speaking about our projection of cognition outward onto flowers, trees, rocks (the process that has, since Ruskin, gone by the name "pathetic fallacy"), since what is at issue is not the lifting of our mental process out onto the flower, but the interiorization of the flower into the brain. It is not *our* intellect that is being conferred on the plant, but the plant's on us. In picturing a flower in the brain, it is the plant's own strange cognition or subcognition that is being used to display the peculiar nature of imaginative cognition. What is imagining like? Like being a plant. What is imagining? It is *not*-perception: it is instead the quasi-percipient, the slightly percipient, the almost percipient, the not yet percipient, the after percipient, of perceptual mimesis. Like the rolled-back pale pink of the daylily Oeakleigh, it is not sentience but sentience rolled back.

Accounts of the sentience of plants often formulate it in terms of either the foreimage or the afterimage of perception. For the poet Louise Glück, for example, the full moment of the flower is the "not yet" moment of spring, "hovering in a doorway," the "preparation," the time "before the appearance."[47] For Ovid it is the afterimage, as in his extraordinary use of the word *still*:

> When her limbs grew numb and heavy, her soft breasts
> Were closed with delicate bark, her hair was leaves,
>
> . . .
>
> Apollo loved her *still*. He placed his hand
> Where he had hoped and felt the heart *still* beating
> Under the bark; and he embraced the branches
> As if they *still* were limbs . . .[48]

When Pan holds Syrinx, he finds the nymph gone and in her place only the afterimage, "only reeds." The word "only" would seem to signal the end of the story or a swerve into frustration. We are given instead an account of the way the soft stirring of their lovemaking produces the flutes of Pan, and he "called them Syrinx, still."[49] Throughout Ovid, the great force of "the perennial"—narcissus, tree, or reeds—comes from its quality of afterimage, of its (even after it has gone) being there *still*.

The attempt to specify with precision the "almost" in the "almost percipience" of plants extends not just to the question of whether or not they nourish themselves, whether they feel pleasure[50] or pain, which sense-modality their own activities approximate, whether they have souls (the third kind of soul, said Plato; incidental souls, says Louise Glück), but even whether or not they are alive. Plato and Aristotle are hesitant to confer yet cannot but confer. Plato says in the *Timaeus*, "Everything that has life has every right to be called a living thing."[51] Yet the assertiveness seems there to answer some prior doubt, as though the full text should read: "The plant is *not* a living creature; yet it *is* alive; so it *must be* a living thing," since (and now the actual sentence) "everything that has life has every right to be called a living thing." Aristotle's treatise on plants opens, "Life is found in animals and plants; but while in animals it is clearly manifest, in plants it is hidden and not evident."[52] If they are not sentient, are they not living? If they are certainly living, are they not certainly sentient?

Pre-image and afterimage, subsentient and supersentient, the plant exposes the shape of a mental process that combines the almost percipient with a kind of transitory exactness. It is as though the very precision required to find the exquisitely poised actuality of the flower's "vague sentience" manifests itself as a form of acuity.

This perceptual acuity entails both vision and touch. The petal becomes the imagination's surrogate retina. It is estimated that the total skin surface in an adult human being is 3,000 square inches.[53] Compared to that expanse, the surface covered by the retinas is a tiny patch of membrane: Rilke calls them small tears in fate.[54] Yet physiologically, 38 percent of all sensory experience takes place against that tiny surface.[55] Eyes are, according to neurobiologists, the direct outcropping of the brain:[56] not content to receive messages by mediation, the brain has moved out to the surface of the skull in order to rub up against the world directly (no wonder it is overwhelming to look into another person's eyes; one beholds directly the moist tissue of the person's brain). As striking as the relation of eye and brain is the relation of eye, brain, and plant. The fifteen-volume *System of Opthalmology* (1958) begins by describing the antecedents of human perception in the membranes of plants, the precedents for the retina in the photochemical reactions of leaves and flowers that liberate energy and produce changes in metabolic activity and variations of movement. Tracing the path from "vague sentiency to apperception," Sir Stewart Duke-Elder writes about the key moment when a "diffuse reactivity" in one-celled organisms gave way to the ability of a multicelled organism to pass signals from receptor tissues to motor tissues. "In this way," he writes, "the effects of light upon metabolism, orientation and pigmentation became correlated through primitive nerve-nets and then became integrated in the ganglia of the central nervous system; and eventually, when the nervous pathways from the eyes were projected into a head-ganglion and ultimately into the fore-brain, the highly complex faculties of vision and apperception evolved."[57]

It was the goal and the accomplishment of Charles Darwin's final book, *The Power of Movement in Plants*, to demonstrate that "light [acts] on the tissue of plants almost in the same manner as it does on the nervous system of an animal."[58] The key transition from "vague" sentience to the "localization of sensitivity" that carries with it the ability to transmit influence "from an excited part to another which consequently moves," was already accomplished in plants.[59] Our nervous system, Darwin writes, is a more perfect transmissibility of the thing plants can already do. Darwin attached delicate instruments to the plants that let them trace on pieces of glass their intricate movements "oscillating up and down during the day." The resulting line drawings fill the book: each looks not like a cardiogram, jig-jagging along regularly, but like the tracing of several constellations superimposed on one another, or like the visual coding system of an elaborate dance. As the parts of the plant above the ground are exquisitely sensitive to light, so the tip of the radicle beneath the earth is so sensitive to touch that it elicits from Darwin periodic outcries: "We believe that there is no structure in plants more

wonderful, as far as its functions are concerned, than the tip of the radicle."
He writes in the final sentence of this, his final work: "It is hardly an exaggeration to say that the tip of the radicle thus endowed, and having the
power of directing the movements of the adjoining parts, acts like the brain
. . . receiving impressions from the sense organs, and directing the several
movements."[60]

Darwin tracks the motion of tiny seedlings, the motion of the tip of the
radicle, the motion of the leaf as it turns its edge to the sunlight to prevent
the injuring rays from falling on its broader surfaces, the overall movement
of a giant acacia tree whose "every growing shoot is constantly describing
small ellipses: as is each petiole, sub-petiole, and leaflet," each "flower pen-
dule," and beneath the earth the "tip of each rootlet endeavour[ing] to
sweep small ellipses or circles" against the resistant ground (409). He also
tracks the intricate patterns of waking and sleeping in the woodbine, the
plant that haunts the third volume of Proust's *Remembrance of Things Past*,
and whose sleep patterns were first recorded by Linnaeus in a flower clock
specifying the regular waking hour of red poppies, speedwell, woodbine,
and white campion.[61]

For both Rilke and Darwin, the petal's sensitivity to light and, equally,
its sensitivity to touch are precocious of our own perception. The plant's
own experience of weight on its leaves, of gravitational excitation during
the curling of a tendril, of its ability to distinguish hard from soft are described at length by Darwin in passages that seem kindred to the felt experience of imagining: the barely perceptible weight of light falling on arms,
the touch of an eyelid glancing across the surface of the eye, the brush of an
image against image. For the Greek poets, the feel of light, not as it
strikes the retina but as it falls elsewhere on the 3,000-square-inch surface
of the human being, is identical with being alive. "The light of the sun
shines on him no more," says Neoptolemus of the dead Ajax and Oedipus
at Colonus, knowing he will in a moment leave the world, holds out his
arm to let the sun fall across their full surface: "O sunlight of no light! Once
you were mine! / This is the last my flesh will feel of you."[62] The child Polyx-
ena, about to be sacrificed by the Greek army, gives the same salutation,
"This is the last time I shall ever see the sun," and calibrates her stay in the
world by the small corridor of light through which she will pass as she
walks to the place of execution:

> O light! I still can say that word; but all the light
> That now belongs to me is what remains between
> This moment and the sword beside Achilles' tomb.[63]

Each responds to the small channel of sunlight, as does Renoir with his anemones ("I think I'm beginning to understand something"), and Manet with the lavender and silver of his lilac-filled water glass. What is the feeling when image rubs against image, when one receives the instruction to glance the image of Golo across the image of the Combray wall, or to flash the light off the solid floor bearing the weight of Des Esseintes, or to throw the shadow on Virginia Woolf's page, or to lift and hold a sheen of starlight a few inches above the grass? The feeling (the almost percipience, the after percipience) of a flower, says Rilke. The felt experience of imagining, the interior brushing of one image against another, is the way it feels when two petals touch one another:

> And then like this: that a feeling begins,
> because flower petals touch flower petals?
> And this: that one opens like a lid,
> and under it lie only eyelids,
> all closed, as if they, sleeping tenfold,
> had to damp an inner power of sight.
> And this above all: that through these petals
> light must pass.[64]

Not Seeing the *Laocoön*?

Lessing in the Archive of the Eighteenth Century

> I will be allowed to think "Greece" without ever seeing it.
> —Martin Heidegger[1]

When the German Enlightenment historian, dramatist, librarian, and anti-quarian Gotthold Ephraim Lessing published his essay *Laocoön oder die Grenzen der Malerey und der Poesie* in 1766, he continued a fervent contro-versy. In the essay, Lessing claimed different aesthetics for different artistic media and thus undid the humanist paradigm of *ut pictura poesis*. Lessing discusses the different aesthetic effects of one and the same subject (the death of the Trojan priest Laocoön and his sons by a god-sent serpent when trying to warn his compatriots of Ulysses' "Trojan horse") in sculptural *ver-sus* epic representation—that is, the ancient *Laocoön* marble group preserved in the Vatican (fig. 6) and the Laocoön-episode in Vergil's epic *Aeneid*. Lessing's challenging semiotics of the arts in his *Laocoön* leaves open ques-tions both anecdotal and central: Did Lessing actually see the sculpture of Laocoön during his trip to Rome? Does it matter, regarding the implica-tions of his essay, if he did or not? Could it be that Lessing's blindness to-wards actual evidence was the condition for theoretical insights? The Greek notion of *theoría* and Latin *spectatio/contemplatio*[2] are involved in this play between blindness and insight (*Anschauung*, to make use of an aesthetic term current in Lessing's age, a kind of divination).[3] Thus Lessing's not see-ing the *Laocoön* is twofold: both a historical (non-)event and, even if it hap-pened, a misreading of what could actually be seen. In starting to look for answers, we first have to check the archival material from Lessing's Italian journey, which does not mention a confrontation between Lessing and the *Laocoön*. Is this a sign of mere absence, of an archival loss and void, or of meaningful silence? One of his biographers likens Lessing's devotion of not "one single letter" to the Laocoön sculpture in Rome to the situation of visiting a learned man "who stubbornly remains silent"—a hermeneutic resistance of the archive that is allegorical of the dissonance between literary evidence and visual arts.[4]

I. Fragments: Lessing's "Italian Notebook"

Western aesthetics has long been trained to transform immediately sensual impressions into literary description. (In this the Western tradition differs, for example, from the Japanese Haiku, which is based on contemplation.) Lessing's Italian journey, though, did not result in a literary description, however rudimentary, but in a register of scattered notes, without any literary pretension: "scholarly annotations of a librarian," Lessing's successor as director of the Wolfenbüttel Herzog August library, Paul Raabe, comments.[5] All that remains is a notebook in *octavo* format of less than 100 pages, some of which are missing; others remain blank. The first entry is pure data: "Turin, 23. August 75." In fact, we are confronted with a ruin of description, currently stored among the Lessing papers in the manuscript department of the Berlin State Library (Unter den Linden).

Most of the entries consist of philological and antiquarian-polyhistorical notes in the "telegram style" (Friedrich A. Kittler) of *collectanea*. Concerning Rome we find some more entries about visits, single works of art and personal contacts, but they are just detailed notes, rather in the descriptive than in the narrative mode. Conrad Wiedemann calls this notebook an "inventory" and asks if this was meant to manifest the author's verdict against description as defined in his theoretical essay *Laocoön*.[6] If Lessing's idea of traveling was the humanistic *iter academicum*, that is as much a literary as a real performance, then discontinuities mark the rhythm of this journey.

The librarian Lessing's point of view of Italy was library-based, an aesthetics which cannot be grasped in the mode of narrative speculations but rather by an insight into his empire of letters, the catalogue of books acquired on his Italian journey being preserved in the Wolfenbüttel library. His sources of information on Italy were books like Burmannus's *Thesaurus antiquitatum et historiarum Italiae* and Pierre Jean Grosley's *Nouveau Mémoires* on Italy, titles (including a *Théâtre*) which hint at the fact that travelling was mainly about authentication of the already literally represented.[7] Lessing mastered the mass of information by critical and comparative reading of printed sources, as indicated by his generic expression *collectanea* for

F I G . 6 . *Laocoön*. The Vatican Museums, Rome. Photo: Ministero per i Beni e le Attività Culturali—Istituto Centrale per il Catalogo e la Documentazione—Fototeca Nazionale, Rome.

his own essay *Laocoön*, which replaced the actual examination of existing collections of art. The largest amount of money spent in Italy was on books bought by Lessing for the Wolfenbüttel ducal library. These lists of books tell a different story of Lessing's journey: they allow us to interpret Lessing's silence (the absence of a narrative on his journey), mirroring the itinerary of a journey which leads more directly into the crypt of his ideas; they represent an implicit commentary by the one who chose them.[8]

Indeed, there was a time when archaeology was still archaeo*graphically* perceived; an author of the journal of the British Society of Antiquaries, *Archaeologia*, wrote in 1803: "the contents of the Archaiology [*sic*] . . . are derived from various collections of old manuscripts," identifying this discipline as a text-based practice.[9] In this sense, Lessing's archaeological aesthetics was based on the medium of the library, reducing visual evidence to the trace of letters (an aesthetic which *nolens volens* we share with him in our attempts to reconstruct evidence on Lessing). Rather reading than seeing, Lessing's Italian journey looks like a voyage into the interior of library space: indeed, he seems to have preferred to visit city libraries rather than collections of art or places of public life.[10]

With his introduction of temporal relativity in topographical description, Lessing's differentiation between the pictorial (momentary description) and the verbal (capacities of temporal representation) as known from his *Laocoön* essay affects the literary aesthetics of his Italian diary. His immediate registering of a series of discrete pictures apparently differs from modes of perception which are already filtered and prefigured by (supplementary or previous) literary narrative time. Joseph Frank was one of the first critics to discuss such qualities and to describe the architecture of a text that works against the "strict causal-chronological order."[11] This is a clue to deciphering Lessing's Italian notebook, and the spatial reordering of his experience of travelling, as collecting information. Thus Lessing's aesthetics may be referred to the *Encyclopédie*, where the essay on description relates directly to the literal meaning of *décrire* used in geometry: "Description is the action of tracing a line, a surface, or some other geometric figure," corresponding with the type of neo-classical outline engravings of ancient sculpture upon which Lessing based his *Laocoön* musings.

Of central interest in his Italian scrapbook is the moment when Lessing might have confronted the *Laocoön* in Rome (fig. 7). Some of the contemporary writers on the *Laocoön* positively saw the statue in the Vatican under various conditions, "others saw only plaster casts or engravings. All saw the *Laocoön* as idea."[12] Johann Bernoulli, for example, saw the Belvedere *Laocoön*

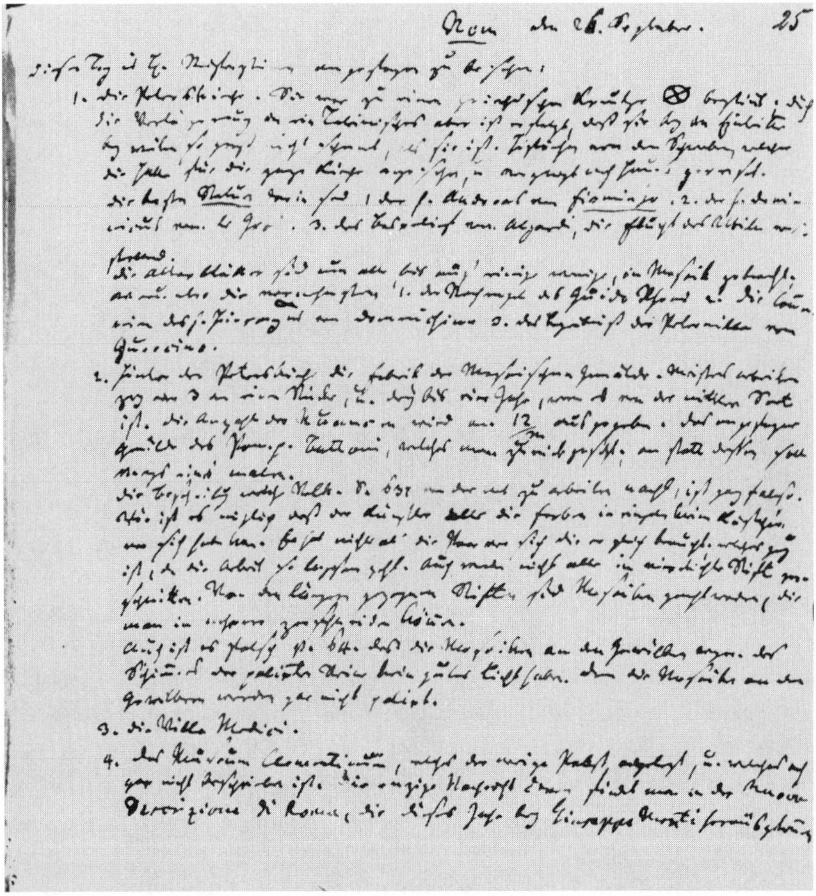

FIG. 7. Gotthold Ephraim Lessing, "Italian Notebook," entry for Rome, 26 September 1775. Preußischer Kulturbesitz Staatsbibliothek (Lessing Collection no. 37, fol. 25), Berlin. Photo: Staatsbibliothek zu Berlin—Preußischer Kulturbesitz—Handschriftenabteilung.

group in the spring of the year Lessing visited Rome—that is, in 1775—but still he valued Lessing's textual insights into the semiotic nature of the sculpture more highly than what could autoptically be seen at close distance.[13]

Since then the canonical predominance of Lessing's media theory of the arts in *Laocoön* has superseded the archaeological perception of the actual marble group; the group has been seen as a document illustrating Lessing's treatise, a derivative sign of its arguments, rather than as a means of checking its validity: "The *Laocoön* has become and is . . . an allegory of itself, its history and the issues that surround it."[14]

In a curious way, Lessing's disregard for the original sculpture and his preference for studying printed engravings depicting it corresponds to the derivative fashion in which academic research on that subject is mostly based on modern text editions and just rarely revisits the archival evidence, Lessing's "Italian Notebook" in the manuscript department of the Berlin Staatsbibliothek. What is true for the textual corpus of Lessing's drafts of *Laocoön* (preserved in the same place) corresponds with its subject's two bodies: "The statue has another body, its material body, its chiseled marble actuality." This is the *Laocoön* of the archaeologists; while the eighteenth century may have seen classical unity in the *Laocoön*, "the statue's real history is a story of fragmentation and indeterminacy."[15]

If Lessing was actually confronted with the *Laocoön*, then locked up in a court of the Vatican Belvedere, he must have been shocked by its fragmentary state (with the right arm still missing) and rough surfaces, which were smoothed in the reproductions he was used to.[16] A similar shock before the actual appearance of the sculpture also informs Simon Richter's recent reconstruction of an interpretive framework for the *Laocoön* as "the body in pain"; Lessing's writings themselves constitute a literary *corpus*, a fragmented body of texts which can hardly be referentially centered any more by supposing (or reconstructing) a coherent individual corpse named Gotthold Ephraim.

Archaeology is involved not only in respect to the antiquarian subject but also to our condition of research into Lessing's *Laocoön*: "What we have actually inherited, however, are fragments, not only the fragments of Greek art and poetry, but the writings, the words and letters, say of Lessing, understood as fragment." This applies above all to the ruinous preservation of the "Italian Notebook"—an accidentally preserved relic.[17] When Lessing's apartment was sealed after his death in 1781, an inventory of his papers mentions "manuscripts for a description of Lessing's Italian journey" *plus* "manuscripts of Lessing's Italian journey." Were there two different sets of Italian papers? Most of these papers subsequently were lost, leaving us with the most common archival aporia: the impossibility of deciding whether the remaining Italian notebook represents only part of a coherent whole or nothing but an originary, primordial fragment "which can only be understood just as a fragment."[18] So maybe Lessing did not remain silent on the *Laocoön* in Rome, and it is just archi(ve)textual transmission that is missing.[19] A similar constellation holds for Lessing's essay on the ancient imagination of death:

> What is given to us with the text of *Wie die Alten den Tod gebildet* is not the spirit or meaning of the work. We inherit its shards and pieces. According to a related and appropriate metaphor, we could say that we inherit its bones, its desiccated skeleton.[20]

II. Contrast: Accounts

There is a different regime of description, though, to supplement the blanks in Lessing's "Italian Notebook" from the hand of a traveling companion who added military rationality to the economy of writing. Appropriately, this additional source is not reported by history, but has to be detected by a different archaeology of knowledge: that is, out of the archive. The document is the account of expenditures of the prince of Braunschweig, whose cicerone Lessing was in Italy. This alphanumerical list was registered by the other of the prince's companions, Lieutenant Karl Bogislaus von Warnstedt (1725–1808), "with uncorrupted precision":[21] thirty-six pages in folio, preserved in the State Archive of Lower Saxony at Wolfenbüttel.[22] Thus, in the case of this town, the neighborhood of an administrative record office and a baroque cultural library (once headed by Lessing) today seems to represent the two differing modes of "description" under discussion here: non-discursive data storage (archive) versus discursive descriptions (the content of libraries) as two conflicting sides of Enlightenment. *Ratio* refers to the question of accounts, of calculation, of (financial) justification as opposed to narrative, literary accounts. Any journey into the archive of the eighteenth century itself has to face the coexistence of both kinds of aggregated evidence—a situation which challenges any one-sided supremacy of the *historio*graphical—that is, narrative—way of confronting and representing the subject.

Warnstedt's way of registering the most important stations of this journey makes a geographical and intellectual topography transparent to the reader, which is completely different from the romantic ways in which "grand tourists" used to praise the beauty of Italy. This alternative account might help to solve the biggest enigma surrounding Lessing's Italian journey: how could the author of *Laocoön* fail to mention any visit to the so-called ancient sculpture in his diary? Raabe believes that Warnstedt's non-narrative financial accounts are the most reliable record of their itinerary: in fact, the entry for a visit to the Vatican museum shows a remarkably high expenditure for gifts to the guardians. Was this a way to open the closet in which the *Laocoön* sculpture remained hidden at that time? Lea Ritter-Santini and Giovanni Chiarini draw our attention to "money: How it was counted and what it tells" [Wie man es zählte und was es erzählt].[23] As long as literary history concentrates on narrative [Erzählung] it fails to perform the kind of archaeology that knows what is being revealed by numbers [Zahlen]. But let us not be trapped by exclusive alternatives such as narrative versus calculation, for any historically given opposition might be so radically "dislocated" or "imbalanced" that *neither* opponent can secure a lasting position of repressive dominance: "The very idea of dichotomous, hierarchical thinking must finally be itself 'problematized.'"[24]

In a way, the absence of the *Laocoön* in Lessing's Italian diary—this blank in a textual body which Ritter-Santini cannot stand to accept without speculative substitution—is a philological equivalent to the aesthetic void that Lessing himself rejects as a disgusting sign of the unimaginable bodily real (the unrepresentable, in Jacques Lacan's sense). The abysmally opened mouth of the *Laocoön* sculpture, so brilliantly analyzed by David Wellbery, as Lessing's effort to defend paternal law (social order, state archival memory) and an idea of beauty that implicitly corresponds to our own privileging of the discourse of history (the discourse of narrative and symbolic order against the real of the archive replete with absences and gaps).[25] In institutional accordance with this aesthetic desire, the curiosity cabinet, one type of assembling artifacts and evidence from the past and abroad with a profusion of uncanny images and monsters, was being replaced in Lessing's epoch by the ideal, art historical order of the neo-classical museum which finally (in the Romantic age) subjected the spatial arrangement of objects to a perceptive mind reasoning in the medium of evolutionary, genealogical narrative—the intellectual "sign of history."[26] The institutionalized museum with top-lit exhibition galleries became the architectural model of literally "enlightened" description and historical aesthetics.[27] When the *Laocoön* group was temporarily on display in Paris (Musée Napoléon), and included in Hubert Robert's designs for redesigning the Louvre galleries, the sculpture could no longer be overlooked.

In the Mannheim collection of antiquities, Johann Wolfgang Goethe first saw a plaster cast of the *Laocoön* in 1769. He later confronted the original statue in 1786/7 during his extended Roman sojourn. In a way no less surprising than Lessing's silence on the *Laocoön* in Rome, Goethe makes absolutely no mention of it either in his correspondence or in his *Italienische Reise*; not until 1798 did Goethe write publicly about the *Laocoön*. "The timing is significant: never before had the statue left Rome or not been available for the public to view. Napoleon's terms for peace in the Treaty of Tolentino (1797) included the transport to Paris of . . . the *Laocoön*. . . . Goethe counters Napoleon's move by erecting a Laocoön in language."[28]

Lessing, who had learned to see with his enlightened mind rather than with seduceable eyes, corresponds with Goethe's attitude towards *Laocoön* in an inverse way: years after refusing to mention the *Laocoön* during his visit to Rome, he polemically (and in an idiosyncratic reaction against Winckelmann's claim for autopsy) remarked that a visitation to the plaster cast collection in Mannheim was more profitable for the artist than a journey to the Vatican museum, where they were stored under literally obscure conditions and could not be touched or looked at from different perspectives.[29] Like the engraved outline drawing, the plaster cast of the *Laocoön* serves as the essential medium of enlightened aesthetics.

III. Travel Journals as Literary Form

In order to understand the nature of Lessing's Italian diary, we have to put it in the context of travel journals as literary form. In 1762 the Göttingen historian Johann David Köhler published his advice for academic journeys, *Anweisung für reisende Gelehrte, Bibliothecken, Münz-Cabinette, Antiquitäten-Zimmer, Bilder-Säle, Naturalien- und Kunst-Kammern u.d.m. mit Nutzen zu besehen*, juxtaposing the awareness of sightseeing with the awareness of manuscripts and ancient documents—that is, by juxtaposing archaeology to the archive.[30] A few generations later, the historian Leopold von Ranke undertook his Italian journey as a voyage into the interior of the Venetian archives.[31] Traveling in space became traveling in time but, in both instances, this happened indexically, following semiotic vectors, when nondiscursive practice was read as inventories. Geographical description (mapping) would finally be transformed into writing history by the medium of narrative.

An anonymous writer in his "letters about traveling" explicitly asked the traveler, especially the historian, to have a "statistical" awareness of what he saw.[32] For the Mainz philosophy professor Anton Joseph Dorsch, in his instruction for scholarly traveling, points of attention were whatever related to humans; the anthropologic turn, the description of social milieus at *mille lieux* (after Pierre Nora) was about to replace the antiquarian description of travelling. Information and news were wanted and registered,[33] but were not necessarily critically reflected upon by an accompanying literary discourse; ways of seeing did not differ from ways of describing in this systemizing of travel.[34] The encyclopedic inventorization of information, common in the age of reason, was then going to be replaced by historical commentaries; since then, statistics and measuring were rivaled by narratives. From the monumental registration to a documentary processing of data, the medium of narrative served for historical contextualization. Individualization, subjectivization, and perspectivization (the "point of view" of Chladenius) revised the systematic encyclopedic travel description.[35]

The eighteenth century continued with the writing practice of a diary of a journey as inventory, as empirical data collection (*apodemics*), culminating in methodological instructions such as Joseph-Marie de Gérando's *Considérations sur les diverses méthodes à suivre dans l'observation des peuples sauvages* (1800).[36] Lessing's Italian diary accordingly looks "like a dusty herbary," closer to Linnaeus's plant classification systems or Buffon's *just description* of natural history than to classical prose writing.[37] The entry on traveling ("Reisen") in J. H. Zedler's universal dictionary reveals his eagerness to inventory almost everything.[38] Historical interest thus took the form of statistics and annalistic or antiquarian writing systems, replacing the temporal coherence of narrative with mechanistic chronological seriation.[39] Maybe reality actually was perceived in the way its description proceeds, as protohistoriographic *annals* of the sort described by Hayden White in his essay on "The Value of Narrativity in the Representation of Reality."[40] Instead of historical remembrance, cultural memory thus was a synchronic function of memory as data storage. Lessing's Italian notebook fits into this aesthetics indeed. But data acquisition was in conflict with the tradition of the aristocratic Grand Tour which, though concentrating on visits to cultural and historical sites, rather culminated in taking into account representative social institutions and events.[41] This was a conflict Lessing had to suffer when travelling with the Prince of Brunswick, whose pragmatic love for visiting military fortresses did not meet the antiquarian's desire.

IV. Lessing's Refusal of Absence: Images of Death

In a way similar to his denial of the actual Laocoön sculpture, Lessing's equivalent topic of research, the antiquarian interpretation of ancient representations of death, is based on what Richter calls "unforgivably bad engravings of the Roman grave monuments he refers to." Lessing's denial in matters of visual evidence strangely corresponds with a methodological blind spot in the same essay marked by "the gulf separating the two components of his argument, ancient literary and later Roman visual sources"— exactly the semiotic relation between word and image to which Lessing in his *Laocoön* essay has shown to be so sensitive.[42] In fact, Lessing's image of death is at odds with the archaeological evidence; his Christian (v)ideology of beauty corrects the data derived from material relics, in a way reminscent of the then current practice of archaeologists who, "trained in the Humanist tradition, interpreted their finds by trying to relate them to the classical literature with which they were familiar, and in these interpretations they often committed understandable anachronisms."[43]

Most of Lessing's prints of ancient representations of death were based on illustrations of ancient Greek and Roman funerary monuments in the Museum Maffeianum at Verona. When Goethe visited the place, his (mis-)reading of such artifacts was from the perspective of life instead of death: "The funerary monuments move the heart and always evoke life."[44] Such was Lessing's perception; he preferred being "the archaeologist of the living."[45] Apparently, visual perception of antiquities was prefigured by a cognitive rhetorical trope of treating mute objects like living beings, *prosopopoeia*, coupled with the explicit meaning of *ekphrasis* as "speaking out." Jean H. Hagstrum defines this rhetorical practice as "that special quality of giving voice and language to the otherwise mute art object" as distinct from "iconic" descriptions.[46] The logocentric accent is on persuasion; that is, rhetoric, the realm of speech. The very perception of past life itself is being generated as an effect of rhetoric. Description becomes prescription.[47]

Lessing's archeo-logo-centrism corresponds with his euphemistic effort to (in fact, mis-)interpret ancient representations of death as *genii* of sleep. Description here serves as deviation. All of Lessing's circumscriptions define death *ex negativo* from the vantage point of life, as sheer absence of life. This fits into the rise of a genuinely *historical* imagination in the late eighteenth century that confronts the temporal absence called "past" in terms of passed life, and tries to make it *speak* in order to confront it dialogically.[48] This has since been a discursive dispositive emblematic of our own way of confronting the "archive of the eighteenth century." Whenever we treat the textual artifacts at our disposal as derivations of real presence, they exist—like Lessing's ideals—only on the stage of our imagination. However well rooted in evidence and research, they exist only as *models* of past configurations of reality. This habit is challenged by the archeology of knowledge proposed by Michel Foucault, who asks us to confront mute monuments (both archival texts and material objects) in terms of pure exteriority, accessible to serial description in its most graphic sense.

V. Surrogates of Laocoön

A different form of figurative description was performed by William Blake, commissioned to engrave the *Laocoön* in 1815 to illustrate John Flaxman's article on sculpture for Abraham Ree's *Cyclopaedia* after a preparatory drawing from the cast in the Royal Academy.[49] Blake adjusted the subject to his own beliefs and produced another Laocoön-engraving "which he filled with aphorisms and observations, sideways, round the figures, and in almost every empty space. Since the words are written higgledy-piggledy, it is difficult to establish the order in which they should be printed."[50] Description, literally, undoes visual evidence. Another contemporary of Lessing in London, Joseph M. Gandy, draughtsman for the architect Sir John Soane, doubted in a diary entry of June 9, 1797, the possibilities of technically rendering a truthful representation of the ancient *Laocoön* in the Vatican by means of engraved reproductions, asking:

> In what do the beauties of the *Laocoön* exist? . . . Can a drawing of this be so correct as the thing itself? I answer no. A drawing will only represent one side whereas to view the original we have all sides—and its effects in different lights & situations.[51]

In contrast to this statement, Lessing did not perceive any defect in confronting artistic monuments only as secondhand reproductions, just as for him "evidence from books is more valid than what appears to the eye."[52] So he could even omit any illustration of the *Laocoön* in his essay on the subject, since everything could be expressed by syntactic arguments.[53] Description here surpasses autopsy, correlating to the supremacy Lessing grants to the literary narrative, i.e. consecutive and temporalizing depiction of Laocoön's death as opposed to his simultaneous representation in sculpture. *Ekphrasis* in this sense is mimetic of the original in the anticipatory sense of *pre*-figuration. Lessing literally *saw* the ancient model in his imagination as a prototype, transforming the plastic image into a literary *topos*, subjecting the work of art to a rhetorical figuration against which autopsy could only be of secondary importance: "neither *narrative* (where description is subordinated to narrative) nor *descriptive* (where it is set free) but *rhetorical*, conferring on the ekphrasis the status of a *figure*."[54] Archaeology here does not deal with the actual artifact, but with primordial knowledge in a Neoplatonic sense, not thinking with the eyes but rather seeing by thoughts.[55] Lessing "confused *knowing* with *seeing*."[56]

VI. Winckelmann versus Lessing (and other writers on Laocoön)

The data from Warnstedt's account book increase the probability that Lessing saw the centerpiece of his writing—the ancient sculpture then as today placed in the museum of the Vatican—since the size of payments made to employees (then called *douceurs*) suggests the outing was important to the traveling party. Nonetheless, the evidence of the payments in Warnstedt's book is inconclusive. Lessing did visit the otherwise unspectacular ruins of Nero's palace, then still known as the Baths of Titus, where the sculpture had been discovered in 1506—another voided place.[57] Even if he did see the group, he viewed it through the lens of engravings which he privileged in his perception. Lessing made semiotic registration *qua* reproduction the point of departure for his theory about the totality of the arts. By contrast, Johann Joachim Winckelmann, a former student of medicine, introduced the literal archeological gaze to the study of art by claiming to perform an autopsy of the original.[58]

Lessing's essay *Laocoön* explicitly asks for the visual arts not to kill the imagination by semiotic over-determination. The *oculus imaginationis* (well known from its engraved localization in Robert Fludd's *Mystery of the Human Mind*, ca. 1620) of interiorized representation was Lessing's stage [Schau-Platz] of reason, as opposed to autopsy (exteriority of the gaze), Winckelmann's archaeological claim.[59] Such was Winckelmann's comment on Jonathan Richardson's *Account of the Statues, Basreliefs, Drawings and Pictures in Italy, France, & etc.* (1754), remarking that the author actually did not see many of the described objects personally, as if those places and works of art had just appeared in Richardson's dreams.[60] On the contrary, the preface to Winckelmann's history of the art of antiquity (*Geschichte der Kunst des Altertums*, 1764) laments the uselessness of current descriptions of Roman antiquities, galleries, and houses for the study of art: "they rather seduce than inform."[61] Derivations from already existing descriptive literature are misleading [verführen] and misreadings actual works of art. Winckelmann coined the term *Unbezeichnung*—the undoing of description—for the idealizing quality of classical beauty.[62] Lessing applied the term to the cloth covering Agamemnon's face in the story of a painting by Timanthes (the sacrifice of Iphigenia) as "a visual silence, the refusal to represent."[63]

Christian Gottlieb Heyne, a professor of classical philology at the University of Göttingen, wrote an essay about the *Laocoön* included in his *Sammlung antiquarischer Aufsätze* (1779). He draws attention to three expressive values of the plastic group: pain, a father's anxiety, and muscular resistance. He develops a close reading of surfaces, "a model of scholarly philological understanding . . . that is at odds not only with Winckelmann's enthusiasm, but also . . . with Lessing's manipulation of classical texts." Johann Wolfgang von Goethe finally, in his essay *Über Laokoon* (1798), established the aesthetic autonomy of the artwork by cutting it off from its mythological context, if not from reference altogether. "He, as it were, 'diagnoses' the body of Laocoön with medical precision" under a truly archaeological gaze.[64]

What we catch is a moment in the late eighteenth century when, accelerated by discoveries such as those at Pompeii and Herculaneum, the discipline of archaeology was about to take a shape different from traditional, text-based antiquarianism. At the same time, the emerging discipline was overshadowed by the kind of art-historical aesthetics and narrative implemented by Winckelmann. This submergence of classical archaeology into a kind of ancient art history (characterized by the "monumental philology" of the German archaeologist Eduard Gerhard)[65] prevented archaeology from becoming a radical alternative (in the sense of material culture studies) to the processing of the past by the literary discourse of history—an epistemological reconciliation[66] that has only been recently questioned by representatives of the *new archaeology*.[67]

VII. Archaeology, Presence, and Restoration

Richter interprets the antagonisms among classical readings of the Laocoön story as an opposition between beauty and the enhancement of pain. He couples this antinomy to those between the ideal and the real, the beautiful and the sublime, classic and baroque, symbol and allegory. To which I would add the antinomy between a historical and a genuinely archaeological reading of data, between narrative and a modular, discrete description. Until January 14, 1506, the *Laocoön* group had been imaginary in a different way: "Before the sixteenth century, no one had seen the *Laocoön* since antiquity, but all were assured that it was an ideal work of art, calling on the authority of Pliny."[68] Kenneth Clark reminds us of the supremacy of ekphrastic imagination, even temporally preceding its actual object: "Pliny's description of the *Laocoön* group had touched the imaginations of Renaissance artists and, even before its excavation, attempts had been made to draw what it could have been like."[69] For the longest time, artistic practice and aesthetic theory has been at odds with "the uneasy contradiction between an aesthetic ideal—the imaginary Laocoön as a repository of artists values and aspirations—and a corporeal real—the material statue in all its determinacy. . . . Only in the twentieth century has it become possible to stand in puzzlement before the statue."[70]

An archaeological difference was introduced in 1905 by Ludwig Pollak's discovery of a piece of that puzzle: the missing right arm of the Laocoön figure in Rome. It was restored to the Vatican original in 1957 by Filippo Magi, vice-director of the Vatican Museums, replacing the plaster supplement created by Giovanni Montorseli in 1523. "In this itself, the *Laocoön* as we know it is profoundly different from that of Goethe and Winckelmann," and still aesthetically misread by modern interpreters: "one might wonder to what extent the reconstruction depends on the idea of the *Laocoön*."[71]

VIII. Conclusion: Archaeology in the Archives

The question whether Lessing actually stood in puzzlement in front of the Vatican *Laocoön* group remains undecidable, between the lacunae of his diary and the non-discursive evidence of Warnstedt's financial accounts—an *argumentum ex silentio* that cannot be transformed easily into a kind of historic speech that would silence the archive of the past. If for Lessing the Italian journey was a journey into the interiority of the archive-library, its logistical interconnection is better reflected by a non-descriptive way of registering information. Navigating through datascapes keeps us aware of the fact that we are dealing with models of the past rather than its reconstruction.[72] The object presented here—Lessing's Italian diary—becomes an allegory of our own reading of the archive of the eighteenth century, which requires an archaeological, "cold" perception (in terms of Marshall McLuhan's media theory) as distinct from a heated historical imagination. We might say that "computing" combines both Warnstedt's kind of writing, which can be used to decipher Lessing's diary, and that described by Recha, the adopted daughter in Lessing's drama *Nathan the Wise*, as book-based knowledge: "dead signs imprinted on the brain." As a reaction formation, this causes prosopopoeic hallucinations when the archaeological perspective is replaced by historical interpretation. Witness Ritter-Santini's claim to be able to decode Lessing's silence on the *Laocoön* in the Roman pages of his "Italian Notebook."

> Among the books bought in Italy some were apt to "imprint dead signs on the brain," if, indeed, even a reader like Lessing was capable of freeing them from the prison of academic misunderstandings and restoring them to their lively, freshly discovered meaning.[73]

"Facts, not moralizing talk." With these words Karl-Philipp Moritz in 1783 asked for a scientific psychology in his journal *Gnothi sauton oder Magazin zur Erfahrungsseelenkunde*. But there is no firm ground for us to assign a single reason for Lessing's not mentioning a visit to the *Laocoön* in Rome when our only ground is an abyss in the archive. Franz Muncker cautions us not to conclude from this silence that Lessing did not actually have such Italian impressions; in fact "Lessing's Italian journey of 1775 and his written documentation can only serve for conclusions *ex negativo*."[74]

Most of Lessing's Italian notes in 1775 were bibliographical and academic extracts from a learned Italian journal called *Efemeridi*, which makes his diary a scrapbook linked to a literally hypertextual space.[75] According to the biography by his brother Karl, Lessing planned to edit his "Italian Notebook" in a more discursive way after a second journey, but Karl's assumption might already be a product of metahistorical imagination in a canonized Lessing myth of enlightenment. Let us not forget that for another contemporary, Johann Gottfried von Herder, it was normal to write the journal of his 1769 journey as a databank report, equating the empirical experience of traveling by navigating through a mass of information, a topography for which an overall classification system no longer existed.[76] Lessing himself preferred road metaphors to describe his intended edition of accidental scraps and notes on the arts, the *Hermaea*.[77] "When actual books do not fit in library catalogues any more, cognitive ruptures become evident": the worn-out library model that arranged knowledge according to academic *faculties* failed, and Lessing died while working out a new system for his Wolfenbüttel library in which he might integrate his Italian acquisitions.[78] His successor, Ernst Theodor Langer, was left to divine Lessing's program for rearranging the books—yet another blank that cannot be grasped by a perception based on narrative hypotheses.[79] One more gap in the archive of the eighteenth century structured as much by voids as by evidence. Although this may also be true for the archives of other periods, the specificity of data storage and processing (both visual and textual) around 1800 is marked by a fragile equivalence of discursive and non-discursive modes of representing reality: if these two modes were no longer integrated into a coherent whole by religious world views, they were not yet held together by the holistic ideologies of the nineteenth century.

For late eighteenth-century *savants*, who were increasingly confronted with an accumulation of unclassifiable data—Herder's *Hierzu immer Data*—an occasional omission could be a strategy to reduce complexity.[80] The next century invented a different medium to cope with the complexity of experience: the discourse of history in its emphatic philosophical sense that supplies data with a meaningful narrative vector and returns to the archive(s) from a different border.

Disparities between Part and Whole in the Description of Works of Art

I. Ekphrasis: Feeling and Knowing

My aim here is to address the particularities of a form of description that sits on the boundaries between scientific knowing and aesthetic experience, a boundary rather differently defined in the eighteenth century than it is now. But of course not entirely differently. Making sense of the distinctions and affinities between Enlightenment regimes of description and present-day ones was a pervasive concern of the conference that gave rise to this volume.

Specifically, I shall be exploring one of the most ambitious and influential exercises in the description of works of art in Enlightenment culture, Johann Joachim Winckelmann's densely wrought evocations of the beauty of famous pieces of antique statuary.[1] These descriptions were quite explicitly presented as guided by the dual imperatives of science and art. This is very evident in the first place from the context in which they were published. They were an important feature of Winckelmann's ambitious archaeological reconstruction of the history of ancient Greek and Roman art, *The History of the Art of Antiquity*, which first came out in 1764. As such, they were designed to direct the reader's attention to what was most significant and distinctive about the statues concerned, and also to make their beauty come alive before his or her eyes. Winckelmann claimed in his introductory comments that this new study was going to do two things previous antiquarian scholarship had almost entirely ignored—it would give a clear and accurate account of surviving works of antique art in their empirical particularity, and it would seek to make evident to the reader "in what their beauty consists."[2]

These elaborate descriptions of a few select "masterpieces," though integrated within his scholarly or scientific project, however, also stood apart from it. They come over as very different from the tabulation and analysis of empirical detail in most of the rest of the text, and they certainly stood apart for most of Winckelmann's contemporary readers, who usually encountered them as independent pieces of writing, as evocations of artistic beauty excerpted from their original context in an archaeological reconstruction of ancient Greek art.[3]

I am concerned here, however, not with the distinctions between Winckelmann's conventional scientific description and his affective evocations of the beauty of antique statuary, but rather with disparities emerging within the latter which have implications for our understanding both of eighteenth-century conceptions of art and of eighteenth-century "scientific" epistemology. What particularly intrigues me in Winckelmann's more ambitious descriptions is the intimation of an anxiety which surfaced from time to time in eighteenth-century culture, one concerning a possible disparity in "exact" empirical description between attending to and articulating individual details, and apprehending a larger totality. In elaborating a full description of an empirical phenomenon, does the accumulation of detail come together naturally to give a coherent picture of the whole, or does the successive definition of individual parts operate at a tangent to apprehending a phenomenon in its totality—and perhaps even get in the way of this? The form in which I have stated this perhaps betrays an anxiety which really only came into focus with the modern critique of nineteenth-century positivism. But it is one that, as other discussion in this volume testifies, intrudes in some form upon the apparently confident empiricism of practices of "scientific" description in Enlightenment culture, and is not just a back-projection of "our" concerns about the possibility of overload and confusion brought to a head by the seemingly unlimited capacities of a computerized recording of empirical phenomena.

The possible disparity between apprehending parts of a phenomenon, and seizing the phenomenon in its totality, emerged as a real issue in eighteenth-century culture where a whole field of scientific inquiry was at issue. In so much as such a disparity was an explicit concern of Winckelmann's, what bothered him was whether he would be able to build up a securely grounded picture of the essential significance of ancient art through accumulating a detailed and systematic knowledge of all its remaining traces.[4] At the same time, the strategies he deployed for negotiating between part and whole in his more elaborate and loaded descriptions of individual statues did impact significantly on his larger project. For Winckelmann, coming to grips with the distinctive forms of these statues was also to understand in general what it was that made antique art so exceptionally beautiful. They were prime pieces of evidence, a kind of intensified summation of what his whole enquiry was about—they embodied, as it were, the larger significance of antique art, the object of his study. What I am suggesting here is that the discrepancies intimated in these descriptions have important ramifications for Winckelmann's whole attempt to fashion a coherent picture of the art of antiquity. They were exercises in demonstrating, in the very fabric of an extended description, how a vivid sense of individual parts might relate to a sense of what made the whole so significant and alive.

But we still must not let drop from view that these descriptions were very different, both in character and function, from anything that would normally pass as scientific or scholarly description at the time. In them, Winckelmann was being self-consciously rhetorical, or literary as we should say now. These were not plain discourse, the discourse normally put to work in exact description, but discourse in the high or beautiful mode, designed to activate the reader's or listener's emotions.[5] Winckelmann took great pride in their literary crafting, and they fall within a long-standing rhetorical tradition of ekphrasis, exercises in the vivid conjuring up of visual images through verbal description. The point of ekphrasis as originally conceived was to offer a demonstration in the rhetorical power of language, not to provide an accurate verbal representation of things observed. Indeed, ekphrasis was often quite detached from the observation of any actual works of art.[6]

In the art world of the mid-eighteenth century, such evocative descriptions of works of art acquired a new significance. This was the moment when a tradition of critical writing about art in the modern sense was taking shape, fostered by the growing body of travel literature and the reviews of works of art at public exhibitions.[7] In such writing, the imperatives of traditional ekphrasis combined with the demands of exact empirical description. The purpose was to try and conjure up for the reader how a work of art looked and also to use the resources of language to convey something of its affective power. To offer an account of the beauty and expressive resonance of a work, it was not enough just to describe its visible forms. It was necessary to evoke the impact it would make on the viewer and to give an account of how and why it was beautiful. Such description had a semiotic as well as an aesthetic dimension. In a cultural context that did not share the modernist belief in the significance of pure form, a description that proceeded to characterize the beautiful parts or aspects of a work would also seek to decode the meaning of these motifs. The issue that interests me is one deeply engrained in such eighteenth-century practices of description, even if rarely explicitly recognized as problematic. A classic work of art, such as the masterpieces of antique statuary being described by Winckelmann, stood in the imagination of the time as the exemplary model of an entity whose parts fused together to form a single resonant whole. How would the elaboration of vivid detail in the description of such a statue or picture square with the evocation of it as a perfect whole that could be taken in at a glance?

Where Winckelmann came closest to offering a theory of his descriptive practice, he envisioned it as an allegorical decoding, a process in which the work was fragmented into a sequence of telling details, each with a distinct "higher" meaning which formed part of the work's ideal or allegorical significance. Yet he was also adamant—more so perhaps than any of his contemporaries or immediate predecessors who engaged in comparably ambitious ekphrasis—that the significance of the work concerned was also conveyed through the vision of an absolute oneness of form and meaning. This latter demand has made people see in Winckelmann's writing a premonition of the Romantic idea of a symbolic embodiment of meaning, and we could characterize the disparities in his descriptive practice as that between a traditional allegorical and a more modern symbolic mode.

The somewhat destabilizing dynamic involved, however, has remained very much a live issue in post-Romantic description of works of art, nowhere more so than where recent high modernist art is involved and such a premium is placed on the formal autonomy and unity of the work. I am thinking above all of the way art critical writing about the Minimalist work of the 1960s put a peculiar pressure on normally unselfconscious assumptions about the integrative relation between part and whole in an art work. On the one hand there was an unusual emphasis on the work immediately striking the viewer as a whole entity uninterrupted by part-by-part articulation, and on the other a strong feeling that its different elements or aspects should maintain their discrete identity. In Donald Judd's accounts of the significant new work of his American contemporaries, for example, there was simultaneously an absolute insistence on the work being viewed as one "single thing," and on the disparate nature of the immediate "specific sensations" it generated.[8] He was categorically antagonistic to compositional strategies which mediated between a vivid sense of the whole and a vivid sense of the part, strategies which produced an illegitimate "gradation or evening out of parts or aspects," subsuming them within the false logic of a deliberately contrived overall structure.[9]

II. The Vision of a Torso with no "Head, Arms and Legs"

Winckelmann took as the exemplary object for his descriptive project the *Torso Belvedere* (figs. 8 and 9), a statue divested precisely of those features which normally would be seen to mediate between the meaning of the individual parts and the character of the work as a whole, namely details of pose and facial feature which had a clearly identifiable expressive significance.[10] There was a logic, however, to Winckelmann's giving priority to the *Torso* over more fully articulated dramatic works such as the *Laocoön* (fig. 6, page 120). Through its very lack of integrity it could be reconstituted in the mind's eye as having a more rigorous formal unity than any image of a whole body.[11] At the same time, it would not suit his purposes if he presented the *Torso* simply as an image of perfect unity entirely divested of particular attributes and meanings. Instead, he offered a close reading of the work in which bodily forms not normally seen as articulating anything definite were singled out and associated with characteristics of the mythological figure he imagined the statue represented, namely a transfigured Hercules. This decoding was based on a highly speculative identification of the statue—the animal skin on which it was seated might be seen as a lion's skin, the traditional attribute of Hercules. Yet the *Torso* did not have the characteristic bruiserish physique of standard images of Hercules, so Winckelmann imagined that it must represent, not the mortal hero in the midst of his great deeds, but the purified and transfigured body of the immortalized figure of Hercules enjoying a state of bliss in the Garden of the Hesperides.[12]

In the description incorporated in the *History of the Art of Antiquity*, Winckelmann begins by singling out a series of evocative features of the work that could be associated with particular stories about Hercules' prowess.[13] He points to the absence of veins and sinews as indicating that this is a deified rather than a mortal body, no longer subject to fleshly needs. The pose as he reconstructs it, seated with back bent forward and upturned head supported on hand, represents a figure sunk in contemplation, at peace with himself, thinking back on his past deeds. The powerfully raised chest conjures up his trial of strength crushing the giant Geryon, and the strong suppleness of the thighs recalls his swiftness pursuing and overcoming the iron-footed stag, and wandering to the farthest reaches of the world.

But then the description takes a different turn, shifting from a singling out of identifiable motifs to a vivid but semantically indeterminate image of

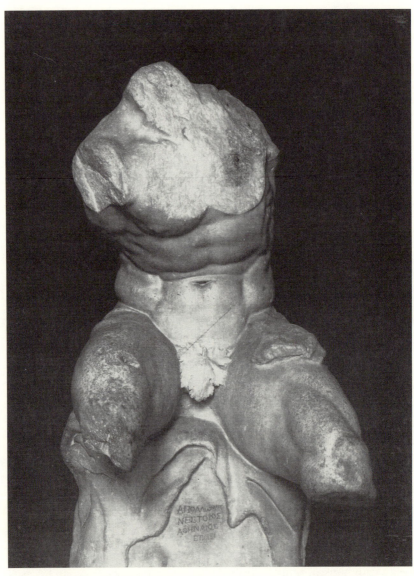

FIG. 8. *Torso Belvedere* (front view). The Vatican Museums, Rome. Photo: Ministero per i Beni e le Attività Culturali—Istituto Centrale per il Catalogo e la Documentazione—Fototeca Nazionale, Rome.

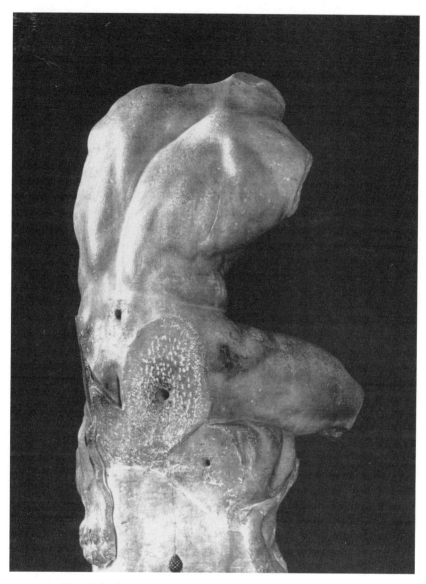

F I G . 9 . *Torso Belvedere* (rear view). The Vatican Museums, Rome. Photo:
Ministero per i Beni e le Attività Culturali—Istituto Centrale per il Catalogo e la
Documentazione—Fototeca Nazionale, Rome.

the whole statue's surface as a play of forms that defies exact characterization: "the artist will admire in the contours of this body the ever changing flowing of one form into the other, floating forms that rise and sink like waves and are engulfed in one another." These contours are so subtly modulated and intermingled, he explains, that they cannot even be pinned down through literal copying, let alone be given definition in a verbal description: "for [their] swing, whose direction one thinks to be able to follow, turns away imperceptibly, taking another direction that leads the hand astray."[14] He concludes with another shift back to empirical particularity—he comments with admiration on the softness of the skin and the perfectly balanced supple fleshiness of the muscles on the legs. But here we are no longer in a realm of higher allegorical meaning—our attention is entirely absorbed by an image of flawlessly beautiful flesh.

In this narrative, the essence of the figure seems to reside in the ideal yet still somewhat physical image of a perfectly modulated flow of curves melting without break into one another, framed by an allegory decoding the bodily traces of the hero's prowess on the one hand, and an image of the exquisitely toned musculature of the thighs on the other. An evocation of the statue's formal wholeness momentarily stalls the decoding of its significant aspects, effecting a caesura in, rather than a climax to, a definition of characteristic attributes of the mythic hero. And when the description does again re-engage with particulars, it plunges us into an erotic delectation of the figure's body rather than returning us to an uncovering of its higher meanings.

From our perspective, Winckelmann's close reading of the *Torso*'s forms has something particularly arbitrary about it because it is so evidently based on associations he himself conjures up between the statue and the figure of Hercules. Such an approach to "decoding" would have been taken for granted in the world of eighteenth-century classical scholarship. But a modern reader more than likely stalls at Winckelmann's starting point, the seemingly contingent identification of a relatively attributionless statue as the image of Hercules. There is also something quite arbitrary, even fanciful, about the way Winckelmann singles out striking aspects of the shaping of the *Torso* to construct a conventional allegorical narrative. Such decoding of bodily form is not mediated by convention in the way that an interpretation of the expressive significance of a gesture or facial expression on a more complete statue might be.[15]

But our awareness of the contingent nature of his decoding of the *Torso*'s meaning also enables us to gain a particular insight into the logic at work in his description. An intensified attentiveness to subtleties of bodily form is suggested through the associations conjured up with the stories about Hercules' heroic feats of strength. The logic of the associations seems not so much dictated by some coding of visual form as by the dynamic of a viewer's shifting and necessarily contingent engagement with different aspects of the statue. And just as in contemplating a statue, a viewer shifts gear between a focus on striking aspects of it and a sense of it as one single entity fully manifest before his or her eyes, so Winckelmann's descriptive narrative is guided by an imperative that echoes this movement, spelling out a series of resonant features alternating with a rather different image of the work as immediately felt whole.

The description is all the more intriguing for the instabilities and disparities that block a modern reader's direct identification with it. We almost cannot avoid being aware of the switch between responses to aspects of the statue which momentarily catch the attention, and the projection of an image of oneness which stands out as being dictated by a less arbitrary, more ideal imperative. For an eighteenth-century reader, the associations binding the former together would appear more natural and hence less contingent and more integrated with the "climactic" image of the statue as an ideal whole.

Such a patterning of the descriptive narrative recurs in the longer and more elaborate version of the *Torso* description Winckelmann included in the treatise on allegory he published in 1766.[16] But here it is more obsessive and insistent because it is repeated several times. He begins by wondering about the apparent impossibility of uncovering the original beauty and significance of a statue that lacks those characteristic features we normally find most immediately striking and expressive:

> How shall I be able to describe this work to you, seeing that it is deprived of the most beautiful and the most significant parts of the body. Like a mighty oak tree that has had its boughs and branches hacked off, and where the trunk alone remains, so this image of the hero sits there abused and mutilated—head, arms and legs and the upper part of the chest are missing.
> A first view will reveal nothing more than a defaced piece of stone; were you able to penetrate into the secrets of art, and contemplate this work with calm eyes, however, you will discover a wonder of art.

Winckelmann is promising to project the reader into a realm where he or she will be able to see into the full significance of this damaged relic. What initially looks little more than a battered lump of stone will be revealed as a complex and subtly articulated configuration of form evoking both the figure of Hercules the hero "in the midst of his deeds" and the divine form he took after his death and deification—"in this piece the hero and the god will simultaneously become manifest to you."

He then proceeds to elaborate on the significance of various aspects of the statue's forms—the powerful contours of the muscles are those of the hero who triumphed over the giants in battle, while the softness of their modulation betrays the lightness and suppleness of build which enabled Hercules to maneuver so fast he was able to overpower the ever metamorphosing river god Achelous in a wrestling match. Each deed of the mortal hero, he explains, is made manifest in particular aspects of the figure's body—the mountain-like form of the remaining right shoulder puts one in mind of the superlative strength which enabled Hercules to bear the entire weight of the world, while the impressive arching of the mightily raised chest embodies a physical power which once crushed the giant Geryon to death.

But the description suddenly enters a different register as it fixes on the beautiful modeling of the muscles on the left side of the torso. A generalized evocation of the finely tuned muscular forms interacting with one another dissolves into an abstract image of pure undulating surface in which the eye loses itself and all sense of articulated bodily shape is lost. The flow of gently modulated pulsing surfaces is likened to the barely perceptible rising and falling of waves on the surface of a calm sea. For a moment the elaboration of the shapes of the hero's body comes to a halt. As Winckelmann puts it: "Here I should like to hold still, so as to give our contemplation room for our perception to look into the depths of such an ever changing image of this side of the body; but the high beauties here are in inseparable fusion with one another."[17]

This again gives way to a renewed evocation of distinctive features of the figure's body, the firmness of the hips characterizing the hero who never bowed down to anyone, the strength and agility of the thighs making one think of his exhausting wanderings through the farthest reaches of the world. But the proliferating perceptions again stall as attention is transfixed by the pure beauty of the musculature on the back. Here again, the roving eye is cut short by the vision of an inhumanly abstract and beautiful modeling of surface that dispels any articulation of bodily form. It is as if we are looking at a fine landscape from afar, our view losing itself in the beautifully modulated spectacle, following the undulations of the hills flowing imperceptibly into the ever widening and narrowing meanderings of the valleys.

After a passage singling out further aspects of the statue's physique which tell of Hercules' legendary trials of strength, Winckelmann moves into another register of association, evoking the serene and blissful composure the hero enjoyed in afterlife, removed from violent action and the perturbations of mortal desire. In this way he can finish with an image of absolute perfection and beauty from which all signs of the feeling, acting mortal body he had been conjuring up earlier have been purged. The attentiveness to details of form and meaning is once more engulfed in an apprehension of form that defies articulation, this time very explicitly "ideal." We are not to think of it as in any way a functioning body "fed on mortal food and coarse elements: he receives the nourishment of the gods, and he seems only to enjoy, not to take things in, to be replete [völlig] without being filled out [angefüllt]." Now the earlier intimations of violence and strength are entirely obliterated. We have a vision of wholeness uncontaminated by differentiations of bodily function and shape, an inhuman perfection, both full and empty, vital and unanimated.

III. Allegory and Beauty—"an indescribable confusion"

Winckelmann's prominent placing of an elaborate description of this kind in a treatise on allegory may seem puzzling, almost perverse to a modern reader, and was quite at odds also with standard practices at the time. A torso so divested of conventional iconographical attributes was not something that even the most ingenious antiquarian scholars of the time would have chosen for a display of their skills of allegorical decoding. Yet the curious juxtaposition of allegory and ekphrasis offers some intriguing insights into how Winckelmann himself conceptualized his description of the *Torso*, which he introduced as follows:

> By way of conclusion I attach here the description of the Torso of Hercules that I have made public elsewhere, because this description can as it were be seen as allegorical in view of the presumed and supposed intentions of the artist in each part of it.[18]

The textual contortions are important—Winckelmann is offering the *Torso* description as an exemplary allegorical reading of a major classical work of art, and yet is also suggesting that this description cannot quite be seen as a conventional allegory—it is only "as it were to be seen as allegorical."

Equally, Winckelmann was also quite explicitly claiming that his description of the *Torso* offered a kind of exemplary allegorical decoding of the significant features of a statue. When spelling out how the subtly modulated shaping of the figure's body could be interpreted as evoking the capacities Hercules displayed in his heroic exploits, he wrote: "In every part of the body is revealed, as in a picture, the whole hero engaged in a particular deed, and just as you can perceive the correct purpose in the structure of a palace, so you can see what use every part has been put to and in which deed."[19]

Yet the semiotic process involved is not at all the same as that in the other allegories he itemizes and discusses in the rest of his treatise. Here, and only here, does he seek to ground allegory in an immediately affective and what we might call naturalistic reading of bodily form. Elsewhere the treatise is concerned with analyzing the conventionalized motifs or attributes by means of which figures in classical art were endowed with a specific significance, and not with the formal subtleties in the rendering of bodily form which might be expressive of particular qualities. His treatise on allegory is concerned with decoding signs rather than with inferring mental or moral attributes from the physical appearance of a figure. Where bodily form enters into consideration, it is only where it can be deemed to have the character of a clearly defined motif with a specific meaning, for example, the unusual, somewhat flattened form of the ear occurring on ancient images of heroes and athletes, which Winckelmann interpreted as a sign of the figure concerned having been a participant in a form of combat combining wrestling and boxing called the Panacration.[20] As he himself makes explicit, his treatise on allegory is concerned with the decoding of signs whose logic is based on the usages of ancient culture rather than on any perceived connection between sign and meaning which might exist for the modern viewer.[21]

In an allegorical image, he explains, there is inevitably a disjunction between the signifying motif and the idea it evokes:

> the true meaning of the word allegory . . . is saying something different from what one wishes to indicate, aiming in another direction from that in which the expression seems to be going.[22]

Allegory was important for Winckelmann because, as he already put it in his earliest published treatise on the visual arts, *Thoughts on the Imitation of the Greeks*, it was the only mechanism whereby "things that are not perceptible to the senses" can be figured through things that are.[23] While the success of an allegory for him depended upon a moment of illumination when the image seemed directly to conjure up the conceptual entity to which it referred, there was nevertheless a structural disparity between the two, one that made allegory essentially paradoxical—like a good baroque conceit.

Is the *Torso* description then being presented by him as an example of how a classical figure might be read "as it were" allegorically, its meaning almost directly manifest to a modern viewer familiar with the better known stories of ancient mythology but not particularly at home with the allegorical motifs of ancient culture? Was this perhaps an instance where the modern viewer could experience the force of the principle Winckelmann enunciated at the outset of his treatise, namely that "every allegorical image and sign should contain within itself the distinguishing features of the thing that is meant, and the simpler this is, the more comprehensible it will become, just as a simple magnifying glass shows things more clearly than a composite one. An allegory should as a result be understandable in itself, and have no need of an accompanying inscription."[24]

At several points Winckelmann returns to a paradox that is of great significance for his supposedly exemplary allegorical reading of the *Torso Belvedere*. In theory, he explains, the best allegories are the simplest ones, and are composed of a single figure that has one clear meaning. Yet he recognizes that this demand is unworkable once the meaning to be projected is at all complex. The latter will involve the use of several attributes that will need to be read sequentially. Those who looked to the ancients to provide a model for modern allegory like Winckelmann would often cite as proof of the ancients' mastery of allegorical signification Pliny's description of a famous image of the Athenian people which supposedly embodied their twelve very different and contradictory qualities in a single figure. But Winckelmann pointedly criticized this as attempting the impossible. It could not work, he explains, unless the figure incorporated a separate symbol for each quality being referred to, and then inevitably, "an indescribable confusion" would result.[25]

Where does this leave the *Torso* description? Winckelmann fixes on the *Torso* as a work where the absence of identifiable attributes would at first sight seem to defy conventional allegorical decoding, and yet whose suggestively charged beauty might nevertheless be made to conjure up a rich array of associations for a modern viewer. There is perhaps a danger, in terms of his own theory of allegory, that his interpreting its battered, almost featureless remains as a dense web of signs evoking the character and deeds of Hercules—every bit as elaborate as any conventional multi-figure allegory—could produce an "indescribable confusion." Certainly such confusion would have resulted had the sculpture offered the image of a figure cluttered with a separate attribute for each deed of Hercules conjured up in Winckelmann's description. The point, however, is that the allegorical attributes Winckelmann momentarily evokes cannot be fixed, but instead melt into one another, like the flow of contour in the modeling of the torso's musculature, thus creating the effect of a shifting, relatively free and also contingent play of vivid associations.

But something else is also going on which I want to dwell on for a moment. Winckelmann's framing of the *Torso* description intimates, if partly unconsciously, that a straightforward allegorical decoding of a classical masterpiece would not be quite adequate to representing its singular beauty as a work of art. At the same time, he also implies that any viable description of such a statue is in some way going to be allegorical. Any intent looking at it cannot be represented solely as fixation on the abstract essence of its beauty, but also entails a contingent, shifting attentiveness to individual aspects of its form, which momentarily strike the viewer as significant. Another way of putting this would be to say that the symbolic identity between form and meaning that Winckelmann projects so suggestively is presented by him as but one moment within a traditional allegorizing of the work of art—one whose fragmenting logic destabilizes the work's symbolic wholeness.

In *The Origins of German Tragic Drama*, Walter Benjamin made the point that Winckelmann adumbrated a conception of the classical ideal as plastic symbol which had affinities with the views of a later generation of German theorists, such as the mythographer Friedrich Creuzer, who insisted on the "difference between symbolic and allegorical representation": "The latter signifies merely a general concept, or an idea which is merely different from itself; the former is the very incarnation and embodiment of the idea."[26] But Winckelmann himself never made an issue of this difference—far from it. As Benjamin recognized, Winckelmann remained deeply attached to Baroque allegory.[27] My point is that the interest for us in Winckelmann's more ambitious descriptions lies precisely in their highlighting a discrepancy which continues to disrupt later regimes of description, even where these sought to distance themselves from traditional allegory.

IV. Description and Desire

We have seen how Winckelmann's descriptions of the *Torso Belvedere* conjure up an image of undifferentiated oneness of beautiful form and also offer a succession of more contingent and particularized projections of form and meaning that echo a viewer's necessarily shifting focus of response when confronting the work. The image of wholeness does not so much mark a climax which absorbs within itself the preceding series of allegorical significations—it is not the underlying meaning which makes them all fuse together—but exists at quite another level.

Winckelmann was too attentive to the unstable conflation of pressures which drove him to his close engagement with the masterpieces of antiquity, and also to the competing demands of vivid sensual particularity and ideal wholeness inherent in the notion of a classical work of art, to allow himself to configure a simple narrative of transcendence out of his descriptions of ancient sculpture.[28] That he had a quite conscious awareness of the tension between offering a comprehensive delineation of parts and conveying a convincing sense of the whole is evident from the traces he left of the process of composing his *Torso* description. The fullest version was one he himself designated as incomplete when he first published it in 1759. Here he indicated that it still remained for him fully to define the particularities of the artistic form of the work.[29] Yet this was an ambition he had in effect already largely abandoned. The published description edits out much of the detailed characterization of specific aspects of the statue found in his early drafts.[30] It was as if he felt that too extensive a part-by-part itemization might not add up to anything significant. Rather than aiming to elaborate a comprehensive definition in words of the work's characteristic aspects, he instead singled out a few particularly resonant features that could be made to evoke a shifting pattern of intensified responses to the work. In the much-condensed version of the description which he published in *The History of the Art of Antiquity*, he pared down the allegorical particulars to the point where he could be even more sure that the image of wholeness would stand out and not be lost from sight.

There is another point I want to highlight here, and that is the peculiar conflation of knowing and desiring evident in the narrative dynamic of the *Torso* description. The repetitive and forever partly frustrated engagement with the object moves to the rhythm of both a scientific and erotic fixation—the two main driving forces of the ambitious form of ekphrasis in which Winckelmann was engaged. Contingent moments of fixation on particularly resonant and vivid details, the moments of differentiation without which a sense of the object in its empirical reality could not be grasped, oscillate with moments of simple oneness promising a kind of perfect union with the object where any resistant concrete particularity melts away. The disparity between the two levels of engagement keeps the descriptive narrative going as it forever seeks to seize and define the object and them merge with it in an experience of undifferentiated oneness. To put this disparity in terms that relate to the images Winckelmann conjures up in his *Torso* description, what does the image of a powerfully muscled and sexy male body, whose forms betray the kinds of strength Hercules displayed in his struggles as a mortal hero, have to do with a vision of perfectly harmonious and softly modulated form, evocative of a state of absolute bliss? That the latter image is suspended in a realm of perfection set quite apart from a body still redolent of the capacity for acts of "brutality" and "uncontrollable desire" is integral to the logic of Winckelmann's description.[31]

The disparity is heavily overdetermined, but one of its more significant determinations has to do with regimes of description, with an acting out verbally of the ambitions and limits of a desire to seize and evoke an art object in all its fullness, in both its fullness as concrete shape and its fullness as object of desire. This dynamic is one perhaps very particular to modern art, and to modern art history, but it also echoes a larger dynamic at work in the modern scientific questing to grasp things. Winckelmann's most ambitious descriptions stage a disparity which neither aesthetic theory nor scientific epistemology in the eighteenth century could quite cope with, a disparity between the shifting and necessarily contingent fixations on particular aspects of an object, and a perfectly satisfying grasp of it as a whole. The latter might just be an illusory ideal, something which grows out of an inner desire, out of one's sense of lack in the manifold of concrete particularity, and which has no substantial grounding in the outside world. The object as one desires to have it, not the changing partial aspects of the object that strike one in one's encounter with it as empirical phenomenon.

The Undescribed

Horizons of the Known

Between Mechanism and Romantic *Naturphilosophie*

Vitalizing Nature and Naturalizing Historical Discourse in the Late Enlightenment

In 1946 Max Horkheimer claimed in an essay that "the collapse of a large part of the intellectual foundation of our civilization is to a certain extent the result of technical and scientific progress."[1] Horkheimer located the origins of this demise—whose process he characterized as "the self-destructive tendency of Reason"—in the Enlightenment. This line of analysis was later expanded and amplified by many commentators: post-modernists who rebel against the so-called "hegemony of Enlightenment rationality," some feminists who decry the Enlightenment's supposed elevation of universality over distinctness, and "converted" philosophers of science, such as Stephen Toulmin, who seek to uncover Modernity's outmoded hidden agenda by searching out the political and social forces that led to its inception. Despite the vast differences separating these critics and the multiple tones of major and minor they sound, the indictment is clear. The Enlightenment in its fascination with science and universalizing reason sired such movements as gender and racial discrimination, colonialism, and totalitarianism.

These are strong words. For students of the Enlightenment there seems to be a radical breach between what is meant by the central signifiers in this critique and what we perceive. Clearly, the major focus in these attacks is the Enlightenment's supposed worship of science, reason, and universality, of a form of power/knowledge, that is invariably characterized in the singular. And we all know what that singular suggests: the triumph in and by the Enlightenment of a mathematically based science, founded upon certain essential presuppositions concerning matter, method, and explanation whose reign has lasted until today. Yet when one begins to query what was really implied beneath this all-powerful engine of cultural and social change, the picture becomes much more hazy, complicating and confusing the new master narratives that are now being forged, and opening, I believe, fascinating alternatives to evaluate what is often called the Enlightenment project.

This is certainly true for the manner in which nature was interpreted in the Enlightenment and how those interpretations were deployed in discourses dealing with human activities. Recently historians of eighteenth-century science have begun to question the assumption that the natural philosophy of the period can be reduced to mathematical mechanism.[2] It is usually conceded that during the first half of the Enlightenment, roughly from the late 1680s to the 1740s, this form of science, usually called Newtonianism, became dominant. During that period, the central project of natural philosophy had been to incorporate the methods and assumptions of formal mathematical reasoning into explanations for natural phenomena. Its overriding impulse was to transform contingent knowledge into certain truth, to reduce the manifold appearances of nature to simple principles. In this process leading proponents of the mechanical philosophy of nature proposed a new definition of matter, established methodological and explanatory procedures to incorporate this definition into a viable vision of science, and evolved an epistemology that authorized these procedures. Matter's essence was streamlined and simplified: it was defined as homogeneous, extended, hard, impenetrable, movable, and inert. The result, in Horkheimer's words was that: "Nature lost every vestige of vital independent existence, all value of its own. It became dead matter—a heap of things."[3]

By the middle of the eighteenth century, however, some of the core assumptions of this new language of nature were no longer considered satisfying or self-evident. For many younger intellectuals mechanism's very success made it suspect, for the brave new world of seventeenth-century mechanism was very easily adapted to support political absolutism, religious orthodoxy, and established social hierarchies.[4] Joined to that was an increasing crisis of assent, expressed in a wave of mid-century skepticism directed against the spirit of systems, against a one-sided reliance upon abstract reasoning in constructing a coherent picture of reality. For leading thinkers of the late Enlightenment, deductive philosophy was deemed incapable of accounting for nature's vast variety. David Hume announced this theme in his essay on the skeptic.

> There is one mistake, to which philosophers seem liable, almost without exception; they confine too much their principles, and make no account of that vast

variety, which nature has so much affected in all her operations. . . . Our own mind being narrow and contracted, we cannot extend our conception to the variety and extent of nature; but imagine, that she is as much bounded in her operations, as we are in our speculation.[5]

Hume's skeptical analysis of causation was but one instance of the re-evaluation of mechanical natural philosophy. George-Louis Leclerc Buffon's attack upon the introduction of mathematical principles into the core of natural philosophical reasoning was probably more typical. In the introduction to the *Histoire naturelle*, Buffon drew a distinction between abstract and physical truths. The first were imaginary products of human invention. The second were real: they existed in nature and were the object of human inquiry. Mathematical proofs belonged to the first category, which were founded upon arbitrarily accepted logical principles. These, in turn, were used to generate equally arbitrary, though more complex principles. All were joined by a method of definition whereby consistency was maintained by rigorously excluding anything that did not agree with the first abstract principle. Physical truths, in contradistinction, were based on things that had actually occurred. They were more than mere constructs of human reason, forever open to manipulation. "They do not stand in our power."[6] In order to understand physical truths, the researcher had to compare and observe similar sets of past occurrences. Science, according to this view, was the description and understanding of real things that have taken place in the world. For both Buffon and Hume, understanding connections in nature was based on repeated historical observations of succession. In Hume's definition, cause "is *an object, followed by another, and where all the objects, similar to the first, are followed by objects of the second.*"[7] In late eighteenth-century terms, the new science was to be a science of facts, observation, and controlled inference.

The mid-eighteenth-century skeptical critique of hypothetical thinking elevated the contingent over the coherent. It became a commonplace that all human knowledge was extremely constricted, because of both its reliance upon sense impressions and its limited scope. If humans were endowed with reason, its power to pierce the veil of the unknown was greatly circumscribed. At the same time, many late Enlightenment thinkers surrendered the idea that nature's operations could be comprehended under the rubric of a few simple, all-encompassing laws. Variety and similarity replaced uniformity and identity as the terms most associated with nature's products. Hume made this clear in his *Enquiry Concerning Human Understanding* where he denied all concepts of inherent identities. Identical things appear so only because we have been accustomed by habit to consider them so. "But there is nothing in a number of instances, different from every single instance, which is supposed to be exactly similar; except only, that after a repetition of similar instances, the mind is carried by habit, upon the appearance of one event, to expect its usual attendant, and to believe, that it will exist."[8]

Nature not only was seen as complex, it also was considered to be in continuous movement. As one author stated, "the world is a theater of continual revolutions," in which old forms of existence are replaced by new ones.[9] In short, nature had a history. This triple movement—the limiting of reason's competence (producing a wide-ranging epistemological modesty), the expansion of nature's complexity, and the historicization of nature—set a new agenda for late Enlightenment natural philosophers. To paraphrase Hume, they were required to rethink the meaning of the terms "*power, force, energy* and *connexion.*"[10]

I.

Generally, one can discern two broad late eighteenth-century strategies designed to satisfy the objections raised by the skeptical critique of reductive rationalism and uniformity. The first, and best known, was formulated by neo-mechanists such as Jean LeRond d'Alembert, Joseph-Louis La Grange, Pierre-Simon La Place and Condorcet, and usually guided by the physical sciences. Though retaining the mechanists' definition of matter as inert, they limited mathematics' role in describing nature to an instrument of discovery instead of considering it a model of reality. In so doing, they put aside those debates concerning the ultimate composition of matter,[11] or the definition of force,[12] which had animated early eighteenth-century thinkers. Rather, they developed the mathematics of probability as the surest guide to direct observational reason, while maintaining an epistemological modesty concerning the truth claims of these activities.

The second response to the skeptical critique was proposed by a loose group of thinkers, less frequently studied, though extremely numerous, whom I call, for want of a better term, Enlightenment vitalists. Their inquiries usually centered on the fields of chemistry, geology, the life sciences, and natural history. Unlike the neo-mechanists, they sought to reformulate the concept of matter, along with those of force, power, and connection in their construction of a science that respected natural variety, dynamic change, and the epistemological consequences of skepticism.

For the vitalists, the basic failure of mechanism was its inability to account for the existence of living matter. Mechanists had posited a radical separation between mind and matter that only the intervention of God could heal, either as the universal occasion for all phenomena or as the creator of a pre-established harmony between mind and matter. This mind/body dichotomy was, according to Stephen Toulmin, the "chief girder in the framework of Modernity, to which all the other parts were connected."[13] Enlightenment vitalists sought to dissolve this dichotomy by positing the existence in living matter of active or self-activating forces, which had a teleological character. Living matter was seen as containing an immanent principle of self-movement whose sources lay in the active powers which resided in matter itself. Thus, we encounter natural philosophers vitalizing the world with living forces such as elective affinities, vital principles, sympathies, and formative drives, reminiscent of the living world of the Renaissance. Rather than considering nature to be Horkheimer's "heap of things," Enlightenment vitalists envisioned it as a teeming interaction of active forces revolving around each other in a developmental dance.

The German physiologist, comparative anatomist, and anthropologist Johann Friedrich Blumenbach provided a typical example. In the complex composition of organized matter (the term usually assigned to living matter), he discerned a number of "common or general vital energies that exist more or less, in almost all, or at least in a great many parts of the body."[14] The foremost of these was the *Bildungstrieb*, which Blumenbach defined as a power that directs the formation of bodies after the miracle of conception, prevents them from destruction, and compensates them through reproduction for any mutilations the body may incur.[15] In addition to these vital powers, Blumenbach posited another vital energy, "namely the *vita propria*, or specific life: under which denomination I mean to arrange such powers as belong to certain parts of the body, destined for the performance of peculiar functions."[16] According to him, "virtually every fibral in the living body possessed a vital energy inherent in itself."[17] An organized body consisted of a complex conjunction of energies and forces of varying intensities and functions that could not be reduced to a single dominating principle. The living body was a constituent assembly of forces.

By reintroducing active, goal-directed forces into nature, Enlightenment vitalists were compelled to reassess their methodological and explanatory procedures. Their conception of matter dissolved the strict distinction between observer and observed; both were related within a much larger conjunction of living matter. Relation, *rapport*, or *Verwandschaft* replaced aggregation as a defining principle of matter. Identity and non-contradiction became degrees of relation and similarity. The world of living matter consisted of a circle of relations, which, seen from the human vantage point, radiated out to touch all forms of matter. The constituent parts of living matter formed a "synergy" in which each conjoined particle was influenced by every other and the *habitus* in which they existed.[18] By emphasizing the centrality of interconnection, Enlightenment vitalists modified the concept of cause and effect. In the world of living nature, each constituent part of an organized body was both cause and effect of the other parts. All forces were symbiotically linked. Further, by re-introducing goal into living nature, Enlightenment vitalists made it the efficient cause of development. An explanation for something's existence took the form of a narrative modeled upon the concept of stage-like development or epigenesis, in which a body evolves through stages from a point of generation. Unique creation and true qualitative transformation were central to the vitalists' vision of living nature.[19]

These shifts in natural philosophic assumptions led Enlightenment vitalists to construct an epistemology capable of validating them. True to the skeptical critique of causation and forces, the vitalists agreed that active life forces could not be seen directly, nor could they be measured. They were "occult powers" in the traditional sense of the term, not as modified by Isaac Newton, who insisted on their quantification.[20] At best outward signs, whose meaning could only be grasped indirectly, announced them. This language of nature reintroduced the topos of locating real reality as something that lurked within a body. Understanding entailed a progressive descent into the depths of observed reality, using signs as the markers to chart the way. Thus, Enlightenment vitalists reintroduced the idea of semiotics as one of the methods to decipher the secrets of nature.

The basic epistemological problem was to understand the meaning of these signs and how to perceive the interaction of the individual yet linked active forces without collapsing one into the other. To resolve this problem Enlightenment vitalists called for a form of understanding that combined the individualized elements of nature's variety into a harmonic conjunction that recognized both nature's unity and diversity. The methods adopted to implement this program were analogical reasoning and comparative analysis.

Analogical reasoning became the functional replacement for mathematical analysis. With it one could discover similar properties or tendencies between dissimilar things that approximated natural laws without dissolving the particular in the general. The fascination for analogies was strengthened by a general preference for functional analysis, in which outward form was subordinated to activity. Comparative analysis reinforced the concentration upon analogical reasoning. It allowed one to consider nature as composed of systems having their own character and dynamics, yet demonstrating similarities not revealed by the consideration of concrete manifestations. Comparison's major task was to see similarities and differences and mediate among them, finding analogies that were not immediately apparent.

In pursuing this program a further epistemological problem arose. If nature was unity in diversity, how could one choose which to emphasize? When should one concentrate upon the concrete singularity and when should one cultivate generalizing approaches? The proposed answer was to do both at once, allowing the interaction between them to produce a higher form of understanding than provided either by simple observation or by discursive logic. This type of understanding was called divination, intuition, or *Anschauung*. Its operation employed the image of mediation, of continually moving back and forth from one to the other, letting each nourish and modify the other. Buffon described this practice in the introduction to his *Histoire naturelle*: "the love of the study of nature supposes two seemingly opposite qualities of the mind: the wide-ranging views of an ardent mind that embraces everything with one glance, and the detail-oriented laboring instinct that concentrates only on one element."[21]

This mediation was supposedly mirrored in the physical world through the action of the life forces. Blumenbach, for example, argued that the *Bildungstrieb* successfully mediated between the "two principles . . . that one had assumed could not be joined, the teleological and the mechanical."[22] Friedrich Schiller, who was trained as a physician, made a similar claim, in his first medical dissertation, for a force that mediated between mind and matter. It was "a force [that] in fact exists between matter and mind. This force is quite distinct from the world and the mind." It was, he claimed, "a force that is spiritual on the one hand and material on the other, an entity that is penetrable on the one hand and impenetrable on the other."[23] Correct understanding formed an analogue to this force as it moved from the concrete to the intellectual and back, mediating in a manner that discursive logic would deny.

In this movement, however, understanding passed through a third, hidden, and informing agent that was, in effect, the ground upon which all reality rested. This hidden middle element, opaque, un-seeable, yet essential was called by such terms as the internal mold (Buffon), prototype (Jean-

Baptiste Robinet), *Urtyp* (Johann Wolfgang von Goethe), or *Haupttypus* (Johann Gottfried Herder). Some writers used the image of a magnetic field to give it visual representation. It was constituted by the magnetic poles, united them, but did not submerge them in a reductive unity. The area of its greatest effect was the middle, where the field encompassed the largest area.

For us, this model of apprehension is difficult to perceive, for it flies in the face of what we consider rational, logical, or scientific. I believe it points to an attempt to answer the skeptical critique of rationalism by seeking to go beyond binary systems of logic and explanation. Binary systems assume that the distance between signifier and signified can be collapsed, that reason can look at the world and it would look back reasonably. What these late Enlightenment thinkers seemed to prefer was a ternary system, which introduced something between sign and signified, what Herder called the *Mittelbegriff*, through which everything was refracted but which could never be seen, grasped, or directly identified. In short, they argued for a harmonic view of nature that organized reality around the figures of ambiguity and paradox central to the skeptical stance, a position that was reluctant to reduce one thing to another but allowed them to be allied. Vitalists often expressed this harmonic ideal in creative oxymorons such as Buffon's "internal mold," or Schiller's concept of "material ideas," which verbally reconstructed the paradoxical *rapports*.

How did the Enlightenment vitalists validate this theory of understanding? What allowed them to proclaim that the tools of analogical reasoning, comparison, and intuitive understanding were objective? The problem was especially acute because of the blurring between object and observer. But it was precisely this mingling that served to justify this approach to science. They argued that humans, being part of living nature, could acquire a living knowledge of nature's processes through sympathetic understanding. Similarity and relationship were the vehicles of understanding, which, by passing through the extended middle, ensured the truth values of these endeavors.

This harmonic view of reality formed the essence of the late Enlightenment vitalists' vision of nature and humanity, differentiating it from early eighteenth-century mechanism and later Romanticism. This view accounted for their fascination with extremes—boundaries and limits—and their mediations. Harmony, the joining of opposites within an expanded middle generated by reciprocal interaction, served as the norm and desired end of each natural process, though that dynamic was continually in motion, leading to ever-changing harmonic combinations. Living nature then became the site where freedom and determinism merged. Its description invoked images and metaphors either drawn from the moral sphere or directly applicable to it. Horkheimer claimed that the "inner logic of science itself tends towards the idea of one truth which is completely opposed to the recognition of such entities as the soul and the individual."[24] Enlightenment vitalists sought to reintroduce entities such as soul and individuality into the inner core of scientific thinking.

For that very reason, Enlightenment vitalism had definite appeal to late Enlightenment thinkers who strove to create what we would call humanistic disciplines by naturalizing their objects of inquiry and explanatory strategies. These elective affinities were further strengthened by the fact that scientific questions were central to the era's discourse. The "great analogy of nature," as Herder termed it, was considered the essential reference point for discussions concerning truth, beauty, and human organization. Therefore any substantial change in a philosophy of nature implied an equally strong realignment of social, political, religious, and cultural sensibilities.

II.

Given the restrictions of space it would be foolhardy to try to demonstrate how the language of vitalism informed the many attempts to create humanistic disciplines in the late Enlightenment. Therefore, I shall concentrate upon one discipline, history. In so doing, I hope that the loss of comprehensive coverage will be compensated by more analytic precision. For I intend to show not just that the historians borrowed a number of metaphors from vitalism, but that they translated that model to serve the ends of constructing a discipline, endowed with its own narrative procedures.

Buffon, in the introduction to the *Histoire naturelle* and also in his *Les Époques de la nature*, drew a direct analogy between natural history and the history of civil society. Both followed analogous methods in attempting to fix specific points in space and time and to chart the moral and physical revolutions that took place on the earth.[25] Throughout the late eighteenth century, historians would take up this analogy and proclaim it their duty to compose a "natural history" of human endeavors, as Herder's definition of universal history illustrates. "The whole of human history is a pure natural history of human powers, actions, and drives located in space and time."[26] The analogy's appeal was founded on the shared belief that everything in the world was ordered by eternal principles. As Herder proclaimed: "The power that thinks and acts in me is according to its nature so eternal a power as that which holds the sun and stars together."[27]

But the laws that governed the human world were not those of physics, which just dealt with Horkheimer's "heaps of things." Adam Ferguson described the nature of this system and the connection of its parts as follows:

> parts that constitute the system of nature, like the stones of an arch, support and are supported; but their beauty is not of the quiescent kind. The principles of agitation and of life combine their effects in constituting an order of things, which is at once fleeting and permanent . . . The whole is alive and in action: the scene is perpetually changing; but in its changes exhibits an order more striking than could be made to arise by mere position or description of any forms entirely at rest.[28]

The goal then was to understand and describe this order of things.

How was this to be done? Let us listen to Ferguson again. For him the material world was a system of "signs and expressions," created by God, but calling for human interpretation.

> It is a magnificent but regular discourse, composed of parts and subdivisions, proceeding, in the original or creative mind, from generals to particulars; but in the observer, to be traced by a laborious induction from the indefinite variety of particulars, to some notion of the general mold of forms in which they are cast.[29]

Included in this vast semiotic field were the past actions and creations of mankind. The historian's task was to order and make sense of these signs, to place them within a system of meaning, and to evolve an adequate way of presenting these hard-won insights.

In late eighteenth-century language this imperative clearly implied that history was to be made scientific, for to systematize was to scientize. But what constituted this system? The German historian August Ludwig Schlözer attempted to answer it. Schlözer drew a distinction between two types of ordering procedures, which he called an *Aggregate* and a *System*. An *Aggregate* arises when "the whole human race is cut up in parts, all of these parts numbered, and the available information about each is correctly presented."[30] But such a picture was unsatisfactory because it did not "give a living representation of the whole."[31] An *Aggregate* corresponded to Ferguson's order of stones in an arch. Its underlying principle was mechanistic. One had to go beyond mechanism, Schlözer argued, and create a true system. This is achieved by looking at things with "a generalizing vision that encompasses the whole; this powerful vision transforms the aggregate into a system, brings all the states of the earth together in a unity."[32] Schlözer's ideal was modeled upon Buffon's characterization of the generalizing view of the natural historian, which, while paying close attention to the particular, encompasses everything in one glance.[33] The goal for both was to establish a real connection that would make clear the "natural, immediate, and obvious connections" between events.[34]

The vitalist call for constructing a natural system was adopted and complemented by its program of proceeding from outward signs to inner reality, designed to achieve a comprehension of the unseen, active, and penetrating forces of living nature and ultimately to acquire an apprehension of the "general mold of forms," an English translation of Buffon's *moule intérieur*. In a similar sense, Herder argued that the historian's goal was to apprehend "the great drama of active forces."[35] But this was not easy to observe, for the major players were hidden from view, performing on a stage located within the depths of living matter. "The ground of the observable lies in the inner, for everything is formed through organic forces which develop from the inner outwards."[36] Real reality could only be perceived through analogical comparisons whose efficacy and truth value were guaranteed according to Herder by two things. First, the universal circle of similarities and interconnections validated our projection of self upon other. The human was, in effect, a composite of all the types of living things that have existed. Humans recapitulated the history of organized life. Hence, they were able to project their understanding onto these forms. Second, this projection was true because it was refracted through and reflected the extended middle—the invisible but organizing *Haupttypus*.[37] For these two reasons analogies became our most powerful analytic tools; they alone gave us the "key to penetrate into the essence of things."[38]

In constructing their research and explanatory agendas, late Enlightenment historians sought to mediate between the dual operations of investigating structure and process, place and time. Structural analysis located the object of inquiry within the total field of external and internal synchronic relations, while the inquiry into process dealt with the "history of the species."[39] According to the first assumption, every social body was influenced by the physical and social environment in which it existed. Thus, historians looked to climate, soil, geography, social and economic organization, government, religion, "opinions," and culture as those elements which form and limit the body social.[40] The specific configurations of cultures and societies resulting from this mediation were treated as "acquired characteristics" or habits. They were ingrained determinants that defined the "characteristics" of a social body, but were not essential qualities. They could be changed.

These external categories did not directly imprint themselves upon the "organized body." Rather, they were redirected or mediated by the active principles residing within that body. Such active powers were seen as analogues to the specific forces in an individual body. Sometimes they were defined as the principles of an activity (e.g. commerce, language) or as the spirit of a group (middle class). In cultures as a whole these powers were considered to reside in those peoples or groups whose activities were hidden from normal observation, neglected by traditional historical discourse.

In emphasizing the action of unseen hidden powers, Enlightenment historians argued that living matter contained an immanent principle of self-movement, which acted directionally. Hence all organized bodies were, as Ferguson called them, "progressive" natures. "Progressive natures are subject to the vicissitudes of advancement or decline," he wrote, "but are not stationary, perhaps in any period of their existence. Thus, in the material world, subjects organized, being progressive, when they cease to advance, begin to decline." By analogy, intelligence and human society were also "progressive natures," continually advancing or declining. Unlike stationary (mechanical) bodies which "are described by the enumeration of co-existent parts . . . subjects progressive are characterized by the enumeration of steps, in the passage from one form of state or excellence to another." This explanation was clearly modeled upon epigenesis in which a body evolves through stages from its point of creation. Each stage in the process had its own integrity, none more privileged or revealing than the other.

But not all progressive development was continuous. At critical junctures it proceeded through a series of changes, "revolutions" in which outward form was altered drastically, followed by gradual development in the newly formed shape. The critical transitions in this process were marked by "astonishing revolutions in almost the whole economy of its system."[41] The image often used for these revolutions was metamorphosis. Schlözer confirmed these views: "The best periodization in the history of states is, without a doubt, the genetic, which details the step-like growth and decline of states (their metamorphoses)."[42]

Late eighteenth-century historians found the idea of epigenesis fascinating because it assumed the dual existence of individuality and regular order, without collapsing one upon the other. The "progression" or "degeneration" of a social body was not arbitrary. Rather, it followed a pattern analogous to that of all living entities. These were shaped by regulative forces such as the internal mold and directed by formative principles such as the *Bildungstrieb*. The regulative patterns became the functional equivalents of general laws. They insured the ordered step-by-step progression or regression of a social body. But these patterns differed from axiomatic laws, for they were not sufficient to account adequately for individual appearances. They dealt only with form, not with specific manifestations of life.

In history, these patterns of change were assumed universal because they were founded upon inherent human drives. However, since drives could only be understood in relation to an object, so too could these descriptive forms only have meaning when placed within a context. As in the world of nature these forms were "empty," that is, they could never predict the specifics of any organic entity. The laws of history were, at best, directional markers that allowed one to use the tools of analogy and comparison to explicate similar forms. Real history had to unite the form with the content and in so doing preserve both the unity and diversity of historical analysis.

III.

To illustrate how historians translated this vitalist view to create a unique narrative regime, I would like to turn briefly to Herder. For many, the choice may appear perverse, since Herder has widely been interpreted as the most significant eighteenth-century opponent of Enlightenment historiography. However, when one looks at his most important historical work, the *Ideen zur Philosophie der Geschichte der Menschheit* (1784-91) through the lens of Enlightenment vitalism, he not only fits the model very well, he emerges as its most passionate advocate.

Herder had immersed himself deeply in this language of nature. He had read widely in the most modern literature, knew or corresponded with many of its leading figures, and supplemented this knowledge by delving into travel reports and anthropological treatises. He also revered the thought of the same natural philosophers being resurrected by Enlightenment vitalists: Hippocrates, Aristotle, Pliny, William Harvey, Francis Bacon, Francis Glisson, Georg Ernst Stahl, and, more covertly, Philippus Aureolus Bombastus von Paracelsus and Jan Baptista van Helmont.[43] Like the vitalists, Herder considered this "ancient" knowledge superior to that of the reigning masters of mechanism.[44]

Herder consciously incorporated vitalism's theoretical and explanatory practices into the *Ideen*. They formed the core around which his explanations were organized. As mentioned above, Herder's explanatory principle posited an essential correspondence between the physical and the moral world. He claimed that all human events must be investigated and explained using the type of critical reasoning applied to natural occurrences.

In narrating history, the greatest truth is to seek to apprehend and judge the total conjunction [of historical phenomena] and never to explain a thing that is or
has occurred, through another, which does not exist . . . . One should seek everywhere what is clearly there. As soon as one sees this, its causes become apparent—why is it not different than it could be? As soon as the mind [Gemüth] ap-
propriates this and makes it into a habit, then it has discovered a sound
philosophy that is difficult to find elsewhere except in natural history and mathematics.[45]

Clearly, Herder desired to establish a discursive realm that not only claimed
equality with natural history and mathematics, but partook of the same in-
vestigative and explanatory procedures. He sounded this theme with fugal
consistency. In essence, "spirit and morality are also physics," all ruled by the
same laws.[46] At the same time, Herder's narrative model did not attempt to
collapse the particular into the general, to adumbrate an essential identity
between nature and morality. He sought to evolve a narrative regime in
which the interaction between the particular and the general led to a deeper
understanding of both the natural laws of history and history's unique and
irreducible concrete manifestations.

To comprehend Herder's attempt to forge a new narrative regime based
on Enlightenment vitalism, a number of important questions must be answered. What is being narrated? What is the formal theory offered to explain events? How are these narrated and what position does the author
take *vis à vis* the reader? What is the plot structure of the story being narrated?

For Herder, the first question was essential, for the *Ideen* was designed
to establish what he considered a new field of historical inquiry and explanation. The *Ideen*'s title defined the historical field in the broadest sense. It
was a study of the philosophy of the history of humanity. But what did this
mean in its concrete application? What did Herder mean by philosophy?
Philosophy, according to Herder, could not be equated with abstract metaphysics. "I believe, however, that such speculations, devoid of empirical observations and analogies drawn from nature, are airy ones that very seldom
lead to the goal."[47] Philosophy's essence was the search for order, for a plan
that organized individual data into a coherent scheme. What was true for
the history of humanity was as true for a colony of ants or any other natural
product.[48] Eternal laws impressed upon primary matter at the beginning of
time bound them all.[49] In one of his typical rhetorical flourishes, Herder
asked: "Is not time ordered as space also is ordered? And are not both twins
of a single fate?"[50] This applied equally to human history. "In physical nature . . . we recognize laws, which we discover to be eternally efficacious,

regular, and invariable; What? And the realm of humanity with its powers, transformations and passions should be excluded from this chain of nature?"[51] The very impossibility of this proposition underscores Herder's extreme naturalization of history.

The twin-like linkage of space and time, held together by conjunctions and mediations, functioned as the central explanatory schema of his massive four-volume work. Space, time, and conjunction were his root organizing ideas, mirroring the vitalist attempt to merge structure and process without submerging one in the other. Given these assumptions, Herder had to design a system of events based on laws that both made general statements yet allowed unique individual content. His work is shot through with generalizing statements. Laws begin and end chapters, numbered subdivisions within sections mark important moments of his narrative. All were designed to demonstrate a "plan." But this philosophic plan was merely formal. It described "empty" relationships that had to be filled in by empirical specification that saved the uniqueness of each historical moment. For example, one of his general laws reads as follows: "Human imagination is always organic and climatic, but also always directed by tradition."[52] This law does not tell anything about any culture's specific imaginative forms. It merely asserts that each culture is shaped within a specific spatio-historical environment (climate in its broadest meaning), that it is subject to a formal pattern of change (organic), and that its forms of imaginative expression were guided by established traditions. The specific imaginative contours of a culture must be generated from empirical research.

Herder's idea of philosophy was grounded upon resemblance, correspondence, and interaction, not identity. Philosophy is the study of a coherent universe, in which each part follows a general pattern established by the natural laws of active matter, which manifest themselves in uniquely individual appearances. Hence, analogy and comparison are central constituents of his philosophy of history. The general laws provided the outer shell allowing one to organize material coherently. Comparison enabled one to see the unity in difference for each historical moment or thing. Analogies served as the essential proof of a statement. They either were drawn directly from "the laws of natural history," from events of a similar kind in different eras, or from different activities within a specific culture. These analogies enabled Herder to explain the unknown from the better known or to reach conclusions not contained in the specific data under examination.

Herder employed analogical comparisons with a vengeance. He roamed freely in the world of physical phenomena to explain specific moral, social, historical, and religious truths as well as to characterize universal occurrences. He was fascinated, for example, with the angle an object had with respect to an established horizontal or vertical plane and the consequences that variation generated. Thus, he discussed at length the importance of the angle of the earth's axis and its effect upon the total development of the earth's ecological system. He incorporated Peter Camper's concept of the facial angle to explain differences between human varieties, and he used the erect posture of humans (the movement from a horizontal axis to a vertical one) as the most important explanation for human uniqueness.[53] On another level, in his attempt to explain the emergence of poetic genius in different cultures without proposing a classical definition of beauty, truth, or eternal norms, he used the analogy of the stages of human growth. Early societies are analogous to youth. They are poetical by nature. As they grow older, they turn to prose. Thus, though Homer can never be duplicated, since Greece's youth can never be re-created, Shakespeare was his functional equivalent, equally admirable, yet totally different.[54] When using analogies to explain activities within a single culture, Herder sought to show how these activities resembled each other. Thus, he discerned a natural analogy between the learning of a "nation" and its political system. For example, in Greece, "the competing schools were what the many republics were in its public affairs: jointly striving but internally competitive forces [Kräfte]."[55] All of these analogies illustrated the metamorphosis of form described by a single principle or law. They attest to the unity in manifoldness that characterizes nature's harmony.

Not only did Enlightenment vitalism guide Herder's definition of "philosophic" analysis, it provided him with the tools to comprehend historical events. As stated above, he discerned three basic interlocking causal categories: space, time, and conjunction. In his historical explanations, space became the metaphor for the effect wrought upon humans by the "habitus" in which they existed. The habitus shaped humans, gave them direction, brought out certain drives while minimizing others. For example, the Greek habitus made it possible for the Greeks to develop their language—the "best formed in the world"—to evolve a culture in which song, dance, and history were its primary expressive forms, to live in a world where ideas and goods circulated freely, and to generate their central passion, the love of freedom.[56]

These "physico-geographical" and cultural causes were modified and opposed by the action of free organic powers [Kräfte], which were forever active. In dealing with them, Herder employed the metaphors of generation [Zeugen] and activity [Wirken]. Generation was a spontaneous process in which a mysterious hidden force is ignited that separates a specific quantity of matter from the mass and gives it a unique and individual form. Herder defined it as follows: "Genesis [Bildung] is an effect of internal powers, acting upon a mass prepared by nature for development."[57] Herder expanded this analogy to cover all creation, ranging from the single organism to the nation and including the generation of ideas. The action between matter and formative drive [Bildungstrieb] was archetypal. This connection itself was paradoxical. Power and matter were joined yet not identical. Matter influenced the direction in which power acts; power shaped matter.

According to Herder, creation was both immediate and inexplicable; it was mysterious, the instantaneous result of inner active forces forming matter. Creation cannot be part of a Great Chain of Being which proceeds continuously through minute shadowings, blurring all real distinctions. Rather, there were leaps in nature, testified to by the appearance of new species, new languages, and new nations.[58] Herder adamantly denied the existence of the Great Chain of Being and the related physiological idea of the preformation of germs, attacking both as mechanical. But he did believe in what he called a ladder of organization—a regular pattern of development from the simple to the more complex—guaranteed by the constant action of internally active forces, following simple laws.

Using an idea formulated by Maupertuis, Herder argued that this "progress" always took place between extremes of *maxima* and *minima*, limiting poles between which healthy life is led. In the history of "nations" those two extremes were represented by "patriotism" and Enlightenment [Aufklärung]. One of the most vivid examples of the confrontation between these poles could be found in Greek history. Here, Herder argued, for the first time in human history did a "nation" progress through all of the phases of a culture's life. "Thus, as natural history can only observe a plant completely if it knows how it goes from seed, bud, bloom to decay, so would Greek history be for us such a plant."[59] In this culture's history, Sparta and Athens represented the two contending poles. Their conflicts, sometimes frivolous and most of the time despicable, generated through their free interplay the "spirit of statecraft and warfare, which still directs the wheel of world events."[60] Through these battles, a harmony was created establishing rules of conduct that constrained the original elemental drives of the participants.

Harmony was a marriage of extremes founded upon complicated interactions of living forces. The greatest harmony entailed increasing the number of interacting forces and widening the distance between the extremes limiting the active forces—leading to an expanded middle realm in which life was experienced. Herder condemned one-sidedness, seeing it as a distortion of nature. The term center or middle [Mittel]—associated with concepts [Mittelbegriff], creations [Mittelgeschöpf, Mittelgattung], class [Mittelstand], and place [Mittelpunkt des Kreises, Mittelstrich der Erde]—was vested with symbolic importance, signifying a location linking freedom with stability. This image of the extended middle was given even deeper meaning by relating it to the ground of being: we are but a chord of the *Haupttypus* at the objective middle of this ground. Its existence validated the harmonic metaphor by assuring that variation did not depend upon chance, or understanding upon pure subjectivity. Herder did not believe that the essence of being could ever be known in and of itself. But its traces could be discovered in the signs of nature and the effects of its unknown causes through analogical thinking. In the continual interaction that defined living entities, the extended middle not only insured the regularity of development, it made understanding possible.

Herder's narrative strategy was typical of late Enlightenment scientific and disciplinary discourse, though colored by Herder's own highly charged rhetorical style. The *Ideen* can best be characterized as Herder's reflections on the philosophy of humanity's history, written in order to engage the reader in a discussion with the author. Herder does not assume the authorial voice of an all-knowing expert delivering wisdom from on high. Nor does he attempt to construct what we may call an uninterrupted narrative. Rather, he places himself directly in the work, exhorting at times, criticizing at others, but encouraging the reader to think along with him or sometimes against him. He interrupts the narrative line by interjections, observations, and pleas for further research. And he places himself in the text as explorer, as struggling researcher, as one who seeks an answer but knows that it will be years before an adequate history of humanity is written, if ever. Of course, all of this may be a sign of false modesty, but it does signal two things: that Herder shared the epistemological modesty of the Enlightenment, and that the idea of reading such a work entailed a process of learning and internal discussion, what might be called a dialogical mode of argument. Herder underscored his points with numerous exclamation points and question marks, indicating, I believe, the spoken, rhetorical ground of his narrative strategy.

In the structure of *Ideen* there is no single, apparent story. This has led many to consider Herder one of the most important proponents of historical relativism, satisfied with demonstrating a basic "humility in the presence of the multiplicity of these forms."[61] Yet, for his eighteenth-century German readers there was very little humility in this work. Herder's history is not a paean to what is and has been, but rather to what can be, based upon the potentialities residing within human history and humanity itself. These potentialities were, Herder believed, products of nature. Humans were the paradoxical animal par excellence—a fragile harmony between animal sensibility and spirit, a *Mittelgattung*, forever unstable, yet capable of achieving an expansion of the *Aufklärung* that was essential to humanity's natural organization. The *Ideen* chart the "progress" humanity has achieved with the hope that historical understanding will encourage us to cultivate those "natural" powers that would enable us to make our future progress towards *Humanität* and *Aufklärung* less tortuous.

IV.

It is, I believe, a major irony that Herder has emerged as an icon representing the first major assault upon the Enlightenment. This has occurred partly because of Herder's deployment of vegetative metaphors and his use of the term organic, which seemed to place him within the ranks of the early Romantic *Naturphilosophen*, and partly because few scholars have investigated the contours of the scientific world in which Herder thrived. Thus, the differences between Romantic organicism and Enlightenment vitalism have not been clearly delineated. Though *Naturphilosophie* employed terms constructed by Enlightenment vitalism, it invested them with new meanings that stood in stark contrast to their original formulations, rendering Enlightenment vitalism either suspect, incomplete, or old-fashioned. A very definite shift in scientific generalizations concerning life, organic processes, matter, and epistemology occurred, leading to a basic transformation from the Enlightenment's harmonic view of nature to one founded upon a philosophy of identity, which conflated matter with spirit.

In *Naturphilosophie*, continuity again became the ruling principle. The *Naturphilosophen* sought to establish a modernized form of the Great Chain of Being. Revolutions in natural history were reduced to surface phenomena. Leaps of nature were deemed impossible. Development was redefined, excising the radical implications of epigenesis by re-introducing the concept of preformed germs, active units created by God. Given the assumed identity between matter and spirit, the *Naturphilosophen* argued that reality consisted in "great ideas," which were God's thoughts. As Lorenz Oken expressed it: "all things are nothing but perceptions, thoughts, ideas of God. . . . Everything that we see are God's thoughts. . . . Since we too are nothing else than thoughts of God, all we can see is the succession of God's thoughts."[62]

Oken's words illustrate a major shift in conceptions concerning change over time between Enlightenment vitalism and *Naturphilosopie*. Though *Naturphilosopie* is often defined as a dynamic philosophy, the meaning of dynamic changed greatly. For the *Naturphilosophen*, development was not a process in which time played a constitutive role. Rather, change entailed a process of unfolding, which takes place in time represented by the play of essential polarities, all replicating the *Ur*-polarity. Time, instead of being a formative force, was transformed into a site where preformed things become manifest.

The *Naturphilosophen* employed a narrative form that recounted the history of the universe, but eliminated essential elements that Herder had championed. They presented an epiphany in which a hierarchy of dyads and triplicities reenacted the dynamics of the initial assertion, negation, and synthesis of creation. Neither time, nor place, nor human agency served as central explanatory categories; phenomena occur in time but the reason for their occurrence is that they replicate the original moment of creation. Causation, contingency, and human agency, central to Enlightenment vitalism, became ephemeral.

The *Naturphilosophen* supported these positions with an epistemology that consciously desired to transcend the epistemological modesty of the Enlightenment. They undertook what Immanuel Kant called a "daring adventure of reason,"[63] which sought to unite what Enlightenment vitalism had sundered: to recapture on a different level the universal vision that had animated the philosophies of Plato, Pythagoras, and Plotinus; to collapse spirit and matter into a uniform, consistent whole, devoid of leaps in nature, empty space, and the distinctions between living and dead matter. They sought to create a new universal *mathesis* where the guiding imperative was the Pythagorean principle: *Geometria est Historia*.[64] The *Naturphilosophen* strove for a form of self-evident knowledge comparable to that of mathematics. Because they assumed an identity between spirit and matter, they collapsed the distance between signifier and signified. They championed a binary form of logic, though radically opposed to the one associated with mechanism. But, like the mechanists, they were convinced of the absolute truth value of their deductions.

These assumptions in *Naturphilosophie* animated the historiography of the founders of what is usually called German Historicism. Their historical reasoning, explanatory strategies, and research agendas were formed within the intellectual climate shaped by Romantic *Naturphilosophie*. This is clear in Leopold von Ranke's vision of historical science. His concentration upon the primacy of international politics only makes sense if the state is conceived as a structurally coherent organism with a fixed character, involved in struggles with other such entities, each with their own preformed characters. External struggle alone leads to real development. Internal struggle indicates a disturbance within an organism.

The internal, spiritual drives corresponded to national characteristics: they were set with the foundation of the state and only required the correct conditions to be released or liberated. Hiding behind phenomenal reality were the essential qualities of the organism, present from its inception. Accordingly, Ranke's historiographical practice was based on relating individuals and events to this essential character. Events and individuals become representative of the whole. Contingency serves only to retard or accelerate the appearance of the preformed categories.

Open any chapter of Ranke's histories and these narrative procedures become evident. In another place, I have attempted a brief analysis of how this happens in a chapter of his *Französische Geschichte* that deals with the Hundred Years War.[65] From such a reading it becomes clear that Ranke is anything but the *Urbild* of the objective, fact-oriented historian, loath to indulge in hypothetical and ideological speculation. It is fascinating to see how often he consciously ignored chronology, violated already established rules of evidence, and avoided specification. Important developments seem to take place by themselves, often without direct connection to specific occurrences. Moments enter [treten ein], things follow quickly after each other [bald darauf], some last a while [eine Zeitlang], only to be replaced by others which force their way in [drängen durch]. How this happens and by whom it is carried out is often left vague or unexpressed, giving the described developments the appearance of being outside the competence of human agency. The deliberate use of anachronisms and of topical, value-laden images reinforce Ranke's message: these were necessary manifestations of the state organism's basic nature. Or, put more simply: what developed is what already was [wie es eigentlich gewesen].

Ranke opted for a radical solution to the question of how to merge synchronic and diachronic analysis that had frustrated many Enlightenment historians. This solution also helps to explain the specific rhetorical devices

Ranke employed so effectively. Events could be manipulated by the all-knowing author who had abstracted himself from the text, their dramatic effect heightened, their significance enhanced, for they served more as proclamations of inward character than as moments within a complex and changing set of existential relations. Ranke's vision of historical change corresponded very closely to Oken's claim that all things are thoughts of God, and that the natural philosopher's task was merely that of charting their succession.[66] In this all-encompassing view, built upon the philosophic concept of identity, the late Enlightenment's epistemological modesty was cast aside in favor of the truth claims often seen by post-modernists as having been forged in the Enlightenment.

This is the final irony. For a careful look at the late Enlightenment might reveal a way of thinking that is much more sympathetic to post-modernism than Romanticism. In its desire to see nature not just as a heap of things, to create a place for soul and the individual, and to avoid the rush to reductionism, the late Enlightenment, at least in part, envisioned an order of things that stood in strong contrast to the instrumental reason with which it is associated. If there is such a thing as the Enlightenment project, it included a healthy respect for uniqueness, free movement, and creation.

Transparency and Utopia

Constructing the Void from Pascal to Foucault

> I plan to show you from this high vantage point everything that is happening in Madrid at this moment. . . . By means of my diabolical power I am going lift up the roofs of the houses and, despite the shadows of the night, I want to uncover the insides to your eyes without veil. At these words, he simply extended his right hand, and immediately all the roofs disappeared. Then the student saw, as if in full daylight, all the interiors of the houses. The spectacle was too novel not to attract his entire attention. . . . He let his gaze wander on all sides, and the diversity of things that surrounded him was enough to occupy his curiosity for a long time.
>
> —Alain-René Le Sage, *Le diable boiteux* (1707)

The two-foot high, limping, "devil on sticks" Asmodée, packaged for the French public by Le Sage from the mid-seventeenth-century Spanish novel by Vélez de Guavara, demonstrated powers of vision that were the envy of the eighteenth-century Enlightenment. The power to lift up the roofs and discover the private world of the inhabitants of the city, was in every way an assertion of the objective, socially precise, and knowledge-seeking sight appropriate to a rational *philosophe*. It was, in the physical world, a fulfillment of the transparency called for by Jean Lerond d'Alembert and his contemporaries in the world of ideas. On an individual level, it served as a metaphor for the soul and its relations to nature and to others—that transparency which Jean-Jacques Rousseau vaunted, for example, or the states of illumination sought by Pierre-Simon Ballanche and his Romantic contemporaries. It was no accident that journalists and guidebook writers from Sébastien Mercier to Charles Nodier found the limping devil an appropriate mascot for their inquiries.

With his magical gesture opening up the roofs of Madrid, the little devil also appealed to those who believed that a rational architecture and urbanism, opened up to light, air, and the free circulation of people and goods, would materially assist the work of Enlightenment—would through their own mechanisms of transparency effect the good society. The tearing away of the roofs became a symbol for the removal of all barriers to sight, a favorite motif of planners from Pierre Patte in the 1760s to Baron Haussmann a century later. The modern technologies of iron and glass made the analogy even more literal. The transparent city as we know it in modernism from Le Corbusier to the present is clearly the heir to such ideals.

As historians, philosophers, architects, and urbanists have imaged it since the end of the eighteenth century, "Enlightenment space" seems simple enough to describe: it is geometrical, rational, gridded, and above all transparent, universal, and seamless, equally illuminated and illuminating. Objects stand in this space as so many clearly defined entities, separate from each other, taxonomically organized in series and hierarchies, as known and knowable as the space that surrounds them. From René Descartes to Immanuel Kant, as Ernst Cassirer had it, rational space is determined by a geometry based on a pure mathematics that carries with it, in Kant's words, "apodictic certainty: that is to say absolute necessity, not based upon experience, and consequently a pure product of reason."[1] In architecture and urbanism, this commonplace of mathematical truth, uncomplicated by Pascalian doubt or Leibnizian critique, and certainly without much introspection, has been accepted as the sign if not the instrument of rational design for two centuries. Enlightenment space, in these terms, found its inevitable expression in the Benthamite Panopticon, at once instrument of social and individual reform, and machine for milling absolute power over mankind by means of architecture (fig. 10).

Here the enlightening vision of the *diable boiteux* demonstrates its other and more obscure character. For Asmodée's ocular trick was, by definition, the exercise of a diabolical power. Its rational pursuit of knowledge covered a more unsavory drive. Voyeuristic, it served the nefarious ends of what the devil himself termed "démon de la luxure" or, more elegantly put, a god of cupidity, "Dieu cupidon." Asmodée had, in the end, to be returned to the glass phial from whence he issued. This was the limping devil who became the mascot of Grub Street, as it pursued its unsavory scandal-mongering, or that of the Marquis de Sade as he deployed the powers of hermetic space on behalf of "freedom to infinity," or that of Charles Baudelaire as the patron saint of the flâneur's gaze when looking with not entirely dispassionate spleen on the follies of Paris.

Following the warnings of Alexis de Tocqueville and the severe critique of Theodor Adorno, and with the experience of two world wars and several

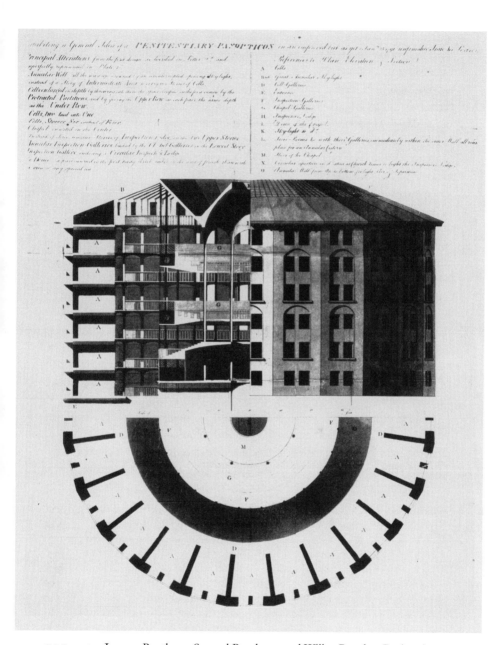

FIG. 10. Jeremy Bentham, Samuel Bentham, and Willey Reveley, *Penitentiary Panopticon*, 1791. University College Library (Bentham Papers), London. Photo: Special Collections, University College Library, London.

industrial revolutions later, we have become only too aware of this side of the apparently brilliant vision of Enlightenment: the "dark side" of Enlightenment, as it has been called, referring in intellectual history to the disturbing works of Sade, or the black visions of Francisco Goya. In spatial terms we might characterize this darkness as relating to similar Sadean and nightmarish evocations—the fundamentally intrusive nature of Enlightenment vision, its relationship to an all-determining technological and antihumanist version of progress—as well as to the deeper psychological implications of Rousseauesque inquiries into the self and its hidden forces. In these terms, the dream of Enlightenment transparency is revealed as a false promise of redemption, dialectically situated between absolute truth and absolute terror, and dedicated to the installation of a machine-like conformity to production and its social laws. The powerful gaze of Enlightenment was in this way founded on a double vision: one promising the triumph of a rational social science and an open politics, yet catering to the worst instincts of the spy and the libertine. As Michael Baxandall has pointed out in his ground-breaking study, Enlightenment theorists and painters recognized many more dimensions to light and shade than the absolute darkness and absolute lightness prescribed by the sublime at its limit points. At the very moment when the theory of vision was being constructed as a science of perception of light falling on bodies, the Enlightenment proposed more than this simplified "dialectic" or rather "opposites" of light and dark.[2]

Indeed, a more careful examination of the *philosophes'* visual ambitions reveals this bifocal characteristic from the outset. We only have to glance at d'Alembert's description of the realm of knowledge in his "Introductory Discourse to the Encyclopedia" to sense that all is not as clear and transparent to the Enlightenment eye as modern commentators have wanted to admit:

> Let us stop for a moment, and cast our eyes on the space that we have crossed. We note two limits, in which are to be found, so to speak, concentrated, almost all the certain knowledge accorded to our natural understanding. On the one side, knowledge of ourselves, leading to knowledge of the divinity and morality; on the other, mathematical knowledge of the general properties of bodies, their extent and size. Between these two terms is an immense gap, where the Supreme Intelligence seems to have wanted to deceive human curiosity, as much by the numberless clouds that it has deployed, as by the few shafts of light that seem to retreat further and further from us in order to attract us. One could compare the universe to certain works of a sublime obscurity . . . a labyrinth through which we have to find the true path with the help of lightning flashes.[3]

This universe of shadows, lit uncertainly by flashes of lightning in the gloom, this space of uncertainty filled with the fear of getting lost, was, as

Cassirer pointed out, Blaise Pascal's legacy for the Enlightenment, and one that all the *philosophes* from Voltaire on, tried to avoid or shrug off.

Michel Foucault provided what has proved the most seductive mapping of Enlightenment spatial devilry, in his contrasting accounts of "universal panopticism" (derived from Jeremy Bentham's architectural model of social surveillance and reform, the Panopticon) and of the Enlightenment's fear of "darkened spaces, of the pall of gloom which prevents the full visibility of things, men and truths."[4] This fear of the dark led, in the late eighteenth century, to a fascination with those same shadowy areas. In an interview entitled "The Eye of Power," published in 1977 as a preface to Bentham's text, Foucault invokes the "fantasy-world of stone walls, darkness, hideouts and dungeons": the precise "negative of the transparency and visibility which it is aimed to establish."[5] This was the world of "dark space" identified in his early essays on phenomenological psychology, the space of nightmares and phantasmic projections that was so poetically identified by psychologists like Eugène Minkowski and Ludwig Binswanger.[6] For Foucault, the moment that saw the creation of the first "considered politics of spaces" based on scientific concepts of light and infinity also saw, and within the same epistemology, the invention of a spatial phenomenology of darkness. Transparency is thus endowed with intimations of terror from the outset, embodying the two sides of Enlightenment.

The implications of Foucault's "architectural" metaphor for Enlightenment vision have been far-reaching, not only in epistemological and historical terms, but also within architectural discourse. First in *Discipline and Punish* published in French in 1975, and then in a series of later interviews and articles, Foucault stressed this architectural connection as both a literal and a metaphoric condition. Responding to the historian Michelle Perrot, Foucault described how his initial studies of the origins of clinical medicine had led to the project for a study of hospital architecture in relation to the medical gaze, and thence to the analysis of prison plans. "So the key was architecture," exclaimed Perrot, with an enthusiasm since registered by dozens of historians and architects.[7]

The architectural connection became even more literal in the work of the research group on hospitals and institutions set up under the guidance of Foucault that included some of the most brilliant architectural historians of the post-1968 generation. In this context, a specifically architectural and spatial methodology made a decisive contribution to Foucault's intellectual development. Stimulated by the tantalizing spatial intuitions of *Histoire de la folie*, a team of historians under the direction of Bruno Fortier produced a research report, *La politique de l'espace parisien*, followed by two books, *Les vaisseaux et les villes* and *Les machines à guérir (aux origines de l'hôpital moderne)*, the last with an introduction by Foucault himself.[8] These researches reinstalled, so to speak, the Panopticon and its correlates in architecture and urbanism, and were invaluable in revealing the socio-political dimensions of the drive towards spatial institutionalization at the end of the Ancien Régime.

Nonetheless, hindsight reveals a less positive effect of this architectural-ization of Foucault's thought, and its subsequent transfer to architectural history. Historians, beginning with Michelle Perrot, were disinclined to accept the totalizing force of panopticism as a singular and unmediated "power" in individual and social terms. In architectural history, the tendency to oversimplify the equation "Panopticon equals circular, centralized, space" led to a corresponding over-simplification of Foucault's thought: his initial understanding of the complex interaction of light and dark, dream and reality, was subordinated to an overall thesis of universal transparency.

The first evidence of the increasing rigidity of Foucault's spatial metaphors appeared following his visit to Attica prison in New York State, after the riots of 1972. In recounting his journey, Foucault directly linked Attica's architectural space and style to penal philosophy:

> At Attica what struck me perhaps first of all was the entrance, that kind of phony fortress à la Disneyland, those observation posts disguised as medieval towers with their machicolations. And behind this rather ridiculous scenery which dwarfs everything else, you discover it's an immense machine. And it's this notion of machinery that struck me most strongly—those very long, clean heated corridors which prescribe, for those who pass through them, specific trajectories that are evidently calculated to be the most efficient possible and at the same time the easiest to oversee, and the most direct.[9]

Foucault joins a critique of the "rational" or "functional" style and construction of the first industrial revolution to an awareness of the stylistic rhetoric of historicism, thus architecturally anticipating the debate between modernist survivals and post-modernist revivals of the next twenty years. When commenting on Tocqueville's initial enquiry into the prison systems of America, Foucault stressed quasi-industrial production as the original aim of this architecture. He noted that the intent of the "factories" of Auburn prison had been to produce "virtuous men." Now, in this architecture, "nothing is produced." But, in equating phony fortresses with display and clean heated corridors with function, Foucault—perhaps unwittingly—reified into a formal opposition what he had treated earlier as dialectical. He produced, in short, a caricature of architectural theory's own over-simplified preoccupation with form and function in the modern period.

This formalization became even more pronounced after Foucault's encounter with a second celebrated site, this time in France. In the fall of 1973, he visited for the first time Claude-Nicolas Ledoux's saltworks at Arc-et-Senans. The famous Saline de Chaux, built between 1774 and 1779 and operated as a salt factory well into the nineteenth century, was restored as a conference center and museum after the Second World War (fig. 11). The semi-circular layout of the Saline, perhaps the only post-encyclopedic factory to incorporate Diderot's ideals of management reform with Rousseau's on social renewal, clustered all the elements of a manufacturing town within a common precinct. Its exaggerated neoclassical architecture, based on the newly rediscovered remains of the Parthenon and the stern Doric order of the Propylaea, was, for Ledoux, rhetorically expressive of the status of salt manufacturing as a money-making monopoly of the crown at the end of the Ancien Régime.[10] Its plan was semi-circular, with the workers' houses around the perimeter and the director's house at the center of the diameter, flanked by the factory sheds. For Foucault, fresh from his "discovery" of Bentham, there was no doubt what this monument represented:

> The perfect disciplinary apparatus would make it possible for a single gaze to see everything constantly. A central point would be both the source of light illuminating everything, and a locus of convergence for everything that must be known: a perfect eye that nothing would escape and a centre towards which all gazes would be turned. This is what Ledoux had imagined when he built Arc-et-Senans; all the buildings were to be arranged in a circle, opening towards the inside, at the center of which a high construction was to house the administrative functions of management, the policing functions of surveillance, the economic functions of control and checking, the religious function of obedience and work; from there all orders would come, all activities would be recorded, all offences perceived and judged; and this would be done immediately with no other aid than a precise geometry. Among all the reasons for the prestige that was accorded in the second half of the eighteenth century, to circular architecture, one must no doubt include the fact that it expressed a certain political utopia.[11]

Foucault presses home his perception of centralized space as a disciplinary apparatus, endowing Ledoux's factory with all the attributes of a pre-panoptical machine. Surely, Ledoux stressed the role of the overseer's gaze, and the controlling function of vision and visibility. Many of his ideal projects for rural workshops develop this theme to a more programmatic degree. The design of a house for the forest guards, for example, is conceived of as "a cage open on all sides . . . everything had to be seen, nothing was to

Vue perspective de la Ville de Chaux

FIG. 11. Claude-Nicolas Ledoux, *Perspective View of the City of Chaux*, from *Architecture* (Paris: chez l'auteur, 1804), pl. 116. Photo: Bibliothèque nationale de France, Paris.

block the eye; the objects of first necessity had to be suppressed at ground level; any obstacle would have been against the principle." Here Ledoux conforms to the idea of an Enlightenment space that was one of perfect visibility, and Foucault, basing his argument on this and other examples, is correct in his understanding of Ledoux's predating Bentham with a kind of panopticism *avant la lettre*.

Yet, it also seems that Foucault, influenced by the more empiricist and pragmatic machine analogies of Bentham, tended to remain blind to any spatial or architectural characteristics that did not conform to his own laws of late Enlightenment, or rather, early industrial practice. For it is easy to demonstrate that there is very little of Bentham in Ledoux's plan: "observation" does not relate with such transparent immediacy to behavior but rather to visual experience and aesthetic sensation. The whole salt-works is less panoptical than theatrical. The plan, rather than being controlled by a literal transparency, allows for a balanced play between the places of living—the pavilions around the edge of the semi-circular courtyard—and those of round-the-clock work. At the center of the composition, the director's house and chapel join, symbolically and practically, both secular and religious power. The entire layout, modeled on the *places royales* of Paris and Dijon, represents a royal crown, while its geometrical proportions and figurative details recall the antique theaters described by Vitruvius and recently revived as paradigms for theatrical reform—notably by Ledoux's friend and colleague, Charles de Wailly at the Théâtre de France, now the Odéon. Ledoux, like most of the architects of his generation, was as invested in the representation of power through symbolic forms and sublime effects as he was in the actual, empirical distribution and implementation of managerial control.

It is not surprising, then, that the architectural analysis developed in *Discipline and Punish* largely ignored the terrifying sublime of Enlightenment space, an aspect acknowledged in Foucault's earlier work on Minkowski. Such terror, as dramatically displayed in the architecture of Ledoux, Étienne-Louis Boullée, and their contemporaries, has a "power" over minds equal to Bentham's machine.[12]

The idea of a sublime architecture, one that by the effect of its forms on the senses would provoke feelings commensurate with the most sublime ideas in poetry and the other arts, was a comparatively modern invention. Inherited from classical antiquity by way of a fragment said to be by Longinus, the term "sublime," as understood by seventeenth-century commentators, had referred to little more than "elevated expression." It was applied with rare exceptions to writing, painting, and sculpture. Boileau, in the Preface to his translation of Longinus, summarized and extended the idea in a way that would become a commonplace in the next century:

> It must be noted that by the sublime, Longinus does not only mean what orators call the sublime style, but rather whatever is extraordinary and marvelous that strikes one in a discourse, that causes a work to uplift, ravish and transport . . . . One must therefore understand by the sublime in Longinus, the extraordinary, the surprising, and, as I have translated it, the marvelous in discourse.[13]

This somewhat idiosyncratic version of Longinus seemed to many to privilege the extraordinary over the high style. Nevertheless, this version extended the applicability of the term, which gradually took on connotations of not only a literary manner but also a form of experience attributable both to the writer and to the objects that inspired such feelings. In this guise the sublime was introduced to architectural theory, most notably by Jacques-François Blondel, educator, contributor to the *Encyclopédie*, and, not incidentally, teacher of Ledoux and Boullée. In outlining the appropriate character for various building types, Blondel recommended an "architecture of sublimity" for temples, basilicas, public buildings, and the tombs of great men. Such monuments acted to confirm their lofty purposes by means of "grand lines." Blondel paraphrased Boileau almost to the letter when he called for a style that would "raise the mind of the observer, seize it and astonish it."[14]

But the decisive intervention had been Edmund Burke's *Philosophical Enquiry into the Origin of Our Ideas of the Sublime and Beautiful*, first published in English in 1757 and in French in 1765. Burke's ideas were popularized in France by Diderot, who used many of them in his art criticism after 1767. Burke's account of the sublime radically extended the ideas of Longinus and his classical interpreters to make of it a fundamental principle of aesthetics founded on the psychology of sensation. Burke detached the sublime from the tricks of style and rhetorical conceits abhorred by the *philosophes*, and reduced it to a "single principle" of terror:

> Whatever is fitted in any sort to excite the ideas of pain and danger, whatever is in any sort terrible, or is conversant about terrible objects, or operates in a manner analogous to terror, is a source of the sublime; that is productive of the strongest emotion which the mind is capable of feeling.[15]

Burke's sublime was based on pain and related sensations—on emotions far more powerful than mere pleasure. He focused on the horror that fear of pain evoked. Any idea of the sublime as specifically stylistic slips away. Otherwise, the astonishment felt by man before the works of nature could not be explained. The continuous chain of association worked from actual pain to anticipated or imagined pain; horror and fear—"apprehension of pain and death"—worked on the mind analogously to real physical hurt. Working from these premises, Burke developed a schema of cause and effect that allowed him to account for possible objects in nature that might stimulate the mind to fear.

Architecture played a major and exemplary role in Burke's account of the sublime: buildings were, after all, experienced in much the same way as nature itself. The difference between a cliff and a wall, a rock and a monument, was that of intention and self-conscious design. Burke illustrated the ability of obscurity and darkness to stimulate apprehension by citing the primitive practice of darkening temples to simulate night:

> Almost all the heathen temples were dark. Even in the barbarous temples of the Americans at this day, they keep their idol in a dark part of the hut, which is consecrated to his worship. For this purpose too the Druids performed all their ceremonies in the bosom of the darkest woods, and in the shade of the oldest and most spreading oaks.[16]

Darkness, confusion, uncertainty, all enhanced the connection between practices of religious domination and the sublime. Similarly, the imaginative experience of infinity, eternity, of supreme and unlimited power such as might be ascribed to a deity, led inevitably to feelings of the sublime. Impressions or experiences of deprivation, including vacuity, darkness, solitude and silence; vastness in every dimension, height, breadth, length and depth; magnificence and splendor: in every case, the sublime might equally be stimulated by nature or architecture. Burke concluded: "To the sublime in building, greatness of dimension seems requisite."[17]

Burke specified in detail the techniques for stimulating the sublime that would become—for Ledoux, Boullée, and later generations of architects— a prescription for ready-made elements of an institutional sublime deployed in every building type worthy of the architect's attention. First was the effect of an artificial infinite produced by combining the succession and uniformity of a building's parts. Burke insisted on the need for absolute uniformity, in geometry or in the parts: whether in a rotunda, where no boundary interfered with the continuous turning of the eye and thence the imagination, or in a row of columns in a temple, basilica or cathedral, where the "grand appearance" is the effect of the "range of uniform pillars on every side."[18] The similarity of each column to the next would, he argued, establish a cumulative effect opposed to the broken rhythm of alternating square and round columns or to the monotonous and un-repetitive effect of an entirely blank wall.[19] Other desirable effects included: a grandeur of dimension, more a question of clever deceit than of real magnitude, since Burke warned prophetically against the diminishing effect of compositions that were too large; a sense of the difficulty overcome to build the structure, including the expense of great strength or labor. Burke's example is Stonehenge, with "its huge rude masses of stone, set on end and piled each on the other." Burke also sanctions feelings of magnificence equivalent to those experienced at the sight of the starry heaven or the dramatic play of light and shade with emphasis on striking contrast. For buildings, "where the highest degree of the sublime is intended," he specifies "sad and fuscous colors, as black or brown, or deep purple." He finds ultimate sublimity in the experience of absolutes, whether darkness or light, the "fiat lux" of Biblical creation.[20]

Architects were well aware of the difficulty of inspiring sublime effects with overblown monuments that might appear as caricatures. They opted instead for effects of light and shade as fundamental instruments of Enlightenment vision. Ledoux, Boullée, and their students sought to evoke the terror that stemmed from meditating on and experiencing the essence of space itself—the void—as represented by absolute light and absolute darkness. This is the void that terrified Pascal and preoccupied Descartes. For late eighteenth-century artists—despite Voltaire's scornful dismissal of Pascal's *horror vacui*—the myth of the agoraphobic philosopher, terrified in the face of the "eternal silence of these infinite spaces," was still active: it authorized a critical examination of mid-century rationalism in favor of spatial mystery and power beyond human control.[21]

Significantly enough, the abbé Boileau joined the memory of Pascal, meditating on the void and experimenting with the vacuum, to an anecdotal account of a supposed malady. Writing in 1737, replying to one of his penitents who suffered from imaginary terrors, Boileau explained:

> Where others see only a smooth path, you see frightening precipices. That reminds me of M. Pascal . . . . This great genius always thought that he saw an abyss at his left side, and he would have a chair placed there to reassure himself. I have this on good authority. His friends, his confessor, and his director tried in vain to tell him that there was nothing to fear, and that his anxiety was only the alarm of an imagination exhausted by abstract and metaphysical studies. He would agree on all this with them, because he was in no way a visionary, and then, within a quarter of an hour, he would have dug for himself the terrifying precipice all over again.[22]

This anecdote was given more force after the discovery in 1740 of the *Recueil d'Utrecht*, which reported for the first time Pascal's supposed accident on the Neuilly bridge:

M. Arnoul de Saint-Victor, the curé of Chambourcy, says that he learned from the prior de Barrillon, a friend of Mme Périer, that M. Pascal, a few years before his death, was going, as was his custom on holidays to walk by the Neuilly bridge with some of his friends in a four or six horse carriage, when the two leading horses, took the reins in their teeth at the point of the bridge where there was no guard-rail, and having fallen into the water, the traces which joined them to the retinue behind broke, in such a way that the carriage remained on the brink of the precipice, which event led M. Pascal to forgo his walks and live in total solitude.[23]

Condorcet's influential *éloge* of Pascal, delivered in 1767, joined these two mythic events to the biographical Pascal, thus forging the portrait of a melancholic philosopher deeply disturbed by the contemplation of space itself. Condorcet held that Pascal's "ceaseless melancholy" was only alleviated by his researches into fluids and "the study of man," a melancholy itself augmented by the incident on the Neuilly bridge: "His imagination, that strongly retained the impressions that it had once received, was troubled for the remainder of his life by involuntary terrors."[24] Thanks to Condorcet's characterization, and to interest in agoraphobia after Carl Westphall named the disease in 1871, Pascal was destined to become the ideal theorist and exemplar of the effects of spatial sublimity. He became a theorist of the void, of "l'horreur du vide," of "l'infini," of "le néant."[25] Ledoux wrote, in a rare architectural appreciation,

Pascal, genius in his taste, irritated by resistance, became more ardent. He managed by the sole force of his penetrating genius to divine up to the thirty-second proposition of Euclid. At sixteen years old, he published a treatise on conic sections. At nineteen, he invented that surprising machine by which one makes all kinds of calculations without the help of the pen and the counter; and he was the first to prove that the effects one attributed to the horror of the void are caused by the thickness of the air.[26]

Ledoux's invocation of the seventeenth-century thinker implied more than a simple association between philosophic and architectural genius. His extended treatment of the spatial sublime is filled with a Pascalian wonder that greatly extends his teacher Blondel's associationism.

Ledoux deploys the sublime on many levels. The interaction of his architectural objects with nature—their variegated masses contrasting with those of the landscape—imply the role of the architect as "the delegate of the Creator on earth." Ledoux attributes high moral purpose to the ideal monuments of his imaginary City of Chaux, designed between the 1780s and his death in 1806. He contemplates immense distances when he imagines the economic and commercial expansion of his salt-works as a center of

FIG. 12. Claude-Nicolas Ledoux, *Cross Section and Plan of the Cemetery of the City of Chaux*, from *Architecture* (Paris: chez l'auteur, 1804), pl. 141. Photo: Bibliothèque nationale de France, Paris.

world trade that links the poles and traverses latitudes—an image evoked by the *Perspective View of the City of Chaux* in which axes stretch to infinity, like those of a similarly depicted Versailles a century earlier (fig. 11). He conjoins memory (the grand antique) and futurology (posterity and destiny) to vindicate the far-sightedness of architecture, whose special modes of vision reveal forms in space.

Most forcefully, however, Ledoux generates the sublime in terms of light and dark. In the lengthy description of Ledoux's project for the *Cemetery of the City of Chaux*, a design probably drawn up around 1785, an entirely pragmatic design for a modern catacomb became an opportunity to reflect on the plight (and flight) of the soul after death and the infinite space of the universe (fig. 12). The project consists of a radial city of the dead established on three underground levels, its streets lined with funerary urns leading to a giant internal sphere. The sphere—half below ground and half above—forms a void lit solely from above like the Pantheon. It symbolizes the universe itself. The allegorical meaning is clearly revealed by an engraving that displays the earth, half submerged in clouds, whirling in the vortex of the universe in the company of the planets: the earth mimics the half-sunken sphere of the cemetery (fig. 13). Ledoux, like Pascal, reflects on the "infinite spaces" of the universe that were being revealed by discoveries of contemporary astronomers like Sir William Herschel (another of the architect's heroes). It is tempting to read the telescope placed by Ledoux at the base of his self-portrait bust on the Frontispiece of *L'Architecture* as assigning the astronomer's extraordinary powers of vision to himself. Ledoux describes his cemetery project with phrases that are correspondingly elevated and intimate the sublime:

> the earth opens up to reveal the caverns of death . . . one travels in the void of terror, one never arrives . . . . if the architect uncovers tenebrous pits whose depth, below the empire of the dead, equals that of the immense spaces that separated the earth from the celestial dome . . . obscure labyrinth . . . abyss . . . this unkind nature gathers her sinister mattocks to excavate her nothingness . . . already the flames of genius spring forth; do you see them electrifying the clouds . . . mingling with the celestial lights? . . . Do you believe that the idea of the earth does not equal its grandeur? This round machine . . . is it not sublime?

Writing of his astronomical engraving, Ledoux speaks of "this sublime harmony that composes the parts of this vast picture." He calls on the viewer to "behold the star with the silver face; time calculates its course . . . a number of worlds revolving in space." The immense vault of the cemetery mimics that of the universe, and confronts the viewer, in Ledoux's words, with the ultimate sublime of "the image of nothingness."[27]

ÉLEVATION DU CIMETIÈRE DE LA VILLE DE CHAUX.

FIG. 13. Claude-Nicolas Ledoux, *Elevation of the Cemetery of the City of Chaux*, from *Architecture* (Paris: chez l'auteur, 1804), pl. 142. Photo: Bibliothèque nationale de France, Paris.

FIG. 14. Étienne-Louis Boullée, *Project for a Newton Cenotaph, Cross Section with Interior Effect of Day,* 1784. Bibliothèque nationale de France—Département des Estampes (Ha 57, pl. 9), Paris. Photo: Bibliothèque nationale de France, Paris.

In many of Ledoux's other projects, the extreme terror of the void seems muted, if present at all. It is displaced, if not replaced, by a delightful frisson, by an endless play of light and shadow changing according to the time of day and the seasons of the year. The building is constituted both to reveal this play (the solid object on which light falls as a means of revealing light) and constituted by this play (itself a thing of degrees of shadow, a purely visual phenomena). Space is no longer a universal truth constructed by geometry, but is transformed into a ceaseless projection and introjection of light.

In my study of the "uncanny" in architecture, I discuss the ways in which the notion of architecture as light and shade was extended under the Terror by Ledoux's contemporary Boullée. His project for a Newton Cenotaph was contemporary with Ledoux's Cemetery (fig. 14). Boullée's sublime was certainly influenced by his reading of Burke, for he exploited all the visual and sensational powers of what Burke had called "absolute light" when conceiving his projects for a Metropolitan Cathedral and a Hall of Justice.[28] He was equally obsessed with absolute darkness as the most powerful instrument to induce that state of fundamental terror that Burke claimed as the instigator of the sublime. Boullée's design for a Palace of Justice confronted the two worlds, light and dark, in a telling allegory of Enlightenment: the cubiform justice halls, lit from above, rest on a half-buried podium containing the prisons. "It seemed to me," Boullée wrote, "that in presenting this august palace raised on the shadowy lair of crime, I would not only be able to ennoble architecture by means of the oppositions that resulted, but further present in a metaphorical way the imposing picture of vice crushed beneath the feet of justice."[29]

Not by chance, Boullée's reflections on the dark were elaborated during the period of his enforced withdrawal from public life during the Terror, an episode described by Robespierre as predicated on the necessities of the "political sublime." During this internal exile, sometime in the mid-1790s, Boullée recounted his experiments in light and shade as he walked by night in the woods surrounding his home:

> Finding myself in the countryside, I skirted a wood by the light of the moon. My effigy produced by its light excited my attention (assuredly this was not a novelty for me). By a particular disposition of the mind, the effect of this simulacrum seemed to me to be of an extreme sadness. The trees drawn on the ground by their shadows made the most profound impression on me. This picture grew in my imagination. I then saw everything that was the most somber in nature. What did I see? The mass of objects standing out in black against a light of extreme pallor. Nature seemed to offer itself, in mourning, to my sight. Struck by the sentiments I felt, I occupied myself, from this moment on, in making its particular application to architecture.[30]

Out of his experiences, Boullée formed a notion of an architecture that would, in his terms, be able to "speak" of death through a true, funereal monumentality. For Boullée, tombs and funeral monuments should be low and compressed in proportions—a "buried architecture" that literally embodied the burial it symbolized. They should express the extreme melancholy of mourning by means of their stripped and naked walls "deprived of all ornament." They should, like the architect's shadow, be made visible by means of shadows:

> one must, as I have tried to do in funerary monuments, present the skeleton of architecture by means of an absolutely naked wall, presenting the image of buried architecture by employing only low and compressed proportions, sinking into the earth, forming, finally, by means of materials absorbent to the light, the black picture of an architecture of shadows depicted by the effect of even blacker shadows.[31]

Boullée imagined a Temple of Death, with its facade etched in shadows on a flat plane of light-absorbent material—a virtual architecture of negativity (fig. 15). Boullée was proud of what he called his "invention," perhaps the first example of an attempt to copyright an architectural manner:

> This genre of architecture formed by shadows is a discovery of the art that belongs to me. It is a new career that I have opened up. Either I fool myself, or artists will not disdain to follow it.[32]

His younger contemporaries were quick to seize on the sublime potential of this abyssal vision of mortuary form.

What is fascinating about Boullée's account is not so much its commonplace references to darkness, nor its fashionable appeal to Egyptian motifs on the eve of Napoleon's expedition to Egypt, but rather its extraordinary notion of projecting what he termed a "skeleton" of architecture based on the example of the human shadow. This shadow, or "effigy" as Boullée called it, prefigured the disappearance of the body into darkness. It was both a haunting double for Boullée himself, and a model for imitation in architecture. On one level, Boullée was following the traditional idea of architecture's imitating the perfection of the human body in its massing and proportions. But he inverted the theory to make an architecture based on the "death form" of the body shadowed on the ground. Boullée created a simulacrum of the buried body in architecture: the building, already half sunken, compressed in its proportions as if by a great weight from above, imitates not a standing figure (as classical Vitruvian theory would have demanded) but a form that is already recumbent, depicted on the ground as a negative space. This prone figure, raised up to mark the facade of Boullée's

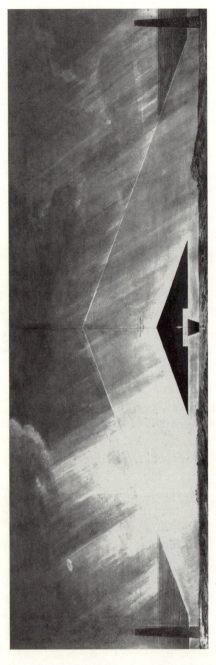

FIG. 15. Étienne-Louis Boullée. *Project for a Funerary Monument*. Bibliothèque nationale de France — Département des Estampes (Ha 55, pl. 29), Paris. Photo: Bibliothèque nationale de France, Paris.

temple, becomes the image of a specter: a monument to death that represents an ambiguous moment somewhere between life and death. A shadow of the living dead. Boullée prefigures the nineteenth-century preoccupation with the double as harbinger of death, as the shadow of the unburied dead.

In this doubling of the double, Boullée was setting up a play between architecture (art of imitation, of doubling) and death (imaged in the double) in a way that gave tangible form to Enlightenment fears. As Sarah Kofman has argued in her analysis of Freud's essay "The Uncanny" (1919),

> Erected to conquer death, art, as a "double," like any double, itself turns into an image of death. The game of art is a game of death, which already implies death in life, as a force of saving and inhibition.[33]

Boullée's death image, with its shadow inscription mirroring the shape of its dark facade or "ground," plays insistently on this theme, that, as Freud pointed out, has to do with "the constant recurrence of the same thing," or repetition. Kofman comments,

> [Freud's] "The Uncanny" indicates this transformation of the algebraic sign of the double, its link with narcissism and death as the punishment for having sought immortality, for having wanted to "kill" the father. It is perhaps no accident that the model of the "double" erected for the first time by the Egyptians, is found in the figuration of castration in dreams, the doubling of the genital organ. Repetition, like repression, is originary, and serves to fill an originary lack as well as to veil it: the double does not double a presence but rather supplements it, allowing one to read, as in a mirror, originary "difference," castration, death, and at the same time the necessity of erasing them.[34]

On this account, Boullée could well be said to have invented the first self-conscious architecture of the uncanny, a prescient experiment in the projection of "dark space." In flattening his shadow on the surface of a building that is nothing but (negative) surface, Boullée created an architecture that has no real depth of its own, but deliberately plays on the ambiguities between absolute flatness and infinite depth, between shadow and void. The building, a double of the death of the subject, translates this disappearance into experienced spatial uncertainty. As Michael Baxandall concludes,

> The shaped and often grotesquely imitative mobility of a shadow, like some parasitical animal, can also be experienced as uncanny. Even in the cool sort of lexicon the eighteenth-century Enlightenment used, established extended senses of *Ombre* include ghost, of course, and chimera; unreal appearance, diminished trace; secret, pretext, concealment; the domination of a destructive presence; threat. Many of these are colored by the thought of denial of light, darkness, which is a strong idea in itself.[35]

To return to Foucault: Boullée's design questions the assumed identity between the spatial and the monumental in Foucault's system. Foucault posited a virtual homology between the institutional politics of panopticism and their monumental crystallizations in building types, from the hospital to the prison and beyond. He set in motion the critique of modernist typologies that takes the *spatial* dimension as a universal flux bonding the political to the architectural or monumental. But our analysis of Boullée suggests that the spatial is a dimension incipiently opposed to the monumental. Space works to contextualize the individual monument within a network of forces stretching from building to city to entire territories. The Situationists, like Henri Lefebvre in another context, recognized this projective phenomenon, but it also operates, by way of the negative bodily projection we have described, to absorb the monument altogether.

Boullée's relentless desire to mimic the engulfing of the subject into the void of death—a desire echoed by Ledoux when he speaks of composing "an image of nothingness" in his Cemetery project of 1785—ended by engulfing monumentality itself. The rational grids and the spatial orders that mark out the panoptical system of the late eighteenth century were, in the Temple of Death, nowhere to be seen. Boullée offered no *plan* for his monument to nothingness. His facade is as infinitely thin and insubstantial as the idea of redoubled darkness, precariously balanced between above and below, vertical and horizontal. The bodily substance of a traditional monument and the palpable spatial identity of a controlling institution dissolve into the projection of a disappearing subject. Space no longer operates as an instrument of monumental construction but as an agent of monumental dissolution. Here, we encounter the origins of the long history of modern agoraphobia first intimated by Pascal's *horror vacui*, the terrifying "eternal silence of infinite spaces." By the end of the nineteenth century, doctors and analysts, critical urbanists like Camillo Sitte, and art historians like Wilhelm Worringer and Aby Warburg will recognize this agoraphobia as the symptom, if not the result, of modern (read Enlightenment) space.

In lieu of the history and theory that constitutes Enlightenment space as the universal and all-controlling gaze wished for by so many of the *philosophes*, and repeated by critics like Foucault, my sense of the shadow in light, the opacity in transparency, the translucency in obscurity, points toward a different history. I recognize and interpret faults in this gaze, "obstacles" as Starobinski calls them when explicating Rousseau's difficulties with transparency. These are not only faults that block and obscure the view of knowledge and control, but also psychological faults, failures to interiorize external impressions and vice versa. These faults are revealed not only by the solids and voids of those apparently clear objects beloved of taxonomists and philosophers, not to speak of architects, but also by the very difficulty of seeing these objects clearly in light and shade. The experimental attitude of Ledoux and Boullée toward an architecture of shadows allows us to extend our understanding of space in the modern period, and to prepare for the profound revolution in our gaze that follows the aphoristic conclusion Freud reached at the end of his life: "Space may be the projection of the extension of the psychical apparatus. No other derivation is probable. Instead of Kant's *a priori* determinants of our psychical apparatus. . . . Psyche is extended; knows nothing about it."[36]

The limits of a Foucauldian interpretation of Enlightenment space become evident when we recognize that it remains tied to the Enlightenment's phenomenology of light and dark, clear and obscure. By insisting on the operation of power through transparency, the panoptic principle resists critical exploration of the extent to which the dialectic between transparency and obscurity is essential for power to operate. The intimate association between the two, their uncanny ability to slip from one to the other, permits the sublime to retain its hold as an instrument of fear by managing an ambiguity that stages the presence of death in life, dark space in bright space.

When Le Sage's limping devil Asmodée was observed again, in Year VII, in the guise of Pierre Jean-Baptiste Chaussard's *Nouveau diable boiteux*, he had abandoned his magic powers of vision in favor of mechanical means.[37] Escaped from the hands of his captor, the enchanter Torribo, he appropriated a balloon from his young pupil, now become an aérostat, and viewed Paris from above. The "Paris or the Discourse in the Air" imagined by the young scholar proclaimed the need to rebuild the city in favor of Mirabeau's physiocratic vision of its forced depopulation, and the repopulation of a fertile and cultivated countryside. Paris would then be endowed with a well-policed order: useful monuments such as "vast baths, abundant fountains, aqueducts similar to the Cloaca Maxima of Rome . . . true commerce . . . straight, wide, and ventilated streets." This state "could be attained only by reducing to rubble half of this gothic city, because, as M. Gabriel well remarked, in this city it should be less a question of building than of demolishing."[38] To Asmodée, this vision of a revived neoclassical utopia, built along the lines of Enlightenment architects like Pierre Patte or Jacques-Ange Gabriel, felt for all the world like "Socrates in a basket in the middle of imaginary space." Few architects and urbanists of the nineteenth and twentieth centuries have been able to resist transparency as a way of ordering a seemingly obscure and unformed reality. Even when their plans have been realized, few have had the effect of magically transforming society for the better. In my view, the radiant spaces of modernism—from the first Panopticon to the boulevards of Haussmann, from the Ville Radieuse to the more recent spate of *grands projets* in Paris—are not calculated on the final triumph of light over dark, but rather on the insistent presence of the one in the other.

DAVID E. WELLBERY

Aesthetic Media

The Structure of Aesthetic Theory before Kant

In 1901, Theodor A. Meyer, a teacher at the protestant theological seminary in the Swabian village of Schöntal, published a book called *The Stylistic Law of Poetry*, the preface to which announces: "The problem and the purpose of my book coincide with the problem and purpose of Lessing's *Laocoön*."[1] Apart from a few important, but delayed and foreign appreciations, Meyer's book met with massive disinterest, which even its re-edition in 1990 seems not to have perturbed. But I want nevertheless to claim for the just quoted sentence, and indeed for the book as a whole, the status of an historical threshold. Meyer's citation of Lessing—and it is, of course, not merely a verbal citation, but the reactualization of an entire conceptual framework, the retracing of a line of inquiry—inaugurates a series of endeavors that includes some of the most penetrating contributions to twentieth-century aesthetic criticism: Rudolf Arnheim's 1938 essay, "A New Laocoön: Artistic Composites and the Talking Film";[2] Clement Greenberg's manifesto on behalf of abstract painting, published in 1940 in *Partisan Review* with a title that seems designed to raise the stakes on Arnheim, "Towards a Newer Laocoön";[3] the third and culminating section of Galvano Della Volpe's forcefully argued *Critique of Taste*, entitled "Laocoön 1960";[4] and finally, Joseph Frank's seminal essay of 1945, "Spatial Form in Modern Literature," the genesis of which Frank recalled in 1990 as follows: "I recall vividly that my ideas only began to take coherent shape once I finally read Lessing's *Laocoön* . . . I have a distinct recollection of the exhilaration I felt after going through Lessing in the little Everyman edition, whose rippled crimson cover I can still feel in my hands and see before my eyes. Here was the systematic clue I had been searching for without knowing it."[5]

What are the historical conditions for this renewed relevance? What is it that, starting in 1901 and continuing until today, makes Lessing citable once again? In our analysis of the modernist return of rhetoric, John Bender and I tried to demonstrate that the key matter in understanding such historical repetitions is to get a view on the gap that preceded them.[6] For repetitions and reactualizations presuppose just that: a hiatus, a forgetting, an interruption of efficacy, and systematic reasons for that interruption. Lessing's *Laocoön* (1766), and with it the discourse of Enlightenment aesthetics of which it is a distinguished, but nonetheless typical representative, had been rendered irrelevant, epistemologically out of contention so to speak, with the advent of the idealist aesthetics of spirit that arose in the wake of Immanuel Kant's *Critique of Judgment*, found its systematically and pedagogically most powerful formulation in Georg Wilhelm Friedrich Hegel's *Lectures on Aesthetics*, and continued its dominance, at least in academic circles, across the nineteenth and well into the twentieth century. To illustrate why, within idealist discourse, the sorts of investigation pursued by the Enlightenment aestheticians are not even candidates for serious intellectual pursuit, a sentence of Hegel's bearing on the status of the sensuous in art may be useful: "For these sensuous figures and tones do not appear in art for their own sake or on account of their immediate appearance, but with the purpose of satisfying, in this appearance, higher spiritual interests, since they have the power of evoking out of the depths of consciousness a resonance and responsive tone in the spirit. In this way, the sensuous in art is *spiritualized*, since the spiritual appears in it as *sensualized*."[7] For Hegel, the sensuous element in art, which he recognizes as one of its defining features, has the status of an externalization or appearance of spirit. Everything hinges on gauging the diminishing force of this *of*, which translates a vigorously subjective genitive. The dictum that art is the "sensuous appearing of the Idea" has much the same reductive tendency, demoting the material texture of the non-verbal arts to a provisional phase in the self-realization of *Geist*.[8] Surprisingly, this demotion is accompanied by a robustly optimistic view regarding the capacity of the poetic word to convey sensuous contents. Poetry, for Hegel, is inevitably imagistic [bildlich], the internal presentation [Vorstellen] of a fully determinate quasi-percept. These two tenets, the one claiming too little, the other too much, are systematically coherent. Since, from the point of view of the subjective genitive of spirit, the only theoretically significant feature of the sensuous element in art is its otherness-to-spirit, its pseudo-objectivity, then this element can enter entire into the domain of poetry, where it finds, finally, its truth as a determination of spirit:

"The power of poetic forming [dichterischen Bildens] consists therefore in the fact that poetry internally shapes for itself a content without proceeding outward to actual external figures and melodious lines and thereby makes the external objectivity of the other arts into an inner objectivity, which the spirit expresses for representation as it is and remains within the spirit."[9] The point is not that Hegel neglects the differences among the arts altogether, rather that these differences are not informative. They are differences that make no real difference, and this because they blend into one another across a transformative process that is the coming-to-itself of what I would call a deep cultural subject.

By 1901, however, at least for acute observers like Theodor Meyer, Hegel's notion that poetry is essentially imagistic had lost its evidentiary force. "Originally," Meyer writes, "I shared this view of the essence of the beautiful and of poetic devices, even if on occasion with a bad conscience: for, had I been honest about the matter, I would not have been able to conceal the fact that those sensuous images of poetic figures and situations which, according to the assurances of our aestheticians, are supposedly awakened by the poetic word . . . simply would not click in in my imagination."[10] Subjectively, it is an apparent defect of imagination, an inability to respond as the inherited theory prescribes, that instigates Meyer's investigation, an investigation that deserves recognition, I believe, as the first systematic treatment in our century of the specifically linguistic character of poetic effect. And, of course, the negative result of this inquiry will be the contention that the idealist tradition in aesthetics is simply confused, claiming intuitive, quasi-perceptual content where there is none and thereby misconstruing the nature of linguistic signification. The point, however, is not that Meyer is right and the idealists wrong, but that the discursive conditions of theoretical work have changed. The Hegelian premise of a spiritual essence, and hence unity of the arts, has lost its capacity to enable and organize observation. Now, in 1901 and still today, it is the disunity of the arts that imposes itself most forcefully, and the reason this is so can be gleaned from the series of cognate endeavors alluded to above. Just as for Meyer poetry derives its specificity from the constraints imposed by language as a medium, the theories of Arnheim, Greenberg, and Della Volpe are all theories of artistic media, and that is to say: of medial differences. Hegel's aesthetics is an aesthetics of the word not as medium but as an expression of spirit, the highest expression this side of the concept, an expression capable of absorbing within itself all the antecedent objectifications of spirit from which no significant divide separates it. It is the aesthetics, in short, of an alphabetized culture for which language is not one medium among others, but, as it were, the meta-medium, and this aesthetic loses its evidentiary force at that historical juncture when aesthetic media become pluralized.[11] The citability of Lessing's *Laocoön*, the resumption of its problem and purpose across the work of Meyer, Arnheim, Greenberg, Della Volpe, Frank, and many others, is made possible by the emergence of a cultural form that has as its field of reference a plurality of media.

Meyer's attention to his own imaginative incapacity, to his failure to respond to poetry as inherited theory claims he should, has an interesting precursor in another Enlightenment aesthetician no less distinguished than Lessing. In the fifth part of his *Philosophical Enquiry into the Origin of our Ideas of the Sublime and Beautiful* (1757) Edmund Burke remarks: "But I am of opinion, that the most general effect even of these words [concrete nouns], does not arise from their forming pictures of the several things they would represent in the imagination; because on a very diligent examination of my own mind, and getting others to consider theirs, I do not find that once in twenty times any such picture is formed, and when it is, there is most commonly a particular effort of the imagination for that purpose."[12] Where Hegel found fully determinate images, Burke, like Meyer a hundred and forty-five years later, could find none. "It seems an odd subject of dispute with any man," Burke himself remarks, "whether he has ideas in his mind or not."[13] And it strikes us as no less odd when we find this dispute conducted between philosophers separated by several decades. My suggestion for diminishing this oddity is to claim that, within the cultural form that Hegel's philosophy codifies, the sort of focused self-observation Burke and Meyer methodically employ just is not possible. Cultural forms determine informational content by determining which differences can make a difference. Hegel could not see the non-seeing that both the Enlightenment and the modernist theoretician take as evidentiary, and this because the leading difference [Leitdifferenz] organizing his observations is that between the spirit and its objectifications. The characteristic structural feature of this distinction is its self-inclusion: the spirit is distinguished from its objectifications, but these are nonetheless—in the sense of the subjective genitive—*its* objectifications, that is, modifications of what they are distinguished from. Hence poetry is the existence in and for the spirit of the determinate sensuous contents of the plastic arts and music. But the cultural form that enables and orients Burke's observations draws its organizing distinction in such a way as to block this reabsorption. Let us call this *Leitdifferenz* (and here I am applying, of course, concepts developed by

Niklas Luhmann) the distinction between consciousness and communication, between perceptual-affective and imaginary experience on the one hand and conceptually elaborated contents on the other.[14] Where this distinction is operatively applied, the sort of focused attention on phenomenological nuance that characterizes the remarks of Burke and Meyer becomes the touchstone of inquiry. Here the questions worthy of investigation bear on the media of transmission, on their differences and limits. The ethos is no longer one of hermeneutic homogenization, as in Hegel, but rather a purist ethos of medial specificity. With the reemergence of the distinction between consciousness and communication and of the ethos it sustains, Lessing's project, subtitled "On the Limits of Painting and Poetry," becomes available for citation.

In order to delineate a bit more sharply the structure of thought that characterizes Enlightenment aesthetics, I need to contrast it with another theoretical endeavor, this one rooted in an earlier cultural form. We are approaching the same issue of attentive focus, but this time from a different angle. In 1730, Johann Christoph Gottsched published his *Critical Poetics*, an important transitional text in that it attempted to ground the seventeenth-century tradition of rhetorical poetics in terms of the rationalist system of Leibniz and Wolff.[15] Gottsched's first chapter enumerates the attributes definitive of what he calls "the character of a poet." A poet must be a skilled imitator of all natural things, he must possess acumen, wit, and imagination, he must have attained a solid grounding in the skills requisite for his art as well as a general erudition. Above all the poet must have a thorough knowledge of mankind, a sound capacity for rational judgment, and a righteous and virtuous spirit. Finally, he must master the rules of his language and write without error. Thus equipped, he can successfully pursue the intention and purpose of his art, which is to contribute productively to the common welfare of his nation. Poetry is conceived here as an office in the full Ciceronian sense, as a role-composite defined not simply in terms of artistry, but also in terms of requisite erudition, practical knowledge, moral character, and civic obligation. Just this capaciousness seems to me to be the historically instructive datum here, a fact that emerges forcefully if we consult the book by the same title that the Swiss Johann Jakob Breitinger brought out ten years later. Despite the fact that his terminology and philosophical references are substantially identical to Gottsched's, Breitinger's theoretical project, which Baumgarten will later acknowledge as a major influence on his own *Aesthetica*, bears on an entirely different object of investigation. Thus, Breitinger's work contains no equivalent to Gottsched's chapter on the poet's character. Instead, his first chapter develops a notion Breitinger designates—with a phrase Lessing will criticize—as "poetic painting." His entire theoretical project, Breitinger avers, is devoted to the exploration of this single capacity: "the highest power of eloquence which imprints images onto the imagination of human beings that are just as lively and touch the heart and mind just as much as those which the art of the painter puts before our corporeal eye and therewith our mind and which often strike our senses with such force, and delight us so that we think we see the things themselves present before us."[16] The juxtaposition of Gottsched and Breitinger makes palpable the labor of isolation and concentration of focus that attended the emergence of aesthetic theory during the first half of the eighteenth century. It is as if poetry had been extricated from the world of social dependencies within which the rhetorical tradition had located it. All the intricate connections that linked the poet to his social circumstance, the ethical and civic responsibilities, the erudition, the schooling, have fallen away; and what remains is an object of attention that had previously not existed: the encounter of a mind, in particular its faculties of perception and imagination, with the media of poetry and painting, and with the forms these media convey.

In seeking out the structures that made this focus of attention possible, I take my cue from John Bender's magisterial study *Imagining the Penitentiary*.[17] Bender demonstrates that the registration of mental processes that characterizes the emergent form of the novel is enabled by frames of observation and self-observation that detach the subject—prisoner or patient—from the turbulence of multiple social relations and interactions. The penitentiary, as institution and idea, is an instrument of abstraction, an isolating frame within the bare space of which the subtlest movements of mind are magnified to noticeable dimensions. By shutting out everything else, the penitentiary restricts the mind to its own operativity, so that the only thing that can be observed is the dynamics of observation itself. But if this device is, as Bender claims, paradigmatic for eighteenth-century culture, it is not because some aggrandizement of power has enclosed individuals in real or virtual cages. Rather, it is because the form of the penitentiary as an abstractive mechanism enabling second-order observations characterizes a range of emergent eighteenth-century institutions. To show this I want to consider briefly two examples decisive for the development of aesthetic theory.

The Earl of Shaftesbury's implicit opponent in *Sensus Communis: An Essay on the Freedom of Wit and Humour* (1709) is a figure he calls (and we must remember that the memory of the religious civil wars is still immediate for the Earl) the "zealot": "I must confess," he writes to his correspondent, "you had reason enough for your caution if you could imagine me at the bottom so true a zealot as not to bear the least raillery on my own opinions. 'Tis the case, I know, with many. Whatever they think grave or solemn, they suppose must never be treated out of a grave and solemn way; though what another thinks so, they can be contented to treat otherwise; and are forward to try the edge of ridicule against any opinions not their own."[18] Zealotry is the symptom of an observational incapacity. While the zealot is capable of critically or caustically observing others' opinions, he cannot suffer such observation of his own; he is the figure in whom the structure of second-order observation remains incomplete, for such observation not only registers the observations of others in their contingency, it grasps the contingency of its own observations, observes itself being observed.[19] This translation of the cited passage into the admittedly more cumbersome terminology of systems theory has the advantage of disclosing the enabling structure of what Shaftesbury calls the freedom of wit and humour. For this freedom is unbounded second-order observation: the submission of every position to the scrutiny of satire, and the subsequent submission of that observation to the same corrective focus. This process unfolds according to the "mighty law of discourse" that Shaftesbury calls "vicissitude,"[20] a constant shifting to an unforeseen otherness of perspective that views every achieved position within "the natural medium . . . of ridicule itself, or that manner of proof by which we discern whatever is liable to just raillery in any subject."[21] No substantial anchorage is allowed, no unassailable tenets abided. The process of second-order observation regulates itself or, as Shaftebury phrases it, "wit is its own remedy."[22] There are many lessons to be gleaned from Shaftesbury's construction of the free play of wit, but I want to call attention here to the one that resonates with Bender's analysis of the isolating function of the penitentiary idea. For the point is that the construction of wit as a self-regulating and hence "free" exchange relies on the same sort of delimitation as that which, in the penitentiary model, enables the observational focus on mental processes. Shaftesbury's free exercise of wit and unbounded skepticism is possible because it takes place in a sphere separated off from the complexly interlaced investments that sustain society at large. "The lovers of mankind," he writes, "respect and honour conventions and societies of men. And in mixed company, and places where men are met promiscuously on account of diversion or affairs, 'tis an imposition and hardship to force them to hear what they dislike, and to treat of matters in a dialect which many who are present have perhaps never been used to."[23] The conversational vicissitudes, in which "fine schemes [are] destroyed, grave reasonings overturned," require that this be "done without offense to the parties concerned."[24] Such disinterestedness, such detachment from personal investment, presupposes enclosure: "For you are to remember, my friend, that I am writing to you in defense of the liberty of the *club*, and of that sort of freedom which is taken among gentleman and friends who know one another perfectly well."[25]

This last reference to the club anchors Shaftesbury's model in a situation of face-to-face oral communication embedded within a hierarchy of estates. But the model is nonetheless generalizable beyond these historical limits and in fact what Kant will describe some seventy-five years later in his famous piece "What is Enlightenment?" as the public sphere evinces exactly the same structure of free self-regulation within the limits of an enclosed domain of exchange. The strategy in both cases is to abstract the exchange of observations and observations of observations from the manifold dependencies of, well, of everything else; to focus, in a manner free of antecedent investments and without the pressuring presentness of decisions, on just this one type of transaction. The observations function, then, much like money, which is notoriously unaffected by the personal history of the hand it comes from. And in this connection it is worth noting that the market, a self-regulating mechanism like Shaftesbury's play of wit, has been described by Luhmann as a system of second-order observation.[26] The market, as a sphere of abstracted transactions—transactions, that is, unfettered by personal, political, or religious investments such that they can find their own proper balance without hindrance—is just the model Shaftesbury himself recurs to: "Liberty and commerce bring [wit] to its true standard. The only danger is, the laying of an embargo."[27]

I turn now to a second application of Bender's argument. The *Réflexions critiques* of the abbé Dubos (1719), a text that remains pertinent to aesthetic theory at least into the 1770s, takes as its starting point the paradox that in painting and poetry the objects that move us and give us pleasure are often flagrantly unpleasant in themselves.[28] This enigma, a theme of art theory at least since Aristotle, finds its solution, as paradoxes often do, in a shift of levels of description. The pertinent distinction, Dubos argues, is not to be drawn with respect to the objects represented, say good or bad, but with respect to the soul attending to the representations, where the relevant disjunction is that between active and inactive. Note here that we have moved from first- to second-order observation, from the what or thematic content of our representations to the activity and effects of our representings. At this level of inquiry Dubos develops his central thesis, which rests on the premise that the soul abhors nothing more than its own inactivity, that it is in constant flight from ennui, and therefore yields itself up to whatever occupies it and stimulates its responsiveness. Activity is the soul's sole hold on existence, to maintain itself the psyche must be moved, and ennui, the prospect of time without affect or interest, therefore signals a threat to its self-preservative instinct. But this thesis would seem to embrace too much and therefore explain too little, for, while occasions energizing the psyche might well satisfy our deepest need and thereby afford us pleasure, it remains unclear what is specific to the pleasures of art. Dubos's counter to this objection is to introduce a further distinction. The specificity of art derives from the fact that its objects, and hence the passions they excite, are not real but, as he puts it, artificial, copies. And, in a reversal of the Platonic verdict against imitation, Dubos claims that precisely this non-real status lends art its singular efficacy and value. The pleasure we feel is not accompanied by any unpleasant consequences, it has no follow-up, entertains no connections with our ongoing experience. It is the pleasure of an emotion or soulful activity cut off from our real or existential situatedness and unencumbered, therefore, by worry or regret, a pure pleasure accessible only in the enjoyment of art. Art is the occasion, then, of the soul's self-presentation and self-mastery, a frame for unburdened self-observation.

Several aspects of this theory call for commentary, but once again I want to direct attention to the overall structural configuration. My argument is that Dubos's use of the concept of imitation has no referential import; it does not connect the representations of art with their prototypes in nature, does not secure the continuity between the natural or moral order and the aesthetic domain. Nor is it, as in Plato, the mark of ontological derivation and deficiency. On the contrary, it is the operator of a distinction that exempts activity from connectedness and consequences, detaches us from our clustered existential, social, and moral concerns. And in this sense it is the psychological correlate of Shaftesbury's social circumscription of the realm of wit. It isolates a domain of second-order observation in which the soul registers the nuances of its own movements in the encounter of mind and medium.

The lesson I draw from these twin examples is that the isolation of aesthetic experience from the intricate entwinements of rhetorical office is accomplished by the institution of a double frame: a social frame that circumscribes a sphere of interchange abstracted from the multiple dependencies of powerfully invested social conventions, and a psychological frame that detaches representational activity from the consequentiality of existential relevance and focuses it on medially transmitted forms of virtuality. So my argument comes down to the apparent paradox that the second precedes the first. That is, the absorptive attention that characterizes aesthetic experience, as the eighteenth century conceives it, is a first-order observation *as* observed from a second-order standpoint, and the attainment of this standpoint presupposes the dual operations of social and psychological containment legible in the texts of Shaftesbury and Dubos.

The strongest argument for this hypothesis, it seems to me, is that it has predictive value. What it predicts, first of all, is that the circumscription of a sphere of second-order observation, while exempting participants from the complex concerns embedded in other fields of activity, nevertheless results in an intensification of complexity within the isolated sphere itself. Complexity increases in the sense that an expanding field of previously unavailable perceptual and affective nuances is disclosed. But it also expands in the sense that what observers observe is that their own observations differ from those of others and, since the connections with other socially available value systems—religion, morality, the political order—have been severed, there is no longer any available benchmark according to which these differences can be measured.

As it develops across the eighteenth century, the discourse of aesthetic theory elaborates two solutions to this immanent structural problem. The first of these is to temporalize the framework of consideration, a process that introduces the concept of novelty, conceived not merely in terms of subject matter, but in terms of the internal history of the system. Value becomes positional value, and position is defined temporally in terms of what has already been achieved. Thus, by mid-century, the predicate of historical novelty nests itself within the concept of beauty, and this not only for nativists like Edward Young, but also for classicists like Johann Joachim Winckelmann, for whom imitation of the Greeks is—paradoxically enough—imitation of their originality. But this solution to the problem of diversity attains predominance only in the last third of the century, for example in the cultural-historical theories of Johann Gottfried Herder. Far more significant in terms of the great decades of Enlightenment aesthetics, the 1750s and 1760s, is the effort to conceive of what I should like to call non-positive norms. In fact, this solution is already limned in Shaftesbury's essay on the freedom of wit, in which the play of second-order observation unleashed by his framing operation is governed by the cognate values of

Providence and Nature. The characteristic feature of these values is that they are unavailable to inspection; they are not given to any single participant in the witty exchange, cannot be recurred to as the anchorage of any individual contribution. Their function, rather, is that of an invisible hand, a guidance immanent to and directive of the process, but thematizable only as a projected or anticipated rationality. My hunch is that this anticipated directionality is what Kant later formulates with his notion of regulative ideas. But the sharpest conception of the matter, it seems to me, was sketched out in David Hume's stunning essay "The Standard of Taste," one of the *Four Dissertations* he published in 1757. The problem of multiplicity of tastes and preferences, certainly one of the central problems in Enlightenment aesthetic theory, is, after all, the problem of complexified second-order observation. Hume's notion, if I read his slippery essay justly, is that this complexity is indeed governed by a standard, but that that standard has no external hold. It is the bent that the play of diversity takes, not an idea, but an empirical fact emergent from plurality. The just standard of taste is just that standard to which the history of tasteful judgments, in the long run, hews.

The second prediction suggested by the hypothesis bears on the structure of activity within the isolated sphere. Once the ramifying network of references has been contained, operative juncture, the linkage of one perceptual-imaginative act to another, can no longer function in an outwardly directed fashion. Thus, operations are compelled to turn back on themselves; they are channeled into recursion, in which they reprocess their own results. This recursive operation can unfold historically, yielding the sort of temporalization described above, but perhaps yet more significant is the tendency toward intensive recursion, which has as its focus an individual work. Or should one not rather say that the very notion of the work as what might be termed an instanding unity is the artifact of this recursive turn? The emergence of a literature of critical description in the 1750s and 1760s— I am thinking of the "Salons" of Denis Diderot and the descriptive writings of Winckelmann, for instance his account of the *Torso Belvedere* (figs. 8 and 9, pages 140–41)—constitute the unity of the work, in the emphatic sense of the term, within a movement of reflection that seeks to account for its own emergence. The notion of aesthetic unity is, of course, an ancient one, but my sense is that in the eighteenth century it undergoes a significant semantic change. That is, in contrast to what might be called the natural model of unity (the living organism, for example), the eighteenth century develops a processual model in which unity is the return of a process of observation to its own point of departure, the closure of an operativity that generates its own elements. One might characterize this kind of unity as auto-productive or, with Humberto Maturana and Luhmann, autopoietic.[29] The theory of genius, which is a theory of the unprecedented emergence of works, can be read, I think, as the mythical script of just such an auto-productive form.

The final prediction suggested by the hypothesis that the second precedes the first brings me back to my opening considerations. For, if Enlightenment aesthetic theory codifies a structure of second-order observation, then it will have as its object just that which, from the standpoint of first-order observation, is invisible. Precisely such invisibility characterizes the media within which first-order observations operate, for it is the distinctive feature of media that their function precludes thematization. One sees through media to that which they mediate, to the forms that establish rigid couplings of elements within the loosely coupled elements of the medium itself.[30] And so it is that the major texts of Enlightenment theory address the question of the capacities and limits of medial transmission. Recall the fascination with examples of blindness and deafness, with the Saundersons and Blacklocks that people the works of Diderot, Moses Mendelssohn, Burke, and Herder. Sensory deprivation provides an isolating test case in terms of which the properties of single-media transmission can be studied. Recall also the influence of theories of sensation and perception as articulated, for example, by George Berkeley, Georges Louis Leclerc Buffon, Étienne Bonnot de Condillac, and Adam Smith. The point here is to focus on the capacities of sensory media to transmit formal values and thereby to delineate the restrictions and combinatory possibilities of media in the construction of artistic forms. The decisive text in this regard might well be the incomparably lucid "Discourse on Music, Painting, and Poetry," which James Harris published as the second of his *Three Treatises* in 1744.[31] I refer to this text rather than to the more famous and, as we have seen, more influential *Laocoön* of Lessing, because it employs a richer array of medial possibilities, distinguishing not merely natural and contractual or arbitrary media, but also imitative media, the class that embraces both the foregoing categories, and sympathetic media that convey, as it were, beneath the level of noematic contents, affective forms. But even where issues other than the classification of the arts enter discussion, as in Burke's *Enquiry* or in Kant's *Observations on the Feelings of the Beautiful and the Sublime* (1764), the question of medial differences remains central. Perhaps the last great contribution to this discussion is Herder's *Plastik* (1778), which, drawing on Berke-

ley's ingenious theory of visual ideas as proleptic signs of physical impinge-
ments, boldly extends the theory of artistic media so as to include tactility.

I conclude by recapitulating briefly the story I have endeavored to tell
here. Enlightenment aesthetics emerges out of the intricate social entangle-
ments of rhetorical theory through a dual process of social and psychological framing that isolates the experience of art as a sphere of self-regulating
second-order observation focused on the sphere of medially transmitted
imaginary forms. Within this frame the discourse of aesthetic theory produces a rich descriptive literature that attends to the threshold between consciousness and communication. But this theoretical paradigm is abandoned, consigned to irrelevance, with the emergence of idealist aesthetics,
which reduces the differential array of expressive means to the status of so
many objectifications of a deep cultural subject. Thus, the idea of self-regulating series is transformed into the shape of an historical narrative, the idea
of form as an auto-productive process of observation becomes the notion
of the work as the correlate of subjective autonomy, and, finally, the field of
medial differences is homogenized as a realm of meaning destined for
hermeneutic appropriation. Wedged as it is between the vast cultural for-
mations of rhetoric on the one hand and idealist hermeneutics on the other,
the fifty-year reign of Enlightenment aesthetics would seem to constitute
but a brief and, as it were, flickering chapter in the history of the theoretical
engagement with art. But, if the cues I have taken from Meyer, Arnheim,
Greenberg, and Frank are the right ones, it may well turn out that this flickering historical moment in fact sheds a revealing light on our modernist
cultural situation. For this situation, defined as it is not by the sensuous media that fascinated the Enlightenment theoreticians, but, rather, by the technological media that shape and extend our sensate capacities, is resistant to
hermeneutic appropriation. The theoretical models pertinent to our reality
are just those that thematize what Hans Ulrich Gumbrecht calls the non-
hermeneutic.[32] And this is why the *Laocoön* of Lessing, and the body of
work that text coheres with, is still available for citation today.

Regimes of Description:
In the Archive of the Eighteenth Century
Conference Proposal

We hope to open a critical space for the discussion of a specific historical moment, but with recourse neither to a pre-shaped notion of the "Enlightenment" nor to the simple chronological limits of the eighteenth century.

Why "Description" as general rubric for the conference? Here our thinking has been affected by the perception—however imprecise—that forms of knowledge in every sector of contemporary culture are being fundamentally reshaped by the digital revolution: music, speech, engineering diagrams, weather conditions, works of visual art, even the words most of us write are now subject, as Jean-François Lyotard points out in *The Inhuman*, to a logic of the *bit*, the elemental unit of electronic information. It is now possible to slice, graft, and splice this knowledge in ways never before imagined using technologies that treat vast bodies of information as a stream of data bits. Programs and technical algorithms specify the criteria for discriminating between the data stream of a Mozart string quartet and the CAT scan of a diseased organ. But are these machine instructions and design parameters *descriptions*, or merely mechanical filters? And if the latter, what constitutes a description of digitally encoded knowledge? Even to pose the question suggests the need for an inquiry into the nature and history of description.

How does this contemporary situation concern the Enlightenment? As Michel Foucault remarked, the eighteenth-century naturalist Georges Louis Leclerc Buffon expressed astonishment that the writings of Ulisse Aldrovandi contained an "inextricable mixture of exact description, reported quotations, fables without commentary," and so on. Most important, Buffon concluded: "There is no description here, only legend." In contrast to Buffon, Foucault points out that the sixteenth century was quite at home with a "non-distinction between . . . observation and relation" that produced a "single, unbroken surface in which observation and language intersect to infinity." Is the digital revolution about to bring the history of knowledge full circle by constructing a new kind of "single unbroken surface"? What might we learn from those eighteenth-century thinkers and researchers who forged from just such an "unbroken surface," the principles of description upon which most—if not all—of the specialized disciplines of modern inquiry were erected?

Such questions cause us to think it timely, and perhaps even necessary, to look again at the assumptions, strategies, and place of description in eighteenth-century culture, and to position the conference as an instance of "rewriting" our modernity for the digital age: "You will ask me," remarks Lyotard, "what relation this practice can have with rewriting modernity. I recall that in working through, the only guiding thread at one's disposal consists in sentiment or, better, in listening to a sentiment. A fragment of a sentence, a scrap of information, a word, come along. They are immediately linked with another 'unit'. No reasoning, no argument, no mediation. By proceeding in this way, one slowly approaches a scene, the scene of something. One describes it. One does not know what it is. One is sure only that it refers to some past, both furthest and nearest past, both one's own past and others' past" (*The Inhuman*).

Where to begin? The entry for "Description" in the *Encyclopédie* is rather brief, and even Jean-François Marmontel's additional four columns in the *Supplément* fail to place it among the longest or most complex of the encyclopedic exposés. Nevertheless, the essays on "description" map the concept across several kinds of knowledge and disciplinary practice: the range of this mapping, and its potential for opening unusual arenas of discussion, has inspired our preliminary thoughts about the conference.

1. The *Encyclopédie* begins with the Natural Sciences, and argues that descriptions must have limits, must be restrained: in short, they must follow certain implicit laws of nature. The general guideline is that complex organisms require longer and more complex descriptions than animals or plants, while descriptions devoted to minerals should be even more brief. A second key principle is that the range of observation, detail, and type of language must not vary when moving within the same domain, yet all three must change when moving from one domain to another. Description is not a normalized activity, but always reflects the relative position of its subject along the chain of being.

This section inspires questions about the linguistic status of descriptions; the relationship between observation and knowledge; and the obscuring effects of iterative statements in any number of disciplines, such as biology, medicine, or the physical sciences. Can we develop a comparative understanding of the issues peculiar to each field of knowledge? What is the descriptive status of probability theory and of probabilistic institutions such as insurance?

2. The essay on "Description" then relates directly to the literal meaning of *décrire* as used in Geometry: description is the action of tracing a line, a surface, or some other geometric figure. A brief discussion of the differences between the concept of a curve as the trace of a single moving point, on one hand, and as the collection of points joined by straight lines, on the other, suggests the impact of contemporary developments in calculus, although the author tends to dismiss these new tools as "more curious than practical or easy to use."

What are the general forms of mathematical descriptions, including the plotting of motion, calculation of inertia, development of differential calculus, or discussions of specific mathematical treatises?

3. The longest section of the essay deals with description in the Humanities [Belles-Lettres]. It opens by comparing descriptions (tool of grammarians) and de-

finitions (required by philosophers): descriptions enumerate attributes (usually accidental qualities) and may seem to be definitions; yet they never "truly reveal something" because they do not "encompass or expose the essential attributes of it." Descriptions catalogue differences among individual members of a group, but not the qualities that distinguish one group from another. Description is thus exiled from philosophy (and, by extension, from absolute truth), but this exile is exactly why it is portrayed as a favorite device of orators and poets. The essay names four areas of knowledge where it is of particular importance: narrating current events, recounting the past, describing remote places, and portraying individuals.

These categories suggest questions about the forms of description deployed across four broad areas of eighteenth-century writing. Journalism, History, Geography, and Biography exercised great power in the political events of Europe and the New World during the course of the century, and each developed specialized strategies of description that continue to affect work in the Humanities today.

4. A final theme raised by the essay on "Description" asks the question: how is it that well-made descriptions of even disagreeable objects or events can be found pleasing? The text suggests that while the description of something beautiful pleases us, we take an even more powerful—almost secret—delight in the description of something terrible that we know cannot physically affect us. In other words, the essay's comments cut across and through contemporary discussions about beauty and the sublime.

An exploration of affective concepts from Edmund Burke—asking how descriptions develop an affective power—may promote innovative discussions across the border between aesthetic theory and eighteenth-century experiments in clinical psychology. Moreover, the broader issue of how to compel opens the question of ideology in descriptions—notably those employed by Economics, Political Theory, and gender-based regimes of social explanation.

5. Marmontel's addition extends the discussion to include comments about theater and the visual arts. His essay begins by emphasizing the role of *choice* in an effective description: not only the choice of subject, but also point of view, moment, salient characteristics, and revealing contrasts. In other words, Marmontel is concerned with what might be called the "staging" of a description—whether on an actual stage or organized within the frame of a picture—and how to manipulate the possible variables to maximum effect. His attention to the material and mechanics of a description, and his advice on how to orchestrate them, suggest that he understands "description" as an artificially induced effect that stands for rather than replicates its object. Indeed, his remarks both summarize the operation of the *Encyclopédie*'s plates and come remarkably close to outlining an alternate proposal for this entire conference.

Notes

Bender and Marrinan: Introduction

1. "Reading the Book of Life; White House Remarks on Decoding of Genome," *New York Times*, 27 June 2000.

2. Technical papers supporting the "official" announcement were not published until mid-February 2001. The principal articles are Eric S. Lander et al., "Initial Sequencing and Analysis of the Human Genome," *Nature* 409 (15 February 2001): 860–921; and J. Craig Venter et al., "The Sequence of the Human Genome," *Science* 291 (16 February 2001): 1304–51. The most important source of official information about the project is the web site of the National Human Genome Research Institute: www.genome.gov.

3. Dr. Robert Waterston, a leading genome sequencer, speaking at a news conference at the National Institutes of Health and reported in Nicholas Wade, "Once Again, Scientists Say Human Genome Is Complete," *New York Times*, 15 April 2003.

4. "Understanding the human genome is expected to revolutionize the practice of medicine," read the *New York Times* on 27 June 2000. "Biologists expect in time to develop an array of diagnostics and treatments based on it and tailored to individual patients, some of which will exploit the body's own mechanisms of self-repair." Since the early 1990s, there has been a steady stream of popular books aimed at framing the ethical and social dimensions of the genome project. For an overview of this bibliography and reviews of specific books, consult the "Book Review Archive," *Genome News Network*: www.genomenewsnetwork.org. For a primer on the human genome, along with extensive rubrics on education, research, medicine, and social issues emerging from the results of the Human Genome Project, consult the Genomes to Life web site maintained by the U.S. Department of Energy: www.ornl.gov/sci/techresources/Human_Genome/home.shtml.

5. Marie Jean Antoine Nicolas Caritat Condorcet, *Sketch for a Historical Picture of the Progress of the Human Mind*, trans. June Barraclough (London: Weidenfeld & Nicolson, 1955), 200. Condorcet's text was originally published in 1795.

6. Ibid., 199.

7. "Human Genome May Be Longer Than Expected," *New York Times*, 1 August 1999; and Kevin Davies, *Cracking the Genome: Inside the Race to Unlock the Human DNA* (New York: The Free Press, 2001), 40–42.

8. "And the Gene Number Is . . . ?" *Science* 288 (19 May 2000): 1146–47.

9. Michael Ashburner et al., "An Exploration of the Sequence of a 2.9-MB Region of the Genome of *Drosophilia melanogaster*: The *Adh* Region," *Genetics* 153 (September 1999): 179–219, esp. 191.

10. John Sulston and James Watson, "Genome Sequence of the Nematode C. elegans: A Platform for Investigating Biology," *Science* 282 (1998): 2012–18; and "Animal's Genetic Program Decoded, in a Science First," *New York Times*, 11 December 1998.

11. "Technology: First Complete Plant Genetic Sequence Is Determined," *New York Times*, 14 December 2000.

12. See the page "So How Many Genes Are There?" on the web site Genomes to Life maintained by the U.S. Department of Energy: www.ornl.gov/sci/techresources/Human_Genome/faq/genenumber.shtml.

13. At a symposium in 1989 Brenner surmised that 98 percent of the human genome was "junk" DNA that "cannot be evaded but there are ways of avoiding it, and, anyway, it is one of the problems that we can and should leave for our successors" (Sydney Brenner, "The Human Genome: The Nature of the Enterprise," in *Symposium on Human Genetic Information: Science, Law and Ethics, Ciba Foundation Symposium* (New York: John Wiley & Sons, 1990), 6–17, at p. 9.

14. Helen Skaletsky et al., "The Male-Specific Region of the Human Y Chromosome Is a Mosaic of Discrete Sequence Classes," *Nature* 423 (19 June 2003): 825–37. On the value of a sustained effort to understand the so-called junk DNA, see Huntington F. Willard, "Genome Biology: Tales of the Y Chromosome," *Nature* 423 (19 June 2003): 810–13.

15. Nicholas Wade, "Comparing Genomes Shows Split Between Chimps and People," *New York Times*, 12 December 2003. This comparative study of the genomes of humans and chimpanzees suggests that some of the genetic changes might have occurred in as little as 100,000 years, which would be an accelerated rate of evolution.

16. Venter's sequencing strategy was first published in Mark D. Adams et al., "Complementary DNA Sequencing: Expressed Sequence Tags and Human Genome Project," *Science* 252 (21 June 1991): 1651–56. It was not until May of 1998, however, that he announced his intention of applying the sequencing strategy to the human genome: see Nicholas Wade, "Scientist's Plan: Map All DNA Within 3 Years," *New York Times*, 10 May 1998. For more information on the technology of sequencing, see www.ornl.gov/sci/techresources/Human_Genome/publicat/hgn/hgnarch.shtml#sequencing.

17. Davies, *Cracking the Genome*, 169–91.

18. In 1989, while defending his call for an approach to the human genome that would simply ignore most of the "junk" material, Brenner clearly articulated a totalizing fantasy of the project: "Rutherford said there were two kinds of science: physics and stamp collecting. But what he forgot is that there are some stamps worth collecting. I like to compare the human genome project with the French En-

lightenment. The aim of the project is to make an encyclopaedia, and to encompass all knowledge of human biology. Some people like to do this. I like it; I get aesthetic pleasure from it" (Brenner, "The Human Genome," 6–17, at p. 17. Needless to say, we believe the essays presented in this volume undermine Brenner's view of the Enlightenment and reshape the ambitions he ascribes to the *Encyclopédie* of Diderot and d'Alembert.

19. Alison and Helmut Gernsheim, *L. J. M. Daguerre: The History of the Diorama and the Daguerreotype*, 2nd ed. (New York: Dover, 1968), 89–90; and Shelly Rice, *Parisian Views* (Cambridge, Mass.: MIT Press, 1997), 7–10.

20. Michel Foucault, *The Order of Things: An Archaeology of the Human Sciences* (New York: Random House Vintage Books, 1994), 239–46, at p. 246.

21. In a forthcoming book, we argue that from the mid-eighteenth century onward a fractured, discontinuous, and non-mimetic form of representation, which we call "diagram," came to challenge the mimetic placing of forms in space (based largely on perspective) that is usually called "tableau." We suggest that a creative interaction between these ways of seeing the world—not simply a debate about their relative validity, functionality, or comprehensiveness—has characterized visual, literary, and scientific culture for more than two hundred years. See John Bender and Michael Marrinan, *The Culture of Diagram* (Stanford, Calif.: Stanford University Press, forthcoming). Anthony Vidler demonstrates the theoretical importance of diagrams in the practice of modern architecture, especially relative to computer-aided design, and many of his conclusions converge importantly with our own: Anthony Vidler, "Diagrams of Diagrams: Architectural Abstraction and Modern Representation," *Representations* 72 (2000): 1–20.

Daston: Description by Omission

1. *Mémoires pour servir à l'histoire naturelle des animaux et des plantes*, in *Mémoires de l'Académie Royale des Sciences, contenant les ouvrages adoptez par cette Académie avant son renouvellement en 1699*, 6 vols. (Amsterdam: Pierre Mortier, 1736), 1: 429, 431. Unless otherwise noted, all translations are my own. A longer version of this paper that dwells more on luminescence and less on description appears as "The Cold Light of Facts and the Facts of Cold Light: Luminescence and the Transformation of the Scientific Fact 1600–1750," *Early Modern France* 3 (1997): 1–28.

2. Carl von Linnaeus, *The Critica Botanica of Linnaeus*, trans. Sir Arthur Hort and rev. M. L. Green (London: Royal Society, 1938), Aphorisms 259, 266, 282, 291; pp. 122, 139, 161, 170–71. The *Critica Botanica*, originally published in 1737, was an elaboration of Aphorisms 210–324 of his *Fundamenta botanica* (1736).

3. "Préface," *Mémoires pour servir à l'histoire naturelle*, 3r.

4. On these strange facts and their function see Lorraine Daston, "Baconian Facts, Academic Civility, and the Prehistory of Objectivity," *Annales of Scholarship* 8 (1991): 337–64.

5. René Descartes, *Passions de l'âme* (1694), in *Oeuvres de Descartes*, ed. Charles Adam and Paul Tannery, 12 vols. (Paris: Libraire J. Vrin, 1957–68), 11: 380.

6. See, for example, Robert Hooke, "A General Scheme, or Idea, of the Present State of Natural Philosophy, and How Its Defects May Be Remedied by a Methodical Proceeding in the Making Experiments and Collecting Observations," in *The*

Posthumous Works of Robert Hooke, ed. Richard Waller (reprint, with an introduction by Richard S. Westfall, New York: Johnson Reprint Corporation, 1969), 61–62.

7. On the history of luminescence in general see E. Newton Harvey, *A History of Luminescence from the Earliest Times until 1900* (Philadelphia: American Philosophical Society, 1957).

8. Francis Bacon, *Topica inquisitionis de luce et lumine* (1612), in *The Works of Francis Bacon*, ed. Basil Montagu, 16 vols. (London: William Pickering, 1825–34).

9. Robert Boyle, "A Short Account of Some Observations Made by Mr. Boyle about a Diamond, That Shines in the Dark" (1663), in Robert Boyle, *The Works of the Honourable Robert Boyle*, ed. Thomas Birch, 6 vols. (reprint, Hildesheim: Georg Olms Verlag, 1966), 1: 797.

10. Boyle, "The Aerial Noctiluca: Or, Some New Phaenomena, and a Process of a Factitious Self-shining Substance" (1680), in ibid., 4: 384.

11. John L. Heilbron, *Electricity in the Seventeenth and Eighteenth Centuries: A Study in Early Modern Physics* (Berkeley: University of California Press, 1979), 76, 219, 229, and passim.

12. On the early modern meaning and valuation of curiosity, see Jean Céard, ed., *La curiosité à la Renaissance* (Paris: Société d'Édition d'Enseignement Supérieur, 1986); Hans Blumenberg, *Der Prozeß der theoretischen Neugierde* (Frankfurt-am-Main: Suhrkamp, 1988); and, on the natural philosophical context, Lorraine Daston, "Neugierde als Empfindung und Epistemologie in der frühmodernen Wissenschaft," in *Macrocosmus im Microcosmus: Die Welt in der Stube: Zur Geschichte des Sammelns 1450 bis 1800*, ed. Andreas Grote (Opladen: Leske & Budrich, 1994), 35–59.

13. Boyle, "A Short Account of Some Observations," 1: 791.

14. Pierre Potier, *De lapide quondam incognito* (Bologna: 1622), quoted in Harvey, *A History of Luminescence*, 308.

15. Jacques de Rohault, *Traité de physique* (Paris: 1671), quoted in Harvey, *A History of Luminescence*, 140.

16. Letter of G. W. Leibniz to Christian Philipp (11/21 April 1682), in Gottfried Wilhelm Leibniz, *Allgemeiner politischer und historischer Briefwechsel*, in *Sämtliche Schriften und Briefe*, ed. Deutsche Akademie der Wissenschaften zu Berlin (reprint, Berlin: Akademie Verlag, 1970), 1.3: 529.

17. Harvey, *A History of Luminescence*, 318.

18. Boyle, "New Experiments Concerning the Relation between Light and Air, in Shining Word and Fish; Made by the Author, and by Him Addressed from Oxford to the Publisher, and So Communicated to the Royal Society" (6 January 1667–68), in Boyle, *The Works of the Honourable Robert Boyle*, 3: 157–69, at 166.

19. Letter of John Clayton to Robert Boyle (23 June 1684), quoted in Harvey, *A History of Luminescence*.

20. Boyle, "The Aerial Noctiluca," 403.

21. Letter of Herzog Friedrich to G. W. Leibniz (4/14 August 1678), in Leibniz, *Allgemeiner politischer und historischer Briefwechsel*, 1.2: 66–67.

22. Boyle, "The Aerial Noctiluca," 382.

23. Ibid., 401.

24. See J. V Golinski, "A Noble Spectacle: Phosphorus and the Public Culture of Science in the Early Royal Society," *Isis* 80 (1989): 11–39; and Christian Licoppe,

La formation de la pratique scientifique: Le discours de l'expérience en France et en Angleterre 1630–1820 (Paris: Éditions de la Découverte, 1996), 88–126, on the audience for such wonders.

25. Boyle, "Short Memorial of Some Observations Made upon an Artificial Substance, That Shines Without Any Precedent Illustration" (1677), in Boyle, *The Works of the Honourable Robert Boyle*, 4: 368.

26. Boyle, "Some Observations About Shining Flesh, Both of Veal and Pullet, and That Without Any Sensible Putrefaction in Those Bodies" (1677), in ibid., 3: 651–55, at 651.

27. Standardized instruments could also help stabilize capricious phenomena. See Heilbron, *Electricity in the Seventeenth and Eighteenth Centuries*, 73–75 and passim; and Simon Schaffer, "Glass Works: Newton's Prisms and the Uses of Experiment," in *The Uses of Experiment: Studies in the Natural Sciences*, ed. D. Gooding, T. Pinch, and Simon Schaffer (Cambridge: Cambridge University Press, 1989), 67–104, on the problem of establishing a standard.

28. C. F. Dufay, "Mémoire sur un grand nombre de phosphores nouveaux," in C. F Dufay, *Mémoires de l'Académie des Sciences: Année 1730* (Paris: Imprimerie Royale, 1732), 524.

29. Bernard de Fontenelle, "Sur l'électricité," in *Histoire de l'Académie Royale des Sciences: Année 1733* (Paris: Imprimerie Royale, 1735), 4–13, at 4.

30. See Lennard J. Davis, *Factual Fictions: The Origins of the English Novel* (New York: Columbia University Press, 1982); also Michael McKeon, *The Origins of the English Novel 1600–1740* (Baltimore: Johns Hopkins University Press, 1987).

31. Dufay, "Mémoire sur un grand nombre de phosphores nouveaux," 531.

32. See, for example "Electricité," in the manuscript "Memoire sur quelques expériences de catoptrique," Archives de l'Académie des Sciences, Paris, fol. 5r, dossier Dufay.

33. Dufay, "Mémoire sur un grand nombre de phosphores nouveaux," 534.

34. Ibid., 18–52, at 52.

35. Dufay, "Sixième mémoire sur l'électricité," in C. F Dufay, *Memoires de l'Académie Royale des Sciences: Année 1734* (Paris: Imprimerie Royale, 1736), 503–26, at 516–18.

36. Ibid., 516.

37. Ibid.

38. Quoted in John L. Heilbron, "Dufay, Charles-François de Cisternai," in Charles C. Gillispie, ed., *Dictionary of Scientific Biography*, 15 vols. (New York: Charles Scribner's Sons, 1970–78), 4: 214–17.

39. Dufay, "Mémoire sur un grand nombre de phosphores nouveaux," 527.

40. Friedrich Steinle, "The Amalgamation of a Concept—Laws of Nature in the New Sciences," in *Laws of Nature: Essays on the Philosophical, Scientific and Historical Dimensions*, ed. Friedel Weinert (Berlin: Walter de Gruyter, 1995), 316–68.

41. Marie-Noëlle Bourguet, "Voyage, collecte, collections: Le catalogue de la nature (fin 17e–debut 19e siècle)," in *Terre à découvrir, terres à parcourir*, ed. D. Lecocq (Paris: Publications de l'Université de Paris 7–Denis Diderot, 1996), 184–207.

42. Marie Jean Antoine Nicolas Caritat Condorcet, "Observations sur le vingt-neuvième livre de *L'esprit des lois*," in Condorcet, *Oeuvres de Condorcet*, ed. F. Arago

224 / *Notes to Pages 23–27*

and A. Condorcet-O'Connor, 12 vols. (Paris: Firmin Didot Frères, 1847–49), 1: 376–81.

43. Marie Jean Antoine Nicolas Caritat Condorcet, *Vie de Turgot* (1786), in ibid., 5: 189.

44. Bernard de Fontenelle, *La république des philosophes, ou Histoire des Ajaoiens* (Geneva: Éditions d'histoire sociale, 1768), 18, 65, 112, 44, 63.

Schiebinger: Nature's Unruly Body

1. Maria Sibylla Merian, *Metamorphosis insectorum surinamensium* (1705), ed. Helmut Deckert (Leipzig: Insel Verlag, 1975), commentary to plate no. 45. Portions of this essay were published in my *Nature's Body: Gender in the Making of Modern Science* (Boston: Beacon Press, 1993) and in my "Lost Knowledge, Bodies of Ignorance, and the Poverty of Taxonomy as Illustrated by the Curious Fate of *Flos Pavonis*, an Abortifacient," in *Picturing Science, Producing Art*, ed. Peter Galison and Caroline Jones (New York: Routledge, 1998), 125–44.

2. *Encyclopédie ou Dictionnaire raisonné des sciences, des arts et des métiers* (1751–65), 17 vols. (reprint, Stuttgart–Bad Cannstatt: Frommann, 1966), s.v. "Histoire Naturelle."

3. Daniel Roche, "Natural History in the Academies," in *Cultures of Natural History*, ed. Nicholas Jardine, James Secord, and Emma Spary (Cambridge: Cambridge University Press, 1996), 127–44, esp. 138.

4. Katie Whitaker, "The Culture of Curiosity," in *Cultures of Natural History*, ed. Nicholas Jardine, James Secord, and Emma Spary (Cambridge: Cambridge University Press, 1996), 75–90, esp. 85.

5. Jacques-Christophe Valmont de Bomare, *Dictionnaire raisonné universel d'histoire naturelle*, 4th ed., 8 vols. (Lyon: Bruyset frères, 1791), 6: 633; David Allen, *The Naturalist in Britain: A Social History* (Harmondsworth, England: Penguin Books, 1978), 30–31.

6. Marie Jean Antoine Nicolas Caritat Condorcet, "Éloge de M. de Linné," in *Histoire de l'Académie Royale des Sciences* (Paris: Imprimerie Royale, 1778), 78.

7. The value of the gold, silver, and precious stones shipped from the East Indies to England in a four-year period from 1759 to 1763 amounted to £600,000. Fernand Braudel, *The Wheels of Commerce*, trans. Siân Reynolds (reprint, New York: Harper & Row, 1982), 222. See also Richard Grove, *Green Imperialism: Colonial Expansion, Tropical Island Edens and the Origins of Environmentalism, 1600–1860* (Cambridge: Cambridge University Press, 1995); and David Miller and Peter Reill, eds., *Visions of Empire: Voyages, Botany, and Representations of Nature* (Cambridge: Cambridge University Press, 1996).

8. Louis-Antoine de Bougainville, *A Voyage Round the World*, trans. Johann Reinhold Forster (London: J. Nourse, 1772), viii.

9. Carl von Linnaeus, "Anthropomorpha," in *Amoenitates academicae seu dissertationes variae physicae, medicae, botanicae* (Holmiæ & Lipsiæ: Apud Godefredum Kiesewetter, 1764), 72–76. Linnaeus also sometimes considered *Homo caudatus* a third species of humans. On Linnaeus's *Homo troglodytes*, see Gunnar Broberg's excellent "*Homo sapiens*," in *Linnaeus: The Man and His Work*, ed. Tore Frängsmyr, Up-

psala Studies in the History of Science 18 (Berkeley: University of California Press, 1983), 185–86.

10. J. Heniger, *Hendrik Adriaan van Reede tot Drakenstein and Hortus malabaricus* (Rotterdam: A. A. Balekema, 1986), 76–77.

11. Harry Burrell, *The Platypus* (Sydney: Angus & Robertson Limited, 1927), 1–45.

12. Lisbet Koerner, "Carl Linnaeus in His Time and Place," in *Cultures of Natural History*, ed. Nicholas Jardine, James Secord, and Emma Spary (Cambridge: Cambridge University Press, 1996), 145–62.

13. Hans Plischke, *Johann Friedreich Blumenbachs Einfluss auf die Entdeckungsreisenden seiner Zeit* (Göttingen: Vandenhoeck & Ruprecht, 1937), 81–82.

14. Foucher d'Obsonville, *Essais philosophiques sur les mœurs de divers animaux étrangers, avec des observations relatives aux principes & usages de plusieurs peuple, ou, Extraits des voyages de M*** en Asie* (Paris: Couturier fils; la veuve Tilliand & fils, 1783), 372–73.

15. Ibid., 365.

16. Edward Tyson, *Orang-Outang, sive Homo sylvestris: Or the Anatomy of a Pygmie Compared with That of a Monkey, an Ape, and a Man* (London: T. Bennett and D. Brown, 1699), 13. Early modern naturalists were still greatly influenced by the ancients who portrayed ape-like creatures (mostly imaginary) walking erect with a staff (Jonathan Swift, *Miscellanies in Prose and Verse*, 3 vols. [London: Sam. Fairbrother, 1732], 3: 101). In anatomical illustrations of this period, ape and monkey were commonly drawn standing erect. Richard Bradley, for example, in comparing the skeleton of a monkey and a human has the monkey drawn in an unnaturally erect posture, thus heightening its human appearance (Richard Bradley, *A Philosophical Account of the Works of Nature* [London: W. Mears, 1721], plate XIX). In the English translation of Georges Cuvier's *Le règne animal*, the skeleton of the chimpanzee is also drawn perfectly erect (Georges Cuvier, *The Animal Kingdom*, 16 vols. [London: George B. Whittker, 1827–35], 1: following 252).

17. Jean-Baptiste Audebert, *Histoire naturelle des singes et des makis* (Paris: Desray, 1799–1800), supplement, 7: 2.

18. Thomas Boreman, *A Description of Some Curious and Uncommon Creatures* (London: Richard Ware and Thomas Boreman, 1739), 25. See also William Bosman, "A New and Accurate Description of the Coast of Guinea," in *A General Collection of the Best and Most Interesting Voyages and Travels in All Parts of the World*, 17 vols., ed. John Pinkerton (London: Printed for Longman, Hurst, Rees and Orme . . . , and Cadell and Davies . . . 1808), 16: 440.

19. Tyson, *Orang-Outang, sive Homo sylvestris*, 15.

20. See the text accompanying Gerard Scotin's illustration of the 1738 London chimpanzee; also Pons Alletz, *Histoire des singes, et autres animaux curieux* (Paris: Duchesne, 1752), 38; Stephen Jay Gould, "Chimp on the Chain," *Natural History* 12 (1983): 18–25, esp. 24; James Prichard, *Researches into the Physical History of Mankind*, 4th ed., 5 vols. (London: Sherwood, Gilbert & Piper [etc.], 1841–47), 1: 286.

21. Renée-Paule Guillot, "La vraie 'Bougainvillée': La première femme qui fit le tour du monde," *Historama* 1 (1984): 36–40.

22. Richard Ligon, *A True and Exact History of the Island of Barbados* (London: Printed for Humphrey Moseley . . ., 1657), 120–21.

23. Ann Shteir, *Cultivating Women, Cultivating Science: Flora's Daughters and Botany in England 1760–1860* (Baltimore: Johns Hopkins University Press, 1996).

24. Johann Friedrich Blumenbach, *The Natural Varieties of Mankind* (1865), trans. Thomas Bendyshe (reprint, New York: Bergman, 1969), 212 n. 2. Blumenbach codified notions long current in the culture.

25. Londa Schiebinger, *The Mind Has No Sex? Women in the Origins of Modern Science* (Cambridge, Mass.: Harvard University Press, 1989), chapter 3; Natalie Davis, *Women on the Margins: Three Seventeenth-Century Lives* (Cambridge, Mass.: Harvard University Press, 1995), 140–202.

26. Hans Sloane, *A Voyage to the Islands Madera, Barbadoes, Nieves, St Christophers, and Jamaica; with the Natural History . . .*, 2 vols. (London: Printed by B.M. for the author, 1707–25), 1: xlvi. Citation slightly altered.

27. Peter Kolb, *The Present State of the Cape of Good Hope*, trans. Guido Medley (London: W. Innys, 1731).

28. Sloane, *A Voyage to the Islands*, 2: 50. Sloane cites Merian's work in an addendum to his text (ibid., 2: 384). Sloane should perhaps not be taken too severely to task for his error; the history of the *flos pavonis* is fraught with ambiguities: A 1981 botanical atlas lists two Latin and up to forty-two common names used within Central America for this particular plant. Julia Morton, *Atlas of Medicinal Plants of Middle America* (Springfield, Ill.: Charles Thomas, 1981), 284–85.

29. See esp. Hendrik Adriaan van Reede, *Hortus indicus malabaricus*, 12 vols. (Amsterdam: Johannis van Someren and Joannis van Dyck, 1678–93), 6: 1–2. See also Jakob Breyne, *Exoticarum aliarumque minus cognitarium plantarum centuria prima* (Gedani: Typis, sumptibus & in aedibus autoris, imprimebat David Fridericus Rhetius, 1678), 61–64; Hans Sloane, *Catalogus plantarum quae in insula Jamaica . . .* (London: Impensis D. Brown, 1696), 149. I have not had an opportunity to consult Paul Hermann's important flora of Ceylon.

30. John Stedman, *Narrative of a Five Years Expedition against the Revolted Negroes of Surinam* (reprint, Baltimore: Johns Hopkins University Press, 1988), 26, 271–72.

31. Sloane, *A Voyage to the Islands*, 2: 50.

32. Ibid., 1: cxliii. Other great "dissemblers" of illness, according to Sloane, were servants, "both Whites and Blacks."

33. John Riddle, *Contraception and Abortion from the Ancient World to the Renaissance* (Cambridge, Mass.: Harvard University Press, 1992), 160.

34. Paul Brodwin, *Medicine and Morality in Haiti: The Contest for Healing Power* (Cambridge: Cambridge University Press, 1996), 28–32.

35. Cited in Barbara Bush, *Slave Women in Caribbean Society: 1650–1838* (Bloomington: Indiana University Press, 1990), 139.

36. My larger project investigates to what extent fertility and anti-fertility agents were collected by early modern European naturalists from abroad.

37. Joseph Raulin, *De la conservation des enfants*, 3 vols. (Paris: Merlin, 1768–69), 1: "épitre au roi."

38. See Angus McLaren, *Reproductive Rituals: The Perception of Fertility in England from the Sixteenth to the Nineteenth Century* (London: Methuen, 1984).

39. Even Merian merely mentioned that the seeds of the *flos pavonis* induce abortion; she did not discuss the manner of preparation—whether they were to be chewed raw, boiled or roasted, or used in a fumigant or pessary—nor did she discuss dosages.

40. Jean Donnison, *Midwives and Medical Men: A History of Inter-Professional Rivals and Women's Rights* (London: Heinemann, 1977); Riddle, *Contraception and Abortion*; Hilary Marland, ed., *The Art of Midwifery: Early Modern Midwives in Europe* (London: Routledge, 1993); Adrian Wilson, *The Making of Man-Midwifery: Childbirth in England, 1660–1770* (Cambridge, Mass.: Harvard University Press, 1995).

41. Barbara Duden, *Disembodying Women: Perspectives on Pregnancy and the Unborn*, trans. Lee Hoinacki (Cambridge, Mass.: Harvard University Press, 1993).

42. Nadia Filippini, "The Church, the State and Childbirth: The Midwife in Italy During the Eighteenth Century," in *The Art of Midwifery*, ed. Hilary Marland (London: Routledge, 1993), 157.

43. A priest reported that in 1659, six hundred women in Paris had confessed to having suffocated the fruit in their womb. Another observer suggested that the number would be much higher if it had included those who took early precautions, before "ensoulment," or quickening. Angus McLaren, *A History of Contraception from Antiquity to the Present Day* (Oxford: Basil Blackwell, 1990), 159–60.

44. McLaren, *Reproductive Rituals*, 102–6; see also Riddle, *Contraception and Abortion* and *Eve's Herbs: A History of Contraception and Abortion in the West* (Cambridge, Mass.: Harvard University Press, 1997), chapter 6.

45. William Stearn, "Botanical Exploration to the Time of Linnaeus," *Proceedings of the Linnean Society of London* 169 (1958): 173–96, esp. 165. Much of the history of botany has been written as the rise of systematics.

46. In fact, however, these traditions often merged in a single botanist. Tournefort and Linnaeus, celebrated as "fathers of modern botany," also collected abroad. Tournefort gathered some 1,356 plants—including wild madder, marigolds, violets, valerian, dwarf cherries, exotic irises, and dragonhead—while traveling through Levant on a pilgrimage to study the reputed marvels of Mount Ararat (where it was believed Noah's Ark had come to rest). Linnaeus' enthusiasm for the fauna and flora of Lapland is well known. He also expended considerable energy on trying to grow economically profitable plants, such as Chinese tea, in Sweden to enrich the coffers of his "fatherland." See Marguerite Duval, *The King's Garden*, trans. Annette Tomarken and Claudine Cowen (Charlottesville: University Press of Virginia, 1982), 42–53; and Lisbet Koerner, "Purposes of Linnaean Travel: A Preliminary Research Report," in *Visions of Empire: Voyages, Botany, and Representations of Nature*, ed. David Miller and Peter Reill (Cambridge: Cambridge University Press, 1996), 117–52.

47. Merian, *Metamorphosis insectorum surinamensium*, introduction, 38.

48. This Latin term was used in both the Dutch first edition and the Latin translation.

49. Breyne, *Exoticarum*, 61–64.
50. Hermann cited in Sloane, *Catalogus plantarum*, 149.
51. Breyne, *Exoticarum*, 61.
52. Merian, *Metamorphosis insectorum surinamensium*, plate 45.
53. From Paulus Hermannus, *Horti academici Lugduno-Batavi catalogus, exhibens plantarum omnium nomina, quibus ab anno 1681–1686 hortus fuit instructus, ut et plurimarum . . . descriptiones et icones* (Leiden: Lugduni Batavorum, 1687), 192. See also van Reede, *Hortus indicus malabaricus*, 6: 1–2. On the scripts used in the *Hortus malabaricus*, see Heniger, *Hendrik Adriaan van Reede*, 148–49.
54. Joseph Pitton de Tournefort, *Elémens de botanique ou Méthode pour connoître les plantes*, 3 vols. (Paris: Imprimerie Royale, 1694), 1: 491–92; 3: plate 391. See also Jean Baptiste Du Tertre, *Histoire generale des Antilles habitées par les Français*, 3 vols. (Paris: T. Jolly, 1667–71), 1: 125–26.
55. Carl von Linnaeus, *Species plantarum*, 2 vols. (Holmiæ: Impensis Laurentii Salvi, 1753), 1: 380.
56. Linnaeus expressly targeted van Reede's *Hortus malabaricus*, where the names for Merian's peacock flower were recorded in Malayalam, Konkani, and Arabic. Linnaeus faulted Merian for what he considered the "absence of names" in her text. Linnaeus, *Critical botanica*, nos. 218 and 229. This stands in contradistinction to more recent international codes of botanical nomenclature that allow "the genus name . . . [to] be taken from any source whatever." W. Greuter, ed., *International Code of Botanical Nomenclature* (Konigstein: Koeltz Scientific Books, 1988).
57. Linnaeus retained "barbarous names" only when he could devise a Latin or Greek derivation, even one having nothing to do with the plant or its origin. *Datura* (a genus in the potato family) he allowed, for example, for its association with *dare* from the Latin "to give, because it is 'given' to those whose sexual powers are weak or enfeebled." Linnaeus, *Critica botanica*, no. 229. Linnaeus did accept some well-established generic names derived from non-European languages, including *Coffea, Datura, Tulipa, Zombia, Camassia, Vanada,* and *Yucca*.
58. Linnaeus, *Critica botanica*, no. 238. See Heinz Goerke, *Linnaeus*, trans. Denver Lindley (New York: Charles Scribner's Sons, 1973), 108.
59. Michel Adanson, *Familles des plantes*, 2 vols. (Paris: Vincent, 1763), 1: clxxiii. On this point, see Joseph Needham, Lu Gwei-Djen, and Huang Hsing-Tsung, *Science and Civilization in China*, 7 vols. (Cambridge: Cambridge University Press, 1954–), 6.1: 19 and 168.
60. In 1905 the International Code of Botanical Nomenclature designated Linnaeus' *Species plantarum* of 1753 the starting point for botanical nomenclature. See Frans A. Stafleu, *Linnaeus and the Linnaeans: The Spreading of Their Ideas in Systematic Botany, 1735–1789* (Utrecht: A. Oosthoek's Uitgeversmaatschappij, 1971), 110.
61. Sander Gilman, *Difference and Pathology: Stereotypes of Sexuality, Race and Madness* (Ithaca, N.Y.: Cornell University Press, 1985); Ludmilla Jordanova, *Sexual Visions: Images of Gender in Science and Medicine between the Eighteenth and Twentieth Centuries* (Madison: University of Wisconsin Press, 1989); Thomas Laqueur, *Making Sex: Body and Gender from the Greeks to Freud* (Cambridge, Mass.: Harvard University Press, 1990); Schiebinger, *The Mind Has No Sex?*; Claudia Honegger, *Die Ordnung der Geschlechter: Die Wissenschaften vom Menschen und das Weib* (Frankfurt:

Campus Verlag, 1992); Felicity Nussbaum, *Torrid Zones: Maternity, Sexuality, and Empire in Eighteenth-Century English Narratives* (Baltimore: Johns Hopkins University Press, 1995); and Anne Fausto-Sterling, "Gender, Race, and Nation," in *Deviant Bodies: Critical Perspectives on Difference in Science and Popular Culture*, ed. Jennifer Terry and Jacqueline Urla (Bloomington: Indiana University Press, 1995), 19–48.

62. Robert Proctor, *Cancer Wars: How Politics Shapes What We Know and Don't Know about Cancer* (New York: Basic Books, 1995), 8 and chapter 5.

63. Susan Bordo, *Unbearable Weight: Feminism, Western Culture, and the Body* (Berkeley: University of California Press, 1993).

Trabant: Mithridates in Paradise

1. Conrad Gesner, *Mithridates: De differentiis linguarum tum veterum tum quae hodie apud diversas nationes in toto orbe terrarum in usu sunt*, ed. Manfred Peters (reprint, Aalen: Scientia Verlag, 1974), 106.

2. Ibid.

3. See Pierre Swiggers, "La culture linguistique en Italie et en France au XVIe siècle," in *Italiano: lingua di cultura europa*, ed. Harro Stammerjohann (Tübingen: Narr, 1997), 59–89.

4. For the history of the seventy-two languages, see Arno Borst, *Der Turmbau von Babel*, 3 vols. (reprint, München: Deutscher Taschenbuch Verlag, 1995); on Saint Augustin see 2: 399ff.

5. *Encyclopédie ou Dictionnaire raisonné des sciences, des arts et des métiers* (1751–65), 17 vols. (reprint, Stuttgart–Bad Cannstatt: Frommann, 1966), 4: 878.

6. Johann Christoph Adelung and Johann Severin Vater, *Mithridates oder allgemeine Sprachenkunde mit dem Vater unser als Sprachprobe in bey nahe fünfhundert Sprachen und Mundarten* (1806–17), 4 vols. (reprint, Hildesheim: Olms, 1970), 2: 316–38.

7. For an elegant modern portrait of English see Ekkehard König, "English," in *The Germanic Languages*, ed. Ekkehard König and Johan van der Auwera (London: Routledge, 1994).

8. *Encyclopédie*, 4: 878.

9. Ibid.

10. I know that this is an exaggeration, that there is the *Donatz proensals* and Palsgrave, for instance (which are grammars for practical uses), but it is nevertheless true in the sense that there is no interest in describing languages as such.

11. See Steven Pinker, *The Language Instinct* (New York: Morrow, 1994).

12. Aristotle, *The Categories: On Interpretation, Prior Analytics*, ed. Harold P. Cook and Hugh Tredennick (London: Heinemann, 1962), 16.

13. The new universalistic linguistics that holds exactly this Aristotelian conviction survives as *linguistics* through a terminological trick: it calls "language" the universal thought behind languages.

14. Jean Denis Lanjuinais, who is perhaps the first historiographer of linguistics, makes this point very clearly. See his "Discours préliminaire," in *Histoire naturelle de la parole ou grammaire universelle à l'usage des jeunes gens* by Antoine Court de Gébelin, ed. Jean Denis Lanjuinais (Paris: Plancher/Eymery/Delaunay, 1816). Another

230 / Notes to Pages 50–60

early attempt at linguistic historiography is Constantin François de Chasseboeuf Volney, "Discours sur l'étude philosophique des Langues" (1820), in *Oeuvres*, 3 vols. (Paris: Fayard, 1989), 2: 423–60.

15. Wolf Peter Klein, *Am Anfang war das Wort: Theorie- und wissenschafts-geschichtliche Elemente frühneuzeitlichen Sprachbewußtseins* (Berlin: Akademie Verlag, 1992).

16. Antoine Arnauld and Claude Lancelot, "Port-Royal," in *Grammaire générale et raisonnée* (reprint of the 1830 edition, Paris: Paulet, 1960).

17. Gottfried Wilhelm Leibniz, *Nouveaux essais sur l'entendement humain* (1765), ed. Jacques Brunschwig (reprint, Paris: Garnier-Flammarion, 1966), iii, ix.

18. Ibid.

19. The enormous wealth of that archive can now be studied in Kurt Mueller-Vollmer, *Wilhelm von Humboldts Sprachwissenschaft: Ein kommentiertes Verzeichnis des sprachwissenschaftlichen Nachlasses* (Paderborn: Schöningh, 1993), where Humboldt's list of linguistic material is published.

20. This will also be the case for the so-called historical comparative linguistics of the nineteenth century, which did not care at all for the marvelous variety of the operations of the human mind.

21. From Lorenzo Hervás y Panduro, *Vocabolario poligloto: Saggio pratico delle lingue*, ed. Manuel Breva-Claramonte and Ramón Sarmiento (reprint, Madrid: Sociedad General Española de Libreria, 1990), 165.

22. Coseriu thinks that Hervás is the inventor of that technique, but Lanjuinais stated already in 1816 that Dumarsais used this instrument and that Pluche took it up. See Eugenio Coseriu, "Lo que se dice de Hervás," in *Estudios ofrecidos a Emilio Alarcos Llorach* (Oviedo: Universidad de Oviedo, 1978); and Lanjuinais, "Discours préliminaire."

23. Hervás y Panduro, *Vocabolario poligloto*, 116.

24. Hervás explains: "*Ma* is an optative and deprecative particle, well translated as *I wish! Yectenehuallo* is composed of *yectli* meaning good, *tentli* meaning lip, and *ehua* meaning to raise: hence *yec-ten-ehuallo* means good-lip-raised; that is, may he be praised with good words. The *lo* ending is a small particle indicating the passive voice." Ibid., 117.

25. Wilhelm von Humboldt, *Gesammelte Schriften*, ed. Albert Leitzmann et al., 17 vols. (Berlin: Behr, 1903–36), 4: 10.

26. Ibid.

27. Ibid., 288.

28. Ibid., 289.

29. "Descriptions would have no limits if they are extended indefinitely … to include every detail of structure or organization" (*Encyclopédie*, 4: 878).

30. Cf. Humboldt, *Gesammelte Schriften*, 4: 421 and 423.

31. See Klaus Zimmermann, Jürgen Trabant, and Kurt Mueller-Vollmer, eds., *Wilhelm Von Humboldt und die amerikanischen Sprachen* (Paderborn: Schöningh, 1994).

32. This task was already assigned to the American people by Count Volney in his famous address to the Congress of 1794.

Poovey: Between Political Arithmetic and Political Economy

1. See William Petty, *Political Arithmetick* (233–313), *A Treatise of Taxes and Contributions* (1–97), and *The Political Anatomy of Ireland* (121–231), all in *The Economic Writings of Sir William Petty*, ed. Charles Henry Hull (reprint, Fairfield, N.J.: Augustus M. Kelley, 1963–64).

2. J. R. McCulloch, *The Principles of Political Economy: With a Sketch of the Rise and Progress of the Science* (Edinburgh: William and Charles Tait, 1825), 2–3.

3. Recent interest in the science of police has been sparked by Foucault's work on governmentality, but, in general, this work has not specified the national differences among the varieties of writing on this subject, nor have Foucault's followers adequately specified the epistemological break that separates political arithmetic from political economy. Graham Burchell has dealt with these issues most effectively in "Peculiar Interests: Civil Society and Governing 'The System of Natural Liberty,'" in *The Foucault Effect: Studies in Governmentality, with Two Lectures by and an Interview with Michel Foucault*, ed. Graham Burchell, Colin Gordon, and Peter Miller (Chicago: University of Chicago Press, 1991), 119–50. Other essays of interest in this volume include: Michel Foucault, "Governmentality," 87–104; Pasquale Pasquino, "Theatrum Politicum: The Genealogy of Capital—Police and the State of Prosperity," 105–19; and Giovanna Procacci, "Social Economy and the Government of Poverty," 151–68.

4. See Richard B. Sher, "Professors of Virtue: The Social History of the Edinburgh Moral Philosophy Chair in the Eighteenth Century," in *Studies in the Philosophy of the Scottish Enlightenment*, ed. M. A. Stewart (Oxford: Clarendon Press, 1990), 87. Sher quotes DeQuincey: "Moral Philosophy, in the large and popular use of that term by the Scotch, offers so immeasurable an expanse, that two people might easily wander there for a whole life and never happen to meet" (87).

5. McCulloch, *Principles of Political Economy*, 59.

6. There were exceptions to this generalization. For British calls for the kind of data collection associated with police, see Daniel Defoe, *Giving Alms No Charity* (London: The Booksellers of London & Westminster, 1704); Henry Fielding, *A Proposal for Making an Effectual Provision for the Poor* (London: A. Miller, 1753); and Jonas Hanway, *An Earnest Appeal for Mercy to the Children of the Poor* (London: J. Dodsley, 1766).

7. My understanding of this problematic is theoretically consistent with the observation Lorraine Daston made at the Stanford conference—that one could write a natural history of (what has counted as) "facts." This, presumably, would belong to the larger project that Daston has christened "historical epistemology." See Lorraine Daston, "The Moral Economy of Science," in *Constructing Knowledge in the History of Science*, ed. Arnold Thackray, special issue of *Osiris*, second series, 10 (1995): 2–24, esp. 23–24.

8. Although he is not concerned with political economy, Peter Dear has associated this problematic with Hume in *Discipline and Experience: The Mathematical Way in the Scientific Revolution* (Chicago: University of Chicago Press, 1995), 15–21. I discuss the relationship between Hume's stabilization of "the problem of induction" and the methodological problematic of political economy in my *A History of*

the Modern Fact: Problems of Knowledge in the Sciences of Wealth and Society (Chicago: University of Chicago Press, 1998), chapter 5.

9. Stewart was professor of moral philosophy at the University of Edinburgh from 1785 to 1810. Stewart played a critical role in the transition between moral philosophy and political economy and in the redefinition of the latter, for he had studied with both Adam Ferguson and Thomas Reid and then taught the young men who founded the *Edinburgh Review*, which was the major organ of political economy in Britain. From 1818, J. R. McCulloch was the chief economic reviewer for the journal, and, although he never studied with Stewart, the latter's influence is evident in McCulloch's work. See Stefan Collini, Donald Winch, and John Burrow, *That Noble Science of Politics: A Study of Nineteenth-Century Intellectual History* (Cambridge: Cambridge University Press, 1983), chapter 1; Biancamaria Fontana, *Rethinking the Politics of Commercial Society: The Edinburgh Review, 1802–1832* (Cambridge: Cambridge University Press, 1985), chapter 1 and 96–104; and Knud Haakonssen, "From Moral Philosophy to Political Economy: The Contribution of Dugald Steward," in *Philosophers of the Enlightenment*, ed. V. Hope (Edinburgh: Edinburgh University Press, 1984), 211–32.

10. Dugald Stewart, *Account of the Life and Writings of Adam Smith, Ll.D.*, in Stewart, *Collected Works*, 11 vols., ed. Sir William Hamilton (Edinburgh: Thomas Constable & Co., 1854), 10: 33.

11. John Millar, *Observations Concerning the Distinction of Ranks in Society* (Dublin: T. Ewing, 1771), xiii, v. Other conjectural historians who address these questions include Lord Kames, *Sketches of the History of Man* (1774), 2nd ed., 4 vols. (Edinburgh: W. Strahan and T. Cadell, 1778), 1: 71; 2: 219; Adam Ferguson, *Essay on the History of Civil Society* (1767), 4th ed. (London: T. Caddell, 1773), 125–33, 326ff.; and David Hume, *The Natural History of Religion*, ed. J. C. A. Gaskin (New York: Oxford University Press, 1993), 137–38.

12. Millar, *Observations*, iv.

13. See my "Science and the Pursuit of Virtue in the Aberdeen Enlightenment," in *Studies in the Philosophy of the Scottish Enlightenment*, ed. M. A. Stewart (Oxford: Clarendon Press, 1990), 127–49. My discussion of the scientism of moral philosophers is indebted to Wood's essay, although I do not reiterate Wood's important observation that the old regent system might have played a critical role in preserving the affiliation between natural and moral philosophies (see 140, 148–49). The most important historical overview of "experiment" can be found in Dear, *Discipline and Experience*, esp. chapters 1, 5, and 8.

14. Lord Kames, *Sketches of the History of Man*, 2: 219.

15. On this element of the conjectural historians' work, see Duncan Forbes, "'Scientific' Whiggism: Adam Smith and John Millar," *Cambridge Journal* 7 (1953–54): 643–70; and Nicholas Phillipson, "The Pursuit of Virtue in Scottish University Education: Dugald Stewart and Scottish Moral Philosophy in the Enlightenment," in *Universities, Society, and the Future*, ed. Nicholas Phillipson (Edinburgh: Edinburgh University Press, 1983), 82–100.

16. See Sher, "Professors of Virtue," 91. On the didacticism of moral philosophy, see also Nicholas Phillipson, "Hume as Moralist: A Social Historian's Perspective,"

in *Philosophers of the Enlightenment*, ed. S. C. Brown (Sussex: Harvester Press, 1979), 140–61; and Nicholas Phillipson, "The Scottish Enlightenment," in *The Enlightenment in National Context*, ed. Roy Porter and Mikulas Teich (Cambridge: Cambridge University Press, 1981), 19–40. See also John Dwyer, *Virtuous Discourse: Sensibility and Community in Late Eighteenth-Century Scotland* (Edinburgh: John Donald Publishers, 1987), esp. 4–7, 30–31, and chapter 2.

17. On eighteenth-century views of Newton and Descartes, see M. Rattansi, "Voltaire and the Enlightenment Image of Newton," in *History and Imagination: Essays in Honour of H. R. Trevor-Roper*, ed. Hugh Lloyd-Jones, Valerie Pearl, and Balir Worden (London: Duckworth, 1981), 218–31. In 1815, this was still a salient contrast for religious men like Thomas Chalmers, the Scottish divine. "In the ethereal whirlpools of Descartes, we see a transgression against the humility of the philosophical character. It is the presumption of knowledge on a subject, where the total want of observation should have confined him to the modesty of ignorance. In the Newtonian system of the world, we see both humility and hardihood" (*The Evidence and Authority of the Christian Revelation*, 1819), cited in Richard R. Yeo, "Scientific Method and the Rhetoric of Science in Britain, 1830–1917," in *The Politics and Rhetoric of Scientific Method: Historical Studies*, ed. John A. Schuster and Richard R. Yeo Dordrecht: D. Reidel, 1986, 276).

18. See H. M. Hopfl, "From Savage to Scotsman: Conjectural History in the Scottish Enlightenment," *Journal of British Studies* 17 (Spring 1978): 26–27.

19. Some modern historians and political theorists have overlooked this strain in the work of the conjectural historians. For the most extreme articulation of this position, see Ronald L. Meek, "A Scottish Contribution to Scottish Sociology," in *Economics and Ideology and Other Essays* (London: Chapman & Hall, 1967), 34–50. For a more considered treatment of this issue, see Andrew Skinner, "Economics and History: The Scottish Enlightenment," *Scottish Journal of Political Economy* 12 (1965): 1–22.

20. See Stewart, *Dissertation: Exhibiting the Progress of Metaphysical, Ethical, and Political Philosophy, since the Revival of Letters in Europe*, in Stewart, *Collected Works*, 1: 4.

21. Adam Smith, "The Principles Which Lead and Direct Philosophical Enquiries; Illustrated by the History of Astronomy," in *Essays on Philosophical Subjects*, ed. W. P. D. Wightman and J. C. Bryce (Oxford: Clarendon Press, 1980), 45–46.

22. Ibid., 105; emphasis mine.

23. Haakonssen makes this point in "From Moral Philosophy to Political Economy," 229.

24. On Stewart's disdain for history, see ibid., 213, 216–17.

25. On Stewart's *Elements* and his indebtedness to Condorcet, see Collini, Winch, and Burrow, *That Noble Science of Politics*, 32–44.

26. Dugald Stewart, *Dissertation*, in Stewart, *Collected Works*, 1: 491–92.

27. Dugald Stewart, *Elements of the Philosophy of the Human Mind* (Boston: James Munroe & Co., 1847), 138 and 149.

28. In his emphasis on introspection, Stewart demonstrated the debt he owed to Thomas Reid. For a discussion of Reid's influence on Stewart and the role of in-

trospection in the Common Sense School, see Phillipson, "The Pursuit of Virtue," 87.

29. Stewart, *Elements of the Philosophy of the Human Mind*, 157.

30. Ibid., 164.

31. Stewart, *Dissertation*, 1: 505.

32. "Systems in many respects resemble machines. A machine is a little system, created to perform, as well as to connect together, in reality, those different movements and effects which the artist has occasion for. A system is an imaginary machine invented to connect together in the fancy those different movements and effects which are already in reality performed" (Smith, "The Principles Which Lead and Direct Philosophical Enquiries," 66). As Knud Haakonssen has phrased it, Stewart's reworking of the argument from design "raises the possibility that it is not the moral rightness of individual actions which justifies the natural system, but that the latter provides some sort of justification for the former" (Haakonssen, "From Moral Philosophy to Political Economy," 228).

33. See Haakonssen, "From Moral Philosophy to Political Economy," 213, 228–29.

34. Stewart, *Elements of the Philosophy of the Human Mind*, 159.

35. McCulloch, *Principles of Political Economy*, 59.

36. Ibid., 121.

37. By the third decade of the nineteenth century, police and data collection had become important again in Britain, although the reasons for this are too complex for a brief discussion. The relevant figures in this regard are Sir John Sinclair, who conducted a statistical survey of Scotland in the 1790s, Jeremy Bentham, who devised a calculus for determining the aggregate happiness of the population, and Edwin Chadwick, who relentlessly pursued the collection of numerical data and the establishment of centralized government agencies throughout the 1830s and 1840s.

38. McCulloch, *Principles of Political Economy*, 17.

39. McCulloch, "Introductory Discourse" to Adam Smith, *An Inquiry into the Nature and Causes of the Wealth of Nations*, new edition (Edinburgh: Adam and Charles Black, 1868), xlv. This "Introductory Discourse" appeared in the 1828 edition.

40. McCulloch, *Principles of Political Economy*, 115; see also 319 and 320.

41. Dickens virtually equated political economy with a numerical form of "fact" in *Hard Times* (1854); Robert Southey blamed the science (and Adam Smith in particular) for all the evils of "the manufacturing system" in "On the State of the Poor, the Principle of Mr. Malthus's Essay on Population, and the Manufacturing System" (1812), in *Essays, Moral and Political*, vol. 1 (London: John Murray, 1832).

42. A full account of the vilification of political economy and of the bifurcation that the science experienced over the issue of theory versus particulars would have to give considerable attention to Robert Malthus and to the split that developed between Malthus and David Ricardo in the 1820s. Here I can only acknowledge the paradoxical nature of the role that contemporary critics of political science assigned Malthus in these developments. Even though Malthus tried to remain faithful to Adam Smith's legacy by keeping political economy a moral and ethical science, which could take account of particular data and formulate general principles, critics

like Southey and Coleridge associated Malthus with the "evils" of political economy *whether* they interpreted political economy as a reductive science (a science of counting particular things) *or* a philosophy so expansive that its theories purported to govern all of modern society. Instead of reading the history of political economy as its contemporaries did—that is, as "Malthusianism"—I am suggesting that McCulloch's taxonomy gives us a way to understand what only a few people grasped in the first decades of the nineteenth century: that "political economy" was potentially composed of (at least) three components, one of which (statistics) was devoted to numerical data collection, and another of which (political economy proper) was devoted to generating theory. David Ricardo promoted a mathematical variant of "political economy" in 1817, but this had less to do with quantification than did either Malthus's notorious arithmetical formulae or the commitment, which he displayed *after* the first edition of his *Essay on the Principle of Population*, to data collection. I discuss Malthus in Poovey, *A History of Modern Fact*, chapter 6.

43. McCulloch, *Principles of Political Economy*, 19–20.

44. This repudiation of theory belonged to a long tradition of English scorn for things French, in which Stewart represents something of an anomaly. On the English disdain for theory, see David Simpson, *Romanticism, Nationalism, and the Revolt Against Theory* (Chicago: University of Chicago Press, 1993), esp. chapters 6 and 7.

45. Dugald Stewart complained about the "common prejudice" against theory and attributed it to the wedge that Bacon had driven—inappropriately, according to Stewart—between empirical observation and the construction of theories. Stewart was particularly sensitive to the prejudice against theory because Thomas Reid, his most influential teacher, was an outspoken critic of hypothesis and conjecture. I suggest that Stewart assigned the phrase "conjectural" history to the work of Smith and other respected moral philosophers primarily to redeem "conjecture" from the disfavor into which Reid and others had cast it. See Stewart, *Elements of the Philosophy of the Human Mind*, chapter 4. On Reid's attitude toward conjecture, see L. L. Laudan, "Thomas Reid and the Newtonian Turn of British Methodological Thought," in *The Methodological Heritage of Newton*, ed. Robert E. Butts and John W. Davis (Oxford: Basil Blackwell, 1970), 102–31.

46. This points to the complex politics of appeals to experience and observation in the 1830s. By that date, such appeals were attractive not only to opponents of political economy like Dickens but also to those, like James Phillips Kay and Edwin Chadwick, who sought to adapt political economy to a version of governmentality that resembles the eighteenth-century theory of police. For a discussion of the role of observation in early social scientific surveys of the industrial cities, see Mary Poovey, "Anatomical Realism and Social Investigation in Early Nineteenth-Century Manchester," in Mary Poovey, *Making a Social Body: British Cultural Formation, 1832–1860* (Chicago: University of Chicago Press, 1995), 73–97.

47. For a discussion of the debates about method among natural scientists, see Yeo, "Scientific Method and the Rhetoric of Science," 259–97.

48. The survey based on first-hand observations was Sir John Sinclair, *Statistical Survey of Scotland* (Edinburgh: W. Creech, 1791–99).

Klein: Problems of Description in Art

1. Fiona Greenwood provided a working English translation of this essay's original German text.
Isaac Newton to Ignace Gaston Pardies, 10.6.1672, cited in Isaac Newton, *Correspondence*, 7 vols., ed. H. W. Turnbull (Cambridge: Published for the Royal Society at the University Press, 1959–77), 1: 164.

2. Voltaire, "Lettres philosophiques" (1734), in *Oeuvres complètes*, 52 vols. (Paris: Garnier frères, 1877–85), 22: 118f., 123.

3. Georg Wilhelm Friedrich Hegel, *Ästhetik*, 2 vols., ed. Friedrich Bassenge (Berlin: Aufbau, 1976), 1: 77, 2: 410.

4. Auguste Comte, "Plan des travaux scientifiques nécessaires pour réorganiser la sociéte" (1822), in Auguste Comte, *Du pouvoir spirituel* (Paris: Le livre de poche, 1978), 139.

5. See discussion of the *longue durée* of writing about culture in Roger Chartier, *Culture écrite et société: L'ordre des livres (XIVe–XVIIIe siècle)* (Paris: Albin Michel, 1996), esp. 27–40.

6. Peter Galison, *How Experiments End* (Chicago: University of Chicago Press, 1987), 277.

7. Jean-François Lyotard, *La condition postmoderne* (Paris: Éditions de Minuit, 1979), 102–8.

8. I have Waltraud Naumann-Beyer to thank for important specifications in these introductory remarks. Her paper "Entmachten statt vernichten. Zwei Typen kritischer Beschreibung: Voltaires Candide und Friedrich Nicolais Sempronius Gundibert," together with texts by Christian Lavagno ("Die unendliche Beschreibung. Zur Vorgeschichte aufklärerischer Beschreibungskonzepte in der Renaissance"), Michael Franz ("Beschreibung im Rahmen einer vergleichenden Zeichentheorie des Sagens und Zeigens. Rhetorische und semiotische Aspekte im ökonomischen Denken von Adam Smith"), and Friedrich Wolfzettel ("Beschreiben und Wissen. Überlegungen zum Funktionswandel der Deskription im französischen Reisebericht"), as well as the present paper, were published in the Leipzig journal *Grenzgänge* in the special issue "Description," 7/1997.

9. The following considerations are treated in more detail in Wolfgang Klein, "Realismus/realistisch," in *Ästhetische Grundbegriffe: Ein historisches Wörterbuch*, 7 vols., ed. Karlheinz Barck et al. (Stuttgart: Metzler, 2000–), 5: 149–97.

10. *Petit Larousse* (Paris: Larousse, 1973), 864.

11. Gustave Flaubert, "Le dictionnaire des idées reçues," in *Bouvard et Pécuchet*, ed. Claudine Gothot-Mersch (Paris: Gallimard, 1993), 506.

12. Eugenio Donato, *The Script of Decadence: Essays on the Fictions of Flaubert and the Poetics of Romanticism* (New York: Oxford University Press, 1993), 10.

13. Ibid., 64.

14. Michel Foucault, "Postface à Gustave Flaubert, Die Versuchung des Heiligen Antonius, Frankfurt/Main 1964," in *Dits et écrits*, 4 vols. (Paris: Éditions Gallimard, 1994), 1: 298.

15. Donato, *The Script of Decadence*, 60.

16. Ibid., 70.

17. Ibid., 103.

18. Gustave Flaubert, *Oeuvres complètes*, 16 vols. (Paris: Club de l'honnête homme, 1975), 15: 615.

19. Ibid., 16:12f.

20. Ibid., 13.

21. Flaubert, *Bouvard et Pécuchet*, 153.

22. Flaubert to Louise Colet, 16.1.1852, in *Oeuvres complètes*, 13: 158. Cf. also Flaubert to George Sand, 6.2.1876, where he even went as far as to stylize himself for the late Romantic writer as a "poor devil . . . of exactitude." Ibid., 15: 435.

23. Flaubert to Louise Colet, 26.8.1853, in ibid., 13: 399.

24. Flaubert to Louise Colet, 18.7.1852, in ibid., 221.

25. I therefore would give Donato's categorical thesis—that since Flaubert's fiction is necessarily unable "to raise the description of reality to intelligibility"—the interrogatory form that Gérard Genette chose in a similar context. Gérard Genette, "Frontières du récit," in *Figures II* (Paris: Éditions du Seuil, 1969), 68–69. See also Patrick Imbert, "La structure de la description réaliste dans la littérature européenne," *Semiotica* 1–2 (1983): 95–122.

26. *Encyclopédie ou Dictionnaire raisonné des sciences, des arts et des métiers*, 17 vols. (reprint, Stuttgart–Bad Cannstatt: Frommann, 1966), 4: 878. There and on the following page are to be found all the quotes from the *Encyclopédie* that follow.

27. John Bender, "Fiktionalität in der Aufklärung," in *Nach der Aufklärung? Beiträge aum Diskurs der Kulturwissenschaften*, ed. Wolfgang Klein and Waltraud Naumann-Beyer (Berlin: Akademie Verlag, 1995), 97, 106; John Bender, "Enlightenment Fiction and the Scientific Hypothesis," *Representations*, no. 61 (1998): 6–28.

28. Cf. Robert Weimann, "Funktion und Prozeß der Weltaneignung: Grundzüge ihrer Geschichte," in *Realismus in der Renaissance: Aneignung der Welt in der erzählenden Prosa* (Berlin: Aufbau, 1977); Martin Fontius, "Das Ende einer Denkform: Zur Ablösung des Nachahmungsprinzips im 18. Jahrhundert," in *Literarische Widerspiegelung: Geschichtliche und theoretische Dimensionen eines Problems*, ed. Dieter Schlenstedt (Berlin: Aufbau, 1981), 197.

29. Leonardo da Vinci, *Trattato della pittura* (Parigi: Giacomo Langlois, 1651), no. 76.

30. Gerd Irrlitz, "Versuch über Descartes," in *René Descartes, Ausgewählte Schriften* (Leipzig: Reclam, 1980), 386.

31. Hans Sanders, *Das Subjekt der Moderne: Mentalitätswandel und literarische Evolution zwischen Klassik und Aufklärung* (Tübingen: Niemeyer, 1987), 165.

32. Voltaire, "Eléments de la philosophie de Newton," in *Oeuvres complètes*, 22: 582.

33. Cf. Rainer Specht, "Über empiristische Ansätze Lockes," *Allgemeine Zeitschrift für Philosophie* 3 (1977); Rudolf Lüthe, *David Hume, Historiker und Philosoph* (Freiberg: Alber, 1991). It appears to me to be overdone, however, to classify Locke in the ranks of a "discursive theoretical knowledge" whose "problem does not begin with the nature of the object, but with the nature of the theory itself" (Cathy Caruth, *Empirical Truths and Critical Fictions: Locke, Wordsworth, Kant, Freud* [Baltimore: Johns Hopkins University Press, 1991], 58f.). It was precisely the fact that the nature of the object was now placed at the center that determined the specific nature of this theory.

34. Ernst Cassirer, *Die Philosophie der Aufklärung* (Tübingen: Mohr, 1932), 8f.

35. Daniel Defoe, "Preface to Robinson Crusoe," in *English Theories of the Novel*, 3 vols., ed. Walter F. Greiner (Tübingen: Niemeyer, 1970), 2: 26.

36. Alain René Le Sage, *Oeuvres* (Paris: Garnier Frères, 1876), 15.

37. Johann Heinrich Merck, "Über den Mangel des epischen Geistes in unserm lieben Vaterland," in *Romantheorie 1620–1880: Dokumentation ihrer Geschichte in Deutschland*, ed. Eberhard Lämmert (Frankfurt-am-Main: Anthenäum, 1988), 159.

38. Svetlana Alpers, *The Art of Describing: Dutch Art in the Seventeenth Century* (Chicago: University of Chicago Press, 1983); cf. Wolfgang Kemp's introduction to the German edition of this book (1985), and Gunter Gebauer and Christoph Wulf, *Mimesis: Kultur—Kunst—Gesellschaft* (Reinbek: Rowohlt, 1992), 208–11.

39. Friedrich Schiller and Wilhelm von Humboldt, *Der Briefwechsel zwischen Friedrich Schiller und Wilhelm von Humboldt*, ed. Siegfried Seidel (Berlin: Aufbau, 1962), 154.

40. Friedrich Schiller and Johann Wolfgang Goethe, *Der Briefwechsel zwischen Schiller und Goethe*, 3 vols., ed. Hans Gerhard Gräf and Albert Leitzmann (Leipzig: Insel, 1964), 1: 80. In a similar vein, Goethe on Diderot in his letter to Friedrich Schiller, 28 February 1798 (ibid., 59f.) and in his "Diderots Versuch über die Malerei" (1798), in Johann Wolfgang von Goethe, *Gedenkausgabe der Werke, Briefe und Gespräche: Erganzungsbäbde*, 3 vols., ed. Ernst Beutler (Zürich: Artemis, 1960), 3: 208f. See also Karl Maurer, "Entstaltung: Ein beinahe untergegangener Goethescher Begriff," in *Leib-Zeichen: Körperbilder, Rhetorik und Anthropologie im 18. Jahrhundert*, ed. R. Behrens and R. Galle (Würzburg: Königshausen & Neumann, 1993), 151–62.

41. Cf. Wolfgang Klein, *Der nüchterne Blick: Programmatischer Realismus in Frankreich nach 1848* (Berlin: Aufbau, 1989), 248–50, 212f.

42. Hegel, *Ästhetik*, 2: 410.

43. Christian Lavagno shows how "Foucault fails to convincingly integrate positivism into his tableau of modernity" in *Rekonstruktion der Moderne: Eine Studie zu Habermas und Foucault* (Münster: Lit Verlag, 2003), 137.

44. Michel Foucault, *The Order of Things: An Archaeology of the Human Sciences* (New York: Random House Vintage Books, 1994).

45. Jakob Michael Reinhold Lenz, "Anmerkungen über Theater" (1774), in *Werke und Briefe in drei Bänden*, 3 vols., ed. Sigrid Damm (München: Hanser, 1987), 2: 647.

46. Henry Fielding, *The History of Tom Jones, a Foundling* (1749), in *The Complete Works of Henry Fielding, Esq.*, 16 vols. (London: William Heinemann, 1903), 4: 189, 187, 186f., 192.

47. Laurence Sterne, *The Life and Opinions of Tristram Shandy*, in *The Complete Works of Laurence Sterne*, ed. David Herbert (Edinburgh: W. P. Nimmo, 1872), 59, 68, 58.

48. David E. Wellbery, "Der Zufall der Geburt: Sternes Poetik der Kontingenz," in *Kontingenz, Poetik und Hermeneutik XVII*, ed. Gerhart von Graevenitz and Odo Marquard (München: Fink, 1998), 309.

49. Denis Diderot, "Eloge de Richardson" (1761), in *Oeuvres*, ed. André Billy (Paris: Gallimard, 1992), 1061f., 1064, 1067.

50. Ibid., 1060, 1064. In regard to the success and to the untransferability of the

English pattern in France, see Wilhelm Graeber, *Der englische Roman in Frankreich 1741–1763* (Heidelberg: C. Winter, 1995).

51. Simon Augustin Irailh, *Querelles littéraires*, 4 vols. (Paris: Durand, 1761), 2: 353; cf. Werner Krauss, "Zur französischen Romantheorie des 18. Jahrhunderts," in *Das wissenschaftliche Werk*, ed. Rolf Geißler (Berlin: Aufbau, 1987), 6: 442–62.

52. Donatien Alphonse François de Sade, "Idée sur les romans" (1800), in *Oeuvres complètes*, 115 vols. (Paris: Pauvert, 1986–), 10: 75, 72.

53. Cf. Martina Thom, "Zum Freiheitsproblem bei Kant," in *Revolution der Denkart oder Denkart der Revolution*, ed. Manfred Buhr and Teodor Oiserman (Berlin: Akademie-Verlag, 1976), esp. 112–17.

54. Immanuel Kant, "Kritik der reinen Vernunft (1781)," in *Gesammelte Schriften* (Berlin: Reimer, 1911), 4: 232.

55. Ingeborg Maus, *Zur Aufklärung der Demokratietheorie: Rechts- und demokratietheorie überlegungen im Anschluß an Kant* (Frankfurt-am-Main: Suhrkamp, 1992), 253, 251.

56. Immanuel Kant, "Kritik der reinen Vernunft" (1781), 4: 231f.

57. Immanuel Kant, "Kritik der praktischen Vernunft" (1788), in *Gesammelte Schriften* (Berlin: Reimer, 1913), 5: 68.

58. Kant, "Kritik der reinen Vernunft" (1781), 4: 232, 231.

59. Ibid., 4: 48.

60. Schiller to Goethe, 28.8.1797, in Gräf and Leitzmann, *Der Briefwechsel zwischen Schiller und Goethe*, 1: 7.

61. Goethe to Schiller, 29.7.1797 resp. 16.8.1797, in ibid., 1: 368, 380; as well Schiller to Goethe, 17.8.1797, in ibid., 1: 381.

62. Schiller to Goethe, 23.8.1794, in ibid., 1: 7.

63. Schiller to Goethe, 31.8.1794, in ibid., 1: 7, 11.

64. Schiller to Goethe, 23.8.1794, in ibid., 1: 6.

65. See Martin Fontius, "Produktivkraftentfaltung und Autonomie der Kunst," in *Literatur im Epochenumbruch*, ed. Winfried Schröder, Günther Klotz, and Peter Weber (Berlin: Aufbau, 1977). Waltraud Naumann-Beyer has shown that the concept of "Heautonomie," which gave the heteronomous its clear ranking in the exchange of letters with Goethe as well, was of "constitutive significance" for Schiller's social and aesthetic utopia. Waltraud Naumann-Beyer, "Kommunikative Beziehungen in Deutschland ende des 18. Jahrhunderts" (Postdoctoral thesis, Berlin, 1986), 42.

66. Cf. Fontius, "Das Ende einer Denkform: Zur Ablösung des Nachahmungsprinzips im 18. Jahrhundert," esp. 202f.

67. Gotthold Ephraim Lessing, "Hamburgische Dramaturgie," in *Lessings Werke*, 18 vols., ed. Robert Boxberger (Berlin: W. Spemann, 1883–90; reprint, Tokyo: Sansyusya, 1974), 10: 157.

68. Wolfgang Heise, *Die Wirklichkeit des Möglichen: Dichtung und Ästhetik in Deutschland 1750–1850* (Berlin: Aufbau, 1990), 261f.

69. Friedrich Schiller, "Über den Gebrauch des Chors in der Tragödie," in *Über Kunst und Wirklichkeit: Schriften und Briefe zur Ästhetik*, ed. Claus Träger (Leipzig: Reclam, 1975), 551.

70. Friedrich Wilhelm Josef Schelling, "Philosophie der Kunst" (1801), in *Früh-*

schriften, 2 vols., ed. Helmut Seidel and Lothar Kleine (Berlin: Akademie-Verlag, 1971), 2: 884.

71. Charles Baudelaire, "Salon de 1859," in *Oeuvres complètes*, ed. Marcel A. Ruff (Paris: Éditions du Seuil, 1982), 396.

72. Georg Lukács, "Nietzsche als Vorläufer der faschistischen Ästhetik" (1934), in *Werke* (Neuwied: Luchterhand, 1969), 10: 326.

73. Georg Lukács, *Die Eigenart des Ästhetischen* (1963), 2 vols. (Berlin: Aufbau, 1981), 2: 803.

74. Georg Lukács, "Es geht um den Realismus" (1938), in *Zur Tradition der deutschen sozialistischen Literatur: Eine Auswahl von Dokumenten*, 4 vols., ed. Friedrich Albrecht (Berlin: Aufbau, 1979), 2: 538.

75. Georg Lukács, *Balzac und der französische Realismus* (Berlin: Aufbau, 1952), 8, and Georg Lukács, *Die Eigenart des Ästhetischen*, 2: 286.

76. Karl Jaspers, from the third interview (10.9.1946), in *L'esprit européen* (Neuchâtel Baconnerie, 1947), 200.

77. Georg Lukács, "Erzählen oder Beschreiben?" (1936), in *Zur Tradition der deutschen sozialistischen Literatur*, 2: 361, 372, 349.

78. Günter Gaus, *Porträts 5* (Berlin: Verlag Volk und Welt, 1993), 92.

79. Jean-François Lyotard, *L'inhumain: Causeries sur le temps* (Paris: Galilée, 1988), 39f.

80. Dietmar Kamper, "Il faut être absolument moderne," in *Jean Baudrillard, Simulation und Verführung*, ed. Ralf Bohn and Dieter Fuder (Munich: Fink, 1994), 15.

81. Klaus Kraemer, "Schwerelosigkeit der Zeichen? Die Paradoxie des selbstreferentiellen Zeichens bei Baudrillard," in ibid., 52f.

82. Jean Baudrillard, *Agonie des Realen* (Berlin: Merve, 1978), 7.

83. Norbert Bolz, "Es war einmal in Amerika," in *Jean Baudrillard: Simulation und Verführung*, 101.

84. Jacques Derrida, *Spectres de Marx* (Paris: Galilée, 1993), 268.

85. Cf. Ingo v. Dahlern, "Bilder aus dem Datenhelm," *Der Tagesspiegel*, 22 April 1995, M 1.

86. Lyotard, *L'inhumain*, 23.

87. Jean Baudrillard, *Die Illusion und die Virtualität* (Bern: Benteli, 1994), 38, 20.

Scarry: Imagining Flowers

1. John Ashbery, "And *Ut Pictura Poesis* Is Her Name," in John Ashbery, *Selected Poems* (New York: Viking Press, 1985), 235. "On Vivacity" appears as chapter 1 of my *Dreaming by the Book* (Boston: Farrar, Straus and Giroux, 1999). The present chapter appears as chapter 4 of the same volume; an earlier version appeared in *Representations* 57 (Winter 1997): 90–115.

2. John Ashbery, "Whatever It Is, Wherever You Are," in John Ashbery, *A Wave: Poems by John Ashbery* (New York: Viking Press, 1985), 63.

3. Seamus Heaney, "Feeling Into Words," in *Preoccupations: Selected Prose, 1968–78* (London: Faber & Faber, 1980), 14. The identification of poets with plants, striking in the case of both Seamus Heaney and Marcel Proust, reaches perhaps its most extreme instance in Rainer Maria Rilke. The place of roses in his self-com-

posed epitaph, and the great part played by the thorn of a rose in "accelerating" his death, are described with great power in the final chapter of Ralph Freedman, *Life of a Poet: Rainer Maria Rilke* (New York: Farrar, Straus & Giroux, 1996), 530, 531, 546, 548. But Rilke's sense of himself as a flower is equally visible in earlier years: the first journal he started (1895) was called *Chicory Flowers* (Wegwarten), a title influenced by the Zurich journal *Sonnenblumen*, as well as by the fifteenth-century Paracelsan legend that "once in each century . . . the chicory flower becomes a living person" (Freedman, *Life of a Poet*, 41, 42). It is not hard to guess what "living person" in particular Rilke might have believed was his century's flower.

4. It might seem tempting to say that imagining is only as inseparable from its object as the perceptual acts (of which imagining is mimetic) are inseparable from theirs: the acts of seeing and hearing, for example, are often almost identical with the objects seen and heard. But, in fact, some perceptual states, such as touch, are much less confined to their object, and even seeing and hearing undergo a level of variation to which imagining is not subject. For a fuller account, see Elaine Scarry, "Pain and Imagining," in *The Body in Pain* (New York: Oxford University Press, 1985).

5. For a more complete account of the difference between the counterfactual and the counterfictional actions of imagining, see Scarry, "On Vivacity."

6. The association of flowers with beauty is long-standing. Plato says in both *Phaedrus* and *Symposium* that beauty, truth, and goodness exist together in the immortal realm, but beauty differs from the other two by having a "clearly discernible" presence in the material world: "Beauty shone bright in the world above, and [on earth] too it still gleams clearest . . . . As things are it is only beauty which has the privilege of being both the most clearly discerned and the most lovely" (Plato, *Phaedrus*, trans. Walter Hamilton [Harmondsworth, England: Penguin, 1973], 250). This "clearly discernible" material thing summons our attention, eventually carrying us to immortal beauty, as well as to its less clearly discernible counterparts, truth and goodness.

It is almost certainly because flowers, whether seen or daydreamed, have this feature of "clear discernibility" that they are so bound up with beauty. Agathon in the *Symposium* says we know we are in the presence of the god Love when we see flowers: "The beauty of [the god's] complexion is shown by his living among flowers; he never settles in any abode . . . that is incapable of blooming . . . but wherever he finds a spot that is flowery and fragrant, there he settles and abides" (Plato, *The Symposium*, trans. Walter Hamilton [London: Penguin Books, 1951], 196b). Thus Marsilio Ficino, in his 1475 *Commentary on Plato's Symposium*, says that "beauty is the blossom, so to speak, of goodness," in Albert Hofstadter and Richard Kuhns, eds., *Philosophies of Art and Beauty: Selected Readings in Aesthetics from Plato to Heidegger* (Chicago: University of Chicago Press, 1976), 217.

This notion of beauty's "clear discernibility," with its inherent power to summon, is intimately bound up with Thomas Aquinas's idea of "claritas" and with Dante's notion of a "greeting." The three phenomena—beauty, flowers, and clear discernibility—continue to be linked both during periods when beauty is greatly honored and during periods when it is rejected or demoted. Both Edmund Burke and Immanuel Kant, in their writings on the beautiful and the sublime, take flowers as the key instance of the former: "It is the flowery species . . . that give us the liveliest idea of beauty" says Burke in *A Philosophical Enquiry into the Origin of Our Ideas of the Sublime and Beautiful*, ed. Adam Phillips (Oxford: Oxford University Press, 1990), 105. Kant contrasts the non–clearly discernible shadows of the sublime's sacred grove with the flower beds of beauty in *Observations on the Feeling of the Beautiful and Sublime*, trans. John T. Goldthwait (Berkeley: University of California Press, 1960), 47. The preference for the sublime in modern thought is a preference for objects that are beyond the radius of our compositional powers, a preference whose timing coincides with the disappearance of beauty's metaphysical referent.

7. In his "Fifth Letter to Madame Delessert," 16 July 1772, in Jean-Jacques Rousseau, *Botany, a Study of Pure Curiosity: Botanical Letters and Notes Towards a Dictionary of Botanical Terms*, trans. Kate Ottevanger (London: Michael Joseph, 1979), 66–85, for example, Rousseau very overtly requires his correspondent mentally to construct the radiating spokes of the umbelliferous family ("Imagine a long and fairly straight stem, with alternate leaves . . ." [70]), periodically interrupting his description to coach and encourage ("If you are able to form a picture of what I have just described to you, you will have in your mind . . ." [72]), and finally after many pages congratulating her:

> Your remarkable progress, dear cousin, and your patience have so emboldened me that, with no regard for your suffering, I have dared to describe the family of the umbellifers without letting you set eyes on a single example; and this must needs have made much greater demands on your concentration. I am certain, however, that reading as you do, after you have looked over my letter once or twice, you will not fail to recognize an umbellifer in flower when you come across one; and at this time of the year, you cannot fail to find several in gardens and in the countryside. (80)

In other letters, Rousseau instructs Madame Delessert to look for, or even pick, an actual flower in bloom at the time of writing, as he does with the lily (first letter), the sweet pea (third letter), and the daisy (sixth letter). Here his instructions (e.g., pull the petal gently from below, gently tear the calyx exposing what is underneath) may be understood either to require a literal act of touching the physical flower or instead to specify a set of mental steps to construct the flower's structure imagistically.

8. Robert Nozick, when invited to try this mental experiment, immediately agreed that the image can be produced as easily in the forearm as in the forehead but questioned whether the image in the forearm is really in the forearm or in a picture of the forearm held in the forehead; Robert Nozick, conversation with author, September 1994.

9. Rainer Maria Rilke, "The Bowl of Roses," in *New Poems*, trans. Edward Snow (revised paperback translation, reprint, San Francisco: North Point Press, 1984), 192–97.

10. Walt Whitman, "When Lilacs Last in the Dooryard Bloom'd," in Walt Whitman, *Walt Whitman: Complete Poetry and Collected Prose* (New York: Viking Press, 1982), 466.

11. Jean Hagstrum comes up with the wonderful term *mental retina* (though he

is not speaking about petals) in *The Sister Arts: The Tradition of Literary Pictorialism and English Poetry from Dryden to Gray* (Chicago: University of Chicago Press, 1958), xx.

12. In the case of Whitman, Ashbery, and William Blake, the flower remains intact even when its petals are used as the surface on which to construct other images. The function of the flower as a template becomes even more strikingly evident in instances where the flower essentially disappears into the other image. Gustave Flaubert's *Madame Bovary*, trans. Francis Steegmuller (New York: Modern Library, 1961), is one of the most flower-filled of all novels; whole runs of pages occur in which a flower appears on every page. Although Flaubert's flowers sometimes remain ravishingly intact as flowers—whether in garden or meadow or window box— at other times they are introduced for their sheer power as template, particularly in constructing the face: an opera singer's pale face emerges beneath "a wreath of orange blossoms in her hair" (253); the "gentle features of the Virgin [Mary] among the bluish clouds of rising incense" are prepared for by a mist "rising among the bare poplars, blurring their outlines with a tinge of purple that was paler and more transparent than the sheerest gauze caught in their branches" (125); a dew that "garnished the cabbages with silvery lace, and joined head to head with long shining filaments" leads to the face of a priest dusted with frost and plaster (71); one woman's face is said to be as spotted as a meadow filled with flowers (169); and of another face, Flaubert writes "Not a hair was out of place in the blond chin whisker outlining his jaw: It was like the edging of a flower bed around his long dreary face with its small eyes and hooked nose" (86). Summarized and made explicit, the images sound humorous, but in context, the flowers are barely noticed yet constantly introduced as though continually to reignite our image-making power with clematis, forget-me-nots, rosettes, and cactus.

13. Stephen Michael Kosslyn, "Measuring the Visual Angle of the Mind's Eye," *Cognitive Psychology* 10 (1978): 381.

14. Kosslyn, in "Measuring the Visual Angle of the Mind's Eye," also describes other experiments suggesting that imaginary mimesis follows the spatial constraints of actual perception. People asked to describe the shape of a horse's ears, for example, answer more quickly than people who (before being asked the shape of the ears) are first asked to picture the place where a horse's tail meets the horse's back: presumably they answer more slowly because they must mentally move the long distance across the horse's back.

15. Joseph Addison, "On the Pleasures of the Imagination," in *The Spectator: With a Historical and Biographical Preface*, 6 vols., ed. A. Chalmers (Boston: Little, Brown & Co., 1872), 6: 147, 148.

16. Virginia Woolf, "The Mark on the Wall," in *The Complete Shorter Fiction of Virginia Woolf*, ed. Susan Dick (San Diego, Calif.: Harcourt Brace Jovanovich, 1985), 84.

17. John Ruskin, *The Queen of the Air: Being a Study of the Greek Myths of Cloud and Storm* (reprint, London: G. Allen, 1903). Scholars disagree about whether *Queen of the Air* is the first reference to Ruskin in Proust's correspondence, but all agree that he speaks of it by December 1899 at the latest. See Richard Macksey's in-

244 / Notes to Pages 102–7

troduction to Marcel Proust, *On Reading Ruskin: Prefaces to La Bible d'Amiens and Sésame et les lys with Selections from the Notes to the Translated Texts* (New Haven, Conn: Yale University Press, 1897), xvii–xix n. 4.

18. Ruskin, *The Queen of the Air*, 112, 116, 117, 118.

19. Jean-Jacques Rousseau, "Third Letter to Madame Delessert," 16 May 1772, in *Botany*, 48, 52; and see "Fifth Letter," 72, 76.

20. D. H. Lawrence, "Purple Anemones," in *Birds, Beasts and Flowers* (Santa Rosa, Calif.: Black Sparrow Press, 1992), 64.

21. Rainer Maria Rilke, "Opium Poppy," in *New Poems*, 185. Rilke's language in the first line cited is "die willig waren, offen und konkav." The two final lines read: "gefranste Kelche auseinanderschlagend, / die fieberhaft das Mohngefäss umgeben."

22. Kosslyn, "Measuring the Visual Angle of the Mind's Eye," 363.

23. All the numbers given here have been rounded off for ease in picturing. A few fairly small paintings appeared in the 1870s or in 1880 (*Portrait of Mallarmé*, 1876, 11 x 14 in.; *At the Café*, 1878, 19 x 15 in.; and *Interior at Café*, 1880, 12 x 18 in.), but they are overwhelmed by the much greater number of large canvases. For reproduction and analysis of the lilac, rose, and water glass paintings, see Andrew Forge and Robert Gordon, *The Last Flowers of Manet*, trans. Richard Howard (New York: H. N. Abrams, 1986).

The account given here about the radius of our compositional powers perhaps holds true even for large paintings. A large landscape painting, for example, brings within the range of our constructive powers the beauty of the actual landscape, which, because of its scale, may—except from a very select viewing point—be outside the range in which the beautiful can be comprehended.

24. This account of Pierre-Auguste Renoir's last day (3 December 1919) is given both by Lawrence Hanson, *Renoir: The Man, the Painter, and His World* (New York: Dodd, Mead, 1968), 294, and by Jean Renoir, *Renoir, My Father*, trans. Randolph Weaver and Dorothy Weaver (Boston: Little, Brown, 1962), 404. A rogue account is given by Ambroise Vollard, *Renoir: An Intimate Record*, trans. Harold L. Van Doren and Randolph T. Weaver (reprint, New York: A. A. Knopf, 1934), 225.

25. Thomas Hardy, *Far from the Madding Crowd* (New York: Harper, 1905), 57. Hardy almost never allows any description to masquerade as the universal case, so when he does say something is the universal case, the sentence carries. "By the time he walked three or four miles every shape in the landscape had assumed a uniform hue of blackness" (91). Uniformity comes before us as an exceptional and extraordinary state.

26. Aristotle, "On Colours," in *The Complete Works of Aristotle: The Revised Oxford Translation*, 2 vols., trans. T. Loveday and E. S. Forster, ed. Jonathan Barnes (Princeton, N.J.: Princeton University Press, 1984), 1: 796a. 796b.

27. Jean-Paul Sartre, *The Psychology of Imagination* (New York: Carol Publishing Group, 1991), 177.

28. Henri Bergson, "The Soul and the Body," lecture delivered in Paris, at Foi et Vie, 28 April 1912, published in *Mind-Energy: Lectures and Essays*, trans. H. Wildon Carr (Westport, Conn.: Greenwood Press, 1975), 63–64. Bergson goes on to apply the same observation to acoustical images, specifically words: "The same word,

pronounced by different persons, or by the same person at different times in different sentences, gives phonograms which do not coincide with one another. How, then can the recollection of the sound of a word—a recollection which is relatively invariable and unique—be comparable to a phonogram?" (64).

29. *Gilbert Wild's Daylilies* (Sarcoxie, Mo., 1991).

30. The painter A. H. Munsell originated his color notation system in 1898 and worked to adjust and perfect it for the next seventeen years. In addition to his widely dispersed color charts, Munsell also developed exercises for helping painters to think about color arrays three-dimensionally. In one exercise, he suggests imagining an orange with five segments pulled slightly apart but still joined at the bottom: "All the reds we have ever seen are gathered into one of those sections, all the yellow in another, all the greens in a third," etc. His choice of an orange is relevant to the present inquiry. It would seem counterintuitive that the act of imagining color could be assisted by mentally displaying all colors more easily picturable despite the competition from a single color: A. H. Munsell, *A Color Notation: An Illustrated System Defining All Colors and Their Relations by Measured Scales of Hue, Value, and Chroma* (Baltimore: Munsell Color Company, 1947), 17. See also A. H. Munsell, *Atlas of the Munsell Color System* (Malden, Mass.: Wadsworth, Howland & Co., 1915), for a supplement to the *Color Notation* handbook with many color charts in two and three dimensions.

31. Random Wit is clearly a racehorse, and See Here is a lipstick.

32. Aristotle, "On Plants," in *The Complete Works of Aristotle*, 2: 822b.

33. Ibid., 2: 823a (emphasis mine).

34. Rainer Maria Rilke, "Blue Hydrangea," in Rilke, *New Poems*, 113.

35. Rilke, "Bowl of Roses," in ibid., 197.

36. Jean-Jacques Rousseau, "Flower," from *Notes Towards a Dictionary of Botanical Terms*, in *Botany*, 134.

37. Friedrich Schiller, *On the Aesthetic Education of Man in a Series of Letters*, trans. Reginald Snell (New York: Frederick Ungar, 1965), 58.

38. Joris-Karl Huysmans, *Against Nature*, trans. Robert Baldick (New York: Penguin Books, 1959), 55, 56.

39. Woolf, "The Mark on the Wall," 83.

40. William Wordsworth, "Evening Voluntaries VI," "To the Same Flower," "To the Daisy," in *Wordsworth: Poetical Works*, ed. Thomas Hutchinson and Ernest de Selincourt (London: Oxford University Press, 1936), 358, 125, 453.

41. Dante Alighieri, *Paradiso*, trans. Allen Mandelbaum (Berkeley: University of California Press, 1982), 30: 61–69.

42. Addison, "On the Pleasures of the Imagination," in *The Spectator*, 6: 154, 156, 157.

43. Diane Ackerman, *A Natural History of the Senses* (New York: Random House, 1991), 12. As Stephen Greenblatt points out to me, Andrew Marvell, in lines 27–32 of "The Garden," delights in Ovid's celebration of cross-species desire: "The gods, that mortal beauty chase, / Still in a tree did end their race. / Apollo hunted Daphne so, / Only that she might laurel grow, / And Pan did after Syrinx speed, / Not as a nymph, but for a reed": see Andrew Marvell, *Andrew Marvell: The*

Complete Poems, ed. Elizabeth Story Donno (London: Penguin, 1985), 100. Marvell promises that if ever he carves the name of a beloved in a tree, it will be not a human name but the name of the tree itself (lines 19–24).

44. Rousseau thought that philosophical cognition also required flowers: "The study of nature separates us from ourselves and elevates us to its own level. It's in this way that one really becomes a *philosophe*; this is how natural history and botany are useful for wisdom and virtue." Letter "À Madame la duchess de Portland," 3 September 1766, cited by Bernard Gagnebin in his introduction to Jean-Jacques Rousseau, *Lettres sur la botanique par Jean-Jacques Rousseau* (Paris: Club des libraires de France: 1962), xxxv.

45. Aristotle, "Sense and Sensibilia," in *The Complete Works of Aristotle*, 1: 444a.

46. Ludwig Wittgenstein, *Culture and Value*, trans. Peter Winch, ed. G. H. von Wright and Heikki Nyman (Chicago: University of Chicago Press, 1980), 24e: "What if I were to say that in both cases my hand feels tempted to draw them?"

47. Louise Glück, "The Doorway," in *The Wild Iris* (New York: Ecco Press, 1992), 33.

48. Ovid, *Metamorphoses*, trans. Rolfe Humphries (Bloomington: Indiana University Press, 1955), bk. 1, ll. 549–50, 554–57 (emphasis mine). Humphries's beautiful threefold repetition of the word *still* is prompted by Ovid's opening *hanc quoque*, which John Dryden also translates *still*, as does the early-eighteenth-century Samuel Garth translation "by various authors." Frank Justus Miller in the 1984 revised Loeb translation and Mary Innes in a 1958 Penguin translation both give the phrase as *even* or *even now*, bringing to mind the etymological connection of *even* with *after* or *following upon* or *late*: see C. T. Onions, *Oxford Dictionary of English Etymology*, ed. C. T. Onions with G. W. S. Friedrichson and R. W. Burchfield (Oxford: Oxford University Press, 1966), s.v. "even"; Robert K. Barnhart, ed., *Barnhart Dictionary of Etymology* (Bronx, N.Y.: H. W. Wilson Co., 1988), s.v. "even", as well as the use of *still* to mean "even now" or "even then" first found in 1535 (Barnhart, ed., *Etymology*, s.v. "still"). Humphries's second use of *still* is prompted by Ovid's *adhuc*, which is widely but not universally translated *still* (Dryden, Garth's "various authors," Innes, Miller). Humphries's third *still* is prompted by the counterfactual *ut* (as when, as if), the *still* intensifying the carrying forward into the present of a condition that is only now an afterimage. The Innes translation is the only one other than the Humphries that explicitly marks this third moment, in her case with the word *even*, and hence is the only one that, like the Humphries, has a threefold repetition in this set of lines. But translators who give two repetitions (Dryden, Miller, Garth's "various authors") often construct the passage so that *still* carries into the lines describing the embrace; even in instances where there is only a single iteration, the word carries throughout the full set of lines, in part because of the sense of "lingering" and "remaining" (see the Brookes More translation and again the A. E. Watts 1980 translation). The force of the word still in part comes from the act of stopping—that is, from the nature of this particular metamorphosis, Daphne's sudden immobilization—and in part from the way the word underscores what is perpetual (perpetually green, bk. 1., l. 567) and enduring (the laurel crown, bk. 1, l. 559) in a world of change. But a special power comes from the sense of an afterimage.

49. Ovid, *Metamorphoses*, bk. 1, ll. 705, 712. Here Humphries's use of the word

still is prompted by Ovid's use of the verb *kept* (*nomen tenuisse puellae*), which many translators also render with a verb: "He took and kept her name" (Miller); "He made her name endure" (Watts); "He preserved the girl's name" (Innes). Dryden, like Humphries, uses the word *still* ("he still retains her name") but Humphries, by making the act of preservation a direct speech act, writes a uniquely beautiful line: "And called them Syrinx, still."

50. Whether the sense of pleasure is rapture (as in Ruskin), exhilaration (as in Virgil), or subdelight (as in D. H. Lawrence).

51. Plato, "Timaeus," in *Timaeus and Critias*, trans. and with an introduction by Desmond Lee (New York: Penguin Books, 1977), 77.

52. Aristotle, "On Plants," in *The Complete Works of Aristotle*, 2: 815a.

53. W. Montagna, "The Skin," *Scientific American* 11 (1959): 58–59. See also Harvey Richard Schiffman, *Sensation and Perception: An Integrated Approach* (New York: Wiley, 1976), 95.

54. Rilke, "The Lace," in *New Poems*, 93.

55. Sir Stewart Duke-Elder, "The Eye in Evolution," in *System of Ophthalmology*, 15 vols. (London: Kimpton, 1958–76), 1: 3.

56. Marcus Meister, "The Retina," lecture presented at the Science Center, Harvard University, Cambridge, Mass., October 1994.

57. Duke-Elder, *System of Ophthalmology*, 1: 4, 6.

58. Charles Darwin, *The Power of Movement in Plants*, in *The Works of Charles Darwin*, 29 vols., ed. Paul H. Barrett and R. B. Freeman (London: Pickering and Chatto, 1986–90), 27: 415.

59. "Vague" in the sense used by Duke-Elder, *System of Ophthalmology*, 1: 4; "localization of sensitivity" in the sense used by Darwin, *Works of Charles Darwin*, 27: 418.

60. Darwin, *Works of Charles Darwin*, 27: 418.

61. Linnaeus's flower clock is described by Duke-Elder, *System of Ophthalmology*, 1: 10.

62. Sophocles, *Philoctetes*, in *Antigone, Oedipus the King, Electra, Philoctetes*, trans. Kenneth Cavander, Michael Townsend, and Francis Ferguson (New York: Dell, 1962), 189.

63. Euripides, *Hecabe*, in *Medea and Other Plays*, trans. and with an introduction by Philip Vellacott (New York: Penguin Books, 1963), 1.410, 2.45–37.

64. Rilke, "Bowl of Roses," in *New Poems*, 193–95.

Ernst: Not Seeing the Laocoön

1. February 1960, in Martin Heidegger and Erhard Kästner, *Briefwechsel, 1953–1974*, ed. H. W. Petzet (Frankfurt: Insel, 1986), 43. See Peter Geimer, "Redundanz einer Reise: Martin Heidegger als Tourist," *Texte zur Kunst* 18 (1995): 125–31; Wolfgang Ernst, "Framing the Fragment: Archaeology, Art, Museum," in *The Rhetoric of the Frame: Essays on the Boundaries of the Artwork*, ed. Paul Duro (Cambridge: Cambridge University Press, 1996), 111–35.

2. Fridericus Astius [Friedrich Ast], *Lexikon platonicum sive vocum platonicarum index*, 3 vols. (Lipsiae: Libraria Weidmannia 1835–38), 2: 67–68.

3. Compare—with a reverse emphasis on visual perception—J. W. Goethe, "Denken ist interessanter als Wisen, aber nicht als Anschauen," quoted in Gottfried

Willems, *Anschaulichkeit: Zu Theorie und Geschichte der Wort-Bild-Beziehungen und des literarischen Darstellungsstils* (Tübingen: Max Niemeyer, 1989).

4. Erich Schmidt, *Lessing: Geschichte seines Lebens und seiner Schriften*, 2 vols. (Berlin: Weidmann, 1884–92), 2: 152.

5. Paul Raabe, "Einige philologische Anmerkungen zu Lessings italiensicher Reise 1775," in *Nation und Gelehrtenrepublik: Lessing im europäischen Zusammenhang*, ed. Wilfried Barner and Albert M. Reh (Detroit, Mich.: Wayne State University Press, 1983), 165.

6. Conrad Wiedemann, "Lessings italienische Reise," in *Nation und Gelehrtenrepublik: Lessing im europäischen Zusammenhang*, ed. Wilfried Barner and Albert M. Reh (Detroit, Mich.: Wayne State University Press, 1983), 152ff. On the inventory as regime of registering between (literally) finding and narrative description, see Thomas Ketelsen, *Künstlerviten, Inventare, Kataloge: Drei Studien zur Geschichte der kunsthistorischen Praxis* (Ammersbek: Verlag an der Lottbek, 1988), parts II and III.

7. Lea Ritter-Santini, ed., *Eine Reise der Aufklärung: Lessing in Italien 1775*, 2 vols. (Berlin: Akademie-Verlag: 1993), 2: 515.

8. Lea Ritter-Santini, *Lessing und die Wespen: Die italienische Reise eines Aufklärers* (Paris: Éditions de la Maison des Sciences de l'Homme, 1993), 22–23.

9. D. P. Dymond, *Archaeology and History: A Plea for Reconciliation* (London: Thames & Hudson, 1974), 11.

10. Gotthold Ephraim Lessing, *Werke 1774–1778*, ed. Arno Schilson, in *Werke und Briefe in zwölf Bänden* (Frankurt-am-Main: Deutscher Klassiker Verlag, 1989), 8: 1133.

11. Quoted by David J. Bolter, *Writing Space: The Computer, Hypertext, and the History of Writing* (Hillsdale, N.J.: Hove, and London: Lawrence Erlbaum Associates, 1991), 159.

12. Simon Richter, *Laocoon's Body and the Aesthetics of Pain: Winckelmann, Lessing, Herder, Moritz, Goethe* (Detroit, Mich.: Wayne State University Press, 1992), 22–23.

13. Bernouilli, reprinted in Ritter-Santini, *Eine Reise der Aufklärung*, 2: 287.

14. Richter, *Laocoon's Body*, 22.

15. Ibid., 23. See also Seymour Howard, "On the Reconstruction of the Vatican *Laocoön* Group," in *Antiquity Restored: Essays on the Afterlife of the Antique* (Vienna: IRSA, 1990), 42–62, esp. 43.

16. Walter Deeters, "Des Prinzen Leopold Von Braunschweigs Italienreise," in *Braunschweigisches Jahrbuch*, ed. J. König (Braunschweig: 1971), 152–53.

17. Richter, *Laocoon's Body*, 80.

18. Raabe, "Einige philologische," 165–66.

19. Ibid., 170.

20. Richter, *Laocoon's Body*, 80–81.

21. Ritter-Santini, *Lessing und die Wespen*, 20.

22. Fund 4 Alt 19; credit for this archival discovery goes to Dr. Matthes (see Deeters, "Des Prinzen Leopold Von Braunschweigs Italienreise," 146 n. 18).

23. In Ritter-Santini, *Eine Reise der Aufklärung*, 1: 201–6.

24. E. M. Henning, "Archaeology, Deconstruction, and Intellectual History," in *Modern European Intellectual History: Reappraisals and New Perspectives*, ed. Do-

minick LaCapra and Steven L. Kaplan (Ithaca, N.Y.: Cornell University Press, 1987), 172.

25. David E. Wellbery, "Das Gesetz der Schönheit: Lessings Ästhetik der Repräsentation," in *Was Heißt "Darstellen"?*, ed. Christiaan L. Hart Nibbrig (Frankfurt: Suhrkamp, 1994), 175–204, 175–204, esp. 192ff.

26. Beate Söntgen, "Schwindel der Sinne: Der Guckkasten und die Optik des achtzehnten Jahrhunderts," *Frankfurter allgemeine Zeitung*, 30 August 1995 (review of Barbara Stafford, *Artful Science: Enlightenment, Entertainment and the Eclipse of Visual Education*).

27. Ludwig Catel, *Museum: Begründet, entworfen und dargestellt nach seiner Urform* (Berlin: Akademie-Ausstellung, 1816), 10. Special thanks to Susanne Holl for pointing out to me this early piece of museology.

28. Richter, *Laocoon's Body*, 164.

29. Remark by Schiller's Thalia, quoted in Schmidt, *Lessing*, 2: 153.

30. Hans Erich Bödeker, "Reisebeschreibungen im historischen Diskurs der Aufklärung," in *Aufklärung und Geschichte: Studien zur deutschen Geschichtswissenschaft im 18. Jahrhundert*, ed. Hans Erich Bödeker et al. (Göttingen: Vandenhoeck and Ruprecht, 1982), 280.

31. Wolfgang Ernst, "Reisen ins Innere des Archivs," in *Philosophie und Reisen*, ed. Ulrich Johannes Schneider and Jochen Kornelius Schütze (Leipzig: Leipzig Universitätsverlag, 1996), 160–77.

32. Bödeker, "Reisebeschreibungen," 276.

33. W. Bonss, *Die Einübung des Tatsachenblicks: Zur Struktur und Veränderung empirischer Sozialforschung* (Frankfurt: Suhrkamp, 1982).

34. Bödeker, "Reisebeschreibungen," 288.

35. Ibid., 294.

36. Ibid., 281. On *apodemics* as the art of travel account, see Justin Stagl, "Die Methodisierung des Reisens im 16. Jahrhundert," in *Der Reisebericht: Die Entwicklung einer Gattung in der deutschen Literatur*, ed. Peter J. Brenner (Frankfurt: Suhrkamp, 1989), 140–77.

37. Schmidt, *Lessing*, 2: 152.

38. Johann Heinrich Zelder, *Grosses vollständiges Universal-Lexikon* (Graz: Akademie Dr. und Verl. Anst., 1742), 31: columns 366ff.

39. Bödeker, "Reisebeschreibungen," 282 and 283.

40. For this article and Hayden White's reply to a critique see Hayden White, "The Value of Narrativity in the Representation of Reality," *Critical Inquiry* 7, no. 4 (1980): 5–27.

41. Bödeker, "Reisebeschreibungen," 279.

42. Ibid., 78.

43. Ludwig Uhlig, "Lessing's Image of Death and the Archaeological Evidence," in *Lessing and the Enlightenment*, ed. Alexej Ugrinsky (New York: Greenwood Press, 1986), 79–85, esp. 80–81.

44. Cited by Ludwig Uhlig, *Der Todesgenius in der deutschen Literatur von Winckelmann bis Thomas Mann* (Tübingen: Max Niemeyer Verlag, 1975), 31.

45. Dieter Hildebrandt, *Lessing: Biographie einer Emanzipation* (München: Hanser Verlag, 1979), 398.

46. Jean H. Hagstrum, *The Sister Arts: The Tradition of Literary Pictorialism and English Poetry from Dryden to Gray* (Chicago: University of Chicago Press, 1958), 18.

47. Murray Krieger, "The Ekphrastic Principle and the Still Movement of Poetry; or Laokoön Revisited," in *The Play and Place of Criticism* (Baltimore: Johns Hopkins University Press, 1967), 109, on the motive of "still" movement and still-life painting.

48. See the discussion of Joseph Wright of Derby's painting *The Corinthian Maid*, 1783–84, linking death, sleep, and absence as a graphic trace of presence in Barbara Stafford, *Body Criticism: Imagining the Unseen in Enlightenment Art and Medicine* (Cambridge, Mass.: MIT Press, 1991), 99 and fig. 60.

49. Abraham Rees, *The Cyclopaedia; or, Universal Dictionary of Arts, Sciences, and Literature*, 39 vols. (London: Longman, Hurst, Rees, Orme & Brown, 1819).

50. William Blake, *William Blake's Writings*, 2 vols., ed. G. E. Bentley Jr. (Oxford: Clarendon Press; Oxford University Press, 1978), 1: 743–44.

51. Quoted from Gandy's unpublished diaries in the collection of Sir John Soane's Museum, Lincoln's Inn Fields, London, that will be edited by Brian Lukacher.

52. Gotthold Ephraim Lessing, *Briefe, antiquarischen Inhalts*, ed. Wilfried Barner, in *Werke und Briefe in zwölf Bänden* (Frankfurt: Deutscher Klassiker Verlag, 1990), 5.2: 353–464, esp. 441.

53. Uhlig, "Lessing's Image," 17.

54. D. P. Fowler, "Narrate and Describe: The Problem of Ekphrasis," *Journal of Roman Studies* 81 (1991): 25–35, esp. 34, referring to an analysis by Alessandro Perutelli.

55. Gotthold Ephraim Lessing, *Laocoön: An Essay on the Limits of Painting and Poetry*, trans. E. A. McCormick (Baltimore: Johns Hopkins University Press, 1984), chapter XI; also Richter, *Laocoon's Body*, 80.

56. Frank Egbert Bryant, *On the Limits of Descriptive Writing: Apropos of Lessing's Laocoon* (Ann Arbor, Mich.: Ann Arbor Press, 1906), 7.

57. Deeters, "Des Prinzen Leopold Von Braunschweigs Italienreise," 153.

58. Walter Rehm, "Winckelmann und Lessing," in *Götterstille und Göttertrauer* (Bern: A. Francke, 1951), 188–91.

59. About the conceptual difference between Lessing and Wickelmann, see Victor Anthony Rudowski, "Lessing Contra Winckelmann," in *Lessing and the Enlightenment*, ed. Alexej Ugrinsky (New York: Greenwood Press, 1986), 69–78.

60. Johann Joachim Winckelmann, *Geschichte der Kunst des Alterthums*, reprinted in Ritter-Santini, *Eine Reise der Aufklärung*, 2: 515.

61. Reprinted in Ritter-Santini, *Eine Reise der Aufklärung*, 2: 514.

62. Richter, *Laocoon's Body*, 206 n. 9.

63. Ibid., 66.

64. Ibid., 19 and 21.

65. Eduard Gerhard, *Grundriss der Archäologie: Für Vorlesungen nach Müllers Handbuch* (Berlin: Reimer, 1853).

66. Dymond, *Archaeology and History*, passim.

67. Michael Shanks and Christopher Tilley, *Re-Constructing Archaeology: Theory and Practice* (Cambridge: Cambridge University Press, 1987).

68. Ibid., 13.

69. Kenneth Clark, *The Nude*, cited in Richter, *Laocoon's Body*, 199.

70. Richter, *Laocoon's Body*, 14.

71. Ibid., 27.

72. Peter Matussek, "Durch die Maschen: Die Vernetzung des kulturellen Gedächtnisses und ihre Erinnerungslücken," paper presented at the conference *Interface III*, Hamburg, 1 November 1995.

73. Ritter-Santini, *Lessing und die Wespen*, 22.

74. Wiedemann, "Lessings italienische Reise," 160.

75. Franz Muncker, "Eine Hauptquelle für Lessings Tagebuch seiner italienischen Reise," in *Germanistische Abhandlungen (Festschrift Hermann Paul)* (Strassburg: K. J. Trübner, 1902), 181–94; 181, 186.

76. Nikolaus Wegmann and Matthias Bickenbach, "Herders 'Journal meiner Reise im Jahre 1769'," *Deutsche Vierteljahresschrift für Literaturwissenschaft und Geistesgeschichte* 71, no. 3 (1997): 397–420.

77. Lessing described his essay on *Laocoön* rather as *collectanea*. On this different meaning of hermeneutics/*Hermaea* (with Hermes, among others, being the Greek god of routes and accidents as well), see Schmidt, *Lessing*, 2: 500–501.

78. Lea Ritter-Santini and Stefan Matuschek, "Topographie unserer Bücher," in Ritter-Santini, *Eine Reise der Aufklärung*, 2: 670–71, referring to Langer's document in the State Archive of Lower Saxony (Wolfenbüttel), fund 2 Alt16409, fol. 31–38, 41–42.

79. Similarly, the editor of Herder's *Journal*, Katharina Mommsen, describes its interrupted narrative as "a missing end"; Johann Gottfried Herder, *Journal meiner Reise im Jahr 1769*, ed. Katharina Mommsen (Stuttgart: Reclam, 1976), Epilogue, 152.

80. Ibid., 128.

Potts: Disparities between Part and Whole in the Description of Works of Art

1. On Winckelmann's descriptions of famous antique sculptures, see Alex Potts, *Flesh and the Ideal: Winckelmann and the Origins of Art History* (New Haven, Conn.: Yale University Press, 1994), 60–65; Hans Zeller, *Winckelmanns Beschreibung des Apollo im Belvedere* (Zürich: Atlantis Verlag, 1955); and Hanna Koch, *Johann Joachim Winckelmann, Sprache und Kunstwerk* (Berlin: Akademie Verlag, 1957).

2. Johann Joachim Winckelmann, *Geschichte der Kunst des Alterthums* (Dresden: In der Waltherischen Hof-Buchhandlung, 1764), XI. The closest precedents for Winckelmann's evocative descriptions of antique statues occur not in archaeological publications but in books directed at artists and connoisseurs. See, for example, François Raguenet, *Les monumens de Rome ou Description des plus beaux ouvrages de peinture, de sculpture et d'architecture que se voient à Rome* (Amsterdam: E. Roger, 1701).

3. The descriptions were widely translated and quoted in reviews and summaries of Winckelmann's writing published in cultural journals such as the *Journal étranger* and *Gazette littéraire de l'Europe*, in guides to the art of Rome and Italy, and

in publications on antique art, whether directed to the general reader or scholarly works such as Ennio Quirino Visconti's major catalogue of the sculpture of the Vatican Museum, *Museo Pio-Clementino*, 17 vols. (Rome: L. Mirri, 1784–1807).

4. Winckelmann, *Geschichte der Kunst des Alterthums*, XXIV. See Potts, *Flesh and the Ideal*, 33–34, 41.

5. I am referring here to the classical theory of the three styles of rhetoric, the high, the middle or ornate, and the plain (Cicero, *Orator*, 75–121), which was still very much part of an educated person's cultural baggage in the eighteenth century: see Donald A. Russell and Michael Winterbottom, *Ancient Literary Criticism* (Oxford: Clarendon Press, 1972), 240ff.

6. On ekphrasis, see Michael Baxandall, *Giotto and the Orators* (Oxford: Clarendon Press, 1971), particularly 85ff.

7. Diderot's reviews of the biennial exhibitions held by the French Academy, which were becoming an important feature of Parisian cultural life at the time, were almost exactly contemporary with Winckelmann's writings on ancient art. Diderot engaged in a similarly elaborate and self-conscious description of works of art, though his ekphrasis tended to be a little more conventional and literary than Winckelmann's in that it mostly entailed interpreting the story being told in multifigure compositions.

8. Donald Judd, *Complete Writings 1959–1975* (New York: New York University Press, 1975), 183, 187.

9. Ibid., 195.

10. The description most often cited in modern studies is the one of the Apollo Belvedere, but this does not tally with the clear evidence we have of Winckelmann's own priorities. Of the four extended descriptions of famous statues in the Vatican in Rome (the *Apollo Belvedere*, the *Laocoön*, the *Belvedere Antinous*, and the *Torso Belvedere*) he incorporated in his *History of the Art of Antiquity*, only that of the *Torso* was ever published by him as an independent essay (*Bibliothek der schönen Wissenschaften und der freyen Künste*, V, 1759, 23–41), reprinted in Johann Joachim Winckelmann, *Kleine Schriften vorreden Entwürfe* (Berlin: De Gruyter, 1968), 169–73. This somewhat more extended version was again singled out by him when he appended it to his treatise on allegory: Johann Joachim Winckelmann, *Versuch einer Allegorie, besonders für die Kunst* (Dresden: In der Waltherischen Hof-Buchhandlung, 1766), 155–58. The *Torso* also had a historical priority for him in that he surmised that it came from a "higher period of art than even the *Apollo*" (Winckelmann, *Geschichte der Kunst des Alterthums*, 370; see Potts, *Flesh and the Ideal*, 174ff.). The *Torso Belvedere* did have one clearly articulated attribute, which was lacking in the other famous antique statues Winckelmann described, namely an inscription giving the artist's name, "Apollonius son of Nestor of Athens." This naming remained rather meaningless, though, in that no references to such an artist could be found in the surviving literature on ancient Greek and Roman art.

11. The "unity" of the very highest beauty, according to Winckelmann, brought with it a "lack of definition . . . it is an image that is peculiar neither to this nor that particular person, nor expressive of any state of mind or movement of feeling, for this would mix alien trait with beauty and disturb its unity" (Winckelmann, *Geschichte der Kunst des Alterthums*, 150).

12. Johann Joachim Winckelmann, *Anmerkungen über die Geschichte der Kunst des Alterthums* (Dresden: In der Waltherischen Hof-Buchhandlung, 1767), V.

13. Winckelmann, *Geschichte der Kunst des Alterthums*, 368–70.

14. Ibid., 369.

15. Winckelmann's apparently more conventional reading of the facial features of the *Laocoön* and *Apollo Belvedere*, however, was so ingeniously subtle in its discrimination that it in the end seems hardly less arbitrary to the modern reader than his interpretation of the play of muscles on the body of the *Torso*.

16. A very slightly different version of this longer description had already been published by Winckelmann as an independent essay in 1759 (see note 10).

17. Winckelmann, *Versuch einer Allegorie*, 156–57.

18. Ibid., 155.

19. Ibid., 156.

20. Ibid., V–IX.

21. "Our times," he explains, "are no longer allegorical as antiquity was, where allegory was based upon and [intimately] connected with religion, and hence generally accepted and known" (ibid., 22).

22. Ibid., 2.

23. Winckelmann, *Kleine Schriften vorreden Entwürfe*, 55.

24. Winckelmann, *Versuch einer Allegorie*, 2.

25. The idea that a visual image could convey the complexity of meaning of an ode, even with the most ingenious use of allegory, he goes on to explain, is "futile" to imagine. Ibid., 22, 30.

26. Walter Benjamin, *The Origin of German Tragic Drama*, trans. John Osborne (London: Verso, 1985), 164.

27. It would be anachronistic and ultimately unilluminating to associate Winckelmann too closely with that new problematizing of allegory that emerged in Western European thought in the late Enlightenment: see Paul de Man, "The Rhetoric of Temporality" (1969), in Paul de Man, *Blindness and Insight* (Minneapolis: University of Minnesota Press, 1983), 187–228. Indeed, for theorists of a later generation such as Herder Winckelmann's understanding of allegory seemed decidedly old-fashioned: see Johann Gottfried Herder, *Denkmal Johann Winckelmanns, eine ungekrönte Preisschrift aus dem Jahr 1778* (Kassel: T. Kay, 1882), 53.

28. This tension pervades Winckelmann's entire discussion of the aesthetics of ancient Greek art. See Potts, *Flesh and the Ideal*, particularly 69ff., 165ff.

29. Winckelmann, *Kleine Schriften vorreden Entwürfe*, 169, 173.

30. The drafts are published in ibid., 280–85. There is an even more marked contrast of this kind between the drafts of the *Apollo Belvedere* description (Winckelmann, *Kleine Schriften vorreden Entwürfe*, 269–79) and the published version (Winckelmann, *Geschichte der Kunst des Alterthums*, 392–94).

31. Winckelmann, *Versuch einer Allegorie*, 158.

Reill: Between Mechanism and Romantic Naturphilosophie

1. Max Horkheimer, "Reason Against Itself: Some Remarks on Enlightenment," in *What Is Enlightenment: Eighteenth-Century Answers and Twentieth-Century Questions*, ed. James Schmidt (Berkeley: University of California Press, 1996), 359.

2. For an excellent analysis of this tendency see Simon Schaffer, "Natural Philosophy," in *The Ferment of Knowledge: Studies in the Historiography of Eighteenth-Century Science*, ed. G. S. Rousseau and Roy Porter (Cambridge: Cambridge University Press, 1980), 53–91.

3. Horkheimer, "Reason Against Itself," 361.

4. Margaret C. Jacob, *The Radical Enlightenment: Pantheists, Freemasons, and Republicans* (London: Allen & Unwin, 1981); Julien Offray de La Mettrie, *L'homme machine: A Study in the Origins of an Idea*, ed. Aram Vartanian (Princeton, N.J.: Princeton University Press, 1960).

5. David Hume, *The Philosophical Works*, 4 vols., ed. Thomas Hill Green and Thomas Hodge Grose (London: Spottiswoode, 1883), 3: 213–14.

6. George Louis Leclerc Buffon, *De la manière d'étudier & de traiter l'histoire naturelle* (reprint, Paris: Diderot, 1986).

7. Hume, *The Philosophical Works*, 4: 63.

8. Ibid., 62.

9. Pierre Nicolas Changeux, *Traité des extremes ou Élements de la science de la réalité* (Amsterdam: Darkstee & Merkus, 1768), 232.

10. Hume, *The Philosophical Works*, 4: 51.

11. The disinclination to engage in the regnant questions of the early eighteenth century was made evident by the German mathematician W. J. G. Karsten in his discussion of the earlier disputes concerning matter, where he dismissed the whole controversy concerning these issues as useless. W. J. G Karsten, *Physische-chemische Abhandlung, durch neuere Schriften von hermetischen Arbeiten und andere neue Untersuchungen veranlasset*, 2 vols. (Halle: Renger, 1786–87), 2: 69.

12. This issue was most clearly evident in the *vis viva* controversy. See Thomas L. Hankins, "Eighteenth-Century Attempts to Resolve the Vis Viva Controversy," *Isis* 56 (1965); Carolyn Iltis [Merchant], "D'Alembert and the Vis Viva Controversy," *Studies in History and Philosophy of Science* 1 (1970); Carolyn Iltis [Merchant], "The Decline of Cartesianism in Mechanics: The Leibnizian-Cartesian Debates," *Isis* 64 (1973); Carolyn Iltis [Merchant], "The Leibnizian-Newtonian Debates: Natural Philosophy and Social Psychology," *British Journal for the History of Science* 6 (1973); Carolyn Iltis [Merchant], "Madam Du Chatelet's Metaphysics and Mechanics," *Studies in History and Philosophy of Science* 8 (1977); David Papineau, "The Vis Viva Controversy: Do Meanings Matter?" *Studies in History and Philosophy of Science* 8 (1977); Giorgio Tonelli, "Analysis and Syntheses in XVIIIth Century Philosophy Prior to Kant," *Archiv für Begriffsgeschichte* 20 (1976); Giorgio Tonelli, "Critiques of the Notion of Substance Prior to Kant," *Tijdschrift voor Philosophie* 23 (1961); Giorgio Tonelli, "The Philosophy of d'Alembert: A Skeptic Beyond Skepticism," *Kantstudien* 67 (1976).

13. Stephen Edelston Toulmin, *Cosmopolis: The Hidden Agenda of Modernity* (New York: Free Press, 1990), 108.

14. Johann Friedrich Blumenbach, *Elements of Physiology*, 2 vols., trans. Charles Caldwell (Philadelphia: Thomas Dobson, 1795), 1: 33.

15. Ibid., 22.

16. Ibid., 34.

17. Ibid., 22.

18. The term *synergy* was coined by Georg Stahl and then used extensively by Paul Barthez in his theory of vital physiology.

19. Kant was much more influenced by this explanatory model than is usually supposed. For an excellent discussion of the vitalistic influences on his philosophy see Wolfgang Krohn and Günther Küppers, "Die natürlichen Ursachen der Zwecke: Kants Ansätze der Selbstorganisation," *Selbstorganisation: Jahrbuch für Komplexität in den Natur-, Sozial- und Geisteswissenschaften* 3 (1992): 7–15.

20. Both Blumenbach and Barthez called their respective concepts of the *Bildungstrieb* and the *Princip Vital* occult powers, and both turned to the authority of Newton. Yet both acknowledged that the only way the powers could be recognized was by their effects, and these were beyond quantification.

21. George Louis Leclerc comte de Buffon, *Histoire naturelle, générale et particulière*, 44 vols. (Paris: Impr. royale, Hôtel de Thou, 1749–1804), 1: 4.

22. Johann Friedrich Blumenbach, *Ueber den Bildungstrieb*, 3rd ed. (Göttingen: Johann Christina Dieterich, 1791), 65–66.

23. Kenneth Dewhurst and Nigel Reeves, *Frederick Schiller: Medicine, Psychology and Literature with the First English Edition of the Complete Medical and Physiological Writings* (Berkeley: University of California Press, 1978), 152.

24. Toulmin, *Cosmopolis: The Hidden Agenda of Modernity*, 364.

25. George Louis Leclerc comte de Buffon, *Les époques de la nature: Édition critique* (reprint, Paris: Diderot, 1998), 4.

26. Johann Gottfried Herder, "Ideen zur Philosophie der Geschichte der Menschheit," in Johann Gottfried Herder, *Sämmtliche Werke*, 33 vols., ed. Bernhard Suphan (Berlin: Weidmann, 1877–1913), 14: 145.

27. Ibid., 13: 16.

28. Adam Ferguson, *Principles of Moral and Political Science*, 2 vols. (Edinburgh: Strahan & T. Cadell, 1792), 1: 174.

29. Ibid., 275.

30. August Ludvig von Schlözer, *Vorstellung seiner Universal-Historie*, 2 vols. (Göttingen: José C. Dieterich, 1772), 1: 15.

31. Ibid.

32. Ibid., 19.

33. Buffon, *De la manière d'étudier & de traiter l'histoire naturelle*, 4.

34. Schlözer, *Vorstellung seiner Universal-Historie*, 1: 46.

35. "Vom Erkennen und Empfinden der menschlichen Seele: Bemerkungen und Träume," in Herder, *Sämmtliche Werke*, 8: 169.

36. Ibid., 13: 129.

37. Ibid., 123.

38. Ibid., 8: 170.

39. Buffon, *Histoire naturelle, générale et particulière*, 1: 20.

40. This program was often derived from Hippocrates. Both Judith Shklar and George Armstrong Kelly show how Montesquieu's analysis of space was derived from Hippocrates. Judith Shklar, "Virtue in a Bad Climate: Good Men and Good Citizens in Montesquieu's *L'esprit des lois*," in *Enlightenment Studies in Honour of Lester G. Crocker*, ed. Alfred Jepson Bingham and Virgil W. Topazio (Oxford: Voltaire Foundation, at the Taylor Institution, 1979), 316. George Armstrong Kelly,

Mortal Politics in Eighteenth-Century France (Waterloo, Ont.: University of Waterloo Press, 1986), 43.

41. Blumenbach, *Elements of Physiology*, 1: 203.

42. Schlözer, *Vorstellung seiner Universal-Historie*, 2: 358.

43. Herder, *Sämmtliche Werke*, 13: 276. This aspect of late Enlightenment science has been virtually suppressed in most histories of science. Amongst natural historians, chemists, and especially life scientists there was a widespread re-evaluation of these thinkers. For many, Hippocrates and Stahl were placed in the same category as Newton and Bacon. See, for example, Pierre Jean Georges Cabanis, *Coup d'oeil sur les révolutions et sur la réforme de la médecine* (Paris: Imprimerie de Crapelet, 1804), 146.

44. Herder, *Sämmtliche Werke*, 13: 276.

45. Ibid., 14: 145.

46. Ibid., 13: 20.

47. Ibid., 13: 9.

48. Ibid., 13: 8.

49. Ibid., 13: 213. Herder interpreted creation in the same manner as Kant. The world was not created perfect, but rather was imbued with specific principles that led matter to develop in the way it has and will continue to do so, all according to a plan.

50. Ibid., 13: 8.

51. Ibid., 14: 144.

52. Ibid., 13: 299.

53. Ibid., 127–32.

54. Ibid., 14: 98–100.

55. Ibid., 130.

56. Ibid., 92–105.

57. Ibid., 13: 173.

58. Blumenbach as a proponent of epigenesis also drew a distinction between dead and living matter, denying in the process the Great Chain of Being: Blumenbach, *Ueber den Bildungstrieb*, 79–80.

59. Herder, *Sämmtliche Werke*, 14: 144.

60. Ibid., 136.

61. Hayden White, *Metahistory: The Historical Imagination in Nineteenth-Century Europe* (Baltimore: Johns Hopkins University Press, 1973), 76.

62. Lorenz Oken, *Lehrbuch der Naturphilosophie*, 2nd ed. (Jena: F. Fromann, 1831), 15.

63. Immanuel Kant, "Kritik der Urtheilskraft," in *Kants Werke: Akademie-Textausgabe*, 9 vols. (Berlin: de Gruyter, 1968), 5: 419.

64. Lorenz Oken, *Abriss der Naturphilosophie* (Göttingen: Vandenhoek und Ruprecht, 1805), 1.

65. Peter Hanns Reill, "History and the Life Sciences in the Early Nineteenth Century: Wilhelm von Humboldt and Leopold von Ranke," in *Leopold von Ranke and the Shaping of the Historical Discipline*, ed. Georg Iggers and James Powell (Syracuse, N.Y.: Syracuse University Press, 1990), 21–36.

66. Ranke virtually repeated this assertion verbatim in one of his most impor-

tant popular essays, "Das politische Gespräch." See Georg Iggers, *The German Conception of History: The National Tradition of Historical Thought from Herder to the Present* (Middletown, Conn.: Wesleyan University Press, 1968), 82.

Vidler: Transparency and Utopia

1. Immanuel Kant, *Prolegomena*, no. 6, cited in Ernst Cassirer, *The Problem of Knowledge: Philosophy, Science and History since Hegel*, trans. W. H. Woglom and C. W. Hendel (New Haven, Conn.: Yale University Press, 1950), 23.

2. Michael Baxandall, *Shadows and Enlightenment* (New Haven, Conn.: Yale University Press, 1995).

3. Jean Le Rond d'Alembert, *Discours préliminaire de l'Encyclopédie* (Paris: Editions Gonthier, 1965), 36–37 (my translation).

4. Michel Foucault, "The Eye of Power," in *Power-Knowledge: Selected Interviews & Other Writings*, ed. Colin Gordon (New York: Pantheon Books, 1980), 153.

5. Ibid., 154.

6. See Michel Foucault and Ludwig Binswanger, *Dream and Existence*, trans. Jacob Needleman (Seattle: Review of Existential Psychology and Psychiatry, 1986).

7. Foucault, "The Eye of Power," 148.

8. Michel Foucault, *Histoire de la folie à l'âge classique* (Paris: Gallimard: 1972); Bruno Fortier, *La politique de l'espace parisien* (Paris: C.O.R.D.A., 1975); Bruno Fortier and Alain Demangeon, *Les vaisseaux et les villes: l'arsenal de Cherbourg* (Brussels: Pierre Margaga, 1978); and Michel Foucault et al., *Les machines à guérir (aux origines de l'hôpital moderne)* (Brussels: Pierre Mardaga, 1979).

9. Michel Foucault, "On Attica: An Interview," *Telos* 19 (Spring 1974): 155–56.

10. I thank J. B. Shank for this insight. For the following citations by Ledoux about the Saline de Chaux see Claude-Nicolas Ledoux, *L'architecture considerée sous le rapport de l'art, des moeurs et de la législation* (Paris: chez l'auteur, 1804). Fuller discussion of many points appears in Anthony Vidler, *Claude-Nicolas Ledoux: Architecture and Social Reform at the End of the Ancien Régime* (Cambridge, Mass.: MIT Press, 1990).

11. Michel Foucault, *Discipline and Punish: The Birth of the Prison*, trans. Alan Sheridan (New York: Vintage Books, 1979), 173–74.

12. See Anthony Vidler, "The Architecture of Allusion: Notes on the Post-Modern Sublime," *Art Criticism* 2, no. 1 (1985): 61–69, and the expanded version "Notes on the Sublime: From Neo-Classicism to Post-Modernism," *The Princeton Journal* 2 (1987).

13. Nicolas Boileau-Despréaux, *Traité du sublime ou du merveilleux dans le discours: Traduit du grec de Longin*, in *Oeuvres diverses* (Paris: chez Claude Barbin, 1685), "Preface," x.

14. Jacques-François Blondel, *Cours d'architecture*, 6 vols. (Paris: Desaint, 1771–77), 2: 377ff.

15. Edmund Burke, *A Philosophical Enquiry into the Origin of Our Ideas of the Sublime and Beautiful*, ed. and with an introduction and notes by James T. Boulton (South Bend, Ind.: University of Notre Dame Press, 1968), 39.

16. Ibid., II, iii, 59.

17. Ibid., 76.

18. Ibid., II, ix, 74–76.

19. Ibid., IV, xiii, 141–42.

20. Ibid., II, xii–xvi, 77–82.

21. Blaise Pascal, *Les Pensées de Pascal*, ed. Francis Kaplan (Paris: Éditions du Cerf, 1982), no. 130.

22. Abbé Boileau, "Lettre de M. B. . . . sur différents sujets de morale et de piété" (1737), reprinted in Blaise Pascal, *Oeuvres complètes*, 4 vols., ed. Jean Mesnard (Paris: Desclée de Brouwer, 1964–), 1: 969.

23. "Extrait d'un mémoire sur la vie de M. Pascal," reprinted in Pascal, *Oeuvres complètes*, 1: 885. The incident with the carriage was the more evocative given Pascal's own supposed involvement with promoting a public carriage system for Paris. See Henri Sauval, *Histoire et recherches des antiquités de la ville de Paris*, 3 vols. (Paris: C. Moette, 1724), 1: 192–93, where Pascal is credited with conceiving a carriage system (*carrosses à cinq sols*) following fixed routes according to a fixed schedule.

24. Marie Jean Antoine Caritat de Condorcet, "Éloge de Blaise Pascal," in *Oeuvres de Condorcet*, 12 vols., ed. A. Condorcet-O'Connor and M. F. Arago (Paris: Firmin Didot Frères, 1847–49), 3: 567–634, citations 592–93.

25. See, for example, Jean-Pierre Fanton d'Andon, *L'horreur du vide* (Paris: Éditions du Centre national de recherche scientifique, 1978).

26. Claude-Nicolas Ledoux, *L'architecture considérée sous le rapport de l'art* (Paris: chez l'auteur, 1804), 123.

27. Ibid., 193–95.

28. See Anthony Vidler, *The Architectural Uncanny: Essays in the Modern Unhomely* (Cambridge, Mass.: MIT Press, 1992), especially the second section of "Dark Space."

29. Etienne-Louis Boullée, *Architecture: Essai sur l'art* (Paris: Hermann, 1968), 113.

30. Ibid., 136.

31. Ibid., 78.

32. Ibid.

33. Sarah Kofman, *The Childhood of Art: An Interpretation of Freud's Aesthetics*, trans. Winifred Woodhull (New York: Columbia University Press, 1988), 128.

34. Ibid.

35. Baxandall, *Shadows and Enlightenment*, 144.

36. Sigmund Freud, *Standard Edition of the Complete Psychological Works of Sigmund Freud*, 24 vols., in collaboration with Anna Freud, translated under the general editorship of James Strachey, with Alix Strachey and Alan Tyson (London: Hogarth, 1953–74), 23: 300. Cited in Victor Burgin, "Geometry and Abjection," in *Abjection, Melancholia, and Love: The Work of Julia Kristeva*, ed. John Fletcher and Andrew Benjamin (London: Routledge, 1990), 25.

37. Pierre Jean-Baptiste Chaussard, *Le nouveau diable boiteux, table philosophique et morale de Paris*, 2 vols. (Paris: F. Buisson, 1798).

38. Ibid., 1: 53–56.

Wellbery: Aesthetic Media

1. Theodor A. Meyer, *Das Stilgesetz der Poesie* (1901; reprint, Frankfurt-am-Main: Suhrkamp, 1990), 23–24.

2. Rudolf Arnheim, *Film as Art* (Berkeley: University of California Press, 1957), 199–230.

3. Clement Greenberg, "Towards a Newer Laocoon," *Partisan Review* 7, no. 4 (1940): 296–310. The title probably alludes not to Arnheim, but to Irving Babbitt's *The New Laokoön* (New York: Houghton Mifflin, 1910).

4. Galvano Della Volpe, *Critique of Taste*, trans. Michael Caesar (London: Verso, 1991), 173–234.

5. Joseph Frank, *The Idea of Spatial Form* (New Brunswick, N.J.: Rutgers University Press, 1990), xiv. This volume includes a reprint of the essay "Spatial Form in Modern Literature" (31–66).

6. John Bender and David Wellbery, "Rhetoricality: On the Modernist Return of Rhetoric," in *The Ends of Rhetoric: History—Theory—Practice* (Stanford, Calif.: Stanford University Press, 1990), 3–42.

7. Georg Wilhelm Friedrich Hegel, *Werke*, 20 vols., ed. Eva Moldenhauer and Karl Markus Michel (Frankfurt-am-Main: Suhrkamp, 1969–71), 13: 61.

8. Ibid., 13: 151–57.

9. Ibid., 15: 276.

10. Meyer, *Das Stilgesetz der Poesie*, 21.

11. Friedrich Kittler, *Discourse Networks 1800/1900*, trans. Michael Metteer and Chris Cullens (Stanford, Calif.: Stanford University Press, 1990), 177–374.

12. Edmund Burke, *A Philosophical Enquiry into the Origin of Our Ideas of the Sublime and Beautiful*, ed. Adam Phillips (Oxford: Oxford University Press, 1990), 152.

13. Ibid., 153.

14. Niklas Luhmann, *Die Wissenschaft der Gesellschaft* (Frankfurt-am-Main: Suhrkamp, 1992), 13–92.

15. Johann Christoph Gottsched, *Versuch einer critischen Dichtkunst* (Darmstadt: Wissenschaftliche Buchgesellschaft, 1962).

16. Johann Jacob Breitinger, *Critische Dichtkunst*, 2 vols. (1740; reprint, Stuttgart: Metzler, 1966), 1: 30.

17. John Bender, *Imagining the Penitentiary: Fiction and the Architecture of Mind in the Eighteenth Century* (Chicago: University of Chicago Press, 1987).

18. Anthony Ashley Cooper, Earl of Shaftesbury, *Characteristics of Men, Manners, Opinions, Times*, ed. John H. Robertson (Indianapolis, Ind.: Bobbs-Merrill, 1964), 43.

19. The notion of observation in systems-theoretical research is quite general, designating the use of a distinction to mark some object or theme. Second-order observation observes not objects or themes, but (first-order) observations of objects or themes. Thus, second-order observation registers the distinctions employed in first-order observation, notes the differences among observations, and marks the fact that its own observing activity can itself be observed from a second-order perspective. Second-order observation is thus distinguished from first-order observa-

tion by the nature of its theme: it observes observations and not things. But second-order observation must itself operate with distinctions in order to isolate and mark its theme and, in this sense, it is also a first-order observation. The most thorough discussion of this topic is Niklas Luhmann, *Die Kunst der Gesellschaft* (Frankfurt-am-Main: Suhrkamp, 1995), 68–121.

20. Shaftesbury, *Characteristics of Men*, 49.

21. Ibid., 44.

22. Ibid., 45.

23. Ibid., 53.

24. Ibid., 48–49.

25. Ibid., 53.

26. Luhmann, *Die Kunst der Gesellschaft*, 106–7.

27. Shaftesbury, *Characteristics of Men*, 45.

28. Abbé Dubos, *Réflexions critiques sur la poésie et sur la peinture*, 4th ed. (Paris: Mariette, 1740).

29. See Niklas Luhmann, *Soziale Systeme* (Frankfurt-am-Main: Suhrkamp, 1984), 15–30.

30. See Luhmann, *Die Kunst der Gesellschaft*, 165.

31. James Harris, *Three Treatises* (London: J. Nourse and P. Vaillant, 1744).

32. Hans Ulrich Gumbrecht, *Production of Presence: What Meaning Cannot Convey* (Stanford, Calif.: Stanford University Press, 2004).

Works Cited

Electronic Resources

www.genome.gov. Official web site of the National Human Genome Research Institute.

www.genomenewsnetwork.org/articles/book_rev_archive.shtml. Book Review Archive on the web site of the Genome News Network.

www.ornl.gov/sci/techresources/Human_Genome/faq/genenumber.shtml. "So How Many Genes Are There?" web page on the Genomes to Life web site maintained by the U.S. Department of Energy.

www.ornl.gov/sci/techresources/Human_Genome/home.shtml. Genomes to Life web site maintained by the U.S. Department of Energy.

www.ornl.gov/sci/techresources/Human_Genome/publicat/hgn/hgnarch.shtml# sequencing. "Sequencing-related Articles" web page on the Genomes to Life web site maintained by the U.S. Department of Energy.

Books and Articles

Ackerman, Diane. *A Natural History of the Senses*. New York: Random House, 1991.

Adams, Mark D., et al. "Complementary DNA Sequencing: Expressed Sequence Tags and Human Genome Project." *Science* 252 (21 June1991): 1651–56.

Adanson, Michel. *Familles des plantes*. 2 vols. Paris: Vincent, 1763.

Addison, Joseph. *The Spectator: With a Historical and Biographical Preface*. Edited by A. Chalmers. 6 vols. Boston: Little, Brown & Co., 1872.

Adelung, Johann Christoph, and Johann Severin Vater. *Mithridates oder allgemeine Sprachenkunde mit dem Vater unser als Sprachprobe in bey nahe fünfhundert Sprachen und Mundarten*. 1806–17. 4 vols. Reprint, Hildesheim: Olms, 1970.

Alighieri, Dante. *Paradiso*. Translated by Allen Mandelbaum. Berkeley: University of California Press, 1982.

Allen, David. *The Naturalist in Britain: A Social History*. Harmondsworth, England: Penguin Books, 1978.

Alletz, Pons. *Histoire des singes, et autres animaux curieux*. Paris: Duchesne, 1752.

Alpers, Svetlana. *The Art of Describing: Dutch Art in the Seventeenth Century.* Chicago: University of Chicago Press, 1983.

"And the Gene Number Is . . . ?" *Science* 288 (19 May 2000): 1146–47.

"Animal's Genetic Program Decoded, in a Science First." *New York Times,* 11 December 1998.

Aristotle. *The Categories: On Interpretation, Prior Analytics.* Edited by Harold P. Cook and Hugh Tredennick. London: Heinemann, 1962.

———. *The Complete Works of Aristotle: The Revised Oxford Translation.* 2 vols. Translated by T. Lovejoy and E. S. Forster. Edited by Jonathan Barnes. Princeton, N.J.: Princeton University Press, 1984.

Arnauld, Antoine, and Claude Lancelot. "Port-Royal." In *Grammaire générale et raisonnée.* 1660. Reprint of the 1830 edition, Paris: Paulet, 1960.

Arnheim, Rudolf. *Film as Art.* Berkeley: University of California Press, 1957.

Ashbery, John. *Selected Poems.* New York: Viking Press, 1985.

———. *A Wave: Poems by John Ashbery.* New York: Viking Press, 1985.

Ashburner, Michael, et al. "An Exploration of the Sequence of a 2.9-MB Region of the Genome of *Drosophilia melanogaster*: The *Adh* Region." *Genetics* 153 (September 1999): 179–219.

Astius, Fridericus [Friedrich Ast]. *Lexikon platonicum sive vocum platonicarum index.* 3 vols. Lipsiae: Libraria Weidmannia, 1835–38.

Audebert, Jean-Baptiste. *Histoire naturelle des singes et des makis.* Paris: Desray, 1799–1800.

Babbitt, Irving. *The New Laokoön.* New York: Houghton Mifflin, 1910.

Bacon, Francis. *Topica inquisitionis de luce et lumine.* 1612. In *The Works of Francis Bacon,* edited by Basil Montagu. 16 vols. London: William Pickering, 1825–34.

Barnhart, Robert K., ed. *Barnhart Dictionary of Etymology.* Bronx, N.Y.: H. W. Wilson Co., 1988.

Baudelaire, Charles. *Oeuvres complètes.* Edited by Marcel A. Ruff. Paris: Editions du Seuil, 1991.

Baudrillard, Jean. *Agonie des Realen.* Berlin: Merve Verlag, 1978.

———. *Die Illusion und die Virtualität.* Bern: Benteli, 1994.

Baxandall, Michael. *Giotto and the Orators.* Oxford: Clarendon Press, 1971.

———. *Shadows and Enlightenment.* New Haven, Conn.: Yale University Press, 1995.

Bender, John. "Enlightenment Fiction and the Scientific Hypothesis." *Representations* 61 (Winter 1998): 6–28.

———. "Fiktionalität in der Aufklärung." In *Nach der Aufklärung? Beiträge zum Diskurs der Kulturwissenschaften,* edited by Wolfgang Klein and Waltraud Naumann-Beyer. Berlin: Akademie Verlag, 1995.

———. *Imagining the Penitentiary: Fiction and the Architecture of Mind in the Eighteenth Century.* Chicago: University of Chicago Press, 1987.

Bender, John, and Michael Marrinan. *The Culture of Diagram.* Stanford, Calif.: Stanford University Press, forthcoming.

Bender, John, and David Wellbery. "Rhetoricality: On the Modernist Return of Rhetoric." In *The Ends of Rhetoric: History—Theory—Practice.* Stanford, Calif.: Stanford University Press, 1990.

Benjamin, Walter. *The Origin of German Tragic Drama*. Translated by John Osborne. London: Verso, 1985.

Bergson, Henri. "The Soul and the Body." In *Mind-Energy: Lectures and Essays*. Translated by H. Wildon Carr. Westport, Conn.: Greenwood Press, 1975.

Bingham, Alfred Jepson, and Virgil W. Topazio, eds. *Enlightenment Studies in Honour of Lester G. Crocker*. Oxford: Voltaire Foundation, at the Taylor Institution, 1979.

Blake, William. *William Blake's Writings*. Edited by G. E. Bentley Jr. 2 vols. Oxford: Clarendon Press; Oxford University Press, 1978.

Blondel, Jacques-François. *Cours d'architecture*. 6 vols. Paris: Desaint, 1771–77.

Blumenbach, Johann Friedrich. *Elements of Physiology*. Translated by Charles Caldwell. 2 vols. Philadelphia: Thomas Dobson, 1795.

———. *The Natural Varieties of Mankind*. 1795. Translated by Thomas Bendyshe. 1865. Reprint, New York: Bergman, 1969.

———. *Ueber den Bildungstrieb*. 3rd ed. Göttingen: Johann Christina Dieterich, 1791.

Blumenberg, Hans. *Der Prozeß der theoretischen Neugierde*. Frankfurt-am-Main: Suhrkamp, 1988.

Bödeker, Hans Erich, et al., eds. *Aufklärung und Geschichte: Studien zur deutschen Geschichtswissenschaft im 18. Jahrhundert*. Göttingen: Vandenhoeck and Ruprecht, 1982.

Boileau-Despréaux, Nicolas. *Traité du sublime ou du merveilleux dans le discours: Traduit du grec de Longin*. In *Oeuvres diverses*. Paris: chez Claude Barbin, 1685.

Bolter, David J. *Writing Space: The Computer, Hypertext, and the History of Writing*. Hillsdale, N.J.: Hove, and London: Lawrence Erlbaum Associates, 1991.

Bonss, W. *Die Einübung des Tatsachenblicks: Zur Struktur und Veränderung empirischer Sozialforschung*. Frankfurt: Suhrkamp, 1982.

Bordo, Susan. *Unbearable Weight: Feminism, Western Culture, and the Body*. Berkeley: University of California Press, 1993.

Boreman, Thomas. *A Description of Some Curious and Uncommon Creatures*. London: Richard Ware and Thomas Boreman, 1739.

Borst, Arno. *Der Turmbau von Babel*. 3 vols. Reprint, München: Deutscher Taschenbuch Verlag, 1995.

Bosman, William. "A New and Accurate Description of the Coast of Guinea." 1705. In *A General Collection of the Best and Most Interesting Voyages and Travels in All Parts of the World*, edited by John Pinkerton. London: Printed for Longman, Hurst, Rees and Orme . . . , and Cadell and Davies . . . , 1808.

Boullée, Etienne-Louis. *Architecture: Essai sur l'art*. Texts selected and presented by Jean-Marie Pérouse de Montclos. Paris: Hermann, 1968.

Bourguet, Marie-Noëlle. "Voyage, collecte, collections: Le catalogue de la nature (fin 17e–debut 19e siècle)." In *Terre à découvrir, terres à parcourir*, edited by D. Lecocq. Paris: Publications de l'Université de Paris 7–Denis Diderot, 1996.

Boyle, Robert. *The Works of the Honourable Robert Boyle*. 1772. Edited by Thomas Birch. 6 vols. Reprint, Hildesheim: Georg Olms Verlag, 1966.

Bradley, Richard. *A Philosophical Account of the Works of Nature*. London: W. Mears, 1721.

Braudel, Fernand. *The Wheels of Commerce*. 1979. Translated by Siân Reynolds. Reprint, New York: Harper & Row, 1982.

Breitinger, Johann Jacob. *Critische Dichtkunst*. 1740. 2 vols. Reprint, Stuttgart: Metzler, 1966.

Brenner, Sydney. "The Human Genome: The Nature of the Enterprise." In *Symposium on Human Genetic Information: Science, Law and Ethics, Ciba Foundation Symposium*. New York: John Wiley & Sons, 1990.

Breyne, Jakob. *Exoticarum aliarumque minus cognitarium plantarum centuria prima*. Gedani: Typis, sumptibus & in aedibus autoris, imprimebat David Fridericus Rhetius, 1678.

Broberg, Gunnar. "*Homo sapiens*." In *Linnaeus: The Man and His Work*, edited by Tore Fränsmyr. Uppsala Studies in the History of Science, 18. Berkeley: University of California Press, 1983.

Brodwin, Paul. *Medicine and Morality in Haiti: The Contest for Healing Power*. Cambridge: Cambridge University Press, 1996.

Bryant, Frank Egbert. *On the Limits of Descriptive Writing: Apropos of Lessing's Laocoon*. Ann Arbor, Mich.: Ann Arbor Press, 1906.

Buffon, Georges Louis Leclerc, comte de. *De la manière d'étudier & de traiter l'histoire naturelle*. 1749. Reprint, Paris: Diderot, 1986.

———. *Histoire naturelle, générale et particulière*. 44 vols. Paris: Impr. royale, Hôtel de Thou, 1749–1804.

———. *Les époques de la nature: Édition critique*. Reprint, Paris: Diderot, 1998.

Burchell, Graham. "Peculiar Interests: Civil Society and Governing 'The System of Natural Liberty.'" In *The Foucault Effect: Studies in Governmentality, with Two Lectures by and an Interview with Michel Foucault*, edited by Graham Burchell, Colin Gordon, and Peter Miller. Chicago: University of Chicago Press, 1991.

Burgin, Victor. "Geometry and Abjection." In *Abjection, Melancholia, and Love: The Work of Julia Kristeva*, edited by John Fletcher and Andrew Benjamin. London: Routledge, 1990.

Burke, Edmund. *A Philosophical Enquiry into the Origin of Our Ideas of the Sublime and Beautiful*. Edited and with an introduction and notes by James T. Boulton. South Bend, Ind.: University of Notre Dame Press, 1968.

———. *A Philosophical Enquiry into the Origin of our Ideas of the Sublime and Beautiful*. Edited by Adam Phillips. Oxford: Oxford University Press, 1990.

Burrell, Harry. *The Platypus*. Sydney: Angus & Robertson Limited, 1927.

Bush, Barbara. *Slave Women in Caribbean Society: 1650–1838*. Bloomington: Indiana University Press, 1990.

Cabanis, Pierre Jean Georges. *Coup d'oeil sur les revolutions et sur la réforme de la médecine*. Paris: Imprimerie de Crapelet, 1804.

Caruth, Cathy. *Empirical Truths and Critical Fictions: Locke, Wordsworth, Kant, Freud*. Baltimore: Johns Hopkins University Press, 1991.

Cassirer, Ernst. *Die Philosophie der Aufklärung*. Tübingen: Mohr, 1932.

———. *The Problem of Knowledge: Philosophy, Science and History since Hegel*. Translated by W. H. Woglom and C. W. Hendel. New Haven, Conn.: Yale University Press, 1950.

Catel, Ludwig. *Museum: Begründet, entworfen und dargestellt nach seiner Urform.* Berlin: Akademie-Ausstellung, 1816.

Céard, Jean, ed. *La curiosité à la Renaissance.* Paris: Société d'Édition d'Enseignement Supérieur, 1986.

Changeux, Pierre Nicolas. *Traité des extremes ou élements de la science de la réalité.* Amsterdam: Darkstee & Merkus, 1768.

Chartier, Roger. *Culture écrite et société: L'ordre des livres (XIVe–XVIIIe siècle).* Paris: Albin Michel, 1996.

Chaussard, Pierre Jean-Baptiste. *Le nouveau diable boiteux, table philosophique et morale de Paris.* 2 vols. Paris: F. Buisson, 1798.

Collini, Stefan, Donald Winch, and John Burrow. *That Noble Science of Politics: A Study of Nineteenth-Century Intellectual History.* Cambridge: Cambridge University Press, 1983.

Comte, Auguste. *Du pouvoir spirituel.* Paris: Le livre de poche, 1978.

Condorcet, Marie Jean Antoine Nicolas Caritat, Marquis de. "Éloge de M. de Linné." In *Histoire de l'Académie Royale des Sciences.* Paris, 1778.

———. *Oeuvres de Condorcet.* Edited by A. Condorcet-O'Connor and M. F. Arago. 12 vols. Paris: Firmin Didot Frères, 1847–49.

———. *Sketch for a Historical Picture of the Progress of the Human Mind.* 1795. Translated by June Barraclough. London: Weidenfeld & Nicolson, 1955.

Coseriu, Eugenio. "Lo que se dice de Hervás." In *Estudios ofrecidos a Emilio Alarcos Llorach.* Vol. 3. Oviedo: Universidad de Oviedo, 1978.

Court de Gébelin, Antoine. *Histoire naturelle de la parole ou grammaire universelle à l'usage des jeunes gens.* Edited by Jean Denis Lanjuinais. Paris: Plancher/Eymery/Delaunay, 1816.

Cuvier, Georges. *The Animal Kingdom.* 16 vols. London: George B. Whittler, 1827–35.

d'Alembert, Jean Le Rond. *Discours préliminaire de l'Encyclopédie.* Paris: Editions Gonthier, 1965.

d'Obsonville, Foucher. *Essais philosophiques sur les mœurs de divers animaux étrangers, avec des observations relatives aux principes & usages de plusieurs peuple, ou, Extraits des voyages de M*** en Asie.* Paris: Couturier fils; la veuve Tilliand & fils, 1783.

da Vinci, Leonardo. *Trattato della pittura.* Parigi: Giacomo Langlois, 1651.

Dahlern, Ingo von. "Bilder aus dem Datenhelm." *Der Tagesspiegel,* 22 April 1995, M1.

Darwin, Charles. *The Works of Charles Darwin.* Edited by Paul H. Barrett and R. B. Freeman. 29 vols. London: Pickering and Chatto, 1986–90.

Daston, Lorraine. "Baconian Facts, Academic Civility, and the Prehistory of Objectivity." *Annales of Scholarship* 8 (1991): 337–64.

———. "The Cold Light of Facts and the Facts of Cold Light: Luminescence and the Transformation of the Scientific Fact 1600–1750." *Early Modern France* 3 (1997): 1–28.

———. "The Moral Economy of Science." In *Constructing Knowledge in the History of Science,* edited by Arnold Thackray. Special issue of *Osiris,* second series, 10 (1995): 2–24.

———. "Neugierde als Empfindung und Epistemologie in der frühmodernen Wissenschaft." In *Macrocosmus im Microcosmus: Die Welt in der Stube: Zur Geschichte des Sammelns 1450 bis 1800*, edited by Andreas Grote, 35–59. Opladen: Leske & Budrich, 1994.

Davies, Kevin. *Cracking the Genome: Inside the Race to Unlock the Human DNA*. New York: The Free Press, 2001.

Davis, Lennard J. *Factual Fictions: The Origins of the English Novel*. New York: Columbia University Press, 1982.

Davis, Natalie. *Women on the Margins: Three Seventeenth-Century Lives*. Cambridge, Mass.: Harvard University Press, 1995.

de Bougainville, Louis-Antoine. *A Voyage Round the World*. Translated by Johann Reinhold Forster. London: J. Nourse, 1772.

de Fontenelle, Bernard. *La république des philosophes, ou Histoire des Ajaoiens*. Geneva: Éditions d'histoire sociale, 1768.

———. "Sur l'électricité." In *Histoire de l'Académie Royale des Sciences: Année 1733*. Paris: Imprimerie Royale, 1735.

———. "Sur un grand nombre de phosphores nouveaux." In *Histoire de l'Académie Royale des Sciences: Année 1730*. Paris: Imprimerie Royale, 1732

de Man, Paul. *Blindness and Insight*. Minneapolis: University of Minnesota Press, 1983.

Dear, Peter. *Discipline and Experience: The Mathematical Way in the Scientific Revolution*. Chicago: University of Chicago Press, 1995.

Deeters, Walter. "Des Prinzen Leopold von Braunschweigs Italienreise." In *Braunschweigisches Jahrbuch*, edited by J. König. Braunschweig, 1971.

Defoe, Daniel. *Giving Alms No Charity*. London: The Booksellers of London & Westminster, 1704.

———. "Preface to Robinson Crusoe." 1719. In *English Theories of the Novel*, edited by Walter F. Greiner. 3 vols. Tübingen: Niemeyer, 1970.

Della Volpe, Galvano. *Critique of Taste*. Translated by Michael Caesar. London: Verso, 1991.

Derrida, Jacques. *Spectres de Marx*. Paris: Galilée, 1993.

Descartes, René. *Oeuvres de Descartes*. Edited by Charles Adam and Paul Tannery. 12 vols. Paris: Libraire J. Vrin, 1957–68.

Destutt de Tracy, Antoine Louis Claude. *Elemens d'idéologie: Vol. II, Grammaire*. 1803. Reprint of the second edition of 1817, Paris: Vrin, 1970.

Dewhurst, Kenneth, and Nigel Reeves. *Frederick Schiller: Medicine, Psychology and Literature with the First English Edition of the Complete Medical and Physiological Writings*. Berkeley: University of California Press, 1978.

Diderot, Denis. *Oeuvres*. Edited by André Billy. Paris: Gallimard, 1992.

Donato, Eugenio. *The Script of Decadence: Essays on the Fictions of Flaubert and the Poetics of Romanticism*. New York: Oxford University Press, 1993.

Donnison, Jean. *Midwives and Medical Men: A History of Inter-Professional Rivals and Women's Rights*. London: Heinemann, 1977.

Du Tertre, Jean Baptiste. *Histoire generale des Antilles habitées par les Français*. 3 vols. Paris: T. Jolly, 1667–71.

Dubos, Abbé. *Réflexions critiques sur la poésie et sur la peinture*. 4th ed. Reviewed, corrected, and augmented by the author. Paris: Mariette, 1740.

Duden, Barbara. *Disembodying Women: Perspectives on Pregnancy and the Unborn.* Translated by Lee Hoinacki. Cambridge, Mass.: Harvard University Press, 1993.

Dufay, C. F. *Mémoires de l'Académie des Sciences: Année 1730.* Paris: Imprimerie Royale, 1732.

———. *Mémoires de l'Académie Royale des Sciences: Année 1734.* Paris: Imprimerie Royale, 1736.

———. "Mémoire sur quelques expériences de catoptrique." Archives de l'Académie des Sciences, Paris: fol. 5r, dossier Dufay.

Duke-Elder, Sir Stewart. *System of Ophthalmology.* 15 vols. London: Kimpton, 1958–76.

Duval, Marguerite. *The King's Garden.* Translated by Annette Tomarken and Claudine Cowen. Charlottesville: University Press of Virginia, 1982.

Dwyer, John. *Virtuous Discourse: Sensibility and Community in Late Eighteenth-Century Scotland.* Edinburgh: John Donald Publishers, 1987.

Dymond, D. P. *Archaeology and History: A Plea for Reconciliation.* London: Thames & Hudson, 1974.

Encyclopédie ou Dictionnaire raisonné des sciences, des arts et des métiers. 1751–65. 17 vols. Reprint, Stuttgart–Bad Cannstatt: Frommann, 1966.

Ernst, Wolfgang. "Framing the Fragment: Archaeology, Art, Museum." In *The Rhetoric of the Frame: Essays on the Boundaries of the Artwork*, edited by Paul Duro, 111–35. Cambridge: Cambridge University Press, 1996.

———. "Reisen ins Innere des Archivs." In *Philosophie und Reisen*, edited by Ulrich Johannes Schneider and Jochen Kornelius Schütze. Leipzig: Leipzig Universitätsverlag, 1996.

Euripides. *Medea and Other Plays.* Translated and with an introduction by Philip Vellacott. New York: Penguin Books, 1963.

Fanton d'Andon, Jean-Pierre. *L'horreur du vide.* Paris: Éditions du Centre national de recherche scientifique, 1978.

Fausto-Sterling, Anne. "Gender, Race, and Nation." In *Deviant Bodies: Critical Perspectives on Difference in Science and Popular Culture*, edited by Jennifer Terry and Jacqueline Urla. Bloomington: Indiana University Press, 1995.

Ferguson, Adam. *Essay on the History of Civil Society.* 1767. 4th ed. London: T. Caddell, 1773.

———. *Principles of Moral and Political Science.* 2 vols. Edinburgh: Strahan & T. Cadell, 1792.

Fielding, Henry. *The Complete Works of Henry Fielding, Esq.* 16 vols. London: William Heinemann, 1903.

———. *A Proposal for Making an Effectual Provision for the Poor.* London: A. Miller, 1753.

Filippini, Nadia. "The Church, the State and Childbirth: The Midwife in Italy During the Eighteenth Century." In *The Art of Midwifery*, edited by Hilary Marland. London: Routledge, 1993.

Flaubert, Gustave. *Bouvard et Pécuchet, avec un choix des scénarios du Sottisier, l'Album de la Marquise, et le Dictionnaire des idées reçues.* Edited by Claudine Gohot-Mersch. Paris: Gallimard, 1993.

———. *Madame Bovary.* Translated by Francis Steegmuller. New York: Modern Library, 1961.

———. *Oeuvres complètes*. 16 vols. Paris: Club de l'honnête homme, 1971–75.

Fontana, Biancamaria. *Rethinking the Politics of Commercial Society: The Edinburgh Review, 1802–1832*. Cambridge: Cambridge University Press, 1985.

Fontius, Martin. "Das Ende einer Denkform. Zur Ablösung des Nachahmungsprinzips im 18. Jahrhundert." In *Literarische Widerspiegelung: Geschichtliche und theoretische Dimensionen eines Problems*, edited by Dieter Schlenstedt. Berlin: Aufbau, 1981.

———. "Produktivkraftentfaltung und Autonomie der Kunst." In *Literatur im Epochenumbruch*, edited by Günther Klotz, Winfried Schröder, and Peter Weber. Berlin: Aufbau, 1977.

Forbes, Duncan. "'Scientific' Whiggism: Adam Smith and John Millar." *Cambridge Journal* 7 (1953–54): 643–70.

Forge, Andrew, and Robert Gordon. *The Last Flowers of Manet*. Translated by Richard Howard. New York: H. N. Abrams, 1986.

Fortier, Bruno. *La politique de l'espace parisien*. Paris: C.O.R.D.A., 1975.

Fortier, Bruno, and Alain Demangeon. *Les vaisseaux et les villes: l'arsenal de Cherbourg*. Brussels: Pierre Mardaga, 1978.

Foucault, Michel. *Discipline and Punish: The Birth of the Prison*. Translated by Alan Sheridan. New York: Vintage Books, 1979.

———. *Dits et écrits*. 4 vols. Paris: Editions Gallimard, 1994.

———. *Histoire de la folie à l'âge classique*. Paris: Gallimard, 1972.

———. "On Attica: An Interview." *Telos* 19 (Spring 1974): 155–56.

———. *The Order of Things: An Archaeology of the Human Sciences*. New York: Random House Vintage Books, 1994.

———. *Power-Knowledge: Selected Interviews & Other Writings*. Edited by Colin Gordon. New York: Pantheon Books, 1980.

Foucault, Michel, and Ludwig Binswanger. *Dream and Existence*. Translated by Jacob Needleman. Seattle: Review of Existential Psychology and Psychiatry, 1986.

Foucault, Michel, et al. *Les machines à guérir (aux origines de l'hôpital moderne)*. Brussels: Pierre Mardaga, 1979.

Fowler, D. P. "Narrate and Describe: The Problem of Ekphrasis." *Journal of Roman Studies* 81 (1991): 25–35.

Frank, Joseph. *The Idea of Spatial Form*. New Brunswick, N.J.: Rutgers University Press, 1990.

Freedman, Ralph. *Life of a Poet: Rainer Maria Rilke*. New York: Farrar, Straus & Giroux, 1996.

Freud, Sigmund. *Standard Edition of the Complete Psychological Works of Sigmund Freud*. Translated under the general editorship of James Strachey, in collaboration with Anna Freud; assisted by Alix Strachey and Alan Tyson. 24 vols. London: Hogarth, 1953–74.

Galison, Peter. *How Experiments End*. Chicago: University of Chicago Press, 1987.

Galison, Peter, and Caroline Jones, eds. *Picturing Science, Producing Art*. New York: Routledge, 1998.

Gaus, Günter. *Porträts 5*. Berlin: Verlag Volk und Welt, 1993.

Gebauer, Gunter, and Christoph Wulf. *Mimesis: Kultur—Kunst—Gesellschaft.* Reinbek: Rowohlt, 1992.

Geimer, Peter. "Redundanz einer Reise: Martin Heidegger als Tourist." *Texte zur Kunst* 18 (1995): 125–31.

Genette, Gérard. "Frontières du récit." In *Figures II.* Paris: Editions du Seuil, 1969.

Gerhard, Eduard. *Grundriss der Archäologie: Für Vorlesungen nach Müllers Handbuch.* Berlin: Reimer, 1853.

Gernsheim, Alison, and Helmut Gernsheim. *L. J. M. Daguerre: The History of the Diorama and the Daguerreotype.* 2nd ed. New York: Dover, 1968.

Gesner, Conrad. *Mithridates: De differentiis linguarum tum veterum tum quae hodie apud diversas nationes in toto orbe terrarum in usu sunt.* 1555. Edited by Manfred Peters. Reprint, Aalen: Scientia Verlag, 1974.

Gilbert Wild's Daylilies. Sarcoxie, Mo., 1991.

Gillispie, Charles C., ed. *Dictionary of Scientific Biography.* 15 vols. New York: Charles Scribner's Sons, 1970–78.

Gilman, Sander. *Difference and Pathology: Stereotypes of Sexuality, Race and Madness.* Ithaca, N.Y.: Cornell University Press, 1985.

Glück, Louise. *The Wild Iris.* New York: Ecco Press, 1992.

Goerke, Heinz. *Linnaeus.* Translated by Denver Lindley. New York: Charles Scribner's Sons, 1973.

Goethe, Johann Wolfgang von. *Gedenkausgabe der Werke, Erganzungsbäbde.* 3 vols. Edited by Ernst Beutler. Zürich: Artemis-Verlag, 1960.

Golinski, J. V. "A Noble Spectacle: Phosphorus and the Public Culture of Science in the Early Royal Society." *Isis* 80 (1989): 11–39.

Gottsched, Johann Christoph. *Versuch einer critischen Dichtkunst.* Darmstadt: Wissenschaftliche Buchgesellschaft, 1962.

Gould, Stephen Jay. "Chimp on the Chain." *Natural History* 12 (1983): 18–25.

Graeber, Wilhelm. *Der englische Roman in Frankreich 1741–1763.* Heidelberg: C. Winter, 1995.

Gräf, Hans Gerhard and Albert Leitzmann, eds. *Der Briefwechsel zwischen Schiller und Goethe.* Leipzig: Insel, 1964.

Greenberg, Clement. "Towards a Newer Laocoon." *Partisan Review* 7, no. 4 (1940): 296–310.

Greuter, W., ed. *International Code of Botanical Nomenclature.* Konigstein: Koeltz Scientific Books, 1988.

Grove, Richard. *Green Imperialism: Colonial Expansion, Tropical Island Edens and the Origins of Environmentalism, 1600–1860.* Cambridge: Cambridge University Press, 1995.

Guillot, Renée-Paule. "La vraie 'Bougainvillée': La première femme qui fit le tour du monde." *Historama* 1 (1984): 36–40.

Gumbrecht, Hans Ulrich. *Production of Presence: What Meaning Cannot Convey.* Stanford, Calif.: Stanford University Press, 2004.

Haakonssen, Knud. "From Moral Philosophy to Political Economy: The Contribution of Dugald Steward." In *Philosophers of the Enlightenment*, edited by V. Hope. Edinburgh: Edinburgh University Press, 1984.

Hagstrum, Jean H. *The Sister Arts: The Tradition of Literary Pictorialism and English Poetry from Dryden to Gray*. Chicago: University of Chicago Press, 1958.

Hankins, Thomas L. "Eighteenth-Century Attempts to Resolve the Vis Viva Controversy." *Isis* 56 (1965).

Hanson, Lawrence. *Renoir: The Man, the Painter, and His World*. New York: Dodd, Mead, 1968.

Hanway, Jonas. *An Earnest Appeal for Mercy to the Children of the Poor*. London: J. Dodsley, 1766.

Hardy, Thomas. *Far from the Madding Crowd*. New York: Harper, 1905.

Harris, James. *Three Treatises*. London: J. Nourse and P. Vaillant, 1744.

Harvey, E. Newton. *A History of Luminescence from the Earliest Times until 1900*. Philadelphia: American Philosophical Society, 1957.

Heaney, Seamus. *Preoccupations: Selected Prose, 1968–78*. London: Faber & Faber, 1980.

Hegel, Georg Wilhelm Friedrich. *Ästhetik*. Edited by Friedrich Bassenge. 2 vols. Berlin: Aufbau, 1976.

———. *Werke*. Edited by Eva Moldenhauer and Karl Markus Michel. Frankfurt-am-Main: Suhrkamp, 1970.

Heidegger, Martin, and Erhard Kästner. *Briefwechsel, 1953–1974*. Edited by H. W. Petzet. Frankfurt: Insel, 1986.

Heilbron, John L. *Electricity in the Seventeenth and Eighteenth Centuries: A Study in Early Modern Physics*. Berkeley: University of California Press, 1979.

Heise, Wolfgang. *Die Wirklichkeit des Möglichen: Dichtung und Ästhetik in Deutschland 1750–1850*. Berlin: Aufbau, 1990.

Heniger, J. *Hendrik Adriaan van Reede tot Drakenstein and Hortus malabaricus*. Rotterdam: A. A. Balekema, 1986.

Henning, E. M. "Archaeology, Deconstruction, and Intellectual History." In *Modern European Intellectual History: Reappraisals and New Perspectives*, edited by Dominick LaCapra and Steven L. Kaplan. 3rd ed. Ithaca, N.Y.: Cornell University Press, 1987.

Herder, Johann Gottfried. *Denkmal Johann Winckelmanns, eine ungekrönte Preisschrift aus dem Jahr 1778*. Kassel: T. Kay, 1882.

———. *Journal meiner Reise im Jahr 1769*. Edited by Katharina Mommsen. Stuttgart: Reclam, 1976.

———. *Sämmtliche Werke*. Edited by Bernhard Suphan. 33 vols. Berlin: Weidmann, 1877–1913.

Hermannus, Paulus. *Horti academici Lugduno-Batavi catalogus, exhibens plantarum omnium nomina, quibus ab anno 1681–1686 hortus fuit instructus, ut et plurimarum . . . descriptiones et icones*. Leiden: Lugduni Batavorum, 1687.

Hervás y Panduro, Lorenzo. *Catalogo delle lingue conosciute*. 1785. Edited by Antonio Tovar and Jesus Bustamante. Reprint, Madrid: Sociedad General Española de Libreria, 1986.

———. *Saggio pratico delle lingue: con prolegomeni, e una raccolta di orazioni dominicali in più de trecento lingue et dialetti*. Cesena: Gregorio Biasini, 1787.

———. *Vocabolario poligloto con prolegomeni sopra più de cl. lingue, dove sono delle scop-*

erte nuove, et utili all'antica storia dell'uman genere, et alla cognizione del meccanismo delle parole. Cesena: Gregorio Biasini, 1787.

Hildebrandt, Dieter. *Lessing: Biographie einer Emanzipation.* München: Hanser Verlag, 1979.

Hofstadter, Albert, and Richard Kuhns, eds. *Philosophies of Art and Beauty: Selected Readings in Aesthetics from Plato to Heidegger.* Chicago: University of Chicago Press, 1976.

Honegger, Claudia. *Die Ordnung der Geschlechter: Die Wissenschaften vom Menschen und das Weib.* Frankfurt: Campus Verlag, 1992.

Hooke, Robert. "A General Scheme, or Idea of the Present State of Natural Philosophy, and How its Defects May Be Remedied by a Methodical Proceeding in the Making Experiments and Collecting Observations." 1705. In *The Posthumous Works of Robert Hooke,* edited by Richard Waller. Introduction by Richard S. Westfall. Reprint, New York: Johnson Reprint Corporation, 1969.

Hope, V., ed. *Philosophers of the Scottish Enlightenment.* Edinburgh: Edinburgh University Press, 1984.

Hopfl, H. M. "From Savage to Scotsman: Conjectural History in the Scottish Enlightenment." *Journal of British Studies* 17 (Spring 1978).

Horkheimer, Max. "Reason Against Itself: Some Remarks on Enlightenment." In *What Is Enlightenment: Eighteenth-Century Answers and Twentieth-Century Questions,* edited by James Schmidt. Berkeley: University of California Press, 1996.

Howard, Seymour. *Antiquity Restored: Essays on the Afterlife of the Antique.* Vienna: IRSA, 1990.

"Human Genome May Be Longer Than Expected." *New York Times,* 1 August 1999.

Humboldt, Wilhelm von. *Gesammelte Schriften.* Edited by Albert Leitzmann et al. 17 vols. Berlin: Behr, 1903–36.

Hume, David. *The Natural History of Religion.* Edited by J. C. A. Gaskin. New York: Oxford University Press, 1993.

———. *The Philosophical Works.* Edited by Thomas Hill Green and Thomas Hodge Grose. 4 vols. London: Spottiswoode, 1883.

Huysmans, Joris-Karl. *Against Nature.* Translated by Robert Baldick. New York: Penguin Books, 1959.

Iltis [Merchant], Carolyn. "D'Alembert and the Vis Viva Controversy." *Studies in History and Philosophy of Science* 1 (1970).

———. "The Decline of Cartesianism in Mechanics: The Leibnizian-Cartesian Debates." *Isis* 64 (1973).

———. "The Leibnizian-Newtonian Debates: Natural Philosophy and Social Psychology." *British Journal for the History of Science* 6 (1973).

———. "Madam du Chatelet's Metaphysics and Mechanics." *Studies in History and Philosophy of Science* 8 (1977).

Imbert, Patrick. "La structure de la description réaliste dans la littérature européenne." *Semiotica* 1–2 (1983): 95–122.

Irailh, Simon Augustin. *Querelles littéraires.* 4 vols. Paris: Durand, 1761.

Irrlitz, Gerd. "Versuch über Descartes." In *René Descartes, Ausgewählte Schriften.* Leipzig: Reclam, 1980.

Jacob, Margaret C. *The Radical Enlightenment: Pantheists, Freemasons, and Republicans*. London: Allen & Unwin, 1981.

Jardine, Nicholas, James Secord, and Emma Spary, eds. *Cultures of Natural History*. Cambridge: Cambridge University Press, 1996.

Jaspers, Karl. *L'esprit européen*. Neuchâtel and Geneva: Baconnerie, 1947.

Jordanova, Ludmilla. *Sexual Visions: Images of Gender in Science and Medicine between the Eighteenth and Twentieth Centuries*. Madison: University of Wisconsin Press, 1989.

Judd, Donald. *Complete Writings 1959–1975*. New York: New York University Press, 1975.

Kames, Lord. *Sketches of the History of Man*. 1774. 2nd ed. 4 vols. Edinburgh: W. Strahan and T. Cadell, 1778.

Kamper, Dietmar. "Il faut être absolument moderne." In *Jean Baudrillard, Simulation und Verführung*, edited by Ralf Bohn and Dieter Fuder. Munich: Fink, 1994.

Kant, Immanuel. *Gesammelte Schriften*. 29 vols. Berlin: Reimer, 1902–.

———. *Kants Werke: Akademie-Textausgabe*. 9 vols. Berlin: de Gruyter, 1968.

———. *Observations on the Feeling of the Beautiful and Sublime*. Translated by John T. Goldthwait. Berkeley: University of California Press, 1960.

Karsten, W. J. G. *Physische-chemische Abhandlung, durch neuere Schriften von hermetischen Arbeiten und andere neue Untersuchungen veranlasset*. 2 vols. Halle: Renger, 1786–87.

Kelly, George Armstrong. *Mortal Politics in Eighteenth-Century France*. Waterloo, Ont.: University of Waterloo Press, 1986.

Ketelsen, Thomas. *Künstlerviten, Inventare, Kataloge: Drei Studien zur Geschichte der kunsthistorischen Praxis*. Ammersbek: Verlag an der Lottbek, 1988.

Kittler, Friedrich. *Discourse Networks 1800/1900*. Translated by Michael Metteer and Chris Cullens. Stanford, Calif.: Stanford University Press, 1990.

Klein, Wolf Peter. *Am Anfang war das Wort: Theorie- und wissenschaftsgeschichtliche Elemente frühneuzeitlichen Sprachbewußtseins*. Berlin: Akademie Verlag, 1992.

Klein, Wolfgang. *Der nüchterne Blick: Programmatischer Realismus in Frankreich nach 1848*. Berlin: Aufbau, 1989.

———. "Realismus/realistisch." In *Ästhetische Grundbegriffe: Ein historisches Wörterbuch*, edited by Karlheinz Barck et al., 7 vols. to date. Stuttgart: Metzler, 2000–.

Klein, Wolfgang, and Waltraud Naumann-Beyer, ed. *Nach der Aufklärung? Beiträge zum Diskurs der Kulturwissenschaften*. Berlin: Akademie Verlag, 1995.

Koch, Hanna. *Johann Joachim Winckelmann, Sprache und Kunstwerk*. Berlin: Akademie Verlag, 1957.

Koerner, Lisbet. "Carl Linnaeus in His Time and Place." In *Cultures of Natural History*, edited by Nicholas Jardine, James Secord, and Emma Spary, 145–62. Cambridge: Cambridge University Press, 1996.

———. "Purposes of Linnaean Travel: A Preliminary Research Report." In *Visions of Empire: Voyages, Botany, and Representations of Nature*, edited by David Miller and Peter Reill. Cambridge: Cambridge University Press, 1996.

Kofman, Sarah. *The Childhood of Art: An Interpretation of Freud's Aesthetics*. Translated by Winifred Woodhull. New York: Columbia University Press, 1988.

Kolb, Peter. *The Present State of the Cape of Good Hope*. Translated by Guido Medley. London: W. Innys, 1731.

König, Ekkehard. "English." In *The Germanic Languages*, edited by Ekkehard König and Johan van der Auwera. London: Routledge, 1994.

Kosslyn, Stephen Michael. "Measuring the Visual Angle of the Mind's Eye." *Cognitive Psychology* 10 (1978): 381.

Kraemer, Klaus. "Schwerelosigkeit der Zeichen? Die Paradoxie des selbstreferentiellen Zeichens bei Baudrillard." In *Jean Baudrillard, Simulation und Verführung*, edited by Ralf Bohn and Dieter Fuder. Munich: Fink, 1994.

Krauss, Werner. *Das wissenschaftliche Werk*. Edited by Rolf Geißler. Vol. 6. Berlin: Aufbau, 1987.

Krieger, Murray. *The Play and Place of Criticism*. Baltimore: Johns Hopkins University Press, 1967.

Krohn, Wolfgang, and Günther Küppers. "Die natürlichen Ursachen der Zwecke: Kants Ansätze der Selbstorganisation." *Selbstorganisation: Jahrbuch für Komplexität in den Natur-, Sozial- und Geisteswissenschaften* 3 (1992): 7–15.

La Mettrie, Julien Offray de. *L'homme machine: A Study in the Origins of an Idea*. Edited by Aram Vartanian. Princeton, N.J.: Princeton University Press, 1960.

Lämmert, Eberhard, ed. *Romantheorie 1620–1880: Dokumentation ihrer Geschichte in Deutschland*. Frankfurt and Main: Anthenäum Verlag, 1988.

Lander, Eric S., et al. "Initial Sequencing and Analysis of the Human Genome." *Nature* 409 (15 February 2001): 860–921.

Lanjuinais, Jean Denis. "Discours préliminaire." In *Histoire naturelle de la parole ou grammaire universelle à l'usage des jeunes gens* by Antoine Court de Gébelin, edited by Jean Denis Lanjuinais. Paris: Plancher/Eymery/Delaunay, 1816.

Laqueur, Thomas. *Making Sex: Body and Gender from the Greeks to Freud*. Cambridge, Mass.: Harvard University Press, 1990.

Laudan, L. L. "Thomas Reid and the Newtonian Turn of British Methodological Thought." In *The Methodological Heritage of Newton*, edited by Robert E. Butts and John W. Davis. Oxford: Basil Blackwell, 1970.

Lavagno, Christian. *Rekonstruktion der Moderne: Eine Studie zu Habermas und Foucault*. Münster: Lit Verlag, 2003.

Lawrence, D. H. "Purple Anemones." In *Birds, Beasts and Flowers*. Santa Rosa, Calif.: Black Sparrow Press, 1992.

Le Rond d'Alembert, Jean. *Discours préliminaire de l'Encyclopédie*. Paris: Editions Gonthier, 1965.

Le Sage, Alain René. *Oeuvres*. Paris: Garnier Frères, 1876.

Ledoux, Claude-Nicolas. *L'architecture considérée sous le rapport de l'art, des moeurs et de la législation*. Paris: chez l'auteur, 1804.

Leibniz, Gottfried Wilhelm. *Allgemeiner politischer und historischer Briefwechsel*. Edited by Deutsche Akademie der Wissenschaften zu Berlin. Vol. 1.3 of *Sämtliche Schriften und Briefe*. Reprint, Berlin: Akademie Verlag, 1970.

———. *Nouveaux essais sur l'entendement humain*. 1765. Edited by Jacques Brunschwig. Reprint, Paris: Garnier-Flammarion, 1966.

Lenz, Jakob Michael Reinhold. *Werke und Briefe in drei Bänden*. Edited by Sigrid Damm. 3 vols. München: Hanser, 1987.

Lessing, Gotthold Ephraim. *Briefe, antiquarische Inhalts.* Edited by Wilfried Barner. Vol. 5.2 of *Werke und Briefe in zwölf Bänden.* Frankfurt-am-Main: Deutscher Klassiker Verlag, 1990.

———. *Laocoön: An Essay on the Limits of Painting and Poetry.* Translated by E. A. McCormick. Baltimore: Johns Hopkins University Press, 1984.

———. *Lessings Werke.* Edited by Robert Boxberger. 18 vols. Berlin: W. Spemann, 1883–90. Reprint, Tokyo: Sansyusa, 1974.

———. *Werke 1774–1778.* Edited by Arno Schilson. Vol. 8 of *Werke und Briefe in zwölf Bänden.* Frankfurt-am-Main: Deutscher Klassiker Verlag, 1989.

Licoppe, Christian. *La formation de la pratique scientifique: Le discours de l'expérience en France et en Angleterre 1630–1820.* Paris: Editions de la Découverte, 1996.

Ligon, Richard. *A True and Exact History of the Island of Barbados.* London: Printed for Humphrey Moseley . . . , 1657.

Linnaeus, Carl von. "Anthropomorpha." In *Amoenitates academicae seu dissertationes variae physicae, medicae, botanicae.* 10 vols. Holmiæ & Lipsiæ: Apud Godefredum Kiesewetter, 1749–90.

———. *The Critica Botanica of Linnaeus.* 1737. Translated by Sir Arthur Hort. Revised by M. L. Green. London: Royal Society, 1938.

———. *Species plantarum.* 2 vols. Holmiæ: Impensis Laurentii Salvi, 1753.

Lloyd-Jones, Hugh, Valerie Pearl, and Blair Worden, eds. *History and Imagination: Essays in Honour of H. R. Trevor-Roper.* London: Duckworth, 1981.

Luhmann, Niklas. *Die Kunst der Gesellschaft.* Frankfurt-am-Main: Suhrkamp, 1995.

———. *Die Wissenschaft der Gesellschaft.* Frankfurt-am-Main: Suhrkamp, 1992.

———. *Soziale Systeme.* Frankfurt-am-Main: Suhrkamp, 1984.

Lukács, Georg. *Balzac und der französische Realismus.* Berlin: Aufbau, 1952.

———. *Die Eigenart des Ästhetischen.* 1963. 2 vols. Berlin: Aufbau, 1981.

———. "Es geht um den Realismus." 1938. In *Zur Tradition der deutschen sozialistischen Literatur: Eine Auswahl von Dokumenten*, edited by Friedrich Albrecht. Berlin: Aufbau, 1979.

———. *Werke.* 17 vols. Neuwied: Luchterhand, 1962–.

———. *Zur Tradition der deutschen sozialistischen Literatur: Eine Auswahl von Dokumenten.* Edited by Friedrich Albrecht. 4 vols. Berlin: Aufbau, 1979.

Lüthe, Rudolf. *David Hume, Historiker und Philosoph.* Freiberg: K. Alber, 1991.

Lyotard, Jean-François. *La condition postmoderne.* Paris: Editions de Minuit, 1979.

———. *L'Inhumain: Causeries sur le temps.* Paris: Galilée, 1988.

Marland, Hilary, ed. *The Art of Midwifery: Early Modern Midwives in Europe.* London: Routledge, 1993.

Martin, Fontius. "Produktivkraftentfaltung und Autonomie der Kunst." In *Literatur im Epochenumbruch*, edited by Winfried Schröder, Günther Klotz, and Peter Weber. Berlin: Aufbau, 1977.

Marvell, Andrew. *Andrew Marvell: The Complete Poems.* Edited by Elizabeth Story Donno. London: Penguin, 1985.

Matussek, Peter. "Durch die Maschen: Die Vernetzung des kulturellen Gedächtnisses und ihre Erinnerungslücken." Paper presented at the conference *Interface III.* Hamburg, 1 November 1995.

Maurer, Karl. "Entstaltung. Ein beinahe untergegangener Goethescher Begriff." In *Leib-Zeichen: Körperbilder, Rhetorik und Anthropologie im 18. Jahrhundert*, edited by R. Behrens and R. Galle. Würzburg: Königshausen & Neumann, 1993.

Maus, Ingeborg. *Zur Aufklärung der Demokratietheorie: Rechts- und demokratietheorie überlegungen im Anschluß an Kant*. Frankfurt-am-Main: Suhrkamp, 1992.

McCulloch, J. R. *The Principles of Political Economy: With a Sketch of the Rise and Progress of the Science*. Edinburgh: William and Charles Tait, 1825.

McKeon, Michael. *The Origins of the English Novel 1600–1740*. Baltimore: Johns Hopkins University Press, 1987.

McLaren, Angus. *A History of Contraception from Antiquity to the Present Day*. Oxford: Basil Blackwell, 1990.

———. *Reproductive Rituals: The Perception of Fertility in England from the Sixteenth to the Nineteenth Century*. London: Methuen, 1984.

Meek, Ronald L. "A Scottish Contribution to Scottish Sociology." In *Economics and Ideology and Other Essays*. London: Chapman & Hall, 1967.

Meister, Marcus. "The Retina." Lecture presented at the Science Center, Harvard University, Cambridge, Mass., October 1994.

Mémoires pour servir à l'histoire naturelle des animaux et des plantes. In *Mémoires de l'Académie Royale des Sciences, contenant les ouvrages adoptez par cette Académie avant son renouvellement en 1699*. 6 vols. Amsterdam: Pierre Mortier, 1736.

Merck, Johann Heinrich. "Ueber den Mangel des epischen Geistes in unserm lieben Vaterland." 1778. In *Romantheorie 1620–1880: Dokumentation ihrer Geschichte in Deutschland*, edited by Eberhard Lämmert. Frankfurt-am-Main: Anthenäum Verlag, 1988.

Merian, Maria Sibylla. *Metamorphosis insectorum surinamensium*. 1705. Edited by Helmut Deckert. Leipzig: Insel Verlag, 1975.

Meyer, Theodor A. *Das Stilgesetz der Poesie*. 1901. Reprint, Frankfurt-am-Main: Suhrkamp, 1990.

Millar, John. *Observations Concerning the Distinction of Ranks in Society*. Dublin: T. Ewing, 1771.

Miller, David, and Peter Reill, eds. *Visions of Empire: Voyages, Botany, and Representations of Nature*. Cambridge: Cambridge University Press, 1996.

Montagna, W. "The Skin." *Scientific American* 11 (1959): 58–59.

Morton, Julia. *Atlas of Medicinal Plants of Middle America*. Springfield, Ill.: Charles Thomas, 1981.

Mueller-Vollmer, Kurt. *Wilhelm von Humboldts Sprachwissenschaft: Ein kommentiertes Verzeichnis des sprachwissenschaftlichen Nachlasses*. Paderborn: Schöningh, 1993.

Muncker, Franz. "Eine Hauptquelle für Lessings Tagebuch seiner italienischen Reise." In *Germanistische Abhandlungen (Festschrift Hermann Paul)*, 181–94. Strassburg: K. J. Trübner, 1902.

Munsell, A. H. *Atlas of the Munsell Color System*. Malden, Mass.: Wadsworth, Howland & Co., 1915.

———. *A Color Notation: An Illustrated System Defining All Colors and Their Relations by Measured Scales of Hue, Value, and Chroma*. Baltimore: Munsell Color Company, 1947.

Naumann-Beyer, Waltraud. "Kommunikative Beziehungen in Deutschland Ende des 18. Jahrhunderts." Postdoctoral thesis, 1986.

Needham, Joseph, Lu Gwei-Djen, and Huang Hsing-Tsung. *Science and Civilization in China*. 7 vols. to date. Cambridge: Cambridge University Press, 1954.

Newton, Isaac. *Correspondence*. Edited by H. W. Turnbull. 7 vols. Cambridge: Published for the Royal Society at the University Press, 1959–77.

Nussbaum, Felicity. *Torrid Zones: Maternity, Sexuality, and Empire in Eighteenth-Century English Narratives*. Baltimore: Johns Hopkins University Press, 1995.

Oken, Lorenz. *Abriss der Naturphilosophie*. Göttingen: Vandenhoek und Ruprecht, 1805.

———. *Lehrbuch der Naturphilosophie*. 2nd ed. Jena: F. Fromann, 1831.

Onions, C. T. *Oxford Dictionary of English Etymology*. Edited by C. T. Onions with G. W. S. Friedrichson and R. W. Burchfield. Oxford: Oxford University Press, 1966.

Ovid. *Metamorphoses*. Translated by Rolfe Humphries. Bloomington: Indiana University Press, 1955.

Pallas, Peter Simon. *Linguarum totius orbis vocabularia comparativa*. 1786–89. Edited by Harald Haarmann. 2 vols. Reprint, Hamburg: Buske 1977–78.

Papineau, David. "The Vis Viva Controversy: Do Meanings Matter?" *Studies in History and Philosophy of Science* 8 (1977).

Pascal, Blaise. *Les Pensées de Pascal*. Edited by Francis Kaplan. Paris: Éditions du Cerf, 1982.

———. *Oeuvres complètes*. Edited by Jean Mesnard. 4 vols. Paris: Desclée de Brouwer, 1964–.

Petit Larousse. Paris: Larousse, 1973.

Petty, William, Sir. *The Economic Writings of Sir William Petty*. Edited by Charles Henry Hull. Fairfield, N.J.: Augustus M. Kelley, 1963–64.

Phillipson, Nicholas. "Hume as Moralist: A Social Historian's Perspective." In *Philosophers of the Enlightenment*, edited by S. C. Brown. Sussex: Harvester Press, 1979.

———. "The Pursuit of Virtue in Scottish University Education: Dugald Stewart and Scottish Moral Philosophy in the Enlightenment." In *Universities, Society, and the Future*, edited by Nicholas Phillipson. Edinburgh: Edinburgh University Press, 1983.

———. "The Scottish Enlightenment." In *The Enlightenment in National Context*, edited by Roy Porter and Mikulas Teich. Cambridge: Cambridge University Press, 1981.

Pinker, Steven. *The Language Instinct*. New York: Morrow, 1994.

Pinkerton, John. *A General Collection of the Best and Most Interesting Voyages and Travels in all Parts of the World*. 17 vols. London: Printed for Longman, Hurst, Rees and Orme . . . , and Cadell and Davies . . . , 1808–14.

Plato. *Phaedrus*. Translated and with an introduction by Walter Hamilton. Harmondsworth, England: Penguin Books, 1973.

———. *The Symposium*. Translated by Walter Hamilton. London: Penguin Books, 1951.

———. *Timaeus and Critias*. Translated and with an introduction by Desmond Lee. New York: Penguin Books, 1977.

Plischke, Hans. *Johann Friedreich Blumenbachs Einfluss auf die Entdeckungsreisenden seiner Zeit*. Göttingen: Vandenhoeck & Ruprecht, 1937.

Poovey, Mary. *A History of Modern Fact: Problems of Knowledge in the Sciences of Wealth and Society*. Chicago: University of Chicago Press, 1998.

———. *Making a Social Body: British Cultural Formation, 1832–1860*. Chicago: University of Chicago Press, 1995.

———. "Science and the Pursuit of Virtue in the Aberdeen Enlightenment." In *Studies in the Philosophy of the Scottish Enlightenment*, edited by M. A. Stewart. Oxford: Clarendon Press, 1990.

Potier, Pierre. *De lapide quondam incognito*. Bologna, 1622.

Potts, Alex. *Flesh and the Ideal: Winckelmann and the Origins of Art History*. New Haven, Conn.: Yale University Press, 1994.

Prichard, James. *Researches into the Physical History of Mankind*. 4th ed. 5 vols. London: Sherwood, Gilbert & Piper [etc.], 1841–47.

Proctor, Robert. *Cancer Wars: How Politics Shapes What We Know and Don't Know About Cancer*. New York: Basic Books, 1995.

Proust, Marcel. *On Reading Ruskin: Prefaces to La Bible d'Amiens and Sésame et les lys with Selections from the Notes to the Translated Texts*. Edited and translated by Jean Autret, William Burford, and Phillip J. Wolfe. Introduction by Richard Macksey. New Haven, Conn.: Yale University Press, 1897.

Raabe, Paul. "Einige philologische Anmerkungen zu Lessings italiensicher Reise 1775." In *Nation und Gelehrtenrepublik: Lessing im europäischen Zusammenhang*, edited by Wilfried Barner and Albert M. Reh. Detroit, Mich.: Wayne State University Press, 1983.

Raguenet, François. *Les Monumens de Rome ou Description des plus beaux ouvrages de peinture, de sculpture et d'architecture que se voient à Rome*. Amsterdam: E. Roger, 1701.

Rattansi, P. M. "Voltaire and the Enlightenment Image of Newton." In *History and Imagination: Essays in Honour of H. R. Trevor-Roper*, edited by Hugh Lloyd-Jones, Valerie Pearl, and Balir Worden. London: Duckworth, 1981.

Raulin, Joseph. *De la conservation des enfants*. 3 vols. Paris: Merlin, 1768–69.

"Reading the Book of Life; White House Remarks on Decoding of Genome." *New York Times*, 27 June 2000.

Rees, Abraham. *The Cyclopaedia; or, Universal Dictionary of Arts, Sciences, and Literature*. 39 vols. London: Longman, Hurst, Rees, Orme & Brown, 1819.

Rehm, Walter. "Winckelmann und Lessing." In *Götterstille und Göttertrauer*. Bern: A. Francke, 1951.

Reill, Peter Hanns. "History and the Life Sciences in the Early Nineteenth Century: Wilhelm von Humboldt and Leopold von Ranke." In *Leopold von Ranke and the Shaping of the Historical Discipline*, edited by Georg Iggers and James Powell. Syracuse, N.Y.: Syracuse University Press, 1990.

Renoir, Jean. *Renoir, My Father*. Translated by Randolph Weaver and Dorothy Weaver. Boston: Little, Brown, 1962.

Rice, Shelly. *Parisian Views*. Cambridge, Mass.: MIT Press, 1997.

Richter, Simon. *Laocoon's Body and the Aesthetics of Pain: Winckelmann, Lessing, Herder, Moritz, Goethe*. Detroit, Mich.: Wayne State University Press, 1992.

Riddle, John. *Contraception and Abortion from the Ancient World to the Renaissance.* Cambridge, Mass.: Harvard University Press, 1992.

———. *Eve's Herbs: A History of Contraception and Abortion in the West.* Cambridge, Mass.: Harvard University Press, 1997.

Rilke, Rainer Maria. *New Poems.* 1907. Translated by Edward Snow. Revised paperback translation. Reprint, San Francisco: North Point Press, 1984.

Ritter-Santini, Lea. *Lessing und die Wespen: die italienische Reise eines Aufklärers.* Paris: Éditions de la Maison des Sciences de l'Homme, 1993.

Ritter-Santini, Lea, ed. *Eine Reise der Aufklärung: Lessing in Italien 1775.* 2 vols. Berlin: Akademie-Verlag, 1993.

Roche, Daniel. "Natural History in the Academies." In *Cultures of Natural History,* edited by Nicholas Jardine, James Secord, and Emma Spary, 127–44. Cambridge: Cambridge University Press, 1996.

Rohault, Jacques de. *Traité de physique.* Paris, 1671.

Rousseau, Jean-Jacques. *Botany, a Study of Pure Curiosity: Botanical Letters and Notes Towards a Dictionary of Botanical Terms.* Translated by Kate Ottevanger. London: Michael Joseph, 1979.

———. *Lettres sur la botanique par Jean-Jacques Rousseau.* Introduction by Bernard Gagnebin. Paris: Club des libraires de France, 1962.

Rudowski, Victor Anthony. "Lessing Contra Winckelmann." In *Lessing and the Enlightenment,* edited by Alexej Ugrinsky. New York: Greenwood Press, 1986.

Ruskin, John. *The Queen of the Air: Being a Study of the Greek Myths of Cloud and Storm.* 1886. Reprint, London: G. Allen, 1903.

Russell, Donald A., and Michael Winterbottom. *Ancient Literary Criticism.* Oxford: Clarendon Press, 1972.

Sade, Donatien Alphonse François de. *Oeuvres complètes.* 15 vols. to date. Paris: Pauvert, 1986–.

Sanders, Hans. *Das Subjekt der Moderne: Mentalitätswandel und literarische Evolution zwischen Klassik und Aufklärung.* Tübingen: Max Niemeyer Verlag, 1987.

Sartre, Jean-Paul. *The Psychology of Imagination.* New York: Carol Publishing Group, 1991.

Sauval, Henri. *Histoire et recherches des antiquités de la ville de Paris.* 3 vols. Paris: C. Moette, 1724.

Scarry, Elaine. *The Body in Pain.* New York: Oxford University Press, 1985.

———. *Dreaming by the Book.* Boston: Farrar, Straus and Giroux, 1999.

Schaffer, Simon. "Glass Works: Newton's Prisms and the Uses of Experiment." In *The Uses of Experiment: Studies in the Natural Sciences,* edited by D. Gooding, T. Pinch, and Simon Schaffer. Cambridge: Cambridge University Press, 1989.

———. "Natural Philosophy." In *The Ferment of Knowledge: Studies in the Historiography of Eighteenth-Century Science,* edited by G. S. Rousseau and Roy Porter. Cambridge: Cambridge University Press, 1980.

Schelling, Friedrich Wilhelm Josef. *Frühschriften.* Edited by Helmut Seidel and Lothar Kleine. 2 vols. Berlin: Akademie-Verlag, 1971.

Schiebinger, Londa. "Lost Knowledge, Bodies of Ignorance, and the Poverty of Taxonomy as Illustrated by the Curious Fate of *Flos Pavonis,* an Abortifacient." In

Picturing Science, Producing Art, edited by Peter Galison and Caroline Jones, 124–44. New York: Routledge, 1998.

———. *The Mind Has No Sex? Women in the Origins of Modern Science*. Cambridge, Mass.: Harvard University Press, 1989.

———. *Nature's Body: Gender in the Making of Modern Science*. Boston: Beacon Press, 1993.

Schiffman, Harvey Richard. *Sensation and Perception: An Integrated Approach*. New York: Wiley, 1976.

Schiller, Friedrich. *On the Aesthetic Education of Man in a Series of Letters*. Translated and introduction by Reginald Snell. New York: Frederick Ungar, 1965.

———. "Über den Gebrauch des Chors in der Tragödie." 1803. In *Über Kunst und Wirklichkeit: Schriften und Briefe zur Ästhetik*, edited by Claus Träger. Leipzig: Reclam, 1975.

Schiller, Friedrich, and Johann Wolfgang Goethe. *Der Briefwechsel Zwischen Schiller und Goethe*. Edited by Hans Gerhard Gräf and Albert Leitzmann. 3 vols. Leipzig: Insel, 1912.

Schiller, Friedrich, and Wilhelm von Humboldt. *Der Briefwechsel Zwischen Friedrich Schiller und Wilhelm von Humboldt*. Edited by Siegfried Seidel. Berlin: Aufbau, 1962.

Schlözer, August Ludvig von. *Vorstellung seiner Universal-Historie*. 2 vols. Göttingen: José C. Dieterich, 1772.

Schmidt, Erich. *Lessing: Geschichte seines Lebens und seiner Schriften*. 2 vols. Berlin: Weidmann, 1884–92.

Schuster, John A., and Richard R. Yeo, eds. *The Politics and Rhetoric of Scientific Method: Historical Studies*. Dordrecht: D. Reidel, 1986.

Seidel, Siegfried, ed. *Der Briefwechsel zwischen Friedrich Schiller und Wilhelm von Humboldt*. Berlin: Aufbau, 1962.

Shaftesbury, Anthony Ashley Cooper, Earl of. *Characteristics of Men, Manners, Opinions, Times*. Edited by John H. Robertson. Indianapolis, Ind.: Bobbs-Merrill, 1964.

Shanks, Michael, and Christopher Tilley. *Re-constructing Archaeology: Theory and Practice*. Cambridge: Cambridge University Press, 1987.

Sher, Richard B. "Professors of Virtue: The Social History of the Edinburgh Moral Philosophy Chair in the Eighteenth Century." In *Studies in the Philosophy of the Scottish Enlightenment*, edited by M. A. Stewart. Oxford: Clarendon Press, 1990.

Shklar, Judith. "Virtue in a Bad Climate: Good Men and Good Citizens in Montesquieu's *L'esprit des lois*." In *Enlightenment Studies in Honour of Lester G. Crocker*, edited by Alfred Jepson Bingham and Virgil W. Topazio. Oxford: Voltaire Foundation, at the Taylor Institution, 1979.

Shteir, Ann. *Cultivating Women, Cultivating Science: Flora's Daughters and Botany in England 1760–1860*. Baltimore: Johns Hopkins University Press, 1996.

Simpson, David. *Romanticism, Nationalism, and the Revolt Against Theory*. Chicago: University of Chicago Press, 1993.

Sinclair, Sir John. *Statistical Survey of Scotland*. Edinburgh: W. Creech, 1791–99.

Skaletsky, Helen, et al. "The Male-Specific Region of the Human Y Chromosome

Is a Mosaic of Discrete Sequence Classes." *Nature* 423 (19 June 2003): 825–37.

Skinner, Andrew. "Economics and History: The Scottish Enlightenment." *Scottish Journal of Political Economy* 12 (1965): 1–22.

Sloane, Hans. *Catalogus plantarum quae in insula Jamaica* . . . London: Impensis D. Brown, 1696.

———. *A Voyage to the Islands Madera, Barbadoes, Nieves, St Christophers, and Jamaica; with the Natural History* . . . 2 vols. London: Printed by B.M. for the author, 1707–25.

Smith, Adam. *An Inquiry into the Nature and Causes of the Wealth of Nations.* New edition. Edinburgh: Adam and Charles Black, 1868.

———. "The Principles Which Lead and Direct Philosophical Enquiries; Illustrated by the History of Astronomy." In *Essays on Philosophical Subjects,* edited by W. P. D. Wightman and J. C. Bryce. Oxford: Clarendon Press, 1980.

Söntgen, Beate. "Schwindel der Sinne: Der Guckkasten und die Optik des achtzehnten Jahrhunderts." *Frankfurter Allgemeine Zeitung,* 30 August 1995.

Sophocles. *Antigone, Oedipus the King, Electra, Philoctetes.* Edited and introduction by Robert Corrigan. Translated by Michael Townsend, Kenneth Cavander, and Francis Ferguson. New York: Dell, 1962.

Southey, Robert. "On the State of the Poor, the Principle of Mr. Malthus's Essay on Population, and the Manufacturing System." 1812. In *Essays, Moral and Political.* 2 vols. London: John Murray, 1832.

Specht, Rainer. "Über empiristische Ansätze Lockes." *Allgemeine Zeitschrift für Philosophie* 3 (1977).

Stafford, Barbara. *Artful Science: Enlightenment, Entertainment and the Eclipse of Visual Education.* Cambridge, Mass.: MIT Press, 1994.

———. *Body Criticism: Imagining the Unseen in Enlightenment Art and Medicine.* Cambridge, Mass.: MIT Press, 1994.

Stafleu, Frans A. *Linnaeus and the Linnaeans: The Spreading of Their Ideas in Systematic Botany, 1735–1789.* Utrecht: A. Oosthoek's Uitgeversmaatschappij, 1971.

Stagl, Justin. "Die Methodisierung des Reisens im 16. Jahrhundert." In *Der Reisebericht: Die Entwicklung einer Gattung in der deutschen Literatur,* edited by Peter J. Brenner. Frankfurt-am-Main: Suhrkamp, 1989.

Stearn, William. "Botanical Exploration to the Time of Linnaeus." *Proceedings of the Linnean Society of London* 169 (1958): 173–96.

Stedman, John. *Narrative of a Five Years Expedition against the Revolted Negroes of Surinam.* 1790. Reprint, Baltimore: Johns Hopkins University Press, 1988.

Steinle, Friedrich. "The Amalgamation of a Concept-Laws of Nature in the New Sciences." In *Laws of Nature: Essays on the Philosophical, Scientific and Historical Dimensions,* edited by Friedel Weinert. Berlin: Walter de Gruyter, 1995.

Sterne, Laurence. *The Complete Works of Laurence Sterne.* Edited by David Herbert. Edinburgh: W. P. Nimmo, 1872.

Stewart, Dugald. *Collected Works.* 11 vols. Edited by Sir William Hamilton. Edinburgh: Thomas Constable & Co., 1854.

———. *Elements of the Philosophy of the Human Mind.* 1792. Boston: James Munroe & Co., 1847.

————. *Studies in the Philosophy of the Scottish Enlightenment.* Oxford: Clarendon Press, 1990.

Sulston, John, and James Watson. "Genome Sequence of the Nematode C. elegans: A Platform for Investigating Biology." *Science* 282 (1998): 2012–18.

Swift, Jonathan. *Miscellanies in Prose and Verse.* 3 vols. London: Sam. Fairbrother, 1732.

Swiggers, Pierre. "La culture linguistique en Italie et en France au XVIe siècle." In *Italiano: lingua di cultura europa*, edited by Harro Stammerjohann. Tübingen: Narr, 1997.

"Technology: First Complete Plant Genetic Sequence Is Determined." *New York Times*, 14 December 2000.

Thom, Martina. "Zum Freiheitsproblem bei Kant." In *Revolution der Denkart oder Denkart der Revolution*, edited by Manfred Buhr and Teodor Oiserman. Berlin: Akademie-Verlag, 1976.

Tonelli, Giorgio. "Analysis and Syntheses in XVIIIth Century Philosophy Prior to Kant." *Archiv für Begriffsgeschichte* 20 (1976).

————. "Critiques of the Notion of Substance Prior to Kant." *Tijdschrift voor Philosophie* 23 (June 1961).

————. "The Philosophy of d'Alembert: A Skeptic beyond Skepticism." *Kantstudien* 67 (1976).

Toulmin, Stephen Edelston. *Cosmopolis: The Hidden Agenda of Modernity.* New York: Free Press, 1990.

Tournefort, Joseph Pitton de. *Elémens de botanique ou Méthode pour connoître les plantes.* 3 vols. Paris: Imprimerie Royale, 1694.

Tyson, Edward. *Orang-Outang, sive Homo sylvestris: or the Anatomy of a Pygmie Compared with That of a Monkey, an Ape, and a Man.* London: T. Bennett and D. Brown, 1699.

Ugrinsky, Alexej, ed. *Lessing and the Enlightenment.* New York: Greenwood Press, 1986.

Uhlig, Ludwig. *Der Todesgenius in der deutschen Literatur von Winckelmann bis Thomas Mann.* Tübingen: Max Niemeyer Verlag, 1975.

————. "Lessing's Image of Death and the Archaeological Evidence." In *Lessing and the Enlightenment*, edited by Alexej Ugrinsky. New York: Greenwood Press, 1986.

Valmont de Bomare, Jacques-Christophe. *Dictionnaire raisonné universel d'histoire naturelle.* 4th ed. 8 vols. Lyon: Bruyset frères, 1791.

van Reede, Hendrik Adriaan. *Hortus indicus malabaricus.* 12 vols. Amsterdam: Johannis van Someren and Joannis van Dyck, 1678–93.

Venter, J. Craig, et al. "The Sequence of the Human Genome." *Science* 291 (16 February 2001): 1304–51.

Vidler, Anthony. *The Architectural Uncanny: Essays in the Modern Unhomely.* Cambridge, Mass.: MIT Press, 1992.

————. "The Architecture of Allusion: Notes on the Post-Modern Sublime." *Art Criticism* 2, no. 1 (1985): 61–69.

————. *Claude-Nicolas Ledoux: Architecture and Social Reform at the End of the Ancien Régime.* Cambridge, Mass.: MIT Press, 1990.

————. "Diagrams of Diagrams: Architectural Abstraction and Modern Representation." *Representations* 72 (Fall 2000): 1–20.

————. "Notes on the Sublime: From Neo-Classicism to Post-Modernism." *Princeton Journal* 2 (1987).

Visconti, Ennio Quirino. *Museo Pio-Clementino*. 7 vols. Rome: L. Mirri, 1784–1807.

Vollard, Ambroise. *Renoir: An Intimate Record*. 1925. Translated by Harold L. Van Doren and Randolph T. Weaver. Reprint, New York: A. A. Knopf, 1934.

Volney, Constantin François de Chasseboeuf. *Oeuvres*. 3 vols. Paris: Fayard, 1989.

Voltaire. *Oeuvres complètes*. 52 vols. Paris: Garnier frères, 1877–85.

von Dahlern, Ingo. "Bilder aus dem Datenhelm." *Der Tagesspiegel*, 22 April 1995.

Wade, Nicholas. "Comparing Genomes Shows Split Between Chimps and People." *New York Times*, 12 December 2003.

————. "Once Again, Scientists Say Human Genome Is Complete." *New York Times*, 15 April 2003.

————. "Scientist's Plan: Map All DNA Within 3 Years." *New York Times*, 10 May 1998.

Wegmann, Nikolaus, and Matthias Bickenbach. "Herders 'Journal meiner Reise im Jahre 1769.'" *Deutsche Vierteljahresschrift für Literaturwissenschaft und Geistesgeschichte* 71, no. 3 (1997): 397–420.

Weimann, Robert. "Funktion und Prozeß der Weltaneignung: Grundzüge ihrer Geschichte." In *Realismus in der Renaissance: Aneignung der Welt in der erzählenden Prosa*. Berlin: Aufbau, 1977.

Wellbery, David. "Das Gesetz der Schönheit: Lessings Ästhetik der Repräsentation." In *Was heißt "Darstellen"?* edited by Christiaan L. Hart Nibbrig, 175–204. Frankfurt: Suhrkamp, 1994.

————. "Der Zufall der Geburt. Sternes Poetik der Kontingenz." In *Kontingenz, Poetik und Hermeneutik XVII*, edited by Gerhart von Graevenitz and Odo Marquard, 291–317. München: Fink, 1998.

Whitaker, Katie. "The Culture of Curiosity." In *Cultures of Natural History*. Edited by Nicholas Jardine, James Secord, and Emma Spary, 75–90. Cambridge: Cambridge University Press, 1996.

White, Hayden. *Metahistory: The Historical Imagination in Nineteenth-Century Europe*. Baltimore: Johns Hopkins University Press, 1973.

————. "The Value of Narrativity in the Representation of Reality." *Critical Inquiry* 7, no. 4 (Summer 1980): 5–27.

Whitman, Walt. *Walt Whitman: Complete Poetry and Collected Prose*. New York: Viking Press, 1982.

Wiedemann, Conrad. "Lessings italienische Reise." In *Nation unde Gelehrtenrepublik: Lessing im europäischen Zusammenhang*, edited by Wilfried Barner and Albert M. Reh. Detroit, Mich.: Wayne State University Press, 1984.

Willard, Huntington F. "Genome Biology: Tales of the Y Chromosome." *Nature* 423 (19 June 2003): 810–13.

Willems, Gottfried. *Anschaulichkeit: zu Theorie und Geschichte der Wort-Bild-Beziehungen und des literarischen Darstellungsstils*. Tübingen: Max Niemeyer Verlag, 1989.

Wilson, Adrian. *The Making of Man-Midwifery: Childbirth in England, 1660–1770.* Cambridge, Mass.: Harvard University Press, 1995.

Winckelmann, Johann Joachim. *Anmerkungen über die Geschichte der Kunst des Alterthums.* Dresden: In der Waltherischen Hof-Buchhandlung, 1767.

———. *Geschichte der Kunst des Alterthums.* Dresden: In der Waltherischen Hof-Buchhandlung, 1764.

———. *Kleine Schriften vorreden Entwürfe.* Berlin: De Gruyter, 1968.

———. *Versuch einer Allegorie, besonders für die Kunst.* Dresden: In der Waltherischen Hof-Buchhandlung, 1766.

Wittgenstein, Ludwig. *Culture and Value.* Translated by Peter Winch. Edited by G. H. von Wright and Heikki Nyman. Chicago: University of Chicago Press, 1980.

Woolf, Virginia. "The Mark on the Wall." In *The Complete Shorter Fiction of Virginia Woolf,* edited by Susan Dick. San Diego, Calif.: Harcourt Brace Jovanovich, 1985.

Wordsworth, William. *Wordsworth: Poetical Works.* Edited by Thomas Hutchinson and Ernest de Selincourt. London: Oxford University Press, 1936.

Yeo, Richard R. "Scientific Method and the Rhetoric of Science in Britain, 1830–1917." In *The Politics and Rhetoric of Scientific Method: Historical Studies,* edited by John A. Schuster and Richard R. Yeo. Dordrecht: D. Reidel, 1986.

Zelder, Johann Heinrich. *Grosses vollständiges Universal-Lexikon.* Vol. 31. Graz: Akademie Dr. und Verl. Anst., 1742.

Zeller, Hans. *Winckelmanns Beschreibung des Apollo im Belvedere.* Zürich: Atlantis Verlag, 1955.

Zimmermann, Klaus, Jürgen Trabant, and Kurt Mueller-Vollmer, eds. *Wilhelm von Humboldt und die amerikanischen Sprachen.* Paderborn: Schöningh, 1994.

Index

Academie Française, 4
Ackerman, Diane, 112
Adanson, Michel, 42
Addison, Joseph, 102, 103, 105, 112
Adelung, Johan Christoph, 46, 47, 53, 55, 56, 57
Adorno, Theodor, 176
d'Alembert, Jean Le Rond, 156, 175, 178
Alberti, Leon Battista, 85
Alpers, Svetlana, 86
Aristotle, 14, 48, 65, 66, 103, 106, 109, 113, 114
Arnheim, Rudolf, 199, 201, 202, 211
Ashbery, John, 95, 100, 101, 109–10
Audebert, Jean, 31

Bacon, Francis, 14, 15, 50, 80
Baldewein, Saxon magistrate, 17, 19
Ballanche, Pierre-Simon, 175
Baret, Jeanne, 34
Barthes, Roland, 86
Bartholin, Thomas, 15
Batteaux, Abbé Charles, 85
Baudelaire, Charles, 90, 176
Baudrillard, Jean, 93, 94
Baumgarten, 203
Baxandall, Michael, 178, 195
Bender, John, 85, 93, 204, 206
Benjamin, Walter, 148
Bentham, Jeremy, 179, 181, 183
Bergson, Henri, 106–7
Berkeley, 210–11
Bernoulli, Johann, 121
Binswanger, Ludwig, 179
Blake, William, 100, 129
Blondel, Jacques-François, 184
Blumenbach, Johann Friedrich, 29–30, 34, 157, 159

Boileau, 184, 186
Bolz, Norbert, 93
Bontius, Jacob, 31
Boreman, Thomas, 31, 33
Bougainville, Louis-Antoine de, 34
Boullée, Etienne-Louis, 183, 184, 185, 186, 192–97
Boyle, Robert, 13, 15–18, 20–23, 64–65, 66
Brand, Hennig, 17–18, 19
Breitinger, Johann Jakob, 203–4
Brenner, Sydney, 2
Bretonne, Nicolas-Edme Rétif de la, 86
Breyne, Jakob, 40
Brosses, de, 51
Brunswick, Prince of, 127
Buffon, Georges-Louis Leclerc, comte de, 26, 127, 155, 160, 161, 163
Burke, Edmund, 68, 184, 185, 186, 192, 202, 203, 210
Burmann, P., 119

Camper, Peter, 168
Canning, Lady Charlotte, 34
Carlyle, 73
Cascariolo, Vincenzo, 17
Cassirer, Ernst, 85, 90, 176, 179
Catherine II (Empress of Russia), 53
Celera Corporation, 3
Cellini, Benvenuto, 15
Champfleury, 86, 91
Chaucer, Geoffrey, 100
Chaussard, Pierre Jean-Baptiste, 197
Chiarini, Giovanni, 125
Clark, Kenneth, 132
Clayton, John, 17
Coleridge, Samuel Taylor, 97
Commelin, Casper, 40–41

Comte, Auguste, 80, 81–82
Condillac, Étienne Bonnot de, 50
Condorcet, Marie Jean Antoine Nicolas
  Caritat, 1–2, 23, 68, 156, 187
Creuzer, Friedrich, 148
Cullen, William, 74

Darwin, Charles, 115–16
Defoe, Daniel, 86
Della Volpe, Galvano, 199, 201, 202
Descartes, René, 14, 66, 85, 176, 186
Dickens, Charles, 73, 75
Diderot, Denis, 26, 27, 29, 88, 181, 184, 209
Dillenius, Johann, 42
Donato, Eugene, 82, 83
Dorsch, Anton Joseph, 127
Dreyfus, Hubert L., 94
Dubos, Abbé, 206–8
Dufay, Charles, 13, 19, 20–24
Duke-Elder, Sir Stewart, 115
Dürer, 16

Encyclopédie, 4, 12, 26, 57, 59, 84, 87, 89, 90,
  91, 121

Ferguson, Adam, 64, 67, 162, 164
Fielding, Henry, 87
Flaubert, Gustave, 82–84, 86, 87, 91
Flaxman, John, 129
Fludd, Robert, 130
Fontenelle, Bernard de, 20, 21, 24
Fortier, Bruno, 179
Foucault, Michel, 4–5, 82, 87, 88, 129,
  179–83, 196
Frank, Joseph, 199, 202, 211, 121, 199
Freud, Sigmund, 195, 197
Friedrich, Johann, 18

Gabriel, Jacques-Ange, 197
Gandy, Joseph M., 129
Gébelin, Antoine Court de, 51
Gérando, Joseph-Marie de, 127
Gesner, Conrad, 15, 44, 45, 46, 55, 57
Glück, Louise, 113–14
Goethe, Johann Wolfgang von, 81, 86, 89,
  128, 131, 132, 160
Gottsched, Johann Christoph, 203–4
Gould, Steven Jay, 33
Goya, Francisco, 178
Greenberg, Clement, 199, 201, 202, 211
Grosley, Pierre Jean, 119

Hagstrom, Jean L., 128
Hardy, Thomas, 105–6
Harris, James, 210
Haussmann, Baron, 176
Hegel, G. W. F., 80, 81–82, 200–203

Heise, Wolfgang, 90
Herder, Johann Gottfried von, 133, 134, 160,
  161, 162, 163, 165–71, 208, 210
Hermann, Paul, 40
Herschel, Sir William, 189
Hervás, Lorenzo, 53, 55, 56
Heyne, Christian Gottlieb, 131
Histoire naturelle, 31, 155, 161
Hobbes, 66
Homer, 112, 168
Horenmann, Friedrich Konrad, 29–30
Horkheimer, Max, 153, 154, 157, 161, 162
Human Genome Project, 1
Humbolt, Alexander von, 53
Humbolt, Wilhelm von, 47, 53, 86
Hume, David, 62, 64, 67, 85, 89, 154–55,
  209
Huysman, Joris-Karl, 111

Judd, Donald, 138

Kames, Lord, 65, 67
Kant, Immanuel, 81, 86, 89, 97, 112, 172, 176,
  197, 200, 206, 209, 210
Klein, Wolf Peter, 50
Kofman, Sarah, 195
Köhler, Johann David, 126
Kunkel, Johann, 17

La Capra, Dominick, 170
Laocoön, 118–34, 139, 199, 200, 202, 210, 211
La Grange, Joseph-Louis, 156
Langer, Ernst Theodor, 133
Lawrence, D. H., 103
Le Corbusier, 176
Ledoux, Claude-Nicolas, 181–90, 196, 197
Lefebvre, Henri, 196
Leibniz, Gottfried Wilhelm, 17, 18, 51, 53,
  57–60
Lenin, Vladimir Ilyich, 82
Lenz, Jakob Michael Reinhold, 87, 88
Lesage, Alain-René, 86, 197
Lessing, Gotthold Ephraim, 90, 118–34, 199,
  203, 210, 211
Ligon, Richard, 34
Linnaeus, Carl von, 11–12, 26, 27, 29–30,
  41–42
Locke, John, 50, 85
Longinus, 183, 184
Louisa Ulrika (Queen of Sweden), 27
Lukács, Georg, 82, 91, 92
Luhmann, Niklas, 203, 210
Lyotard, Jean-François, 79, 93, 94

McCulloch, J. R., 61–63, 70–76
Magi, Filippo, 132
Manet, 99, 104–5, 117

Marx, Karl, 82
Mattheuer, Wolfgang, 92
Maturana, Humberto, 210
Maupassant, Guy de, 83
Maupertius, 169
Merck, Johann Heinrich, 86
Merian, Dorothea, 34
Merian, Maria Sibylla, 25–26, 34–35, 37–38, 39–40, 41, 42
Meyer, Theodor A., 199, 201, 203, 211
Millar, John, 64–65, 67
Minkowski, Eugène, 179, 183
Montesquieu, 23
Mortiz, Karl-Philipp, 133

Newton, Isaac, 14, 65, 66, 75, 80, 85, 158

Obsonville, Foucher d', 30–31
Oken, Lorenz, 172, 174
Ovid, 112

Pallas, Peter Simon, 53, 55
Paris, 4, 197–98
Paris Académie Royale des Sciences, 11, 19, 24
Pascal, Blaise, 179, 186–87, 189, 196
Patte, Pierre, 176, 197
Perrot, Michelle, 179, 180
Petty, William, 61–63
Place, Pierre-Simon La, 156
Plato, 114, 207
Poinci, Louis de Louvilliers, 41
Pollak, Ludwig, 132
Potier, Pierre, 17
Pritchard, James, 33
Proctor, Robert, 43
Proust, Marcel, 98, 104, 116

Raabe, Paul, 119, 125
Ranke, Leopold von, 126, 173–74
Ree, Abraham, 129
Reede, Hendrik Van, 42
Renoir, Pierre-Auguste, 99, 104, 117
Richardson, Jonathon, 130
Richardson, Samuel, 88
Richter, Simon, 123, 131–32
Rilke, Rainer Maria, 100, 103, 110, 112, 115, 116, 117
Ritter-Santini, Lea, 125
Robert, Hubert, 126
Robertson, Dennis H., 64
Robespierre, 192
Rohault, Jacques, 17
Romanticism, 160, 171, 174
Rousseau, Jean-Jacques, 98, 104–5, 110, 175, 181, 196

Royal Academy, 129
Ruskin, John, 104, 113

Sade, Marquis de, 88, 176, 178
Sartre, Jean-Paul, 96, 106
Schelling, Friedrich, 91
Schiller, Friedrich, 81, 86, 89, 90–91, 110–11, 159, 160
Schlegel, Friedrich, 55
Schlözer, August Ludwig, 162–63, 164
Shaftesbury, Earl of, 204–6, 207–8
Shakespeare, William, 168
Shaw, George, 29
Sitte, Camillo, 196
Sloane, Hans, 35, 37–38
Smith, Adam, 64, 67–68, 72
Southey, Robert, 73
Stedman, John, 37
Sterne, Laurence, 87–88
Stewart, Dugald, 63–64, 67, 68, 69–70, 72–73, 75

Tocqueville, Alexis de, 176, 180
Toulmin, Stephen, 153, 157
Tournefort, Joseph Pitton de, 11–12, 41, 42
Turgot, Anne Robert Jacques, 23
Tyson, Edward, 31–33

Vater, Johann Severin, 46, 47, 53, 56
Venter, J. Craig, 3
Vergil, 112
Vinci, Leonardo da, 85
Voltaire, 80, 85, 179, 186

Wailly, Charles de, 183
Warburg, Aby, 196
Warnock, Mary, 96
Warnstedt, Karl Bogislaus von, 124–25, 132, 133
Wellbery, David, 88
Westphall, Carl, 187
White, Hayden, 127
Whitman, Walt, 101
Wiedemann, Conrad, 119
Wild, Gilbert, 107–9
Winckelmann, Johann Joachim, 130, 131, 132, 135–50, 208, 209
Wittgenstein, Ludwig, 113
Wood, P. B., 65
Woolf, Virginia, 102, 111, 117
Wordsworth, William, 100, 112
Worringer, Wilhelm, 196

Young, Edward, 208

Zola, Emile, 84, 86, 91